PARIS IN THE TERROR

JUNE 1793–JULY 1794

By Stanley Loomis

PARIS IN THE TERROR:
June 1793–July 1794

DU BARRY
A Biography

PARIS

IN THE TERROR

JUNE 1793 - JULY 1794

by STANLEY LOOMIS

DORSET PRESS
New York

This edition published by Dorset Press,
a division of Marboro Books Corporation,
by arrangement with Harper & Row
1989 Dorset Press

ISBN 0-88029-401-9

Printed in the United States of America
M 9 8 7 6 5 4 3 2 1

CONTENTS

I. THE MURDER OF MARAT

JULY 1793

I

On june 2, 1793, a mob incited by Jean-Paul Marat invaded the Tuileries and by force of arms evicted twenty-two elected representatives of the French people from the National Convention, which sat in session there. These twenty-two men were the backbone of a political party known as the Gironde. Although that party and the twenty-two men have receded into the background of history, they were once redolent of all that the Revolution ideally represented: eloquence and idealism, youth and noble aspiration.

The French Revolution was four years old in that month of June 1793, and in the course of those years had undergone many radical changes. Two senates, the Constituent and the Legislative Assemblies, had come and gone. The heroes of one day had become the villains of the next. The monarchy that had presided over these upheavals for more than three years had been overthrown by a mob that entered the Tuileries on August 10, 1792. Five months later, in January of 1793, Louis XVI was executed. And five months after that—on June 2—the Girondins, many of whom had voted for the King's execution, were themselves uprooted by the whirlwind.

Pre-Revolutionary France had presented the curious spectacle of a people technically at the mercy of medieval monarchic law enjoying freedom in a way that would not for an instant be tolerated by many of today's republican societies, where conformity of idea as well as of manner is often considered to be the ideal. An ill-administered, ineffectual tyranny induces a climate hospitable to ideas in which are planted and nourished the seeds that grow into revolution.

It is ironic that of all countries in Europe, France was the only one that could have had a revolution—not because she groaned under the lash of tyranny, but, on the contrary, because she tolerated and even invited every conceivable dissension and heresy. Restlessness, a passion for novelty and the pursuit of excitement were everywhere in the air. They were the fruits of idleness and leisure, not of poverty.

Paris was a "storm-tossed sea, blown perpetually by contrary winds." When, in 1789, the Revolution finally arrived it was everywhere acclaimed. It was not a single, self-contained or unified uprising, but a succession of revolutions. One after another, various men or parties emerged to seize power. One after another, they were swept away by forces stronger than themselves. So violent were these insurrections, so torrential the flow of events that today's reader, like many people who lived through the time, often finds himself without bearings. Were the French Revolution to be depicted on canvas, the composition of the painting might find its point of unity in that day of June 2, 1793.

The overthrow of the Girondin party by Marat's mob is one of those crucial or pivotal events on which the reader and the historian might conveniently establish a vantage point from which to view that phase of the Revolution that followed it, the Reign of Terror. The uprising of June 2 corresponds with the beginning of the Terror, while the intrigues, hostilities and rivalries that provoked the downfall of the Girondins contributed to the establishment of the Terror.

Anarchy, represented by Marat, preceded the institution of the Revolutionary Tribunal; dictatorship followed it.

Marat, the man who organized and brought to pass the insurrection of June 2, was the bitterest enemy of the Girondins. With twitching face and rolling eyes he behaved in his hour of triumph like a man demented. Backed by the cannon of his "general," a drunken ex-valet named Hanriot; supported by his "army," the dregs of the Paris gutters, Marat entered the hall of the National Convention and demanded the arrest of twenty-two elected representatives of the French people. The Paris mob, which had twice before invaded the Tuileries and had toppled the Crown and outraged the Constitution of 1791, had now finally dared violate the French representation, the sacrosanct body of the Revolution itself. And such was Marat's power at that moment that the Convention was hardly consulted in his selection of the men whom he wished evicted.

An hour later the Girondins were ignominiously led from the hall to be placed under house arrest. Proscription and prison quickly followed. Four months later they were sentenced to death, and all through the winter of 1793 and 1794 those of their party who had escaped were hunted down by bloodhounds in the caves of Normandy, Brittany and the Gironde.

One of their number, a man named Lanjuinais, became inspired that day when he spoke his prophetic and parting words to the National Convention. "I foresee civil war set afire in my country," he declared, "spreading its ravages everywhere and tearing France apart. I see the monstor Dictatorship advancing over piles of ruins and corpses, swallowing each of you up in his turn and finally overthrowing the Republic."

In the ruin of the Girondins was comprehended the ruin of many hundreds, many thousands of obscure people. The uprisings that had been taking place in Paris since the outbreak of the Revolution in 1789 had been followed in the provinces by observant eyes. Dispute had begun to rage as fiercely in the villages as in the cities. Lyons, Toulon, Marseilles and the Vendée were already in armed revolt against the men whom, rightly, they believed to be the usurpers of Paris.

In Normandy, in the ancient town of Caen, there lived a comely young woman who was a passionate admirer of the Girondins. Her name, Marie-Charlotte de Corday, was unknown to them. For many months she had followed in the Girondin newspapers the waning of their fortune. In the weeks preceding Marat's triumph she had been in the habit of retiring to the solitude of her bedroom, where on little slips of paper she would write, over and again, the question "Shall I or shall I not?" Her preoccupied air, her dreaming eyes suggested to friends and relatives that the young lady was in love. The good souls of Caen were people of limited experience and few of them could have known that wilder passions than love will sometimes seize possession of a high-minded woman's heart.

The news of the overthrow of the Girondins reached Caen two days after the event. Five days later, on June 9, a remnant of the Girondins who had managed to escape house arrest in Paris arrived in Caen. Here, hoping to raise an army and march on Paris to liberate the captured city, they set up headquarters at a local hostelry and awaited other members of their party who might make their way to Caen. All Calvados thus heard firsthand the story of the insurrection of Marat's rabble against the elected government. Inflammatory placards appeared on every wall. Everywhere, and with horror, was heard the name Marat. The once sleepy town of Caen crackled with excitement. But the young woman who was so dedicated an admirer of the Girondins seemed calm. Sometime during those days she had ceased tormenting herself with that question, "Shall I or shall I not?" She had made up her mind.

In Paris, the exhausted Marat now spent his days at home. Helped by his common-law wife, Simonne Evrard, he superintended the publication of his newspaper, wrote articles and corrected proof. The disease which appeared to be consuming his flesh—an ailment which doctors of the time diagnosed as "scrofula"—had worsened and Marat now worked while soaking in his hip bath, a portable, copper-lined contraption shaped like an old-fashioned high-buttoned shoe. Minerals and medicines were added to his bath water, and here with a bandana soaked in vinegar wrapped about his head, and with a moist towel thrown over his shoulders, the sick man would sit hour after hour, kept alive by the same demonic fury which was killing him.

2

THE HOUSE OF CORDAY into which, in 1768, the murderess of Marat was born was among the most ancient in Calvados. It is related that on the night of Charlotte's birth the surrounding marshes were beaten by peasants to silence the frogs, a feudal tribute that cannot have been much compensation to the impoverished family to whom it was offered. The baby was born in a *manoir,* but little more than the name distinguished that rudely beamed and plastered cottage from the neighboring huts of the peasants.

The Cordays had been noble since 1077, and their arms, on which were emblazoned the insignia of counts, showed thirty-two quarterings of nobility. Their nobility was of the "sword" rather than of the "robe"—a significant distinction in the social scheme of those times, for the first implied the honor of unrewarded service while the second suggested the taint of favor and even, indeed, of commerce. For nearly five centuries the purest Norman blood had flowed in the Cordays' veins. But if, during those centuries, their house had been unsullied by trade, neither had it been invigorated by industry. They bred with the indifference of their livestock, and their once extensive property, though protected by the laws of primogeniture, had been divided and subdivided many times. In the generation of Charlotte's grandfather it had been reduced to four or five farms, a château in disrepair, and several *manoirs,* in the least and meanest of which, "Lignerie," Marie-Charlotte was born. Her father was a third son and consequently disinherited of all but a few castoff morsels of his ancestral lands, a fact that was central in the formation of his view of life. Characteristically, though M. de Corday railed and ranted at the injustice of laws that reduced him to living in a peasant's hovel, he does not appear to have troubled himself much about any division in his own children's poor inheritance; for he continued to breed with the recklessness of his more opulent ancestors. Two sons and three daughters—of whom Charlotte was the middle daughter—were soon dependent on his support. In his sons M. de Corday, like many a father who has not prospered, hoped to see a renewal of fortune. That which had been lost by his hands might be retrieved by theirs. Poor though he was, he managed by sacrifices and economies that reduced his family to patched-up rags to scrape enough from the bottom of the barrel to send his sons to a training school for officers in the King's army. As gentlemen they were eligible for commissions, and the army was then an honorable and occasionally even a lucrative calling.

Poverty and pretension: such for the most part, was the condition of the French aristocracy of the *ancien régime,* whom the writers of historical fiction have pictured in silk stockings, minuetting across the polished floors of Versailles. A short visit to Lignerie or the countless households like it would have stilled a few of these fluent pens. In many of these houses the countess would breed her children beneath a roof shared by the rutting hogs and cattle of her husband's barnyard. The proximity of the manure pile, which added its own moist leachings to the muck and mire dropped by geese and pigs, lent to the scene a rustic character of a kind that has not been conveyed to us by the novels of Rousseau or the canvases of Fragonard. In the descriptions of the *ancien régime* which have come down to us from that period no mention is made of flies; the imagination must add these to the picture, swarming in profusion about the *fumier* and the hogpen. On more than one such *seigneurie* the count or marquis wore wooden shoes like his peasants and dressed little better than they. An intricate system of law and tradition prohibited these gentlemen from entering the world of trade or negotiation. Even had convention permitted, it is unlikely that many of them would have chosen that particular path to prosperity. For the contempt these pedigreed peasants felt for the rising and wealthy class of men who traded in goods and money was matched only by the resentment the burgess class felt for the tattered and arrogant provincial nobility. The banker's wife wore jewels and scent, the countess's clothes were patched and often she smelled of the barnyard, but there was no question in the mind of either as to who was to the manor born. The French nobility, though often poverty-stricken, then occupied a legal position attached to which were certain symbolic prerogatives, such as having the frogs silenced during childbirth, and certain concrete privileges, such as immunity from taxation.

It would be easy to dismiss with scorn the pretensions of such families as the one into which Charlotte Corday was born. What there is about these families that invites our admiration if not our sympathy is of more elusive definition. By the middle of the eighteenth century the words "honor" and "obligation" had come to mean as little to the fine-feathered aristocracy of Versailles as they mean to the greater part of the world today. Some portion of that toughness of spirit, that strength of character without which honor can be no more than a word, remained with the provincial nobility, a legacy perhaps of their Renaissance ancestors. They may have been poor and, in the management of their affairs, ineffectual. But they were not weak. At certain standards one may smile, but the maintenance of those standards in face of adversity can only command respect. Courage, unlike honor, had not yet lost its meaning. It was characteristic of M. de Corday that he did not hesitate to send his sons to college. The money he spent on their education might have supported an easier old age for him, but in the next generation his blood would have sunk to the level of his peasants. His sons went to college, and in the Corday household the pinch of need grew sharper.

A third daughter, Éléonore, was born to the family shortly after Charlotte. With her birth their circumstances grew more restricted still. Éléonore and Marie-Charlotte (there was a third and older sister who rarely makes an appearance in the few records which have come down to us of this period in Charlotte's life) were raised in the changeless traditions of their class: household duty and the dedication of self to family and to God. Needlework and cooking represented the domestic accomplishments, while at Mesnil-Imbert, the nearby manor house of their grandfather M. de Corday's father, a little oratory was fitted up in a closet above the stable, where, taught by their mother, the children learned to say their prayers. Mesnil-Imbert, a typical Norman farmhouse of plastered brick hatched by rough wooden beams, was hardly more imposing than Ferme au Bois, the one-story farm to which Charlotte's parents had moved after her birth. However, Glatigny, the residence of

Charlotte's uncle, was more impressive. Known as "the château," Glatigny was traditionally the seat of the head of the Corday clan. Since, like all the Corday farms, it was but a few kilometers' distance from Ferme au Bois the girls were frequent visitors at Glatigny, where, at those family gatherings so dear to the provincial French, they would meet an endless variety of cousins, uncles and aunts.

Although the scope of Charlotte's world was little more than this small cluster of farm villages, from time to time she would be taken to visit an uncle who was curé in the more distant community of Vicques. It was through this uncle, the Abbé de Corday, that Charlotte was introduced to an influence that was central in the formation of her character. Through her father, Charlotte was the great-granddaughter of the celebrated seventeenth-century dramatist Corneille. The Cordays, and in particular the Abbé de Corday, were understandably proud of their distinguished ancestor. Never for a moment did the Abbé permit his niece to forget that the blood of genius flowed in her veins (though not the blood of a gentleman, for the marriage of a Corday to Corneille's granddaughter constituted, genealogically speaking, the only blot on an otherwise pure escutcheon). The young niece and the elderly uncle, who more properly should have been instructing her in her catechism, closeted themselves for long stretches of time in the Abbé's study, where they pored over the tragedies of Corneille and compared the meanness of their own times with the elevated virtues of that Classical Age depicted in exalted verse by their ancestor.

The dramas of Corneille, which, like the canvases of Poussin, drew much of their inspiration from the wellspring of antiquity, are at their best of a loftiness of tone, a grandeur and dignity unsurpassed in the literature of the theatre. But they were written in the middle sixteen hundreds for the court of Louis XIV; their virtues and faults are the virtues and faults of that mannered and sumptuous time, not of ancient Rome. No vulgar emotion (and in consequence no recognizable life) ever animates the effigies who proclaim, hour after asphyxiating hour, those perfectly polished couplets. They move like priests or acolytes reciting the Mass. The protagonists of Corneille's dramas always subordinate passion to the stern obligations of duty, a fact that takes on a certain sinister significance in any study of Charlotte Corday, a girl who, in the solitude of a room above the bakehouse of her grandfather's farm, dreamed her days away in the company of these purposeful heroes. Everywhere in Corneille the power of the will is exalted over the meanness of circumstance or the selfishness of personal emotion. Sacrifice, stoicism and patriotism—these alone are the sentiments that stir the hearts of Corneille's pasteboard Romans. On the wings of sublime verse the impressionable girl was daily transported into this fantastic world. Degree by imperceptible degree the ideals of these seventeenth-century Romans became her ideals, and the impossibly elevated standards by which they lived her standards. They fortified her and became sources of a secret strength. She went about her dull daily chores like someone in the initial stages of a love affair, impervious to reality. Her chores, it may be added, she did well, for she was a Norman and a noble, but they were distractions which never trespassed upon the rich and better world that she bore within her.

As she entered adolescence, the influence of her beloved Romans grew rather than diminished. Corneille led her to Plutarch, whose *Lives* celebrates in appropriate style the same austere and self-sacrificing Romans who already occupied her dreams: Manlius, who put to death his disobedient son; Brutus, another stern father who sacrificed his son to the laws of the Republic; above all, Marcus Junius Brutus, who stabbed Caesar, his patron and friend, in the hall of the Senate in order that liberty might be restored to his country.

The girl who mused in the loft of her grandfather's farmhouse was not alone in her admiration of these heroes of antiquity. The vogue for Republican Rome was spreading like a disease through France, a country that has always been susceptible to such superficial contagions of the intellect. It found its victims largely among the provincial middle classes, professional men such as lawyers and doctors for whom ancient Rome offered an inspiring contrast to the banal facts of their own existence. When the Girondin deputies came up to Paris for the Legislative Assembly, they brought with them an ample stock of classical quotation. In more than one shabby portmanteau there might have been found a well-thumbed set of Cicero or Plutarch—more often than not, alas, in translation, for the education of these men was not always equal to their enthusiasm. No wonder then that when, in 1791, the Girondins were elected to make their entrance onto the stage of the Revolution, they were to capture the adulation of this unknown Norman gentlewoman. Clairvoyantly, Charlotte Corday walked with them in the same trance and partook, though from afar, of the same dream.

Plutarch led Charlotte to Tacitus and Tacitus to Cicero, and all of these influences were to lead inevitably to that fatal addition to the Roman hodgepodge, Rousseau. Yet, all the while, on another plane of existence, that of humdrum reality, a series of small but heartbreaking events were taking place in Charlotte Corday's life.

The happenings that from 1782, Charlotte's fifteenth year, almost engulfed her father and his family do not belong to the elevated order of tragedy. There is nothing Roman about them, but unlike the dramas of Corneille they belong to the mainstream of recognizable humanity. Across the chasm of time man can touch hands with man where their common portion has been financial worry, grief and the disappointment of hope. Such plain matters bring us suddenly close to the little Norman family whose distress, but for the dramatic act of its daughter, would have been long lost in that oblivion which casts its shadow over the anxieties and failures of most men. It is not easy to share with Charlotte her high-minded fantasies, but the grey outward circumstances of her life still can touch us. That is an irony of which Charlotte Corday would not be appreciative.

3

In 1782, harassed beyond endurance, M. de Corday entered upon a lawsuit against his brother-in-law. A lawsuit in those days was no mean undertaking. Medieval tradition, conflicting statutes, confusion, prejudice and favoritism characterized the courts. Nor did cases brought up for judgment ever seem to terminate. Lawsuits, instead of property, were bequeathed from generation to generation; some suits dated back to the time of the Norman conquest. This condition of the courts and the pressing need for reform are not the least of the many reasons that have been given for the advent of the Revolution.

To pursue his ill-advised scheme it became necessary for M. de Corday to leave his farm in the country and move into Caen, the ancient capital of Calvados and the central city of the Cordays' province. So, at the age of twelve, Charlotte left the Ferme au Bois where she had spent her childhood. At Caen, M. de Corday rented a cramped and dilapidated house in a poor quarter of the city. The contrast between the dark confinement of a miserable city dwelling and the freedom of the woods and open meadows of the lovely Norman countryside must have been a painful one for this dreaming girl who had a more than natural love of solitude. The Norman landscape to which Charlotte Corday now bade farewell is so much a part of her character and appearance that along with the writings of Corneille and Plutarch it must be considered an important element among the influences that governed her destiny. The possibility of her having come from some other province is inconceivable.

In the time of Charlotte Corday the ancient provinces of France still remained cultural enclaves, each with its own traditions, habits and even language. The system of the "Departments" was introduced with the Revolution, but it takes more than the decrees of a government to separate a people from the roots of its ancient custom. Even today Normandy remains uniquely "Norman." Unlike Brittany, rock-bound and drawing its livelihood from a stormy and often treacherous sea, Normandy, which scarcely touches upon the open Atlantic, is a rich agricultural province. Even today a picture of it can be sketched in sound, sight and smell: the lowing of cattle, the early-morning crow of the inevitable rooster, the haystack and nearby the ever-present rick; in the barnyard, geese, ducks and chickens; over all the rich smell of the dungheap as redolent as Normandy's splendid cheeses where so many of them are, in fact, ripened. To this picture one should add some suggestion of the chaste and shimmering beauty of the Norman spring, that ecstatic season when the apple trees come into blossom, and along the shallow streams that feed the rich pastureland the meadow flowers and water herbs begin to show. In such a place at such a time the soul of a young and impressionable girl might well begin to tremble and to hear, carried on the fragrance of a blossom-scented breeze, the whispers of another world.

Bound to her land by the deep roots of ancestry, Charlotte Corday here came to the threshold of puberty. Under the influence of the land she had grown healthy and strong of limb. Nearly all who saw her or who were to meet her in the few days of her notoriety in Paris were to comment, some of them with an insinuating leer, on her robust good health. She was compared to the farm produce of Normandy, to butter, cream and eggs, to peaches, pears and apples. For she was well fleshed, robust and in every way a comely young woman. Much of this healthful appearance, startling to a starved and haggard city, she owed to her early years at Ferme au Bois. She owed much of her character too to her Norman background. The winters of Normandy are long. Grey day follows grey day for weeks on end. The summers are cool and overcast. That lax and frivolous acceptance of life that is engendered in weak people by too much sunlight or happiness, and which sometimes leads to indiscriminate and vulgar bursts of passion, is rarely to be found in the Norman character. Precaution, common sense and a regard for the proprieties direct the Norman towards his well-considered decisions; tenacity holds him on the path to their accomplishment. It was no impetuous stiletto thrust, the whim of an instant—such as might have been expected of someone from the southern or central provinces of France—that informed Charlotte Corday's blow at Marat. It was the outcome of long and measured consideration, of resolution quietly but firmly taken, after the Norman fashion. One observes with interest that during her trial Charlotte's self-possession was upset only once—when the Public Prosecutor implied that she was experienced in the use of the dagger.

"Good heavens!" she cried out in dismay. "He takes me for a common assassin!" Well-bred Normans, when they commit murder, do so with premeditation and leave the *crime passionelle* to such excitable folk as Gascons or Provençals.

Caen was in 1782 (as, until the invasion of 1944, it remained) a semimedieval town linked to its great and stormy past by a number of churches dating back to the time of William the Conqueror. In the imposing cathedral of the Holy Trinity, attached to which was the convent of the Abbaye-aux-Dames built by Queen Matilda of Flanders, the Conqueror's headstrong wife, in expiation of her sins, the Queen's body had lain since 1083. For seven hundred years nuns of the order of St. Benoît had prayed for the repose of that tempestuous soul. On an opposite eminence the Conqueror had caused to be built the Abbaye-aux-Hommes in expiation of his particular sins. The Church of St. Gilles dated from the eleventh century, as did that of St. Étienne. The historic walls of these edifices exhaled a dank smell, the chilling and fetid breath of the centuries. Everywhere the remote past impinged on the present, not only in the churches but in the many half-timbered second stories that perilously jutted out over dark, crooked alleys; in the beautifully carved wood of Renaissance date that embellished certain doorways; and especially in the powerful unseen forces of legend and tradition.

In the year 1782 Caen was a typical provincial capital of the *ancien régime*. Madame de Sévigné somewhere speaks of it as "the Athens of northern France," a reserved tribute that refers perhaps to the university at Caen, which was devoted to scholarship in the medieval tradition. Caen was also an important garrison town which lent the city a certain pallid luster. Though rank in those times was unassailably established, snobbery was none the less active in both its aggressive and defensive expressions. Prim and proud, the nobility of Caen immured itself behind the high walls of its ancestral *hôtels particuliers,* a haughty breed made the haughtier by an awareness of its insignificance in the great world of affairs. It was in such towns as Caen and among the *petite noblesse* that the hatred for Marie Antoinette, for the Court and all that in the popular imagination these things stood for, was most virulent.

In this community, where it may be imagined that genteel distress was a familiar presence, the Corday family occupied an ambiguous position. Threadbare and proud, M. de Corday did not move as freely among the nobility of Caen as his rank and background might have entitled him to do. His attitude towards Caen was probably similar to the attitude of Caen towards Paris. His pride, rising in direct proportion to the decline of his estate, would not permit him to receive favors from the hands of his equals. It is possible that the aristocracy of Caen no more wanted to see M. de Corday than he them, for there is a point beyond which genteel distress becomes simply distress and the act of according charity to one's unfortunate neighbor ceases to please and begins to depress. M. de Corday was a reminder of what could happen to them all.

In his dark rooms, far from the tree-lined streets down which rolled the insolent equipages of the rich, Charlotte's father buried himself with his misery and sought, picking his way through the debris of philosophic speculation and political literature that had begun to flood France, an answer to his many problems. He was an educated man, but he does not appear to have been either wise or intelligent. Like so many of his kind and generation, he heard an echo of his private confusion in the wider confusion of his times. The limits of his Revolutionary ardor were set entirely by the nature of his private circumstances. It thus seemed to him that the major purpose of a revolution in France should be an annulment of the unjust law of primogeniture that had caused him so much suffering. To his mind there was something wrong with a system whose laws permitted a gentleman such as himself to live in poverty. M. de Corday thus warmly embraced the oncoming Revolution and began himself to write pamphlets, most of them on the law of primogeniture. But, in Lamartine's words, "either from lack of genius, restlessness of temperament or that malevolence of fortune which sometimes restrains the highest spirits in oblivion," M. de Corday achieved no renown as a pamphleteer. In nothing "was he able to make his way through events."

Some months after the Corday family moved to Caen, sorrow paid a call on them. Charlotte's elder sister, a shadowy figure who passed from the scene without having noticeably entered it, died suddenly of causes not recorded. No letters remain to commemorate the bereavement. But the sorrow that M. de Corday and his family may have felt at this loss was soon overwhelmed in a greater grief.

After the move, the health of Charlotte's mother began perceptibly to fail. Hardship and anxiety had taken their toll when in 1783 she was brought to bed of another child, her sixth. She died a few hours after its birth. The baby survived her by but a day. Though the outline of this woman, too, is vague because she takes an unassuming place in the shadow cast by her husband, the few glimpses we are able to catch of her testify that she was a good wife and a conscientious mother. One ray of light appears to have illuminated the sorry tale of M. de Corday's life; his happy marriage to this excellent woman. They had been inseparable and so unashamedly in love that they were known archly to their friends as "Baucis and Philemon"—pathetic echo of a long-passed fashion for elegiac and pastoral euphuism.

M. de Corday was prostrated by the death of his wife. We can only imagine Charlotte's feelings. She was fifteen years old, an age when such a loss would make its deepest impression on an imaginative girl. In the close quarters of that house she would have heard the sounds and seen the sights that are the heart-rending and physical part of birth and death. It was a day when such experiences were considered to be a natural part of existence. Death particularly was of interest. Children of the tenderest age were brought trembling to the bedside of a dying parent to exchange farewells and be given some final admonition. Moans of anguish, from the dying as well as the survivors, lamentations and even screams, more often than not accompanied these emotional scenes. The arrival of the priest, the low murmur attending the Last Rites, the final convulsion or hush, the tender closing of the eyes and folding of the hands were part of every child's earliest experiences. Lest a drop of the brew go wasted the child would often be exhorted over the corpse of a deceased mother or father to consider the possibility of his own approaching dissolution, the flames of Hell awaiting him on one hand, the angels of Paradise on the other. The flesh is conceived in corruption and to corruption does it return: that was a lesson in which

Charlotte Corday, like all children of her faith and time, was instructed young.

An echo of the emotions that she may have felt at the time of her mother's death is to be detected in a little prayer that she wrote a few years later in one of her notebooks. "Oh, Jesus," she wrote, "I recommend to you my last hour and all which must follow it. When my pale and livid cheeks inspire terror and pity in those who are by my side, when my ears, about to be closed to the voices of men, strain to hear the words of Judgment pronounced—*oh miserere mei.*"

Heredity, her readings in Plutarch and natural inclination made a stoic of Charlotte Corday, a strain that was to develop more markedly in her with the passing of time. At fifteen she faced the altered circumstances of her life with equanimity. As eldest daughter of the family, she now took over the management of her father's household. In these tasks she was helped by her sister Éléonore. It is said that M. de Corday, in order to demonstrate the confidence that he had in his daughters' domestic efficiency left his money in an open drawer to be taken by them when it was needed. Engulfed by sorrow, he retired to the privacy of his bedroom, where he quaffed yet more copious draughts of the works of the *philosophes* and Rousseau—a regimen that in his situation was ill calculated either to alleviate distress or to inspire hope.

4

IT WAS THROUGH her father that Charlotte made her acquaintance with the writings of Jean-Jacques Rousseau, effervescent addition to a mixture of Corneille, adolescence and grief. The effect on her, as on so many others in the France of 1785, was explosive. Mme. Roland, Egeria-to-be of the Girondin party, who was nourished, like Charlotte Corday, on a diet of Plutarch and Corneille, said of Rousseau: "I read him too late, and a lucky thing that was for me, because he would have driven me mad and I should never have read anything else." In another provincial capital, Arras, another fervent admirer of Rousseau, Maximilien Robespierre, mused with chastely fluttering soul over those same pages turned in Caen by Charlotte Corday and at Lyons by Mme. Roland.

Rousseau spoke to a varied audience, and the secret of his success, if so coarse a term may be applied to an influence and celebrity that probably transcend anything achieved by any writer since his time, is to be discovered at a homely and familiar source: sex. But, curious and significant introduction to the literature of pornography, he ravished not the body but the soul of his reader. Suffering from a peculiar physical ailment, Rousseau's "fulfillment" was further thwarted by certain unassuageable desires awakened in him by the birch rod of his schoolmaster's daughter, one Mlle. Lambercier, and quite frankly diagnosed by him in his celebrated *Confessions*—confessions that in an extraordinary exhibition of psychic masochism admit freely to a series of bizarre lesser faults but mask at all times the more commonplace and less interesting larger ones. Idealizing women, he was driven by forces stronger than recollections of Mlle. Lambercier to place them upon a pedestal and himself in a position prostrate and expectantly quivering. It was not, however, woman whom he wished to exalt, but rather himself whom he wished to mortify. In every relationship he set very carefully and always with his own hand the trap into which he planned to fall—when the complicated conditions under which his ruin might be most pleasurably effected had all been satisfied.

To this powerful flow of masochism was added another current, a passionate recollection of adolescent flights of soul, an ardent and, as he grew older, a desperate, dedication of his whole sick and troubled being to ecstatic inner whispers once heard in the meadows and forests which descend to the gentle shores of the Lake of Geneva. These raptures, inner and entirely personal, belonged to that order of experience which is the source of poetry and mysticism, the voice regretted by Wordsworth and followed by Jeanne d'Arc. Those who have voyaged any distance into that mysterious land can never be the same as other men, nor, once they have returned, can the pursuits and distractions of other men be of consequence to them. That many people have in some degree and at some period in their lives experienced them is perhaps true, but the recollection is soon obliterated by domestic anxieties and their compensations, and the struggle towards those goals which, if one is to survive in this world, must be pursued.

Far indeed had nature removed the unfortunate Rousseau from the possibility of domestic solace. A cottage there was and women to share it with him, but under circumstances so unhappy, indeed so bizarre, that they can be said to bear no resemblance at all to the cozy hearthside of sentimental tradition—that tradition furthered, if not indeed begun, by Rousseau himself. His private life is a record of almost uninterrupted squalor and misery. His quarrels with David Hume, Baron Grimm and Mme. d'Épinay were of a pettiness and complexity scarcely credible. Powers beyond his control obliged him to bite the hand that fed him, and many hands, impulsively generous, were at one time or another extended to that harassed and unhappy creature. Every friendship, whether with men or with women, concluded in a quarrel. He lived his life within a net of animosity, jealousy and a terror of conspiracies against him, of plots that might be hatching behind his back or of coalitions formed against him by his friends. This net, as he grew older, was drawn closer and closer about him until, in 1778, he died, paranoid and almost catatonic.

Feeding this mire of misery bubbled the clear sweet spring of those intimations of immortality once whispered to him by the shore of the Lake of Geneva. From these waters Rousseau drew the inspiration for his works. His sanity went into his writing. Sex-ridden, emotionally avid, physically and psychologically thwarted, Rousseau created in his books the world in which he fain would pass his days, a world, it scarcely need be added, in which the real Rousseau or the real anybody could not have survived for an instant. Far from the birch rod of Mlle. Lambercier, far, apparently, from all base and fleshly cravings, the creatures of his dream world exist in a perpetual pursuit of one another's souls, philosophizing as they go. No conquest of the gross or physical order is ever achieved. On the surface a paean to the exquisite satisfactions of chastity, Rousseau's books actually were inducements to sensuality of a most delicious and novel kind. He introduced sex to the soul, not to the soul that is the precinct of saints and theologians, but to the ardent, sentimental soul of the adolescent—that repository of yearnings not yet directed to their natural outlet, the breeding place of idealism and discontent, of theories in only the slightest way related to human nature as it is, of musings, cravings and rebellion. Rousseau's characters share one another's tears, never their beds. Like Rousseau, but for different reasons, they are thwarted of the satisfactions which might staunch their tears. They perch perpetually, in delectable anguish, on the brim of relief to their longings.

The plots of these novels are preposterous; the characters can scarcely be called stereotypes since their like has never existed before nor since. But "the writing," the prose in which Rousseau describes his dream world, is of an order less lightly dismissed. He had in the first place a considerable narrative gift. In reading him one is reminded of occasional stories that are to be found in today's confession magazines. Deficient in style, taste, insight, humor and practically every other quality that might recommend their author, the ignorance and vulgarity that inform these stories are occasionally transcended by a gripping quality in the narration. However preposterous both the story and the characters may be, one is impelled to turn the page. Voltaire, the realist, wise and well read in the secrets of the human heart, the least vulgar and most amusing man of his age, is today almost unreadable. One must turn (apart from *Candide*) to his lucid and wonderful letters to begin to appreciate how Voltaire had been able to hold his age spellbound. The *Confes-*

sions of Rousseau, on the other hand, if edited with an eye towards making the events that are related in it appear to be contemporary—many people find it difficult to believe that any event taking place before their birth ever actually occurred—could be profitably serialized in any popular periodical and be read attentively in the dentist's office, the hairdresser's salon or in bed.

Rousseau wrote his sentimental novels in a limpid, easy and sensuous style that fell upon the arid landscape of eighteenth-century France, a country withered by cynicism and weary of rationalism, wit and paradox, with the welcome freshness of soft and gentle rain upon a desert. Appearing at the time they did, his works appealed to the widest variety of men. To the poor because Rousseau ennobled their condition, presaging at the same time change in that condition. To the rich because the rich, as usual, were bored. (This was the period in French landscape design when hamlets and water mills began to make their appearance to complement or in some cases to replace the rigid geometry of Lenôtre's classic designs.) To the chaste because Rousseau unctuously preached the delights of chastity—and the chaste have always comprehended a larger segment of every population than is popularly supposed. To the vicious because purity is the most tantalizing of seductions. In a loose society it is always the prim prostitute who commands the highest price, and prudery, skillfully flaunted, will awaken the interest of the weariest *débauché*. To the imaginative, to the lonely, to the idealistic, to all who found life cruel or insufficient, Rousseau's novels came as an intoxicant of the most effervescent kind.

Had the author of *La Nouvelle Héloïse* contented himself with a description of the problems of his unhappy characters, the French Revolution might have taken a different course or assumed a different character than it did. Unfortunately, in their lachrymose meanderings Rousseau's creatures must stop on every other page to rhapsodize, philosophize and make solemn sermons on the human condition. Rousseau thought of himself, and has come to be thought of, as a philosopher and political theorist rather than a novelist. Like their author, the characters in Rousseau's fiction are adolescent and —to borrow from the vocabulary of our own times—"disturbed" at that. Neither humor nor common sense—two qualities that the Rationalists, whatever their deficiencies, usually possessed—ever manifest themselves in Rousseau. "Teen-agers," past or present, have

30

rarely been conspicuous for their sense of humor. So, with Rousseau, whether in the novels or the political treatises, all is solemn, as though heaviness of manner were in some way the same as weight of idea—a naïve and most un-French assumption, which reminds us that Rousseau, after all, was not French but Swiss and from the canton of Calvin at that.

In his political treatises Rousseau stepped out from behind his characters and spoke his mind. These works, and especially the *Contrat Social*, were to have the widest imaginable influence on the thinking of his contemporaries. When, in August 1789, after the storming of the Bastille, the newly formed Assembly wished to give utterance to the high purposes by which it would be directed, it drew up a Declaration of the Rights of Man, a noble and, in its time, a moving document, informed largely by the precepts and ideals of Jean-Jacques Rousseau. The utterance of this credo was accompanied by the enthusiasm, indeed the hysteria, that was to attend the promulgation of most of the declarations, constitutions and rescripts of the Revolution: hats were flung into the air, tears of joy were shed, weeping deputy clutched weeping deputy and many such strange couples began to dance wildly about the room, "kissing and embracing one another in a transport." Unfortunately, when this fever abated and ambition, jealousy and expediency returned to preside over the Assembly, no more attention was paid to the Rights of Man than to the constitutions that followed it, all of which were written on the finest of parchment and in a hand of matchless curlicues and flourishes. It takes more than idealistic phrases and high-minded resolutions, however passionately their authors may believe in them, to divert humankind from its customary paths for very long.

Rousseau wrote his novels and treatises on the assumption that men were what he believed they ought to be—content, for instance, in the bosom of their family, or, given the necessary conditions, content to live in harmony with their neighbors. Had he for an instant examined his own heart, which was devoured by suspicion and envy, or looked at the unpleasant facts of his own life—at his children, for instance, whom he put up for adoption—he might have noticed the significant discrepancies that exist between life as ideally one might wish it to be, and life as, in fact, it is.

"Man is born free and everywhere he is in irons." This, his most celebrated statement, is characteristic of Rousseau. It has a ring about it that stirs the heart as it pleases the ear. The fact that it is not true, that man on the contrary is born into almost complete dependence on others and must remain so at least until his tenth or twelfth year, is a fact that one hesitates to introduce in the face of Rousseau's ringing assertion to the contrary. Rousseau's idealization of "nature," his recommendation that men return to that bosom for their livelihood and inspiration, is equally distant from the world of reality. It is possible that property owners on the Lake of Geneva might have found "nature" refreshing; it is doubtful that the inhabitants of Africa, Asia and the two continents of the New World would have found it so.

There is an important connection, direct and clearly definable, between thinking such as this, which combines the weakness of sentimentality with the stubbornness of conviction, and the storm that was to break over France during the Reign of Terror. Robespierre was among the most impassioned admirers of the writings of Rousseau. Like Charlotte Corday, he was among the chaste of the philosopher's followers, and he found in Rousseau's fervent pages a tribute to his own chastity, or, as he and Rousseau preferred to call it— horrible word that was to haunt the Terror—his "Virtue." "Terror without Virtue is bloody; Virtue without Terror is powerless." That ugly sentence would have been different had Robespierre not read Rousseau. With their repeated references to "purity," "virtue" and the delights of domestic simplicity, Robespierre's speeches are not only marked by the idiom of Rousseau, they are informed more profoundly by the same looseness of thought and the same sentimentality which masks that most dangerous of luxuries: self-deceit. Highflown words were scattered everywhere by Robespierre: "liberty," "virtue," "freedom"; but the exact definition of these words, on which depended the animosity or favor of Robespierre, was governed by the exigencies of the moment. By "liberty" Robespierre usually meant liberty as he happened to see it at the time. Rousseau dreamed the dream. It was given to Robespierre, who for a time had the power of life and death over men, to attempt to realize that dream. But he never learned, no more than did Rousseau, that men cannot be carried for very far or very long by abstractions. The fact that many men, frail creatures, continued to pursue such gross goals as sex and money grieved and angered him. To fit men into the inflexible shape of his Utopia it became necessary to do a little squeezing and finally, when they refused to fit the unyielding contours, to slice off the resisting portion.

What makes the Utopias of Rousseau and Robespierre singularly unattractive is that these societies are informed not only with bad judgment but in the large with bad taste. They remind one of a candy box or the biblical illustrations that might be found on a calendar sent out by some small-town undertaker. Men have slaughtered men in the name of many creeds; but the "truths" of Rousseau, as filtered through Robespierre, strike an odd note in the massacres of history, for they are of the simplest order, many of them manifestly false, most of them platitudes—vague, sentimental little niceties. To the victim it can be but a matter of passing moment whether he is put to death in the name of the Holy Trinity or of lower-middle-class virtue. But the reader of history can permit himself a more detached view. Not least among the things that startle him in the Reign of Terror is that the roots of its philosophical justification are in the naïve, adolescent and vulgar idealism always passionately felt, often passionately expressed, of Jean-Jacques Rousseau.

5

WHEN, TOWARDS 1784, Charlotte Corday happened on the works of Rousseau, that exceptional man had been dead for six years, buried on an island fringed with weeping willows at Ermenonville, to which shrine pilgrims in ever-increasing numbers annually made their way. Robespierre, a young law student, went there to visit Rousseau in 1778, shortly before the philosopher's death. There is reason to believe that he may secretly have gone to Ermenonville again in 1793, during the Terror. Charlotte Corday did not feel the need of such a pilgrimage. Knowing nothing of the scandal and squalor of his private life, she was content to bathe in the luscious, rosy-tinted reveries that the philosopher in his still-living voice had bequeathed to France.

These moments of communion with Rousseau, Plutarch and Corneille were snatched between hours of household chores of a commonplace and even menial kind, but she never appears to have felt herself at odds with the world. *"Elle était douce, calme et douée d'une raison au-dessus de son age"*—such is the testimony of a neighbor who recalled her from this time. "She was sweet, calm and sensible beyond her years." Her dreams cushioned her from the buffets of fortune, the alterations of circumstance that frighten or embitter the common portion of men. She moved through the storms of life unruffled by any wind. The waves that swamped other vessels beat upon hers in vain. She was one of those people who, though they partake cheerfully enough of any gathering, remain aloof. This tranquility, which set her apart in her youth and which had a faintly disconcerting quality about it, was to astonish the men whose paths she crossed in the turbulent finale of her life. It astonishes us as much today. There was that in her manner which caused men, even of the mob, instinctively to pull away from her. The officials who examined her, the jury who condemned her, the sightseers who turned out at her trial were as one disconcerted by her untroubled gaze. Her condemnation was heard in uneasy silence—the silence of social embarrassment. There is no case quite like hers in the short and terrible history of the Revolutionary Tribunal. She went to her death still silent, still alone, still apart, inviolable though violated.

Although he despised the *ancien régime,* M. de Corday by no means despised certain of the privileges that for men of his class were attached to it. Ruined in fortune and depressed in mind, he decided to return to his farm at Mesnil-Imbert and to put his two daughters, whom he could no longer support, under the protection of one of those monastic institutions then flourishing in France. There was in that day a convent to suit the requirements of women of every class and temperament. The daughters of M. de Corday, genteel and needy, belonged to a large category, and ample provision had been made for their kind in the conventual system of old France. A cousin of M. de Corday, a nun in the Abbaye-aux-Dames named Mme. de Louvagny, began to take an interest in the unfortunate situation of her relatives. Mme. de Louvagny was a friend of the Abbess of the Abbaye-aux-Dames, Mme. de Belzunce. The Abbess was then aged sixty-five, a woman of great rectitude, piety and presence—the picture, in every way, of what the abbess of a celebrated convent should be. When she learned of the father's need and the situation of his two daughters, Mme. de Belzunce concerned herself with the case. A foundation had been established by Matilda of Flanders in the eleventh century for the education and maintenance of five deserving noble girls without means. Only on the recommendation of the King himself were such students supposed to receive appointments, but the positions had long gone unfilled, and the year before the Abbess had made several exceptions to the rule by inviting her niece Alexandrine de Forbin and a certain Mlle. de Recorbin, who was the daughter of a friend, to enter the Abbaye as boarding students. She now invited M. de Corday to send his daughters to join these girls, who were of their own age. Her invitation was gratefully accepted, and M. de Corday then returned to his land at Mesnil-Imbert. Except for brief intervals, Charlotte was not to see her father again. Politics and the events of the Revolution put a distance between them that was farther than that between Caen and Mesnil-Imbert.

Her entrance into the Abbaye began another phase in Charlotte's life. She was to remain there for six years, years that for France were to comprehend events of the most extraordinary kind, leading to the downfall of the monarchy and the establishment of a republic. Charlotte Corday entered the convent an idealistic and dreaming girl on the threshold of maturity; she left it a woman of character and competence, but singular in this: the dreams of the girl lived on side by side with the practical common sense of the woman. The combination, although not unique, is rare and rather curious.

The Abbaye-aux-Dames, which still stands although the medieval character of its surroundings was destroyed in the invasion of 1944, spreads itself like a fortress upon a hill overlooking Caen. Its outer appearance has not greatly changed since the day when Charlotte Corday arrived there as a student boarder. At the entrance to the abbatial compound rises the Church of the Holy Trinity surmounted by a spire of Gothic design. Here, in the choir, beneath a slab of black marble, rest the bones of Queen Matilda, whose slumber has twice been interrupted since she was entombed—during the Religious Wars of the sixteenth century and again during the Revolution in 1793. In the time of Charlotte Corday masses were said daily for the repose of the soul of that passionate queen who seven centuries earlier had defied a papal interdiction in order to marry the soldier who had had the courage first to beat and then to rape and abduct her. Below the choir there is a crypt of gloomy, unadorned beauty, a "forest of columns" supporting a succession of bare vaults. To this crypt, fit spot for prayer and introspection, Charlotte Corday would often secretly make her way.

Within the compound are still to be found the Abbess's house, a kitchen, administrative buildings, a cloister around which are the nuns' quarters, orchards and a park. In the eighteenth century the park contained a maze worked in a hornbeam hedge. At its center was a clearing that commanded a magnificent view of the city below. An *allée* of ancient elms then shaded the convent walls, while within the park there were avenues of pleached linden and groves of elm and yew through which, two by two, the nuns of St. Benoît glided on noiseless feet. The whole made a picture of unalterable tranquility and unchanging custom, for in these convents of old France century merged unnoticed into century. Even in the year 1785 the wind of the rising storm stirred no leaves behind the walls of the cloister of the Abbaye-aux-Dames.

The four girls who met in the convent that year were of the same background; they had all been instructed by their parents in the manners and accomplishments that in those days were considered suitable for young women of condition. The submission of self to obligation, the inner discipline that is traditionally considered inseparable from good breeding, already marked their deportment. Charlotte learned what it meant to be a Corday and to be able to surmount her arms with a count's coronet. Fine needlework, music and the making of altar lace represented the amusements of the place. Acts of goodness, charitably offered among the poor and sick of Caen, long vigils of prayer and unquestioning submission to authority, represented the duties. Betweentimes, by the old hornbeam hedge, along the avenue of elms or in the crypt, there were opportunities for reverie. An unexpected liberality governed these religious retreats of the *ancien régime*. Charlotte's favorite authors, Rousseau, Plutarch and Corneille, came with her unchallenged behind convent walls. The nuns could see no threat to their way of life in such books as these. So she read and reflected. As she grew older the novels of Rousseau ceased to interest her, and she began to read his political treatises and works of philosophy. The *Contract Social* especially enthralled her and was never far from her side.

Mme. de Louvagny was in charge of the Corday girls' religious education. Years later she was to recall Charlotte as her most difficult pupil, who had disputed every step of the rocky way leading from Faith to Dogma. The Abbé de Vicques, who had handled Charlotte's earlier education, was to say the same thing of her. "She argued everything," he recalled. "She rarely gave in." Charlotte's arguments were dealt with patiently but firmly. The nuns, well versed in the ways of religious dispute and familiar with most of the doubts of idealistic young ladies, had an answer to their pupil's questions. From time to time the Abbess would be summoned to settle some fine point or to rein in a too coltish spirit. The daily routine of prayer, work and meditation, "the soothing force of habit," gradually quelled the storm. The subtle influences of her surroundings—the dank grey stone of the cloister, witness to so many centuries of piety; the linden-shaded garden; the visits to the crypt—began their calming work on her questioning spirit. Temperamentally an extremist and unattracted by compromise or by any middle path, she soon became a *dévote* and hoped to dedicate her mystical propensities to the contemplation of God.

At this time in her life, when she was sixteen, one detects in Charlotte Corday certain makings of the saint *manquée*, one of those nuns who become the legend of their convent, whose spirit lingers on long after the passing of the body to edify novices and the sisters who follow them. Had the times been with her, curious thought, it is possible that Charlotte Corday might one day have become a modest candidate for beatification, for in her visits to the crypt, such was the excess of her zeal that she would sometimes be thrown into a trancelike state; at other times strange spasms would cause her limbs to tremble. These curious seizures would be followed by waves of an ineffable sweetness redolent of ecstasy.

Such solitary pleasures were complemented by her work in the world, and by her many mundane acts of charity. In the poor quarter of St. Gilles, where, with a little band of nuns, she went about her daily rounds, she became known as a *"sainte personne."* But in her transactions with the world she brought to bear a brisk common sense that was part of her Norman heritage and was in no way at odds with the mystical strain rooted in the deeper part of her being. The mystic, having nothing to gain in the world and nothing to lose, can often deal with its affairs with more confidence and therefore more competence than can the materialist, to whom such things appear to be of final importance. Recognizing the girl's practical ability, the Abbess, when Charlotte was a few years older, put her in charge of household purchasing for the convent. An efficient little note from Charlotte Corday to a shopkeeper in the rue Dauphine in Paris still exists; it deals with matters of credit and a letter of exchange. In later years when the Revolution issued the assignats, which made foreign purchases difficult, she was foresighted enough to lay up a good stock of lace that might be used as barter. Hoarding, and indeed even the mechanics of the black market, would have been no mysteries to her. She may have been a *sainte personne;* she was also a Norman.

For Charlotte, occupied with good works, with instruction and an intense inner life, the convent years passed swiftly by. She became a woman, and her appearance became that of the Charlotte Corday who murdered Marat, made immortal by Hauer in his startling portrait of her sketched a few hours before her execution. Was she beautiful? "She was very tall and very beautiful," writes a contemporary of her own sex who knew her shortly after she left the convent. "Her figure was robust but it was noble, her complexion of a dazzling whiteness and of the most wonderful freshness. The tissue of her skin was very fine—you could see the circulation of her blood. She blushed easily and then she became truly ravishing. Her eyes were deep-set and lovely, but their expression was veiled. Her chin was too long and there was something obstinate about it, but her appearance was full of charm and distinction and had an expression of surpassing purity and frankness. The sound of her voice was indescribably low and sweet. Her hair was light chestnut. She did not always have the best posture. Her head often seemed to droop a little."

Like much eighteenth-century portraiture, whether in words or paint, such descriptions leave us with only a vague picture of their subject. They must be compared in their salient points with other descriptions, and by taking what is common to them all one might hope to piece together some resemblance to the original. All descriptions (except, oddly, the one on her passport) agree on her height and build. She was tall and large-boned. "Hoydenish" according to the reporter of the Revolutionary Tribunal, "with a distinctly masculine demeanor." "Strongly built," according to less prejudiced sources, "and statuesque." Hauer's portrait of her confirms these words. It is of a comely but robust woman. Seeing it, one has an immediate sense of the strength and physical good health of its subject. The masculine appearance spoken of in the Revolutionary press, though present in Hauer's portrait, is better suggested by certain facts in Charlotte's life, which in turn illuminate certain facets of her character. The heroines of antiquity held no interest for her; it was the heroes whom she wished to emulate. She instinctively resisted the use of those allurements traditionally considered feminine: ribbons, dress and jewelry. There was a bluntness about her, an aversion to ruse or affectation that might be called "tomboyish" if not actually masculine in character. Under the garish circumstances following her execution, it was discovered that she died *virgo intacta*. Certain of her earthy compatriots have seen this fact as instrumental in producing a state of spiritual exaltation that prompted her to crime. "If Corneille's great-granddaughter had been a wife and mother," one writer was to observe in 1850, "the blood that surged through her brain and made her mad might have filled her breasts with mother's milk to nourish children. The angels who whispered into the ear of Jeanne d'Arc were the same as those who urged Charlotte Corday to murder Marat: they were her womanhood and her rebellious blood. . . ." The French, though they have given the world quite a few mystics and martyrs, have small respect for them.

Her eyes were "blue and piercing." Some describe them as being "veiled" in their expression. They appear at least to have been arresting. Her hair was very fair. Her skin was more than naturally fine and susceptible to the sudden reddening that is characteristic of abnormally thin tissue. The hostile reporter of the Revolutionary Tribunal speaks of "erysipelas," while her admirers refer to "blushes." Her features, apart from a too long and prominent chin, were regular. Her general appearance was informed by an air of good breeding. That in her manner which, for so big a woman, might have been gawky or awkward had been transmuted by her convent education into a composure and presence that were arresting.

Taken all in all, she appears to have been a remarkably handsome woman, though her beauty was not of that kind to exercise sway over ordinary men. After her death many legends and stories were inevitably to arise telling of secret amours, of men she loved who had incited her to vengeance, or of men who loved her and died of that love. All but one of these stories is false. The one strange and authentic case was Adam Lux, a fervent young envoy to the Assembly from Mayence. The downfall of the Girondins spelt for him, as for Charlotte Corday, the end to dreams of a regenerated Europe. In the death of Charlotte Corday he saw the perfect expression of that noble self-sacrifice which both he and she so intensely admired. And so, with Charlotte Corday's name reverently on his lips, he went deliberately to his own death. He had seen her only once, swaying in a tumbrel on her way to the same scaffold where he too chose to die. The recollection of her dignity and beauty at that moment possessed him totally. In Adam Lux Charlotte Corday might have found a man worthy of her disturbed and passionate heart.

6

In 1789 Charlotte turned twenty-one. In that crucial year, the most significant perhaps in French history, she decided to take the veil and, renouncing pomps and vanities she had never known and for which she had no taste, to retire behind the walls of her convent. It was an ill-chosen hour to decide to become a nun. The swiftly approaching end of the Abbaye-aux-Dames and all places like it was prophetically written in the epic events that rocked France during that year. The storm, which was to last five years, broke out in May 1789, when, after the summoning of the States-General, the Third Estate—the People—separated from the Nobility and the Clergy and declared itself to be a National Assembly invested with the authority to represent national interest, and dedicated itself to the task of giving France a constitution. This audacious act was everywhere greeted with the wildest enthusiasm. One may be sure that behind the walls of the Abbaye-aux-Dames Charlotte Corday contributed her tears of joy to that ocean of tears that was wept during those happy weeks. In July the Bastille, symbolic stronghold of feudalism, was stormed and taken. In August came the Declaration of the Rights of Man: "We wish to make a declaration for all men, for all time, for all countries, to be an example for all the world," pronounced the Assembly. Surely, if events had gone as well as the Declaration of the Rights of Man assumed that they would go, the millennium was at hand.

Unfortunately the Assembly soon became a political body like any other, finding itself divided into a Right, a Left and a Center. Among its members were to be found certain men who aspired to positions of more authority than their fellow representatives. There were those among them who believed that their ideas alone represented the best interests of the French nation and that anyone who did not agree with them was consequently an enemy of the nation. From its inception the Assembly was rent by quarrels of the most bitter sort. This representative body was first to be a Constituent Assembly, then a Legislative Assembly, before finally convening in 1792 as the National Convention. The unending battles for control of it—by the Constitutional Monarchists and the Republicans, by the Girondins and the Maratists, by the city of Paris and the country of France, by the Jacobins and the Cordeliers, by Danton and Robespierre, by the Committee of Public Safety and finally by certain members within the Committee of Public Safety—represent the political history of the French Revolution. No event of the Revolution or of the Terror is separate from that struggle. The assassination of Marat is as closely tied to it as is the final fateful enmity between Fouché and Robespierre that brought the Terror to its close. Revolt was to follow revolt within the Assembly, and he who had been on the Left in one month found himself taking the place of a vanished Right in the next.

In the rosy morn of its inception few could have foreseen the dark dramas that were to be played before the National Assembly. While in her convent Charlotte Corday was rejoicing, in Paris Marat, hearkening to the distant roar, abandoned his medical practice and founded his newspaper, *L'Ami du Peuple*. During those summer months a man by the name of Lavaux happened into the Cordeliers' Convent, central meeting place of the Cordeliers' "District" of Paris, where he saw an orator of the wildest appearance leaping up and down upon a table and "in a frantic voice" exhorting his fellow citizens to take up arms and save themselves from the Royalist brigands who were about to destroy them. Drawing closer, he was astonished to recognize in the convulsed features the familiar face of his friend Georges-Jacques Danton, a respectable lawyer and happily married *bon bourgeois* of the quarter.

Not far from this scene, which astonished Lavaux, a lonely deputy from Arras had set up temporary lodging in the rue de Saintonge. The high hopes that this deputy had entertained of making a great name for himself in Paris had been dampened by the presence of more than seven hundred other deputies. In 1789 the name Robespierre meant no more than any other of those obscure names. After the Assembly moved into Paris from Versailles in October, Robespierre began to attend the evening meetings of the Society of the Friends of the Constitution, recently set up in the Jacobin Convent. The Jacobin Club, as this organization soon became known, served in those days as a clearing house in Paris where friendless or lonely deputies might meet one another and discuss the issues of the day. As a social agency its initial function was oddly akin to that which has been taken unto themselves by many of today's churches. Because he had little else to do of an evening—the pleasures of the flesh held no interest for him—Robespierre spent more time than most men at the Jacobin Club. And here, not in the Assembly, he slowly began to acquire that reputation which in three years' time was to carry him to high places.

Those months of general joy were not without certain ominous undertones for timid spirits or those who were less readily transported by enthusiasm. A wave of anarchy swept over France; in the provinces châteaux were burned, and in several instances their luckless owners with them. Provincial records were tossed into the flames. In Paris "the mob," that newborn monster of many faces, showed a frightening fondness for heads and hearts on the end of its pikestaffs. The epithet "aristocrat" lent itself to a wide interpretation and became an excuse for acts of outrage, vandalism and murder. Woe betide the innocent individual singled out for attention by this roaming wolfpack. From the first days of the Revolution it became apparent that the law, in the courtroom as well as on the streets, could not offer its customary protection. What help is a handful of policemen against a crowd of five hundred men and women? As often as not the police themselves would become a part of the mob. Nor could the National Guard always withstand the power of these mobs. The position of individuals who composed the police or militia was at all times equivocal. To whose orders, in the rapid succession of mutually hostile factions that governed France, were they subject?

The provinces were not wanting in examples of anarchy. At Caen Charlotte Corday was close to a grim event that rudely intruded upon her pure and noble dreams of France's approaching Golden Age. Mme. de Belzunce, the Abbess of the Abbaye-aux-Dames (who died in 1787, two years before this episode), had a relative, one Henri de Belzunce, who was second in command of the Bourbon regiment garrisoned at Caen. He was twenty-four, "slim, elegant and good-looking." He also appears to have been an arrogant and ignorant fop, in whose strutting figure we can distinguish the outline of much that must have made the *ancien régime* intolerable to ordinary people. Invested with too much power and giving themselves airs far out of proportion to their modest talents, young officers like Belzunce ill represented the Crown in such innately conservative provincial towns as Caen. When the National Assembly established itself, Henri de Belzunce did not trouble to conceal his contempt and chagrin. He sweepingly referred to the honest burghers and tradesmen of Caen as "canaille" and swaggered through the town followed by an escort of soldiers, his pistol more often than not menacingly drawn.

On June 29 a celebration was held in the main square of Caen to honor the newly formed Assembly. Here a wooden pyramid painted to resemble marble was set up and decorated with wreaths and flowers; inscribed on its three faces were the legends *Vive le Roi!* and *Vive les Trois Ordres!* This rejoicing annoyed Belzunce, who seized and placed under arrest a small boy who had been setting off fireworks. He aimed his ever-present pistol at a citizen who attempted to take the boy's part. The crowd murmured ominously. Exasperated, Belzunce summoned his soldiery, who surrounded the pyramid and put an end to the day's celebration. The effect of this particular event, disagreeable in itself, was to confirm the unpleasant impression that the young officer had already made in Caen. The rumor circulated swiftly—and was believed—that it was his intention to burn the town and massacre all its inhabitants.

The fuse which was attached to this keg of powder was finally lit on August 11, when Belzunce incited some of his soldiers to tear Necker's medal portrait from the throat of their comrades who were wearing it. Belzunce himself joined in this assault, which, understandably, was bitterly resented by the victims. Certain of the soldiers who had been attacked spread the story about the town, provoking indignation everywhere. Finally gunfire was exchanged by one of Belzunce's men and some of the civil guard of Caen. In the excitement the old rumor that Belzunce planned to destroy the city began to spread like wildfire. That evening the city fathers sent a message to him requesting his presence at the Hôtel de Ville. In addition to being arrogant Belzunce appears also to have been stupid, as fops so often are. Very foolishly he agreed to see the city fathers, and immediately (in bedroom slippers and nightshirt—interesting testimony to his haste and to the hour) left the security of his garrison for the Hôtel de Ville, which was in another quarter of the town. He set out alone. No sooner was he detached from his soldiery than a vast and angry crowd surrounded him. "For his own safety" the city fathers ordered that he spend the night in the municipal château, or—in blunter words—the city fortress. The meaning of this move cannot have been lost on him, for in the course of that night he made out his will.

On the following morning he again set out for the Hôtel de Ville. Since dawn the tocsin, that augury of civil strife whose wild summons was to clang across the eve of every upheaval of the Revolution, had been calling together the townspeople of Caen. Armed, some with scythes, some with muskets, they gathered from near and far. When Belzunce left his prison he had to make his way through a howling mob that demanded his head. Rather than be torn limb from limb by the mob, he decided to kill himself on the spot. He tried to wrench a gun from one of his guards. The guard knocked him down. In an instant the mob was on him. He was clubbed to death. The mob tore his body to bits. One man ripped open his chest with a pair of scissors and pulled out the still-palpitating heart. The grisly token was tossed about in the air like a child's plaything. A woman finally caught it, impaled it on a pike and, screaming all the while like one gone mad, devoured it. Unspeakable atrocities were perpetrated on the rest of his body. His head was cut off, taken to a hairdresser where the bloody locks were washed and curled, then carried to the convent of the Abbaye-aux-Dames to be shown to the Abbess—the mob did not know that, luckily for her, Mme. de Belzunce had been dead two years. The gruesome crime was thus brought very close to Charlotte Corday. Charlotte's closest friend at the convent, Alexandrine de Forbin, was in fact a cousin of Belzunce.

7

CHARLOTTE CORDAY would have had scant respect for the behavior
and opinions of Henri de Belzunce. She was already outspoken in
her enthusiasm for the Revolution. But her gentle and generous
dreams, which in that year of 1789 were the dreams of many
thoughtful people, could not comprehend a murder so savage as that
of Belzunce. The circumstances of his death came to her as a great
shock. She saw for the first time that face of the Revolution which,
rising as though out of the fog of nightmare, menaced the noble
hopes of her beloved philosophers. Not yet was that face the face
of Marat. His name was still unknown to her, though in Paris it was
already beginning to appear prominently in the police registers. Pursued by the agents of Lafayette, Marat had begun to lead his life
below ground, in holes, cellars and sewers.

Once on its feet the Revolution moved forward with swift steps.
In October a mob from Paris marched to Versailles, stormed the
palace and on the following day brought a captive King and Queen
back with them to the capital. The Tuileries, that palace of ill-omen,
became the residence of the monarchy. For the royal family the
Tuileries was the antichamber of their imprisonment, the first room
in a narrowing succession of rooms leading to the Temple Tower
and to the scaffold. Titles of nobility, and with them many out-
moded prerogatives, were abolished in August. On April of the
following year the Assembly dealt with the growing menace of national bankruptcy (it had been to solve this problem that the States-
General was convened in the first place) by seizing the vast lands
and chattels of the Church and issuing against these confiscated
riches a currency known as "assignats." The assignats, beautifully
engraved slips of paper, were in no convenient way convertible into

46

the real estate that they represented. The ease with which this currency could be printed in order to give the illusion of wealth was a temptation the government was unable to resist. The fixing of prices and the consequent intricate series of maneuvers by the government to inject into its currency a value that it did not have were the inevitable outcomes.

Inevitable too was the appearance of speculators, that persistent and mysterious breed which is never to be seen in clear weather but which under the darkening skies of trouble appears as though from nowhere. These vultures flocked from far and wide, ready and able to make profit from the abuse of government regulations. Safely nested down in such places as Switzerland or the Rhenish provinces, few were apprehended. It was their agents or those ordinary individuals, unpracticed in dishonest ways, inept enough to be caught exchanging gold for real estate or even for a loaf of bread, who were hailed before the Revolutionary Tribunal and dispatched on the Place de la Révolution. When the Terror ended, these new rich moved with impunity into the palaces of the former nobles, which they had bought for a song, and began to enjoy the fruits of their acumen. The confiscated church lands did not always lend themselves to such profitable or comfortable use as the *hôtels particuliers* of the nobility. The buildings themselves were often uninhabitable. "The nation can set up workrooms in those once barren houses of prayer in which poor people can find subsistence by working"—such was a suggestion for their disposal by Le Chapelier, a deputy. "Thus," he continued, "there will be no more poor people in France except those people who choose to remain poor"—a sequence of reasoning that must have been difficult for even the most advanced of Rousseau's disciples to follow.

Convents were not effectively suppressed until the following year. At the Abbaye-aux-Dames Charlotte Corday, following with close attention the long-hoped-for events taking place in France, continued to manage the household affairs of the convent. She bartered lace and bought comestibles. With her friend Alexandrine de Forbin she continued to do acts of charity among the poor of the city. She wore the uniform of her calling without fear. The flames of civic idealism began to burn again in her breast, and as she read with freshened interest the *Contrat Social* and the biographies of Plutarch, it seemed to her that the time was at last at hand when the virtues of that better age were to return to earth and establish their reign over men. She began to dream of playing some part in the events of the time or of demonstrating the exaltation which flooded her soul.

In June 1791 the royal family, after months of secret and careful preparation, managed to escape from the Tuileries and make their way towards Metz. They were apprehended at Varennes, a few miles from the frontier, and were escorted back to Paris in circumstances of great ignominy. In the heat and horror of that two days' journey the Queen's hair turned white. From that moment courtly words ceased to disguise from the King the true nature of his position. Three months later the Crown enjoyed the last flicker of an expiring respect when the Assembly presented to the nation the Constitution, on which for the past two years it had been working.

The principles enunciated in the Constitution of 1791 were of the loftiest kind, but they belonged to that order of regulation which governs the general rather than the particular or specific. At those points where it did touch upon the definite, small provision was made for the judicious use of compromise, for the timely sacrifice of private animosity as well as private ambition or for that hard work which contributes as much to realizing the aspirations of the state as to realizing those of the individual.

It has never been difficult to design elaborate constitutions or covenants; the difficulty has always been in making them work. "It is very easy to draft on paper great changes or great innovations, for paper offers no resistance," wrote the astute Mme. de Sabran, "and it is a great deal easier to write books than it is to govern men." High ideals, so facilely phrased, so readily believed in, are not, in the end, to be realized easily. This was a fact overlooked in the apparently universal joy that greeted the short-lived Constitution of 1791.

For many persons less skeptical than Mme. de Sabran that Constitution spelled the end of the Revolution. The nation's demands had been satisfied and the threat of aggression from abroad seemed to be over. The monarchy had been saved, liberty had been achieved. It was supposed that now the French people could return to their daily occupations, pick up their lives where they had left off and profit by the improved condition of things.

Such was not to be the case. Pandora's box had been opened. Dark forces, more powerful than the restraints of the law, were abroad in the land. Not only had the Paris mob tasted blood, which it liked; its leaders had tasted power. On the rue St. Honoré, in the former Convent of the Jacobins, the onetime "social club" was well on its way to becoming the dictator of France. Through its three hundred members in the Assembly; through its other members who controlled the Commune and the Paris mob; through its wide and loyal membership in the recently established provincial affiliates—a network that was soon to cover the whole country—the Jacobin Club held in its fingers the reins of enormous power. Who controlled the Jacobins might well control France. Intrigue began to make its stealthy way behind those walls of sinister name. A succession of public expulsions from membership had already begun. Rival clubs were hurriedly formed. The name Robespierre, the Jacobins' most assiduous member, began to be heard in the remote regions of France.

It was Robespierre who proposed to the Assembly that when that body dissolved itself—its allotted task of presenting France with a constitution now being complete—it should not reconvene with the same members. Members of the first Assembly, the so-called Constituent Assembly, were to be ineligible for election to the second Assembly, known as the Legislative Assembly. The motives behind this apparently disinterested proposal, which made Robespierre himself ineligible for election, were clear. Through its member clubs in the provinces who were at the command of the central club in Paris, the new Assembly, by pressures prudently applied in the proper places, could be composed largely of deputies who were Jacobins and who received their orders from the Jacobin Club rather than from their provincial electors, most of whom, relative to the political climate of Paris in 1791, were now conservative. Robespierre and his admirers, dominant powers at the Jacobin Club, could thus exert a greater influence over the destiny of France than they could as mere members of the Assembly. Robespierre's proposal was accepted.

"The Jacobins," writes one witness to these maneuvers, "made use of their provincial affiliates, which were everywhere, to make themselves masters of the new elections. Many cranks and agitators were chosen to go to Paris and represent the nation. Few wise or experienced men were chosen. The new Assembly was composed of men with the most hostile views towards the King, although they publicly affected to 'adore' the Constitution."

In the new Assembly the colleagues of Lafayette, the Constitutionalists who in the first Assembly had sat on the left and who only two years ago had been regarded as red-hot revolutionaries, now took their place in "that pillory," the Right. Those who sat on the left composed themselves about a voluble group of deputies from the country around Bordeaux who, in honor of the river that flows through that peaceful southern valley, were soon, popularly, to be known as the Girondins. A smaller but more startling group on the left represented the Paris Sections, a ragged and filthy band whose sinister appearance was that of thieves and cutthroats and whose raucous interruptions struck an unpleasant chord in the debates of the gathering. This group, known as "the Mountain" because it sat in the high upper benches on the left of the President's tribune, was supported by a menacing audience in the galleries, screaming fish-wives and hooligans of criminal aspect, a persistent and ominous re-minder to the new deputies that their sessions were being held in the center of the city of Paris from whose slums and gutters was evoked the now famous "mob." The power of the party of the Mountain seemed incarnate in its self-appointed leader, the terrible Marat.

"I am the rage of the people," he declared. And, indeed, in that sick and twitching face seemed written the past suffering and the approaching vengeance of all the beaten, rejected and despised. Dressed in greasy rags, caked with filth, wracked by disease, Marat made the strongest tremble and the boldest keep his distance. It was noticed that even the men of his own party chose not to sit too close to the reeking and unwashed figure of their leader, whose skin was covered by the scabs and pustules of eczema, rumored among the ignorant to be, in fact, leprosy.

From the opening sessions of the Legislative Assembly the two groups of the Left, the Mountain and the Gironde, were at daggers drawn. The death struggle did not begin until the end of 1792, when the Assembly once again dissolved and reassembled as the National Convention. In the National Convention the Girondins were to find themselves men of the Right, Lafayette and the frayed remnants of the Constitutionalists having fled the land that they had set aflame, thus anticipating Queen Marie Amélie's remark to Thiers in 1848: "You ignited this fire, Monsieur Thiers. Try now to put it out." The downfall of the Girondins was eventually to deliver the Convention into the hands of the Extreme Left, which then immediately divided into its own rival factions and parties. The overthrow by Marat of the Girondin deputies on that June day in 1793 marks the real beginning of the Reign of Terror.

Who were these deputies whose fate was to bring Charlotte Corday to Paris with the crime of Judith in her heart and who were one day to be the inspiration of Lamartine and of the Romantic poets? Inescapably we must see them through nineteenth-century eyes, the eyes of the Romantics of whom the Girondins, for all their affectation of Classicism were the harbingers. Tradition depicts them on their final night of life gathered together in their common cell at the Conciergerie in a symposium at which the afterlife was calmly and philosophically discussed in a scene worthy of the pen of Plato and the presence of Socrates. We glimpse them on the following day in the tragic radiance of their youth advancing up the steps of the scaffold. The story of the symposium is no more true than is the picture suggested by their death, though in the case of the symposium it might, with irony, be said, *Se non e verro e ben trovato*. For, had circumstances allowed, it is probable that the Girondins might indeed have spent their final hours in talk—though not for reasons flattering either to themselves or to the legends that have sprung up around them. They were as garrulous a group of men as ever composed a political party, intoxicated by words, obsessed with phrases and the sound of their own voices uttering them.

Certain of these deputies, Vergniaud in particular, were gifted with splendid elocution. Declaimed in a golden voice from the rostrum of the Assembly, many of their fine-sounding phrases appeared for a moment to have some bearing on reality; a great round of applause would follow their utterance. The Girondins would be carried away by the applause, and they would often find themselves saying terrible things that they did not mean to say. "They went far beyond the limits of their real feelings, and often, as they left the Assembly, they would blush for what they had said." So reports an observer of these frequently hysterical sessions which the Girondins, passionate admirers of the Roman Republic, fondly imagined to resemble the grave gatherings of antiquity.

"The gangrened limb should be amputated in order to save the rest of the body." That fine phrase, casually uttered by Isnard in 1791, contains the whole philosophy of the Terror. Isnard did not foresee its application to himself. Denouncing alleged plots by the monarchy, Brissot once cried out, "Why should we find proofs of this? Conspiracy never provides proof." The Public Prosecutor of the Revolutionary Tribunal would borrow that phrase less than two years later and use it against Brissot himself. "It is permitted to any nation to cast from its bosom those who attempt to harm it." Vergniaud uttered this sentiment in speaking of refractory priests. It was to be used with fatal effect against him by Camille Desmoulins in 1793—and in turn against Camille in 1794.

Orating from the Tribune, the Girondins were not above the use of grandiloquent gesture or stage effects. Toga-like cloaks and large flowing bows of muslin worn as cravats became the uniform of their "party." Their long hair, hanging loose and cut in a Brutus fringe, set them apart from the common run of deputies. In addressing the Assembly they made frequent use of their profiles, lifting and slightly turning their heads away from their audience. Barbaroux, whose nose was much admired as being "Roman," made frequent use of this conceit. Their passion for the Rome of Plutarch, the Rome of Charlotte Corday's dreams, carried them beyond reasonable limits. One of their number, Gaudet, never referred to "God" in his oaths; he always spoke of "the gods." Vergniaud preferred to have it said that he and his group were deputies from the Peloponnesus rather than from the homely Gironde. Louis XVI was generally either "Tarquin" or "Caligula"; their references to Cato, the Gracchi, to Brutus and to Caesar became as tiresome as they were cryptic.

Posterity has described them as "men of letters," a compliment that is open to some question. They wrote copiously, it is true, and with all the postures and flourishes that marked their public speaking, but they had been educated neither in the school of experience nor in that of the textbook. In consequence, when read today, their writings remind one of some flaking, ornate façade of stucco behind which there is nothing. In the arena of politics, long words or classical references are poor substitutes for a useful idea. They are no substitute at all for an organized police force, ammunition and a loyal National Guard.

In the months that preceded the downfall of the Girondin party, Paris was on the brink of a famine worse than any suffered under the monarchy. The average man's hospitality to political theory diminishes rapidly in proportion to his hunger and discomfort. Few Frenchmen in February 1793 were as interested in Cicero, Plutarch or Rousseau as they were in a good meal. The Girondins, heedless of the dangers inherent in this situation, unwisely continued to spout their beloved philosophers. They thus invited a general sympathy with the drunken Hanriot's remark on the day of their downfall: "We don't want any more empty words."

Their affectations, their naïve idealism and their weakness helped bring ruin upon France as well as upon themselves. It is possible that had they been able to rise above the petty rancor that they felt towards Danton and been willing to make an alliance with him against Marat and Robespierre, France would not have plunged into the abyss before which in the spring of 1793 she was poised. Politicians have never found it difficult to sacrifice their friends. The test of statesmen is the warmth with which they are able to embrace their enemies. The Girondins were idealists, not statesmen. And indeed, while lamenting their fate, we should remember that for all their idealism they too did not hesitate to call upon the mob when it served their purpose. They had turned to the rabble-rousing Santerre, just as the Mountain finally turned to Hanriot. It was the Girondins, not the Mountain, who brought the fearsome *Marseillais* to Paris, an act they lived bitterly to regret.

For all their obvious faults, there remains a quality about these doomed deputies that even from this distance in time invites respect. "To this devoted band of men whose whole career was Justice and Virtue no one has dared to be contemptuous and history on every side has left them heroes. . . ." Hilaire Belloc has expressed it too vigorously perhaps. More temperately, it might be said that the Girondins belonged to that category of men who can no more be disparaged without qualification than they can be admired without reservation. Their useless brilliance, their unavailing courage, their uncompromising convictions evoke in us today the same mixed emotions as divided France in 1792. The Girondins were foolish, but at least they were consistent. The ideals that inspired them were childish, but the Girondins lived by them and died for them.

The impression that these high-minded young men made on the France of 1791 is best measured by the enthusiasm with which their arrival on the scene was greeted by Charlotte Corday, who was but one of many of the young and hopeful who had been following the Revolution with quickened pulse.

8

THE CONVENTS had been closed and their inhabitants dispersed by that autumn of 1791 when the Girondin party began to make its appearance in Paris. Charlotte Corday and her sister returned to their father's farm at Mesnil-Imbert. Charlotte's friend Alexandrine de Forbin, refusing to abandon the veil, had emigrated. The letters that she wrote Charlotte from across the frontier, petitioning that her name be removed from the lists of the emigrated and that her property be restored to her, were one day to serve as pretext for Charlotte's introduction to the proscribed Girondins and for her fateful trip to Paris.

No violence had disturbed the Norman countryside since the murder of Henri de Belzunce. From the autumn of 1789 until the spring of 1792 the Revolution had progressed swiftly and without bloodshed. Even so, for many men and women who had been advocates of change in 1789, progress by 1791 had become too swift by far. Such a one was Charlotte's father, who, though he may have advocated the destruction of feudalism (and particularly that part of feudal law which excluded younger sons from the inheritance of property), could never have been sympathetic to assaults upon the person or prerogatives of a constitutional king. He may, like many, have desired the destruction of the *ancien régime,* but he did not comprehend in its destruction any loss of his own small privileges. He wished the Revolution to stop at the point where it most benefited him; his view was essentially the view of all the provincial nobility, who desired nothing better than to see the haughty lords of the Court and of Paris brought low. They forgot that the prosperous bourgeoisie, a notch below them on the social scale, a group excluded from positions of rank in the army or civil service, because for all its wealth the individuals who composed it could not quarter their arms, viewed them with the same resentful eyes as they themselves view the glittering parasites of Versailles. On the whole the provincial nobility had been supporters of Lafayette and of the Constitutional Monarchists. The bourgeoisie, on the other hand, supported the Girondins, a party it mistakenly believed to represent its own class. The animosity between these two groups found its parallel only in the hatred of Marat and the Extremists for the Girondins.

When she returned to her father's farm after an absence of six years Charlotte Corday was aflame with revolutionary enthusiasms of a kind that in her father's eyes made her appear to be a spokesman for Danton or Marat. Not least among the disagreeable symptoms of discordant times is the rude intrusion of politics at the dinner table and by the hearthside. Dissension does not restrict itself to the tribune of the senate but, like a blight, makes its way everywhere, dividing the oldest of friends, separating the closest of families.

"The worst part of this deplorable revolution," wrote Mme. de Sabran to her lover the Chevalier de Boufflers, "is the discord sown by it in private circles, among families and friends and even between lovers. Nothing is free from the contagion . . . hatred will always carry the day in hearts withered by politics, and then farewell to the charm of life."

M. de Corday's household was soon shaken by discordant political opinion and heated by dispute. Éléonore took her father's part against her older sister. Charlotte went about the business she had learned in the convent, teaching the girls of the village to sew, visiting the sick and encouraging the infirm, but the disturbances of the time, reflected in her father's family, weighed on her heart. In June 1791, only a few months after her return to the Ferme au Bois, she decided to go back to Caen and solicit lodging there in the household of an elderly and distant aunt, one Mme. de Bretteville.

Unmarried, without funds, and no longer able to retreat to a convent—the usual path of escape for young ladies in her position—Charlotte's future at this moment in her life seems prefigured with a painful clarity. One sees service with a succession of aged female relatives such as Mme. de Bretteville—disgruntled women, not rich themselves, resentfully doling out bread and board in exchange for servitude. One sees her finally, old herself, a destitute maiden aunt living in the back room of a third-class boarding house with a bird and a few plants—possibly in England, for Charlotte's middle age would have corresponded with the dawning Victorian age, when French governesses came into vogue. But the times were to cheat the world of its retired governess as they had of its pious nun.

Mme. de Bretteville was a woman in her sixties, bent, prematurely aged and soured by misfortune and disappointment. She was the only daughter of a rich and eccentric man who had been at once a libertine and a miser, managing this feat by denying to his daughter and wife that which his insatiable appetites obliged him to spend on mistresses and prostitutes. The suitors who had come to his door to ask permission to marry his daughter were quickly discouraged by the meanness of her dowry. Long after hope of marriage had been abandoned, her hand was finally asked for and her father's miserly settlement accepted. M. de Bretteville was hardly a *grand parti,* but he was a husband and he had a name with the requisite *de* in front of it. A gambler at heart, he accepted the lesser immediate sum, the dowry, with the larger inevitable sum, the inheritance, not distant from his vision. Lechery and age were beginning to tell on the old gentleman, and M. de Bretteville, though far from young himself, confidently foresaw the day when his wife would fall heir to a very sizable fortune. His optimism proved ill founded, for instead of dying his father-in-law appeared to grow younger. Year followed year and the old man lived on, wasting his substance on vices that should have been the end of him. All the while the state of the Bretteville household grew more and more wretched. To her husband's continual recriminations ("What good are succulent meats and fine dishes," he is reported to have asked, "when you no longer have teeth in your head to chew them?") Mme. de Bretteville could only retort, "You can't expect me to murder my father just to please you." The couple invested all their hopes in the only issue of their unhappy union, a daughter. Mme. de Bretteville directed her energies towards the eventual marriage of this girl, hoping to do for her daughter what her own father had not done for her. But the future could no more be commanded by Mme. de Bretteville than by her husband. In 1789, at the age of seventeen, the daughter died. On that same day Mme. de Bretteville's father, now in his ninetieth year, married his mistress.

"I had hoped to marry my daughter and bury my father," the afflicted woman cried out, "but the reverse has happened!"

When Mme. de Bretteville's father finally died a few months after his marriage, the better part of his fortune went to his new wife. His daughter received an annual income of 40,000 livres (which, although but a portion of her father's wealth, was a substantial sum of money and made her a rich woman in Caen, as indeed it would have in Paris). She was left her father's furniture as well. M. de Bretteville, advanced in years himself, was unable to survive the dissipations into which, too late, he now flung himself, and soon followed his father-in-law to the grave, offering to all who knew his story a stern lesson in the futility of such schemes and the danger of gambling with dowries.

Mme. de Bretteville was too old and too set in her ways to leave the gloomy house at 148 rue St. Jean where she had spent the long lean years of her marriage. Though located in the most aristocratic street in Caen, it was of meaner proportion than its neighbors, unadorned by heraldic emblems and set back from the street by a dark and narrow courtyard in the center of which were a pump and well. Its kind is still to be come upon in the older quarter of certain French cities, somber relics of a bygone age that do not at all suggest high-living such as the writers of historic fiction have often depicted it.

The ground floor of the house was rented out to a carpenter named Lunel. Above his shop were the two floors comprising Mme. de Bretteville's apartments. Entry to the house was through a small door at the far side of the courtyard. One entered a dark narrow passage at the end of which was a stone staircase leading to Mme. de Bretteville's rooms on the second floor. The building no longer stands, but a guidebook to Caen written in 1850 gives us a picture of it and of the room that Charlotte Corday once occupied. Because it was the house in which Charlotte conceived her plan of saving France by the murder of Marat, by 1850 it had become something of a *monument historique* and a visiting place of tourists. "The apartment of Mme. de Bretteville communicated by means of a narrow corridor with the room that Charlotte Corday occupied at the other end of the house. Charlotte Corday's room, situated on the second story at the end of the courtyard, has undergone very few changes. The same stone staircase leads to it and the same door serves as an entrance. With the exception of the fireplace, which today occupies less space, the construction of the room is just as it used to be. The floor is of stone; the beams of the ceiling are not carved. All is very plain. The window, however, that overlooks the courtyard has changed its shape. In those days there were small panes on which some witnesses still recollect having seen Charlotte make little drawings and amuse herself by tracing designs. She was very fond of drawing, and it was to the eldest son of the carpenter Lunel, still alive today, that she presented at the moment of her departure for Paris a portfolio containing her drawings and her pencil case."

Mme. de Bretteville led a life that was regulated by a minute and undeviating routine, most of it centered about the needs of her cat Minette and her dog Azor. When it was announced to her that a distant relative, Charlotte de Corday, was on her doorstep and had come to solicit board and shelter, she was astonished. She later confessed to a friend that she did not know the girl "from Eve or from Adam either"; but in this she perhaps exaggerated, for she had certainly seen something of Charlotte during her niece's residence at the nearby Abbaye-aux-Dames. Charlotte's sudden appearance became the main topic of conversation among the elderly Royalists of Caen, who were the old woman's only friends. As a relative, Charlotte was accepted without question into Mme. de Bretteville's household and escorted by the housekeeper to her bedroom.

The gloomy chamber where she was to live for nearly two years was lit by the cold light of two mullioned windows that faced north onto the courtyard. The floor was of uncarpeted stone or brick. A huge oaken chest over which hung a tarnished mirror dominated the room. A few hard chairs covered with worn tapestry were scattered here and there across the bare floor. It was a room that was cold in winter and dank in summer, its single interest perhaps being the view onto which it opened across the court to the street on the opposite side. Here, unobserved, one could watch the comings and goings of the people of Caen. The Hôtel de l'Intendance, the town's most important hostelry, was visible from Charlotte's bedroom and was one day to become the object of her interested scrutiny; here the proscribed Girondins who had managed to elude arrest in Paris were to be lodged. On the other side of the courtyard lived a young man who was a student of the *clavecin*. On warm summer evenings the music of this instrument would often drift through Charlotte's open window, appropriate accompaniment to the melancholy reveries to which in the solitude of her darkened chamber she would often abandon herself.

Charlotte's position in her aunt's household became that of paid companion. In Mme. de Bretteville's dingy little salon she would help the old lady receive her dwindling circle of friends and relatives: the Marquis de Faudoas, the Marquise de Beaurepaire, Mme. Levaillant and her two daughters—the names alone suggest the tone of the society. As the Revolution progressed, many of these provincial Royalists began to emigrate or to remove themselves to quieter communities than Caen. Rouen, untouched by Jacobin excesses, was one such place of retirement. Mme. de Bretteville, a creature of habit, never found the strength to leave the house in Caen that had been her home for so many years. In the evenings Charlotte would dine with her; the old lady sat at one end of the table, Minette the cat by one hand, Azor the dog by the other. Charlotte sat at the far end. The conversation cannot have been lively. Mme. de Bretteville was not interested in the speculations and musings that were so large a part of her young relative's inner life. In its initial stages, the revolution was for Mme. de Bretteville a source of annoyance; in its later stages, a source of fear. Through it all she probably had but the vaguest notion of what actually was taking place. In the evenings after dinner Charlotte would read to her—often turning to certain favorite passages from the dramas of their illustrious ancestor. For these services she was given shelter and a small allowance.

Mme. de Bretteville was an ignorant, selfish and small-minded old woman, but she was not wanting in a certain dignity, the result of a profound and unquestioning attachment to outward manner and small ceremony. She was one of those aristocrats of legend who would have gone to the guillotine with icy dignity, a posture that was rather one of good manners than of defiance or courage; for it would have constituted unpardonable rudeness to embarrass the lower classes with an exhibition of one's private feelings. Although Charlotte Corday appears to have respected her aunt's attachment to these standards and to have viewed her whims with a wry humor, the atmosphere in that dull, provincial household must have hung heavily upon her. Fortunately she was not long in making friends, some of whom were as fascinated as herself by the events that were taking place in Paris.

One of these was a young man named Augustin Leclerc. He worked as steward or man of affairs in her aunt's household, supervising his employer's investments and managing the accounting of her income and expenses. His wife was Mme. de Bretteville's housekeeper. The couple did not live in the house with Mme. de Bretteville, but came and went as circumstances demanded. Augustin Leclerc was an intelligent man, self-educated in a wide variety of subjects, ranging from astronomy to law, from medicine to agronomy. The principles that informed the dawn of the Revolution filled him with the greatest enthusiasm, for he was an avid admirer of the *philosophes* and the Encyclopedists, many of whose books he owned.

Of the Encyclopedists, those extraordinary men whose fire had so brilliantly illuminated the second half of the eighteenth century, lighting for France its road to freedom, only one remained alive in the year 1791. This was the Abbé Raynal, author of the celebrated *Histoire des Deux Indes,* an imaginary travel story of a kind extraordinarily popular in eighteenth-century France. The European, made deceitful and rapacious by his civilization, is scornfully contrasted with the uncorrupted natives of the two Indies, into whose idyllic life the European intrudes. Published in two volumes (Diderot had some hand in its revised edition), the *Histoire des Deux Indes,* although ostensibly a travel book, was, in fact, an open attack on King, Church and most of the institutions of the *ancien régime.* It was denounced by the Provincial Parliaments, and the Abbé Raynal, in the honorable tradition of his fellow Encyclopedists, had been obliged to flee France to escape prosecution.

Charlotte Corday, like her friend Augustin Leclerc, was an admirer of the Abbé Raynal and his works. In reading the luscious descriptions that form so large a body of the *Deux Indes* we can still today share vicariously with Charlotte Corday some of the excitement of her imagined travels and some of her indignation too at the institutions that wrought suffering on the innocent natives of the two Indies. The book is a mirror, cracked and darkened by time, but in it we can catch a glimpse of the youthful features of Charlotte Corday affixed with intensity to those spellbinding pages.

In 1791, after many years of exile, the Abbé Raynal returned to Paris. He was shocked to find that the country for whose liberty he had suffered was poised on the brink of anarchy, and to learn that the principles that had been the inspiration of the Encyclopedists were being violated by ambitious leaders of the many factions within the Assembly. The dangers inherent in the political clubs, the Jacobins' and the Cordeliers', especially disturbed him. The ominous outbreaks of mob violence and the atrocities committed by these wandering mobs shocked him.

The Abbé Raynal now did a courageous thing. He addressed a long, blunt letter to the Assembly, dissociating the *philosophes* from its errors, indicating at the same time the path by which France might return to stability. In essence his recommendations were for a stronger central government that should find its point of unity in the person of the King—an arresting suggestion from a man who under the old monarchy had been the most tireless and courageous opponent of tyranny.

9

THIS LETTER, read before the Assembly in May 1791, is an extraordinary document that has too often been ignored by historians. It should be quoted not only because it is directly connected with Charlotte Corday's assassination of Marat, but because it describes clearly the condition of France a few weeks before the King's flight to Varennes—a moment when the Revolution might have taken another turn. At the time of the Abbé Raynal's letter the prison massacres of September 1792 had not yet taken place and the Reign of Terror was nearly two years distant. As may be imagined, this document caused the greatest commotion in the Assembly. It was delivered to the President and read aloud—after a vote had been taken —to the assembled deputies.

"Returning to this capital after a long absence," the Abbé Raynal began, "my heart and thoughts are turned towards you. You would have seen me before the feet of this august assembly if my age and infirmities allowed me to speak to you of the great things which you have done and of those other things which now need be done in order to establish in this unhappy land that peace, liberty and happiness which it is your intention to procure for us.

"Not long ago I dared to speak to kings of their duty. Suffer me today that I speak to the people of its mistakes and to the people's representatives of the great dangers which menace us. . . . I shall not hesitate to say that I am profoundly grieved by the crimes which are covering our nation in mourning. I am appalled to realize that I am one of those who, once battling against arbitrary power, may have given arms to license rather than to liberty. . . ." Here, speaking for the *philosophes,* he disavowed all association of these vanished men with the events that were currently taking place in

France. "You cannot, without falling into the greatest error, attribute to us the false interpretations which have been made of our philosophy.

"About to die, very soon to leave this great family whose happiness has been my life's most ardent wish, what do I see about me? Religious dispute, civil dissension, fear on the part of some, tyranny and ambition on the part of others, a government which has become a slave to the forces of the gutter and become a sanctuary for men who want alternately to dictate or to violate the law, soldiers without discipline, heads of state without authority, ministers without means, power over the state existing in certain clubs where gross and ignorant men pass judgment on political matters. . . ."

At this point a great outcry arose from the Left, followed by a demand that the reading of Abbé Raynal's letter be immediately discontinued. Invoking the name of liberty, the President managed to calm the indignant members of the Jacobin Club, and the reading went on.

"Such, and I tell you the truth, is the real state of affairs in France. I dare to tell you so not only because I must, but because I am eighty years of age, because no one here can accuse me of regretting the *ancien régime,* because in denouncing in your presence those citizens who have irresponsibly set fire to our kingdom or who have perverted public opinion by their writings [a reference to Marat and *L'Ami du Peuple*] no one can accuse me of being insensible to the value of the freedom of the press. I was full of joy and hope when I saw you laying the foundations of public felicity, abrogating feudal abuses, proclaiming the Rights of Man and bringing the divers regions of our nation under a common law and a uniform government. My eyes fill with tears when I see unscrupulous men using the lowest kind of intrigue to taint this revolution, when I see the honorable name of 'patriot' prostituted and behold license triumphantly marching under the banner of liberty [here, according to a stenographer's notation there were 'a great many murmurs']. . . . I tremble when I hear certain insidious voices fill you with false fears in order to distract your attention from real dangers. I tremble particularly when, looking at the new life of this people which wishes to be free, I see so conspicuous a misunderstanding of those social virtues Humanity and Justice, which are the only bases of real liberty. I see this same people welcoming with avidity the germs of a new and worse corruption, permitting itself to become enchained in a new slavery. In this city, which has been the city of light and of civilization, I see this people welcome with ferocity the most culpable of propositions and see it smile at accounts of murder, boasting of its crimes as though they were conquests. Such people do not realize that the smallest crime can be the beginning of an infinity of calamities. The lightheadedness of this people laughing and dancing on the brink of an abyss has disturbed me more than anything else."

Raynal now made a series of lucid and sensible suggestions to the Assembly as to how it might regain that centralizing authority without which both it and France would be lost. The *philosophes,* in addition to expressing themselves with precision, were also generally realistic in their ideas. Unlike the Girondins, they did not make easy use of such words as "liberty," "tyranny" or "virtue"; such abstractions were usually qualified by them with at least a semblance of definition. The Abbé's well-reasoned arguments won him no support from the deputies of the Left, who interrupted this part of his letter with a barrage of sarcastic and threatening comment.

The letter concluded with another attack on the Jacobin Club and another warning of the terrible fate that awaited France if the incessant attacks on the Assembly by the factions and rabble-rousers, Marat's minions, were not ended: "How, having consecrated France to the principle of individual freedom, can you tolerate within your bosom an institution which is a pretext for every kind of insidious inquisition which a restless faction has sown throughout the nation? . . . What sort of government can withstand the domination of these political clubs? You have destroyed vested power, yet over your heads has risen the most monstrous imaginable expression of aggregate power. All France is now divided into two distinct groups: one, of decent people, moderate spirits who stand aside dumb and appalled, while that other group of violent men terrifies the nation and ferments a frightful volcano which vomits forth a lava capable of destroying us all. . . .

"I have gathered all my strength to speak to you in the austere language of truth. Forgive my zeal and the love which I have for my country should my remonstrances appear too free. Believe in my ardent wishes for your glory as well as in my deepest respect for you."

The effect that this letter, written indeed in "the austere language of truth," had on the Assembly was, according to all present, "impossible to describe." The Right applauded, the Left hooted; the Center, as usual, stirred in agitated but silent consternation. Twenty members of the Left stormed the rostrum demanding a hearing. Robespierre, the most energetic representative of the Jacobin Club, managed to seize the opportunity. His answer to Raynal's letter was characteristic of him, for Robespierre's public utterances always struck a cautious balance between the danger of offending his own faction and that of making too pronounced a commitment against a party still in power. It was only when they were on their way to the guillotine or safely dead that Robespierre ever publicly covered with his invective those whom he called his "enemies." He was able to achieve this difficult and delicate balance by repeated invocation of such exemplary qualities as "tolerance," and "fairmindedness," and by unctuous references to the "virtue of the people"—vague concepts before which men have been traditionally obliged to bow and for which no one, politicians least of all, has ever had the slightest regard. The tone of Robespierre's speech on this day was that of sanctimonious forgiveness of others' faults, his attitude that of a shocked but forgiving moralist. The shock kept him safely on the side of his own faction, while the forgiveness—in case of trouble— could not entirely alienate him from the possibly resurgent forces of "reaction."

"Far be it from me," he pronounced, "to wish to direct the severity with which the name of this man who is still great must be judged— I do not say 'judged by this Assembly,' but by public opinion. As for myself, I find sufficient excuse for him in a circumstance which he has already called to our attention, namely his great age. I am even able to forgive those who applauded this letter because the letter will have a far different effect on the People than was perhaps intended by its author. . . ."

Robespierre cannot have imagined the effect that the letter was to have in the house of Mme. de Bretteville in Caen. It was published privately, as were many such speeches given before the Assembly, and was distributed widely throughout the kingdom. Augustin Leclerc showed his copy of it to Charlotte Corday, who had just arrived in Mme. de Bretteville's household. Not only did it express precisely and courageously many of her own ideas on conditions in France (and was there not something "Roman," something reminiscent of an Athenian Elder about the Abbé's dignified warning?), it contributed several new ideas to Charlotte's already ample store of thoughts. *On ne doit pas la vérité à ses tyrans:* the phrase, which came from one of the Abbé's earlier writings, returned to her now and was echoed in her own scribblings: "One does not owe the truth to one's oppressors."

10

Not yet had her hatred for the forces of ambition and destruction fixed itself on Marat. That name was now known to her, but it was still one of many in the dark and rising torrent that Raynal feared would soon engulf France. Until now the acts of pillage and murder that shocked the famous *philosophe* had been of an isolated and sporadic nature. The real atrocities, organized and cold-blooded, were not to begin until the September Massacres. It was then that the name of Marat, like a lightning rod, attracted the accumulated force of Charlotte's loathing. It was the fault of Charlotte Corday (as it was of the more experienced Raynal; as indeed it often has been of many idealists) that her generous spirit could not recognize the existence in others of such passions as ambition, spite, envy and malice. In refusing to make allowances for their existence, the idealists often exhibit an intolerance that can well match the intolerance that they deplore in others. History has consistently demonstrated that such idealists when in a position to design constitutions or to promulgate law—as the Girondins briefly were—do poor service to their nation.

Another friend whom Charlotte Corday made during her stay at Mme. de Bretteville's was Mlle. Levaillant, a young lady of her own age. Some years after Charlotte's execution Mlle. Levaillant published, when it was safe to do so, a memoir of her friendship with Charlotte Corday. The book is filled with small inaccuracies when it refers to dates of political events. In what pertains to Charlotte Corday, however, it would appear to be generally correct. Mlle. Levaillant (writing under her married name, Mme. de Maromme) recounts one of the most frequently cited stories about Charlotte. On St. Michael's Day (September 29) in 1791, a few months after Charlotte's arrival at Mme. de Bretteville's, her aunt gave a dinner party as a farewell to several of her friends—Mme. Levaillant and her daughter among them—who had decided to leave Caen until the storm abated. Among those present were Charlotte's younger brother François, who was going off the following day to join the Royalist army at Coblenz, and her father. Towards the end of the meal the health of the King (whose ignominious return from Varennes had taken place a few months earlier) was proposed. All glasses were raised save that of Charlotte, who sat with her eyes firmly lowered. An embarrassed silence fell over the little group of embattled Royalists. M. de Corday shot his daughter the severest look; her cousin gazed at her reproachfully.

"How is it that you can refuse to drink to a king who is so virtuous?" her friend Mlle. Levaillant whispered to her.

"I believe that he is a good king," answered Charlotte Corday, who was covered with blushes, "but how can a weak king be virtuous? A weak king can only bring misfortune to his people."

There is something in this part of the anecdote, as Mlle. Levaillant relates it, that does not entirely correspond with the character of Charlotte Corday as it is revealed to us in her letters and in other anecdotes. She may have committed murder in the name of her principles, but it is unlike her to be impolite. Nowhere does she show herself to be so priggish as to embarrass in quite this manner a room filled with relatives and friends. Without questioning the gist of Mlle. Levaillant's anecdote, one wonders if this particular speech is accurately quoted and if there were not some small but mitigating *politesse* on Charlotte's part.

The meal continued, the talk resumed. Again the dinner party was interrupted, this time by a commotion on the street below. It was Claude Fauchet, the newly elected Bishop of Calvados, being sent off to his see at Bayeux to oust from it his predecessor, who had refused to renounce allegiance to Rome. The matter of "juring" priests (those priests who had taken an oath to support the Constitution and thus had been obliged to renounce all attachment to the authority of Rome) and of "nonjuring" priests—those who refused to take the oath—had split France asunder. It was the Revolution's first step towards the militant anti-Christian movement that was to usher in the Terror. In the initial stages of anticlericalism these juring priests were despised by that sizable portion of the French people who remained faithful to their religion; later, when the more courageous priests who refused to take the oath were butchered (more than twelve hundred of them during the September Massacres) or guillotined during the Terror, the juring priests became hated. For all her pseudo-Roman enthusiasms, Charlotte remained a Catholic. Whatever her religious views, she would have despised a man such as Bishop Fauchet because he was an opportunist and a coward.

The disturbance on the street below broke up Mme. de Bretteville's little supper party. Two of her guests, young François de-Corday and a M. de Tournelis, went to the window and were so outraged by the sight that met their eyes that they were prepared either to call down insults or to go down and try to break up the demonstration. The other guests hurriedly drew them from the window. Charlotte Corday was particularly urgent in her warnings.

"Such an act of bravado might be the ruin of us all!" she exclaimed.

M. de Tournelis turned to her reproachfully. "Only a moment ago you offended us by not toasting the King in order to be true to your sentiments. Why should I not avow mine?"

"What I did," came the answer, "compromised only myself. What you planned to do, without gaining any useful end, might have endangered the lives of everybody about you."

Mme. de Bretteville's dinner party brought the curtain down on such small social gaiety as might have cheered Charlotte's stay in her aunt's household. On the following day all the guests left Caen for their various destinations. Gloom and apprehension, like the drizzle of a Norman winter, settled over the household on the rue St. Jean. Mlle. Levaillant's departure was a particular loss for Charlotte Corday. Although in matters of philosophy or politics they shared no common point of view, Mlle. Levaillant had given Charlotte affectionate companionship and agreeable distraction. After her return to Rouen with her mother, she and Charlotte entered into a correspondence, exchanging gossip and ideas. None of Mlle. Levaillant's letters to Charlotte survive. When she left Caen never to return, Charlotte carefully destroyed all papers in which the police might find the names of friends who could be compromised by the discovery. Of Charlotte's letters to Mlle. Levaillant only two survive. Mlle. Levaillant's mother, panic-stricken when the news of Charlotte's dramatic act struck Normandy like a bolt of lightning, tossed the rest into the fire. We have very few of Charlotte's letters today. At the time the letters were written, their recipients did not consider them of sufficient significance to be saved; after the murder of Marat those that had not been thrown away took on too much significance to be left lying about the house. During the Terror more than one person was sent to the guillotine for possessing an innocuous letter from some unfortunate friend who had been executed.

Charlotte's two surviving letters to her friend in Rouen therefore have an interest that is distinct from the small events they recount. In them one is able to catch a glimpse of their author and to hear her speak. These letters, like her other remaining letters (especially that extraordinary one written to Barbaroux the day after her arrest), reveal a sensible, unaffected and high-spirited young woman. A wry humor glints here and there between the lines. She gives the impression of examining events with the interest and dispassion of a laboratory technician. The collapse of her world and her hopes fills her with sorrow, but not with fear or despair.

"You ask me for news," she writes in the first letter, dated March 1792, some six months after the departure of her friend from Caen and a time when the Revolution was about to begin in earnest. "At the present moment, dear friend, nothing at all is happening in our town. People who have any sense have pulled themselves together and left. The curses which you threw down on Caen have all been fulfilled, and if grass is not growing in the streets here it is because it is not yet the season for it. The Faudoases have left, even taking some of their furniture. M. de Cussy is in charge of the flags. I suspect he's rather sweet on Mlle. Fleuriot. With this exodus we are very quiet. The fewer there are of us, the less danger there is of insurrection.

"If it were only myself that I had to consider I should increase the number of refugees in Rouen, not because I am afraid, but just to be with you. . . . My aunt thanks you for your kind wishes. Her health and tastes prevent her from finding solace in anything. She awaits future events with confidence, not having lost all hope. She asks you to express her thanks to your mother for her kind message. She misses you very much and is afraid, as I am too, that you will never return to a town which you so properly despise.

"My other brother left a few days ago to join the ranks of the knights-errant. Perhaps they will meet a few windmills along the way. I cannot believe, as do our too famous 'aristocrats,' that they will make a triumphant entry without encountering some resistance, particularly since the nation is very well armed. I agree that its soldiers are not well disciplined, but this idea of Liberty inspires them with something very much like courage; despair too will serve them well. I am far from calm. What is the fate which awaits us? A terrible despotism if the people are again chained down. We will fall between Scylla and Charybdis. . . .

"I seem to have written you a newspaper instead of a letter as was my intention. These lamentations cure nothing. I am opening this letter to say that M. de Faudoas has just come back. Nobody knows why. His conduct is most mysterious. Adieu, *mon coeur*."

Charlotte Corday's second letter was written two months later, soon after an outbreak of violence known locally as the "Verson Affair." Mme. de Bretteville had a farm at Verson, a community not distant from Caen. The place was well known to Charlotte, as were the details of the "affair." Several priests at Verson had refused to take the oath and continued to celebrate the Mass. Hearing this, the authorities at Caen had dispatched the National Guard to Verson to arrest them. Forewarned, the culprits managed to escape. When the Guard arrived, it had to content itself with looting the presbytery, using their swords to cut off the hair of the curé's sister and the canon's mother, and branding several other women. They took some fifty people prisoner, most of them women, tied them with ropes and made them walk barefoot to Caen. Now and again the guards would seize a torch and singe the hair of those women whose heads had not already been shaved. The episode was a local one but characteristic of the sporadic violence that had broken out in the opening phase of the Revolution (and that had been the source of the Abbé Raynal's distress) and had now started up again. It caused considerable consternation in Caen, further alienating many who might once have been sympathetic to the National Guard and the cause it supported. Charlotte Corday was shocked:

"You ask me what happened at Verson. Every imaginable abomination. About fifty people were beaten and their hair cut off. It seems that it was largely women they had a grudge against. Three of them died a few days later. The rest are still ill . . . among the women were the Abbé Adam's mother and the curé's sister; the mayor of the parish was also taken. One of the peasants was asked by the municipality whether he was a patriot. 'Indeed, gentleman, I am,' he replied. 'Everybody knows that I was the first to steal the property of the clergy, and you know that honest people wouldn't do that!' I don't believe a witty man could have given a better answer than this poor lout. Even the judges found it hard not to smile. The whole parish has now veered around. You would think it was a political club.

"That's enough about them. All the people you ask about have gone to Paris, and today the rest of our decent people depart for Rouen. We are now almost entirely alone. I should have loved to take up residence in your community, especially as each day brings us nearer the threat of insurrection. One dies only once, and what consoles me in the midst of these horrors is that no one will lose much in losing me. . . . When the present offers nothing and there is no future, one must take refuge in the past and look there for the ideal life which does not exist in reality."

Alone in that deserted and frightened town, she did indeed begin to take refuge in the past, drawing closer to the heroes of classic times who had never been far from her side. In the pages of Corneille and Plutarch she found in abundance those virtues so conspicuously lacking in the France of 1792: constancy, uncompromised high-mindedness and the elevation of the state above self. For Charlotte, closeted in her cold bedroom with the heroes of *Cinna* and *De Viribus,* the raucous shriek of reality receded. The dismal winter of 1792 came to its end. With summer the sound of her neighbor's *clavecin* once more drifted through her open window. Here in the evenings she would sit for hours, wrapped in reveries and thoughts that she confided in no one.

"You are foolish to think so much of the past," someone chided.

"Perhaps," she answered. "But I wish I had lived then. In Sparta and Athens there were many courageous women."

II

In AUGUST of that year the Tuileries was stormed by a mob directed by an insurrectionary Paris Commune. The King and his family were seized and taken to the prison of the Temple Tower. The monarchy at last came to its end; the Republic, once so ardently desired by Charlotte Corday and by so many like her, was now at hand. It was not to be officially declared until September 21, when the National Convention, the new representative assembly, held its first sitting; for directly after the storming of the Tuileries on August 10 and the deposition of the King, the Assembly voted to dissolve itself and called for immediate election of a new body, which was to be called the "Convention." Between the downfall of the monarchy and the first meeting of the National Convention occurred the September Massacres, that bloody marker at the parting of the ways in the Revolution. One must look to certain powerful ambitions that centered about these elections to discover at least one rational reason for the appalling events that took place in Paris between September 2 and September 8 in 1792.

The September Massacres have been viewed, and properly so, as an example of the phenomenon called "revolutionary neurosis," in which there occurs a complete breakdown of those instincts and restraints that keep at a deep and usually harmless level the maniacal forces that flow beneath human consciousness. Just as an individual, subjected to certain inner pressures beyond his endurance, will suddenly go mad and destroy himself or those around him, so too, apparently, can a segment of society take leave of its senses and deliver itself to the forces of destruction. The protective coating that separates the maniac from the human being, thin at best, is thinner in some people than in others: that is one of those natural inequalities which legislature is not likely to alter or to cure. Less than three hundred men (many of them neither Parisian nor Frenchmen) committed the atrocities which took place in Paris during that September. The better part of the Parisian populace can be credited with only the negative virtue of having stayed indoors or otherwise having closed its ears to the screams that rose day and night during that week of horror.

Though the roots of this outbreak of savagery may be found in certain obscure elements within the human personality, the error should not be made of dismissing the September Massacres as some accidental outburst of passion. They were coldly and carefully organized. In early August the Duke of Brunswick, speaking for the armies of Europe that had united against the French Revolution, had issued his ill-advised manifesto threatening the "total ruin" of Paris if the King or his family were injured, and a most terrible chastisement to Paris and those citizens of France "who dared defend themselves." Towards the end of August the French armies had met with serious reverses.

At the beginning of September Paris was electrified by the news that the enemy had broken through the frontier near Verdun and was marching towards the capital. Without a king, without leaders, and rent by a thousand dissensions, the Assembly, about to be dissolved, was thoroughly disorganized. Its power had, in fact, fallen into the hands of the Paris Commune; and the Commune, whose animating spirit was Marat, now took measures to confirm that power and to show in no uncertain terms who was master of Paris.

The September Massacres have been conventionally and facilely attributed to the panic brought on by the advancing armies of the Duke of Brunswick. The massacres were represented to their time (as they have been to posterity) as "an irrepressible popular effervescence" caused by the approach of Brunswick and the discovery of many "conspirators" in the prisons of Paris. Contemporary evidence—of men not in collusion with the carefully laid schemes of the Commune—by no means confirms this. "With the Prussians in Champagne you might have supposed that great alarm would have existed in many minds," writes Mercier, an acute observer of the contemporary Paris scene. "Not at all. The theatres and restaurants, all of them full, displayed only peaceful newsmongers. All the boastful threats of our enemies, all their murderous hopes, were not listened to. The Parisians believed their city to be unassailable, and defense plans were laughed at. It was impossible to make them feel terror of the enemy."

There was an Englishman living in Paris at that time, one Dr. John Moore, whose journal makes fascinating reading. He too, noted, and with astonishment, the bland indifference of the average Parisian to the approaching threat of Brunswick. "The Champs-Élysées were crowded with strollers of one sort or another. A great number of small booths were erected where refreshments were sold and which resounded with music and singing. Pantomimes and puppet shows of various kinds were here exhibited and in some parts people were dancing. 'Are these people as happy as they seem?' I asked a Frenchman who was with me. 'They are as happy as that,' he answered. 'Do you think that the Duke of Brunswick never enters their thoughts?' asked I. 'You can be sure that the Duke of Brunswick is the last person in the world they are thinking about,' was his answer."

"Popular effervescence," though undoubtedly present during those troubled August days, is not at all the explanation of the September Massacres; it is their excuse or justification. The explanation is to be found in the well-laid plans of the men who had seized control of the municipal government of Paris and established the Commune. The proofs of this, which are to be found both in documents and in the testimony of reliable witnesses, are beyond question. The registers of the Commune (destroyed in 1871 by another equally desperate Commune, but not destroyed before they had been examined, copied and published in extract by dispassionate scholars) indicate very clearly that the greater part of the assassins were hired, at twenty-four livres each, a sum equivalent to twenty-four dollars. A list of their names, addresses and professions has been published by M. Granier de Cassagnac. Many were chosen from the ranks of the *Marseillais*, "a scum of criminals vomited out of the prisons of Genoa and Sicily," as Blanc-Grilli, himself a deputy from Marseilles to the Assembly, was able with truth to testify.

This horde of brigands had arrived in Paris at the end of July. Their fearful appearance struck terror in all hearts. They were neither French nor from Marseilles but were "a collection of foreign vagabonds, the dregs of all nations, Genoese, Corsicans and Greeks. They had as their principal leaders a man from the Indies and a Pole named Lazowski."

The Girondin ministry, inspired by Roland, had made the fatal mistake of summoning these cutthroats to Paris in the hope that they would support its tottering power. But instead of putting themselves at the disposal of the feeble Girondins or the Assembly, the *Marseillais* and their leaders made a pact with the Paris Commune and Marat.

By what strange distortion of fact they have come to be pictured as a liberty-loving band of romantic volunteers gaily singing the song that they appropriated to their name, it is difficult to imagine. The song was written in a moment of patriotic fervor by Rouget de Lisle in Strasbourg and had nothing to do with the city of Marseilles. "What is this revolutionary hymn which is sung by a group of bandits on their way across France with which your name is associated?" wrote Rouget de Lisle's mother to her son. The composer was imprisoned during the greater part of the Terror. Less known than the "Marseillais" is the anthem that he composed in honor of the restored Bourbon monarchy.

"It was the thirtieth of July, a month before the outbreak of the September Massacres," recalls Thiébault, a deputy, "that these hideous confederates belched up by Marseilles arrived in Paris. I do not think it would be possible to imagine anything more frightful than these five hundred madmen, most of them drunk, wearing red caps and with their arms bare, followed by the dregs of the people from the Faubourgs St. Antoine and St. Marceau fraternizing in tavern after tavern with bands as fearful as the one they formed. Thus they proceeded in 'farandoles' through the principal streets, where the orgy to which they had been bidden by Santerre was preceded by dances which were satanic."

In addition to this group, the Commune had at its disposal the services of certain men in its prisons—murderers, felons and others who had been convicted of crimes of violence. These were released from prison before the beginning of the massacres. The organization of the massacres was undertaken by the newly formed Committee of Surveillance of the Commune. The meetings were attended by Billaud-Varennes and Collot d'Herbois (both of whom during the

Terror were to be appointed to the Committee of Public Safety), and by Danton, Tallien, Panis and Marat.

Marat, who through his newspaper had been keeping the city in a fever for the past three years, had at last come into his own as a power. He now began to act. He appointed himself head of the Committee of Surveillance and immediately and without the slightest authority to do so signed an order for the arrest of his enemy Roland, who had some weeks earlier refused to give him a grant out of the Secret Service fund: for that and for many other reasons Marat was determined to catch the Girondins in the net that was about to be cast over Paris and then to have them massacred. To this plan Danton was opposed: "You know that I do not hesitate at such things when they are necessary," he is reported to have said, "but I disdain them when they are useless." On this point at least he overrode Marat.

At these meetings it was determined to arrest some three to four thousand persons. Gathered together behind prison bars, the victims could be murdered in whole groups. The exact means of dispatching them came up for early discussion. According to Prudhomme, a witness: "Marat proposed to set the prisons on fire, but it was pointed out to him that the neighboring houses would be endangered; someone else advised flooding them. Billaud-Varennes proposed butchering the prisoners. 'You propose butchering them,' someone said, 'but you won't find enough killers.' Billaud-Varennes answered warmly, 'They can be found.' Tallien showed disgust at the discussion, but did not have the courage to oppose it."

The arrests began in the evening of August 29, four days before the massacres. The exact number of those arrested will never be known. It is believed to have been about four thousand people, many of whom were released before their final and fatal imprisonment. All were persons considered "suspect" by the Commune: many priests, a few nobles and a vast number of ordinary people.

When Marat and his Committee of Surveillance had completed their own list of "suspects," the matter was handed over to the Sections, those forty-eight districts into which Paris, headed by the Commune, had been divided. Each Section had its own revolutionary committee; surveillance of civic enthusiasm was easier in small city units, where neighbor could spy on neighbor. Private animosity, vindictiveness and jealousy probably aided the Section committees in the drawing up of their lists. One thing is certain: it was the intention of the Commune that, in addition to being murdered, its victims were also to be robbed. For this reason, such persons as the Sections believed might have valuable possessions on them—watches, jewelry or snuffboxes—were added to the list. Upon arresting the many priests who were detained as suspects, the police of the Commune informed them that they were about to depart on a long journey. The deluded priests would thus take along with them what small change they could lay their hands on. Looting and old-fashioned robbery were never the least motives for much Revolutionary enthusiasm.

Human clay being what it is, many individuals were less susceptible to political exaltation than such idealists as Robespierre would have liked to believe. At the height of the massacres, Billaud-Varennes, learning that his paid assassins were supplementing their stipend with loot from the corpses—loot that the Paris Commune intended to take for itself—hurried to one such scene of carnage in order to harangue the murderers. He was seen there by several witnesses, among them a certain Abbé Sicard, who was one of the few priests to escape slaughter. Abbé Sicard recalls his words: "My good friends," cried Billaud-Varennes, "the Commune sends me to you to say that you are dishonoring this beautiful day. They have learned that after executing justice on them you have been robbing these aristocratic wretches. Leave all the jewels and all the money and goods which they have on them in order to pay the expenses of the great act of justice you are exercising. The Commune will pay you as it was arranged. Be as noble, great and generous as the profession which you follow. May everything on this splendid day be worthy of the people whose sovereignty is entrusted to you!" It is not recorded that Billaud-Varennes's speech had its desired effect.

The massacres began on the afternoon of September 2, a Sunday, when several carriages filled with priests were delivering their load of prisoners to the jail of the Abbaye de St. Germain des Prés. Just before entering the prison gates, the carriages were halted in the narrow street by a thick and menacing crowd. A prisoner in the first vehicle, "a tall young man, clad in a white dressing gown on whose dark hair could still be discerned the bluish trace of a tonsure," was forced from the carriage, where he was huddled with his companions, all of whom were struck dumb with terror. Faced with the men who were employed to murder him, he seemed to hesitate a moment, then raised his arms and whispered "Mercy! Mercy!" These words broke the spell. He was cut down by ten sabre blows. The guards who had been assigned to "protect" the prisoners were among his murderers. The carriages jolted forward a few feet more towards the prison doors. The crowd could wait no longer. One by one the remaining prisoners, twenty-four in all, were torn from the carriages. All of the prisoners but one, the Abbé Sicard, were brutally put to death. The Abbé managed to escape, to face adventures yet more terrible in the hours that were to follow. He survived to write his memoirs.

No sooner were these priests murdered than the mob, now well on its way to madness, roared on to the Carmes, the nearby Carmelite Convent, which had been converted into a prison, where it was known some 150 more priests had been incarcerated. Here the September Massacres began in earnest. Certain priests confined at the Carmes, the Archbishop of Arles among them, had sought refuge in an oratory in the garden, and here the mob found them in attitudes of prayer and resignation. They were instantly dispatched with pike thrusts, sabre cuts and blows from such implements as axes and shovels. Many of their brethren were less resigned to their fate and fled through the garden, hoping to conceal themselves behind statues or trees or in some way to elude their howling pursuers. A few of these priests, driven by sheer terror, managed to leap over a ten-foot wall at the foot of the garden and escape into the neighboring rue Cassette. The rest were quickly cut down.

In the meanwhile a sinister individual by the name of Maillard had arrived on the scene. This strange personage, whose function it was to lend an air of justice to the massacres, and who had been sent to the scene by the Commune, was to preside over several of the butcheries of that week, hurrying from one prison to another with the bustling activity of some *petit commissaire*. At the Carmes, he ordered that "trials" should be instituted. A table was set up in the corridor of the convent that led into the garden. The surviving priests were shepherded into the chapel and in pairs were summoned before Maillard's "popular" tribunal. Condemned, they were pushed down

79

the corridor to the steps descending into the garden. At the foot of these steps the murderers awaited them. In less than two hours 119 men were killed.

The Carmes still stands, and the scene in which the massacres took place is still today very much the same as it was then. The dank and narrow corridor in which Maillard's table stood, the flight of steps down which the victim was thrown to meet his death, the untended and strangely unpleasant garden, are today almost exactly as they were then. In the eighteen sixties certain excavations were made in the garden, and in an abandoned well a great quantity of human bones were found, the jawbones fractured, and the skulls almost without exception broken by blows from a variety of blunt instruments. The men whom the Commune had hired to carry away the bodies, apparently growing weary of the task, had simply tossed them down a well, which they then covered with debris: brooms, wine bottles, market gardeners' cases, plates and dishes. These articles, among them such curious objects as a curling iron, several pots of jam, and a few grease pots, have a macabre air of immediacy. Along with the skulls, many such objects were removed to a chapel in the basement of the building, where, human bones and all, they may be viewed by the visitor today.

Night had begun to fall when the assassins finished their work at the Carmes. Without a pause they roared back to the Abbaye, before the doors of which they had started the massacres that afternoon. Behind the walls of the Abbaye and its adjoining two prisons, nearly three hundred more prisoners were incarcerated to await in terror their own doom; for the rumor of the terrible happenings at the Carmes had penetrated the walls of the Abbaye. Two enormous bonfires were lit in the Abbaye courtyard, and here by the garish light of torches carried by the murderers and their drunken henchmen the scenes at the Carmes were repeated with a renewed fury. Maillard and his committee presided here as before; few escaped the terrible sentence, which was pronounced with the ironic words "Let so-and-so be released." Believing himself free, the unfortunate prisoner docilely followed his guard to the courtyard of the prison, where an indescribable sight met his eyes; everywhere the dying and the dead, many of them hacked limb from limb, the howls of the murderers mingling with the cries and groans of their victims. All night and into the dawn the slaughter continued. A young man named Philippe Morice happened to be returning home from the theatre (it is one of the curiosities of the September Massacres that the ordinary life of Paris continued throughout them) and passed not far from the Abbaye. The gutters of the rue de Seine were running with blood.

"I had hardly reached the rue de Seine when I observed an unusual light and heard a great clamor, which seemed to proceed from the direction of the rue Sainte-Marguerite. I approached a group of women who were assembled at the corner of the street and inquired the cause of this noise.

" 'Where does this one come from?' one of the women asked, looking at her neighbor. 'Do you mean to say you don't know that they're taking care of the goods in the prisons? Look! Look down there in the gutter.'

"The gutter ran red with the blood of the poor creatures whom they were butchering in the Abbaye. Their cries were mingled with the yells of the executioners, and the light which I had caught a glimpse of from the rue de Seine was the light of bonfires which the murderers had lit to illuminate their exploits."

Philippe Morice fled in horror from the neighborhood, but the terrible sounds followed him as far as the rue de Grenelle. On that same night the prisons of the Châtelet and of the Conciergerie were invaded by two separate bands of assassins. At the Conciergerie 328 persons were murdered; at least 225 more lost their lives at the Châtelet. At about the time that Morice was returning from the theatre, the Englishman Dr. Moore sat in his hotel bedroom making an entry in his journal. In an intuitive flash he saw what many historians have refused to see: the cold-blooded organization that lay behind these murders and the direct complicity in them of certain interested politicians.

"Is this the work of a furious and deluded mob?" he asked. "How is it that the citizens of this populous metropolis remain passive spectators of so dreadful an outrage? Is it possible that this is the accomplishment of a plan concerted two or three weeks ago, that those arbitrary arrests were ordered with this view, that rumours of treasons and intended insurrections and massacres were spread about to exasperate the people and that, taking advantage of the rumours of bad news from the frontiers, orders have been issued for firing the cannon and sounding the tocsin to increase the alarm and terrify the populace into acquiescence; while a band of selected ruffians was hired to massacre those whom hatred, revenge or fear had destined to destruction, but whom law and justice could not destroy?

"It is now past twelve at midnight and the bloody work still goes on! Almighty God!"

The bloody work went on for five more days and nights. On the morning of the third, the prison of La Force was entered, and here took place the murder of the Princesse de Lamballe, the most celebrated victim of the September Massacres. The frenzy of the crazed and drunken murderers appears to have reached its highest pitch at La Force. Cannibalism, disembowelment and acts of indescribable ferocity took place there. The Princess, a timid but loyal spirit, had returned to France from the safety of England to be by the side of her friend Marie Antoinette during the troubled days of 1792. She had been arrested in the Temple Tower, where she had accompanied the royal family in its imprisonment, and was returned to La Force, where she met her end a few weeks later. Brought before Maillard's "tribunal," she refused to swear her hatred of the King and Queen and was duly handed over to the mob. She was dispatched with a pike thrust, her still beating heart was ripped from her body and devoured, her legs and arms were severed from her body and shot through cannon. The horrors that were then perpetrated on her disemboweled torso are indescribable; traditionally they have remained cloaked in the obscurity of medical Latin. Because of Mme. de Lamballe's rank her murder is the best known of those that occurred during the September Massacres. It has been loosely assumed, therefore, that most of the other victims were, like herself, aristocrats—an assumption that for some curious reason is often supposed to mitigate these crimes.

Very few victims were, in fact, of the former nobility—less than thirty out of the fifteen hundred who were killed. The massacre that took place at the prison of Bicêtre poignantly testifies to the position of "the People" during that bloody week. Bicêtre had always been the prison of the people; it is, in fact, ironic, that instead of Bicêtre it had been the Bastille, handsomely furnished and providing an excellent table for its aristocratic prisoners, that had been stormed in July 1789. Had the leaders of the mob wished to free some really unfortunate prisoners, they would have gone to Bicêtre, a sinkhole worthy of the attention of a Piranesi.

The mob that descended on it in September 1792, however, was in no mood to liberate any of the 170 unfortunates who were incarcerated there, many of them beggars and the homeless castoffs of society. All without exception were murdered. Among their number were 33 boys between the ages of twelve and fourteen. The atrocities committed at Salpetrière, another prison of the people, were worse. Here girls of ten were put to the sword. "If you knew the terrible details!" wrote Mme. Roland about Salpetrière. "Women brutally violated before being torn to pieces by these tigers . . . you know my enthusiasm for the Revolution; well, now I am ashamed of it; it has been dishonored by this scum and it has become hideous to me."

Mme. Roland's despairing cry was echoed throughout France. The September Massacres mark a crucial turning of the road. Between the Girondins and the men of the Mountain, whom the Girondins believed to be responsible for the murder of fifteen hundred helpless people, there was now never to be any hope of reconciliation —a fact that contributed directly to the institution of the Revolutionary Tribunal and of the Terror.

Out of the ashes of the massacres three men rose to dominate the new Convention: Robespierre, Danton and Marat. Politically and, more important, temperamentally incompatible, the three had in common only their determination to destroy the Girondins. With the downfall of that party Marat was removed from the triumvirate by the hand of Charlotte Corday and the great battle between Robespierre and Danton was the inevitable outcome.

12

THE SEPTEMBER MASSACRES introduced to all France that "sick and passionate creature," Jean-Paul Marat. Until then he had been known only in Paris, largely for his inflammatory journal, *L'Ami du Peuple*. In his Section, that of the Cordeliers, he was known as one of the more restless and energetic of those residing in that asylum of agitators. After the September Massacres, of which he was undoubtedly the animating spirit, he achieved a position of power independent of his publication. He had a mob at his command that had demonstrated in very clear terms the "enthusiasm" of which it was capable. It was thus a grinning and confident Marat who came into prominence at the Convention, the elected representative there of the Paris Commune. The men of the Left viewed him with consternation; those of the Right, with terror. His appearance disconcerted all.

Who was this strange man who, though he died on the threshold of the Terror, was, as Mercier justly says, "the father of all the horrors which followed his horrible reign"? He had been born in Switzerland in 1743 (thus he was forty-nine years of age when elected to the Convention and fifty when he died), the son of a Sardinian father and a Swiss mother. Like so many men who have fished in France's troubled waters, he was not French himself. He was one of six children, of whom only one other, his sister Albertine, retains any identity. An expert watchmaker, Albertine shared Marat's quarters in Paris and helped take care of his household. Her name has thus been preserved for posterity, though she was absent on a visit to Switzerland on that sultry July afternoon in 1793 when Charlotte Corday came to call.

Marat has often been represented to the readers of history as a gross, illiterate boor and a product of the lowest class. This was not the case. His father was a chemist and a teacher of languages, and Marat was raised in the precepts of Calvinism, a background that may certainly be described as "respectable." The twelve heavy volumes that Marat published between 1773 and 1789, on subjects as varied as optics, electricity and philosophy, testify to their author's erudition. Marat could read and write English, Italian, Dutch and German—a heritage, perhaps, from his father. How then did it happen that this man of respectable Swiss background, distinguished by his scholarship and education, was in 1792 dressed in rags, the leader of a maddened mob, the incarnation of ferocity and hatred? The answer is to be found in part by a consideration of those twelve books that, testifying to their author's education, speak too of his aspiration.

"I ever sought the truth," Marat once wrote in a description of himself that was published during the Revolution, "and I must flatter myself that I did not miss my goal, if I am to judge by the low persecutions to which the Royal Academy of Science subjected me for over ten years. This persecution began at the moment the Academy realized that my discoveries about the nature of light upset its own work on the subject and that I hadn't the slightest interest in entering its ranks. Since the d'Alemberts, the Condorcets, the Moniers, Monges, Lavoisiers and all the other charlatans of that scientific body wanted to hog the limelight for themselves, and since they held the trumpet of fame in their hands, it isn't difficult to understand why they disparaged my discoveries throughout Europe, turned every learned society against me and had all learned publications closed to me so that I was obliged to use a pen name in order to get my works published. For over five years I put up with this cowardly oppression.

"The Revolution announced itself with the convocation of the States-General. I quickly saw how the wind was blowing, and at last I began to breathe in the hope of seeing humanity avenged and *myself installed in the place which I deserved. . . .*"

It was always one of Marat's few charms that he called a spade a spade, and this frank description of himself leaves little to be added but the details.

It was his family's wish that he should study medicine, a calling that the young man eagerly pursued. Methodical, hard-working and little susceptible to fanciful distractions, he was, in fact, eminently suited to work in the sciences, those new and fascinating branches of knowledge that opened vistas of such promise in the mid-eighteenth century.

Marat's character inclined him to the laboratory rather than the consulting room. Closeted alone, theorizing and experimenting, he was happy; brought into touch with men, however, he grew truculent and suspicious, and troubles of one sort or another, quarrels, disappointments and failures, soon followed. He was one of those men, common to every time and society, who are not temperamentally disposed to close contact with their fellow beings. It is remarkable that of all the men of the Revolution Marat alone allied himself with no organized "cause" and belonged to no party. This alienation, fruitful for certain men and frequently beneficial to society, was for Marat the cornerstone on which he was to build a terrible edifice.

In another passage of his autobiography, Marat refers to his devouring appetite for *gloire*. "From my earliest years I was consumed with a love of glory, a passion which often changed its object in the divers periods of my life, but which has never left me for a moment. At five I wanted to be a schoolmaster, at fifteen, a professor; author at eighteen, a creative genius at twenty. . . ." In Marat's case this *gloire* so ardently desired might aptly be translated as "fame," or even more coarsely as "notoriety." It was to elude him until the Revolution; but all who know the story of Marat's life will take his word for it that his craving for fame never for an instant left him. Its achievement came when disappointment and ill health had turned his love of *gloire* into the blind fury of a man gone mad.

The study of medicine took him to Bordeaux, to Toulouse, to Paris. He was able to support himself in his wanderings by teaching. His studies did not stop at medicine; industriously he applied himself to philosophy, literature, political theory and physics. Driven by his ungratified appetite for recognition, he began to travel about Europe. He lived for a while in Holland, first in Utrecht, then The Hague, then Amsterdam, always studying, always alone. Obscurity covers these years. One can readily imagine him, nourished by little more than his ambition; indifferent in any case to the pleasures of the table, which temperament as much as poverty had put beyond his reach; indifferent to the small pleasures of society; indifferent, too, to the delights of knowledge which ruthlessly he grabbed and gathered as a miser collects gold. One can only imagine the myriad unknown hurts to which poverty and thwarted ambition made this oversensitive man susceptible.

The year 1772 found him in England, and here, for a moment, the obscurity lightens. In that year he published a book in English called "An Essay on the Human Soul," a curious examination of the soul in terms of anatomy and medicine. It enjoyed a small success in England, and in the following year was expanded and translated into French under the title *Essai Philosophique sur l'Homme*. Although the work was described as "a challenge to Helvétius," in Paris, among the sacrosanct circle of the *philosophes* it was greeted with contempt. Voltaire dismissed it with a few sharp sentences, and the doors of that precious sanctuary that dominated French letters were banged rudely shut on the aspiring Dr. Marat. In 1774, still in England, he published another book, *The Chains of Slavery*, which, as its title suggests, was of a revolutionary nature, "an exposure of the intrigues among the princes of Europe against their peoples." This book won him the attention of certain English radicals. In his own country it was ignored. In the following year he went to Scotland, where he was awarded a degree in medicine by St. Andrew's University. He returned to London, where he set up practice in Pimlico, dedicating his spare moments to writings of a scientific character. Optics and electricity were of particular interest to him, and his research in these fields brought him some attention.

In 1777 he returned at last to France, where he accepted a situation in the household of the Comte d'Artois as brevet-physician to that royal prince's guard. The appointment was of no mean order, and Carlyle, in contemptuously referring to Marat as "a horse-leech" in Artois's stables, is far from the truth. Marat received his keep and the annual stipend of a sum equivalent to five thousand dollars. Considerable distinction attached to this position, but it is odd to find the future revolutionary referring to himself at this period in his life as "the Chevalier Marat." Still more surprising is a letter written in his hand petitioning the *juges d'armes* for confirmation of his nobility ("You will not refuse me these arms when you see how firmly my family has been established in the nobility of Spain as in France . . ."). His attachment to the household of the King's brother permitted him to charge high fees in the office that he opened in his house on the rue de Bourgogne. He was reported to have cured a woman who was dying of pulmonary tuberculosis. The rumor brought more patients to his door. As such things are measured by most men, Dr. Marat, at this moment in his life, was a success. But Dr. Marat was not like other men. The collecting of fees and the honor, only vicarious, that attended his brevet could only remind him of his subjection to other men and to a society that he despised. The comfort of his apartment and the size of his fees afforded little of the *gloire* that haunted him and that, as his fortieth year approached, seemed still to have eluded his grasp.

He began to neglect his patients, never a congenial group to him, and to devote his time to laboratory work. There is at least one instance on record of a scuffle between Marat and the servants of one of his patients that terminated in a lawsuit. Ill health and frustration wore at his frayed nerves, and his temper, naturally irascible, began to grow morbidly quick. The effort he put into his work was prodigious. When he wrote *Chains of Slavery,* he worked on it twenty hours a day, keeping himself awake with draughts of coffee. He once wrote of himself, "I devote only two out of twenty-four hours to sleep, and only one to my meals and domestic necessities. I have not had fifteen minutes' relaxation for more than three years." Such a regimen suggests both the cause of his physical ailments and the symptom of his emotional ones. Ambition of manic proportion was met by overwhelming frustration. For, in Taine's words, "between his talents and his aspirations there lay too great a disproportion."

Hard work and ambition, necessary though they might be to achievement, are in the end no substitutes for talent. It is not of importance that—as many who have read them feel—his works may be a hodgepodge of commonplaces and badly digested truths borrowed from other writers, all presented in a shrill tone and wanting in imagination, humor and style. What is of importance is that they were treated as such by Marat's contemporaries, by the "vested interests" and the various academies of letters and science that were then guardians of the gate to fame and glory. These societies, annoying enough in any century, were distinguished in the eighteenth century by a complacency and arrogance since unmatched. The works of Dr. Marat were ignored by them.

"Impervious to the joys of life, Marat spent all his means upon experiments in physics. He would have been content with bread and water if he could have had the pleasure of humiliating the Academy of Science. That was really the *ne plus ultra* of his ambition"; so wrote Brissot. In 1784 Marat entered a competition initiated by the Academy with a thesis on Newton's optics. His entry received a cutting rejection. Soon after this disappointment there occurred another rebuff, which had an even more irritating effect. An opening appeared in the Spanish Academy of Sciences at Madrid for which Marat applied, again submitting his work to the judgment of men whom he considered inferior to himself. He failed to get the position. The job was "stolen from him by the insidious machinations of his enemies." This disappointment probably alienated him forever from all organized society.

It has been observed by a scholar versed in Marat's life that after the rebuffs from the Royal Academy in France and from the Academy in Madrid, Marat published little more. From 1784 he begins to speak of his "enemies" and of dark, insidious maneuvers behind his back. These are suspicions that cannot be entirely dismissed as paranoid by one familiar with the intellectual world of eighteenth-century France. The men and women of letters of that time were malicious and vindictive, and many were quite capable of those intrigues that Marat, with his sick mind, believed to be going on around him.

The existence of jealous and intriguing enemies, imaginary or not, now became necessary to support Marat's self-esteem. Only through them could he reconcile the high opinion he held of his accomplishments with the failure of his works. In his period of power he was to recall these dark days in his newspaper, *L'Ami du Peuple*. The events as he describes them vary conspicuously from the facts: "The street in front of my house was always blocked with carriages. People from all quarters came to consult me. . . . The abstract of my experiments on light finally appeared, and it created a prodigious sensation throughout Europe; the newspapers were all full of it. I had people from the Court and the City in my house for six months. The Academy, finding that it couldn't stifle my findings, tried to make it appear that they were its own discoveries. Three different academic bodies visited me on the same day trying to persuade me to present myself as a candidate. Several crowned heads sought me out on account of the fame of my works!"

This reminiscence gives us an interesting insight into the unhappy man's mind. The presence in his house of "several crowned heads," the waiting throng outside his door, the academies hopefully proffering their laurels: such were the naïve visions that constituted Marat's picture of *gloire*. He was one of those men who are more interested in the rewards of work—celebrity and the deference of others—than they are in the work itself. For such mean ambitions failure paid him back in mean wages. Between 1785 and the outbreak of the Revolution he was in a condition of mental and physical deterioration, an example of one of those men who have isolated themselves behind an impenetrable wall of hatred, suspicion and suffering.

After 1785 Marat was abandoned by his patients. He resigned (or more probably was asked to resign) his position in the household of the Comte d'Artois. That demonic energy of which all who knew him speak, that devouring ambition which drove the man to work for twenty hours at a stretch, was no longer dedicated to research in optics or to the writing of theses; in a paroxysm of elemental fury it now became devoted to a far different purpose: the destruction of the society that had maimed him.

Arms flailing about in all directions, he waded into the Revolution with the reckless rage of a lunatic. Certain extracts from the newspaper which he established in 1789 make significant reading: "Rise up, you unfortunates of the city, workmen without work, street stragglers sleeping under bridges, prowlers along the highways, beggars without food or shelter, vagabonds, cripples and tramps. . . . Cut the thumbs off the aristocrats who conspire against you; split the tongues of the priests who have preached servitude." His recurrent incitements to bloodshed and murder suggest a strain of homicidal mania in Marat's make-up. In reading his journal one is certainly left with the impression of a man in a delirium. "To ensure the public tranquility two hundred thousand heads should be cut off." "A man who is starving has the right to cut another man's throat and devour his palpitating flesh."

The editor of such an inflammatory sheet could not avoid trouble. In its opening years the Revolution remained under the influence of idealists, intellectuals or men whose ambitions were of a moderate and rational order. Lafayette, a leader of very limited ability but of inordinate conceit, was in command of the National Guard, and the lash of Marat's invective was soon directed at this smug and condescending altruist. ("I'll tear the heart out of that infernal Lafayette right in front of his battalion of lackeys.") Between Marat, who knew what it was to suffer, and Lafayette, who had arrogated to himself all the pretty platitudes of idealism in order to conceal from everyone, himself included, his vanity and ambition, there could be no conceivable agreement. As early as September 1789, the government had issued an order for the arrest of the seditious and rabble-rousing journalist.

Thus began a history of midnight flights, of concealment in cellars, in caves and attics. Once, according to his friend Panis, Marat spent six weeks in a room no bigger than a cell, "crouched down on one buttock." He lived like a bat or owl, always hidden from the light of day. He sought refuge in the Cordeliers' District of Paris, a section of the city now occupied by the College of Medicine and its environs. In those days the Cordeliers' District was a hotbed of the most advanced Revolutionary sentiment, a self-proclaimed and defiant republic within a kingdom, an enclave independent of the rest of the city, which, because it was vigorous and had Danton as its leader, soon came to dominate all other sections composing the city government. The District was then a warren of dark alleys, culs-de-sac and crooked streets that led nowhere. Marat was welcomed by its leaders with open arms and "treated like a prince." From this position of safety he took up his attacks on Lafayette with renewed vigor. Goaded into attack, the government, in January 1790, dispatched an army of three thousand men into the rebellious district with orders to arrest Marat. This challenge to the self-established sovereignty of the Cordeliers made a great sensation. In the course of Danton's negotiation with the government, Marat, in disguise, managed to escape.

He went to England, but unwilling even at the risk of arrest to abandon his publication he returned to Paris after a few months. In September 1790 the police were again on his track. His printer's shop was entered and the presses smashed. Marat's hatred of constituted authority had by this time clearly passed the restraints of sanity. His health had become seriously affected, and now began those ailments that henceforth were to harass him and to alter his appearance, at best unprepossessing, into the hideous mold that his contemporaries are as one in describing.

"By his compulsive, brusque and jerky walk one recognized him as an assassin who had escaped from the executioner, but not from the Furies, a man who wished to annihilate the whole human race."

"Physically," recalls another, "Marat had the burning, haggard eye of a hyena. Like a hyena's his glance was always anxious and in motion. His movements were rapid and jerky, his features were marked by a convulsive contraction which affected his way of walking. He did not walk; he hopped."

"His countenance," describes still another, "toadlike in shape, marked by bulging eyes and a flabby mouth, was of a greenish, corpselike hue. Open sores, often running, pitted this terrible countenance."

The exact nature of his disease—there were probably several—remains unclear. Dr. Cabanès, something of an expert in these matters, has pronounced it to have been eczema "in one of its most dolorous and revolting manifestations. . . . A suppurating tetter ran from the scrotum to the perineum and maddened him with torment." His skin blistered with running sores, he was racked by headaches and intolerable pains in his legs and arms. Often in a fever, the sick and suffering man was in a condition that from this distance in time defies accurate diagnosis. Some mysterious interaction of body and mind was assuredly at work within him, and the committee of "patriots" who, after visiting his sickbed, reported him to be suffering from "a suppression of too furious a patriotism" was probably correct in its analysis. Frustration had wrought its worst upon the ravaged little body, while pain and fever in their turn had poisoned and possessed the spirit.

Sometime during the winter of 1790 an unexpected influence entered Marat's life. Men such as he who are consumed by some single idea are not usually susceptible to the distractions of love. Their passions nourish their fanaticism; little energy remains for those interests that are considered necessary to ordinary men. They do not, like Robespierre, dislike women. Rather they do not have enough time to think about them or the opportunity, in a life such as Marat's, to meet them. These considerations apart, what makes Marat's liaison with Simonne Evrard astonishing is that any woman could have fallen in love with this man, whose appearance was so repulsive that the wildest extremists of the Left and their minions from the gutter were always careful to keep a distance of several benches between themselves and him.

Simonne Evrard was one of three sisters who had come to Paris from the little town of Tournus in the Saône-et-Loire in order to make their living. She had been a laundress and, at the time she met Marat, was employed in a factory that made watch parts. She and her sisters, respectable, hard-working provincials, had been living in Paris for nearly twelve years when the Revolution broke out. She was twenty-seven years of age when Marat entered her life, "a comely woman of decent behavior with soft brown eyes, a large mouth and a grave expression." They met when Marat sought asylum in their house from the agents of Lafayette. Unwilling to compromise the sisters by his presence, he stayed only a night and then moved on. But that brief visit aroused in this quiet, respectable woman a passion that caused her to dedicate her life to him. She became his nurse, his servant, his cook—and his wife. They were married *à la Rousseau* before an open window. "It is in the vast Temple of Nature," pronounced Marat, "that I take for witness of the eternal fidelity which I swear to you, the Supreme Being who hears us."

The vow may have been unconventional, but the devotion of this strange couple never faltered. After his death Simonne Evrard was always spoken of as "the Widow Marat"; Marat's family publicly declared her to have been his legal wife. From 1791 until his death she kept house for him, sharing that task with Marat's sister Albertine. When Marat needed money to re-establish his newspaper she unhesitatingly turned her savings over to him, a small sum perhaps, but one that represented a lifetime of thrift and hard work.

Her affection does not appear to have softened the enraged rabble-rouser. His political life probably interested her only to the extent that it was his. She remained apart from it, soliciting favors from him for no one, while Marat went on his turbulent way. With the September Massacres he came into his own. The dissolution of the Assembly and the new elections to the National Convention brought the extremists of the Left, Danton, Robespierre and Marat, into power. What once had been the Left, the Girondin party, now belonged to the Right. Lafayette and the Moderates had either fled or been arrested. From the time of the September Massacres until May 1793, Marat's rage was to be concentrated on the Girondins.

From the moment of his election to the Convention until his death, Marat's name was known throughout France. In provincial eyes he was the incarnation of the elemental forces from the gutters of Paris that were destroying the Revolution and disgracing France, a creature risen from the regions of Hell whose extinction was most devoutly to be desired. The *gloire* that too late he had achieved, that fame so dear to his heart, was to destroy him. After the expulsion of the Girondins, his death warrant was filled out. Sometime in May or June of 1793 it was finally signed. Although she effected the deed, Charlotte Corday was not alone in wishing death on the man who had brought death to so many others.

On the whole Marat has been represented to posterity as he was to the law-abiding "liberals" of his time—a monster. Nonetheless he has not gone without his defenders, some of them men of scholarship and insight. For those who are too attached to political jargon, who equate contemporary parties and positions with those of the past (a futile task that both diminishes the deeper drama of history and distorts its facts), Marat will always remain either monster or saint. For those, on the other hand, who are more interested in the human heart than in political parties and who measure men less by their political position than by their motives, the character of Marat is not without certain qualities that recommend an attempt at understanding, if not sympathy.

He himself despised all politicians and all abstract political theory, no mean point in his favor when one realizes the horrors shortly to be unleashed upon France in the name of such theories—and for the benefit of those politicians. His was the raucous, persistent voice of dissent, shrill, defiant—and brave, a thorn in the side of the successsive factions who believed, each in its turn, that they had achieved the Revolution and that with them the Revolution would stop. He belonged to no party. His ambitions did not extend to dictatorship. He was never a hypocrite. His advocates speak of his great pity for the poor and have depicted him with a heart brimming over with compassion. That is a picture which is open to doubt. In any case the poor, the derelict and the dispossessed do not always want or need pity. Many of them are more interested in vengeance. And, driven by his own anger, Marat was prepared to offer vengeance in full. "I am the rage of the people," he pronounced. They were words to make the complacent and the prosperous tremble. And from the faceless masses they brought forth many who were eager and willing to fight beneath Marat's banner.

It might, in the end, be said of Marat that he was the embodiment of certain forces present in every society. "Might" may not always make "Right," but it assuredly makes governments. That is not always an agreeable truth to governments or to individuals who have come to a position of wealth, importance or comfort through forebears who have been stronger than themselves. Too readily do the prosperous begin to believe that their chattels and property are protected by divine ordinance rather than by the police. Such self-deception is often one of the first fruits of an individual's wealth—as it is of a nation's. The government that is unable to deal with its Marats or to resist the rigors of challenge is almost certainly doomed. For better or for worse the Marats have always been present in this world, providing, as certain historians have seen it, that friction or resistance which may be necessary to the ultimate health of a state.

There is a story, related with disgust by the Girondins, that in a brief, illuminating flash seems to describe Marat perfectly. Towards the end of 1792, a time when Marat was in the midst of his campaign to destroy the Girondins, the actor Talma gave a reception to General Dumouriez, the hero of Valmy and the strongest remaining support of the Girondins' fast-collapsing hold on power. While the guests were enjoying refreshments to the accompaniment of music from the harp and the piano, a great clatter was heard on the stairs and Marat burst into the room. He was dressed in a "carmagnole," his sockless feet were sheathed in dirty boots, a red bandana was bound around his head and bits of greasy hair caked with dirt stuck out here and there along its fringes. His twitching grin made the women's blood run cold. He was accompanied by several rough-mannered members of the General Security Committee.

"Citizen," he bawled at Dumouriez, "a group of those who love liberty went to the war office this evening to communicate certain dispatches that concerned you. They went to your house and didn't find you there either. We are dumbfounded to find you in a house like this surrounded by a flock of whores and counterrevolutionaries."

Dumouriez answered, "May I not rest from the fatigues of war in the midst of the arts and my friends without having them outraged by your indecent epithets?"

Marat spat on the floor and shook his fist at the shocked assembly. "This house," he cried, "is the house of counterrevolution!" He turned on his heel and left, but not before he had uttered a great many threats of the most terrifying kind. After his departure one of the guests went about the room with scent in order to purify the air after this strange visit from "the dirty beast."

Marat's complicity in the September Massacres has been questioned by certain historians. But once it has been accepted that the massacres were organized by the Commune—as they were—there can be little doubt not only that Marat was implicated in the affair but that his was the guiding hand behind it. It is possible that he may have felt some remorse when a sober dawn broke over the ashes of that which his torch had set afire. The possibility arises from no evidence, but from an estimate of his temperament: he was probably not the sort of man who would kill with his own hands—a subtle but significant distinction. Remorse was an emotion felt too late by other rabble-rousers of those times. Camille Desmoulins, whose reckless pen helped to provide the Revolutionary Tribunal with the false evidence it needed to convict the Girondins, burst into tears when he heard them sentenced to death and was heard to cry out in the courtroom, "It is I who have killed them!"

A proclamation sent out by the Commune of Paris to its brethren throughout the provinces testifies to the complicity of Marat in the September Massacres. It is dated September 3 and is signed at the bottom by Marat:

"The Commune of Paris hastens to inform its brothers in the Departments that many ferocious conspirators detained in its prisons have been put to death by the people—acts of justice which seemed to be indispensable in order to terrorize the traitors concealed within its walls at a time when it was about to march on the enemy. The whole nation will without doubt hasten to adopt this measure so necessary to public safety, and all the French people will cry out as did the Parisians, 'We will march on the enemy, but we will not leave brigands behind us to murder our wives and children.'"

This dispatch, a cold-blooded incitement to violence in the provinces, admits, in terms that could not be clearer, the concurrence of the Commune in those atrocities that conventionally have been attributed to "a popular effervescence." Its cynical reference to "ferocious conspirators" evokes a picture of those women and girls of Salpetrière, the 170 derelicts and the 33 fourteen-year-olds of Bicêtre, of the defenseless priests of the Abbaye and the Carmes. . . .

Marat, if only because of this document, is suddenly placed beyond the pale of humankind. One can understand him as a bacteriologist may be said to "understand" the pneumonia virus—as much a manifestation of nature as are the trees and brooks so touted by Rousseau. But one's sympathy resists the arguments of his few admirers.

13

WHATEVER others may since have believed about the matter, Charlotte Corday had no doubt about Marat's complicity in the massacres. She said so very bluntly in the course of her interrogation by the police. When asked why she had killed him she answered, "Because it was he who caused the massacres of September. . . ." And when asked what proof she had of this she replied, "I can give you no proof. It is the opinion of all France. The future will one day discover the proof."

The proof lay in that inflammatory proclamation that found its way to Caen as it did to other provincial centers. At Caen the document was directly responsible for at least one murder, that of the government's Deputy Attorney-General in Normandy, a man named Bayeux, who was known to Charlotte Corday. Bayeux, "a gentle and upright man of culture who had translated Ovid and published several essays," belonged to that class of men which was associated with the Girondin party. In favor during the first act of the Revolution, in August 1792 he was in prison on some vague charge, as were many of the doomed "suspects" of Paris. His wife, who was pregnant, was determined to save him and accordingly set out for Paris not only with the proofs of his innocence but also with letters of introduction to influential people. The trip from Caen to Paris at that time normally took two days. Mme. Bayeux did it in fifteen hours. She arrived in Paris on the fifth, in the midst of the massacres—and somehow managed to secure an order for her husband's release. She hurried back to Caen with this precious bit of paper in her hands. Marat's proclamation to the provinces was issued on the third; it arrived in Caen on the fifth, on the same day that Mme. Bayeux was hurrying from Paris back to Caen. Incited by Marat's call to crime, the Jacobins and the political adversaries of Bayeux went about Caen raising a mob. Mme. Bayeux thus arrived home in time to secure her husband's release, but not in time to save him from the wild horde that waited outside the prison gates. He was cut down by a bayonet in front of his wife and twelve-year-old son. His head was severed from his body and borne triumphantly through the town on the end of a pole. An excited mob, eager to find fresh victims, followed the grisly trophy.

Charlotte Corday, avid reader of every kind of political literature, was able to follow the violence that rocked France after Marat's election to the Convention. Scarcely had the Convention assembled when an undignified quarrel broke out between Marat and his fellow representatives. One deputy rose to accuse him of having provoked the massacres. "In this assembly I have a large number of personal enemies," he replied. "All of us! All of us!" came the answer. Even Danton and Robespierre now recoiled from him. Danton, indeed, who at this time was attempting to make an alliance with the Girondins, did not hesitate to demonstrate his contempt for Marat and made several sarcastic references to "that man's writings."

Furious, Marat rose to justify the massacres and, indirectly, to warn the Convention of the power that was at his command. "The people," he said, "were obedient to my voice. They saved France by appointing themselves to the dictatorship in order to kill traitors." This pronouncement caused a great outcry, and the deputies of the Left and Right began to hurl accusations at one another. In the midst of the commotion Marat pulled a pistol from his belt and, wildly brandishing it, threatened to shoot himself at the foot of the Tribune should the delegates attempt to prosecute him. All in all, it was hardly a scene worthy of that senate depicted in the dignified pages of Plutarch.

In December came news of the trial of the King. This issue was the rock on which the men of the Mountain hoped to wreck the Girondins. Their scheme did succeed to the extent of hopelessly dividing their ill-organized opponents. When it became apparent that the Mountain was going to petition the Convention for a decree ordering the King's immediate execution without trial, the Girondins fought for a trial—thus entering the trap that the Mountain had set for them. Certain Girondins then countered with the proposal that the matter be put to the direct vote of all the people of

France. Robespierre's sanctimonious argument against this was characteristic: "It would be unwise to appeal to the people," he declared, "because Virtue has always been a minority on this earth." His disciple St. Just expressed his doubts more bluntly: "An appeal to the people might mean a recall of the monarchy," he said.

The King's trial was decided on; and his guilt, on January 15, pronounced. The question of his sentence next arose. Again the Girondins fought for an appeal to the people, but the King's sentence was a foregone conclusion. The Commune had no intention of putting so dangerous a weapon as a popular vote into the hands of its opponents in the provinces. Voting among the deputies began at eight in the evening of January 16. Mercier, who was a witness of the drama, has probably given the best description of it. "There passed into the Tribune countenances rendered the more somber by the dim light. In slow and sepulchral voices only one word was heard, 'Death!' Face passed after face. The tone of voice was in a different key. Some men calculated whether they had time to dine before giving their vote. Deputies fell asleep and were awakened in order to give their opinion. Of all that I saw that night no idea can be given. It is impossible to imagine the reality. Fiction would not be able to approach it." One is left with the flickering impression of a vast and darkened room and of many indistinct faces, haggard in that central pool of light which was the Tribune.

One by one the deputies stepped forward, some to utter those unadorned words *la mort,* others to recommend mercy. Robespierre seized the opportunity to make a long, self-centered speech, which he began with the words, "Everybody here knows how much I dislike making long speeches. . . ." No one laughed. Their sense of irony, not to mention humor, had long since been put into storage by most Frenchmen; it was not to be taken out again for many months. Robespierre disliked levity. In his thousands of recorded words there is not a sentence, not a turn of phrase, to suggest that delicate fusion of irony and gaiety, that laughter which has always been the heritage of the French of every class.

In the procession of 721 men who stepped up to the rostrum during those hours, there was one who, with Robespierre, might have captured the attention of those present who were endowed with the gift of prescience. He was a frail, bloodless, retiring creature with the reddish eyes of an albino, eyes whose lids and lashes were so pale that they seemed not there at all. He appeared in the light for a moment and then was gone, back to the shadows that were his natural habitat. His verdict was "Death," and that one word, uttered by him with well-concealed reluctance, was to alter his life and with it, very probably, the destiny of France. His name was Joseph Fouché. He had been sent to the Convention in September by the voters of Nantes in Brittany. Before the closing of the religious orders he had been a lay priest and a teacher of physics to the pupils of the Oratorian fathers. He was to apply with consummate agility the principles of that science to his own extraordinary life. In the opening days of the Convention he had sat on the right with the Girondins. His constituency in Brittany was, like most provincial constituencies, conservative, a fact unlikely to deter Joseph Fouché from taking the course that seemed to him most profitable. The inherent weakness of the Girondin "party" became clear to him during the King's trial. The Girondins' doom was written in their division. Fouché's knowledge of the relation between force and movement assured him that the complete swing of the Revolutionary pendulum had not yet taken place. Twenty-four hours before he cast his vote he had coolly assured his associates of the Right that it would be in the King's favor. In the rostrum however he uttered the word "Death" with neither hesitation nor explanation. His long public life thus began on an appropriate note: the betrayal of his colleagues.

The political purposes of this man who, as agent of the Directory and Minister of the Consulate and the Empire, was to become one of the most powerful and enigmatic in France were inalterably fixed by that word which made him a regicide. He was to publish a hundred thousand words in order to explain that one word; he would have paid a fortune to unsay it. "That week," writes the historian Madelin of the King's trial, "which was so heavy with destiny, was to be the death of some, such as Vergniaud and Robespierre, before two years were out. In the rest, those who survived, it was to cause a sort of mental *alienation*—in the true sense of that word—which was to send all their lives astray. For them a change had come over all things and they were never to look at life again save across the guillotine of Louis XVI."

Fouché's alienation was less mental than political; it was never to be forgotten (least of all by himself) that the Duc d'Otrante, cloaked in ermine and glittering in the many medallions of his high office, had once been the regicide Joseph Fouché. His brief appearance before the Convention on that historic night was informed with more immediate significance, however, because this was the man who in eighteen months' time was to meet Robespierre in the political arena and destroy him. No one, not even so astute an observer of political affairs as Joseph Fouché, could have seen beyond the darkness that obscured the twisting path ahead.

The King was guillotined on January 21, 1793, and his head defiantly thrown at all the kings of Europe. Within weeks France was at war with England. The first of those many coalitions that were to witness the rise and fall of Bonaparte had begun. The King's execution brought those responsible for it into closer league. "The roads have been broken behind us," a member of the Convention was to write, "and we must march on, whether we would or no." The community of their crime became a bond between many dissimilar men.

But from the French people the King's execution evoked a curiously hollow response. The fanatics, whether Monarchist or Jacobin, responded vociferously according to their convictions. The bulk of the people looked on in silence. Louis XVI the man had never been unpopular with them. Had he been the tyrant that the extremists accused him of being, there would have been no Revolution. He was, in fact, gentle, simple in his tastes and charitable. Posterity has dismissed him as "weak." The evidence indicates the contrary. He stood firmly by his principles. There had been many times when he might have availed himself of Bonaparte's "whiff of grapeshot," and by meeting violence with violence have brought an end to the disturbances that rocked his realm. He did not do so, because bloodshed violated the principles by which he lived. "I cannot shed the blood of my People." He was to repeat that statement many times and in many crises when by the use of force he might have saved his fast-dwindling authority. His successor on the throne was not to be troubled by such scruples. The fault of Louis XVI was his inability to separate himself as a man from himself as a monarch. The monarch, because he failed, might be considered weak; the man was not.

14

THE NEWS of Louis XVI's execution was a great shock to Charlotte Corday. She, who only a few months earlier had refused to toast him and who by her own admission had been a Republican, wept when she learned of his death. "You have heard the frightful news," she wrote to a friend, Rose de Fourgeron, "and your heart like mine must be quivering with indignation. Poor France, at the mercy of these wretches who have already done us so much harm! God only knows where all this will end. . . . I shudder with horror and indignation. This event presages unimaginable horrors for the future. I despair of that peace which a little while ago I thought possible. These men are nothing but butchers! Let us weep for the fate of our unhappy country.

"I know that you are sad, and I hesitate to make you weep further by a recital of our own sorrows. All our friends are persecuted and my aunt has been subjected to every kind of trouble because it was discovered that she gave shelter to [a relative] on his way to England. I too would go to England if I could do so, but *God keeps us here for other destinies. . . .*"

From this moment some intimation of her own destiny begins to gleam from Charlotte Corday's letters. To her friend Mme. Levaillant she had already confessed her "contempt for life and disdain for an existence without purpose"; she spoke repeatedly of "the disenchantment of a spirit that finds itself deceived after having cherished so many beautiful illusions." Self-renunciation, the necessity of dedication to some aim, the deep purpose of life—these were themes and questions that began to occupy her thoughts and that were reflected in her conversation. Early in April she secured a passport in order to visit her father at Ferme au Bois. A few weeks later, in the company of a friend who was applying for a passport to Paris, she impulsively had her own passport viséd for Paris. She mentioned this caprice to no one.

That month of April brought the Girondins another step closer to destruction. Dumouriez, the general in whom they had invested their faltering hopes, lost the battle of Neerwinden and defected to the Austrians. Danton, provoked by Mme. Roland and her circle, angrily threw in his lot with the extremists of the Mountain. "To save himself and his friends," remarked an observer, "Danton now crossed many Rubicons." Marat became president of the Jacobin Club, a position that he used to denounce the Girondins to the Club's provincial affiliates, proclaiming them throughout France to be "traitors."

This time the Girondins struck back at Marat. They secured a vote from the Convention ordering his arrest and appearance before the newly created Revolutionary Tribunal, where the editor of *L'Ami du Peuple* was to be judged for his own treasonable activities. The move was a mistake, not only because it established the unwise precedent of throwing members of the Convention to the Tribunal, but because treason is a crime that is open to the interpretation of those who happen to control the state. What is called treason by one faction might very well be called patriotism by another. The cynical and experienced Talleyrand put it succinctly: "Treason," he declared, "is merely a question of dates." The National Convention was the state, but the bulk of its 720 members were faceless, frightened men without character or identity who in these quarrels were pulled with little resistance towards the side of the greater force. Infuriated by Marat's arrest, the Commune of Paris wasted no time in showing the Convention who was its master—and in deciding for it who was the traitor.

Marat's appearance before the Tribunal (the jurors of which were all agents of the Commune, as was the Public Prosecutor Fouquier-Tinville) was a fiasco. The scene that attended his acquittal has been described by one historian as "perhaps the strangest of all the grotesque scenes of the Revolution." The "People's Friend" was carried from the courtroom by a frenzied mob of admirers. The greasy bandana that usually swathed his brow was discarded and its place taken by a crown of laurels—"a Caesar in rags." He was borne from the Palais de Justice to the Convention; his howling attendants smashed open the door of the hall where the deputies were in session. The cruel smile curling across his mouth forecast his approaching revenge. He spoke a few words to the Convention and then was carried off by his rabble to the Jacobin Club, where, amidst hysterical acclaim, he was enthroned on the president's chair. With this apotheosis Marat's dream of *gloire* at last was realized.

Such scenes can have left the Girondins with very few illusions about their own fate. The Commune in fact was already busy with preparations for their final destruction. There is some evidence indeed that at this moment the Commune was planning another massacre along the lines of the one in September. The Girondins were not deaf to the rumor. A speech given by Isnard, one of their number, before the Convention reflects both their bitterness and their fear. "Listen to what I am about to tell you," he declared from the rostrum. "If in one of the insurrections which have occurred without cease since March 10 any attack were made on the representatives of the nation, I declare to you in the name of all France that Paris would be destroyed. Yes! The whole of France would avenge the outrage and men would soon be wondering on which bank of the Seine Paris once stood."

While the Girondins talked and threatened, the Commune acted. It seized control of the National Guard by appointing one of its own men to the crucial post of Commander-in-Chief. The Girondins in the meanwhile had instituted a committee—they leaned strongly to committees—called the Commission of Twelve, which was appointed to "examine matters." Until now the Girondins had always retained a certain theoretical power.

The actuality of power, however, the power of an organized mob and of an insurrectionary army, lay in ruder hands. The Commune of Paris had already carefully tested and found safe the ground on which it was about to trespass. The National Convention indeed had come to such a pass that it now submitted to any group of petitioners, however small, from the Paris Sections. These raucous and ragged "deputations," as they were called, burst into the Convention at every hour of the day, rudely interrupting its sessions with many demands and threats. The Convention, part of it terrified, part of it in collusion with the schemes of the Commune, always listened with a groveling deference to the caterwauling fishwives and drunken hoodlums who composed the deputations. Robespierre would usually seize the opportunity which such occasions offered to hurry to the Tribune and utter an ingratiating speech on the "virtue of the people"; the demand, whatever it might be, would then be acceded to amid the applause of the deputies.

The Commission of Twelve became the pretext for the *coup d'état* that took place between May 31 and June 2 of 1793. The mystery is that the Girondins had lasted as long as they did. The scene which took place that June day in the garden of the Tuileries and the subsequent scene within the palace, when Marat contemptuously read off the names of the men who were to be expelled from the Convention, brought down the curtain on one act of the Revolution.

Broken and humiliated, the Convention on that day ceased to exist as a representative body. The expelled deputies were put under house arrest, a liberality that poorly disguised the Commune's ultimate intentions and that provoked one of the victims to cry out, "Give Couthon his glass of blood; he is thirsty." They were not under any illusions, and during the night of June 2-3 certain of them, in disguise, made their way out of Paris.

The news of the *coup d'état* in Paris had reached the provinces ahead of them, striking in many places with the force of lightning. Lyons was already in full revolt against the government of Paris. Unable to bear the arrogant and brutal behavior of the Jacobins' representative there, a man named Chalier, the enraged *Lyonnais* had recovered their sovereignty and sent Chalier to the guillotine, thus defying Paris in much the manner that Paris was defying the provinces. Lyons was to pay dearly for its audacity when the government recaptured that unhappy city in November. Other cities now raised the standard of revolt: Marseilles, Bordeaux and Nantes. At least twenty departments were in full rebellion. Seventy more registered the strongest protest in Paris. The fire of civil war was thus ignited in a nation already beset by war abroad.

The Girondins who had escaped from Paris hoped to profit from the situation in the provinces by raising an army to march on the capital and overthrow the usurpers who had seized the government. Had they gone about this in any practical or realistic way they might possibly have achieved their goal, but they were no more strategists than they were statesmen. Bordeaux, capital of the province from which many of them hailed, would have been the logical place in which to establish their base. Lyons could have joined forces with Marseilles to the south and with Bordeaux to the west and thus have made a concentrated and formidable resistance south of Paris. Unfortunately they were persuaded by one of their number, Buzot, to go to Normandy instead. They forgot that the nearby revolts in Brittany and the Vendée were entirely Royalist in nature. And the Royalists were to them (as the Girondins were to the Royalists) as odious as their common enemy the Paris Commune. To the end, these stern idealists were unable to make compromises.

Normandy was already in revolt when, on June 9, the first of the Girondins arrived there, bringing with them a full account of those events that the indignant Normans had already read of in hundreds of conflicting newssheets and placards from Paris. "How is it that these excesses are tolerated?" Charlotte Corday heard a friend of her aunt cry out. "How is it that these monsters are endured? Are there no men left in France?" The friend was later to remember that Mlle. de Corday made no answer to these agitated queries. Through the excitement of the ensuing weeks she remained calm.

The Norman resistance had been organized by a General Wimpffen, and it was he who arranged for the proscribed deputies to be lodged and fed. One by one or in scattered groups of three they began to arrive in Caen. They were billeted at the Hôtel de l'Intendance, and this hotel, which was visible from the window of Charlotte Corday's bedroom, became the headquarters of the martyred men who might have brought to France that Republic of virtue which had long occupied the thoughts of Charlotte Corday. Standing at the window of her aunt's salon, she could see the agitated crowds that gathered about the hotel and hear drifting scraps of the endless harangues and speeches that went on all day and far into the night.

15

On june 20 the Girondin leader Charles Barbaroux was informed that a young lady was at the hotel requesting an interview with him. By way of introducing herself to him she mentioned that they had a friend in common, Alexandrine de Forbin, and that she wished to see him on a matter of business relating to this friend. She gave her name as Marie-Charlotte de Corday.

Barbaroux was one of the most famous of the Girondins. He was from the South, twenty-six years of age and admired as much for his handsome appearance as for his brilliance as an orator and pamphleteer. Only a few days earlier he had written and signed a fiery denunciation of Marat and his crimes that had been posted throughout Caen: ". . . may this vilest of men perish, cursed with all his kind by the heavens." With his dark lustrous eyes, with his sharply-cut profile, as fine as might have been found on a Roman coin, this passionate "Antinoüs" of the Girondin party had never wanted for the love of women. His southern temperament was responsive to women's charms, but sensitive too to their reservations. When he greeted his unexpected visitor, he recognized at once that the Norman gentlewoman who awaited him in the salon of his hotel with a servant quietly in attendance—Augustin Leclerc had accompanied her—was not soliciting his attention for any romantic purpose. Louvet, a friend of Barbaroux's who was in the room on the occasion that Charlotte first met him, recalled the moment in his *Memoirs:* "At the Hôtel de l'Intendance, where we were lodged, a handsome young woman of well-bred and decent appearance presented herself to speak to Barbaroux. There was something about her face and bearing, a mixture of pride and sweetness, which spoke of an exalted soul. She always came accompanied by a servant and always waited for Barbaroux in the salon." During this and future meetings she met the notorious lady-killer with the utmost discretion, thus giving the lie to the inevitable stories that she had been seized by an ungovernable passion for Barbaroux, who had incited her to kill Marat.

The southerner politely asked his caller what he might do for her. Charlotte Corday replied that she had received from their mutual friend Alexandrine de Forbin a request that the pension to which she was entitled, and which had been canceled because she was an *emigrée*, be reinstituted. She thought that Barbaroux was the man to whom she might best turn for help in the matter. She had brought the papers pertaining to the case with her and she now showed them to Barbaroux. She had, in fact, already been in communication with the Ministry of the Interior about the matter and six months before had forwarded certain documents to Paris. Barbaroux said that without those documents her case would prove difficult. All the same he promised to do what he could for the citizeness—"though I very much fear," he added with a smile, "that the recommendations of a proscribed deputy will not much help your friend."

"Perhaps then you know someone in the Convention to whom you might introduce the matter and who would be of help?" she enquired.

Barbaroux recalled that he did indeed have a friend in the Convention, a certain Lauze Duperret, who was his intermediary with those Girondins such as Mme. Roland who had not escaped Paris and who were now in prison. Barbaroux was in constant communication with Duperret and promised to include a recommendation for Mlle. de Forbin in a letter he would write that very evening. He suggested that his caller return in a week to see how the business had progressed. Charlotte Corday then took her leave of him.

A week later she duly returned to the Intendance and for a second time obtained an interview with Barbaroux, who told her that there had been no news from Paris. She informed him that she had now decided to go to Paris herself and would be leaving Caen very soon. She asked him for a letter of introduction to Duperret and offered in exchange to carry any papers that Barbaroux might wish delivered to his friend. She said that her date of departure was not yet determined, since she had many things to settle before leaving. Barbaroux begged her to call on him before she left, when he would give her a letter to Duperret along with some books and pamphlets he would like to have delivered. This she promised to do, saying that she would return in another week.

She now prepared to die, putting her house in order with a tidiness that would have done credit to the neatest of Norman housewives. She returned all the books she had borrowed. For some time she had been working on a piece of petit point that she wished to give Mme. de Bretteville's maid as a present. She knew now that she could not stay to finish it. She brought it to a local needlewoman for completion, paid for it in advance and arranged for delivery to the maid. Perhaps she foresaw that this scrap of needlework would one day have a value of its own because it came from her. Much of her activity in the ensuing days suggests that she was aware that she was about to make her appearance in history. She was determined that this appearance should be as she chose it to be—*à la romaine.*

She went to her shoemaker and ordered a pair of shoes suitable for the streets of Paris. He offered to make her a pair according to her specifications, but when she learned that it would take two or three weeks she replied that there wasn't time and bought a ready-made pair, the heels of which she had altered. She visited her friends, but being unable to convey to them the knowledge that her farewell was final, she left them with various souvenirs or the recollection of certain phrases that, after the event, would take on their true significance. She gave her book of lace designs to Mme. Paisan: "I shall have no more need of lace." To another friend she gave her earrings: "I shall have no more need of these," she said with a smile as she removed them from her ears.

A few days before her departure she drove out to Verson, the village near Caen where her aunt had a farm. A friend, Mme. Gautier de Villiers, lived there. Charlotte Corday found her in the garden shelling peas with her cook. "I have come to say good-bye to you," she said. "I have a journey to make and I didn't wish to leave without embracing you." She appeared to be excited, and as the two women spoke of the troubles that were disturbing their country Mme. Gautier received the strong impression that "though her person was at Verson, her spirit was elsewhere." All at once Charlotte seized a handful of peas, crushed them in her fingers and threw them to the ground. She leapt up, embraced Mme. Gautier, and with no further words, hurried away.

Her words to Mme. de Pontécoulant, former Abbess of the Abbaye-aux-Dames had a more sinister ring. Charlotte visited her to return a history of the Knights of Malta that she had borrowed. She announced her imminent departure for Paris.

"Will you be gone for long?" asked the Abbess.

"That," replied Charlotte Corday with a smile, "depends on the turn which my business there will take."

June 1793 had been unusually warm all over France. In Normandy, always freshened by a breath of sea air, the weather was superb. Everywhere those flowers that have caused that province to be called the "Garden of France" bloomed in extraordinary profusion. The sun shone beneficently over the unhappy land, casting shadows through the ancient avenues of lime and oak, bringing into early fruit and flower the produce of the rich and beautiful Norman countryside. As she went from friend to friend making her careful adieux, there must have been a larger farewell in her heart to the land of which she was so entirely the child. Not even she could have estimated the numberless invisible ways in which that country had exalted her heart with purpose as it was to steel her hand with resolution. To the fiber of her being she was Norman, the descendant of knights who counted it more important for a man to be brave than rich.

She informed her aunt that she was leaving soon to visit her father at Argentan, but Mme. de Bretteville had heard other rumors and was aware of her niece's preparations. Every evening Charlotte would burn great quantities of pamphlets and political literature in her fireplace. Once her aunt unexpectedly entered Charlotte's bedroom to find the girl sitting alone in the summer dusk, weeping bitterly.

"Who would not weep, dear Aunt, in such times as these?" she demanded. "Who knows who may be struck down next? Which of us is safe so long as Marat lives?"

On July 5 she bought a one-way ticket to Paris on the stagecoach that was to leave Caen on Tuesday July 9. On July 6 she packed her modest trunk and sent it to the booking office to be held for shipment with her on the ninth. On July 7 the Girondins, led by General Wimpffen, held a great rally in the public square, hoping to enlist many volunteers under their banner to go to Paris and deliver the government from the usurpers. There were parades, bands, refreshments and many stirring speeches, but the sorry result of this patriotic demonstration was only seventeen volunteers instead of the many hundreds who had been expected.

Charlotte Corday was present at the review, standing not far from Barbaroux's friend Pétion, the former mayor of Paris. The statuesque young woman of noble birth had piqued Pétion's curiosity from his first sight of her in the hotel salon. He suspected that she wished to seduce Barbaroux and that her Girondin sympathies were affected to further this purpose. The idea of aristocratic women succumbing to rough, Republican embraces apparently fascinated Pétion. When, as mayor of Paris, he had been sent to escort the captured royal family back from Varennes he had persuaded himself that in the course of that tragic trip the King's young sister Princess Elizabeth had conceived a violent passion for him. He turned now to Charlotte Corday and asked insinuatingly, "And would you be sorry if they did not go?"

She did not answer his question, but when she came home that evening she betrayed her feelings to the family of the carpenter who occupied the ground floor of her aunt's house. Lunel and his wife were playing a game of cards in front of their door when Charlotte returned from the rally. They asked her how the day had gone. Her answer was passionate and unexpected. "No!" she cried, "No! Marat will never rule France!" Blinded by tears, she hurried upstairs.

On the following day she called on Barbaroux for the last time, asking him for the letter of introduction that he had promised her. He said he would mail the letter to Duperret in the morning. She replied that she was leaving for Paris immediately and that it would be better if she took it with her. It was recalled by those present that she asked many questions about the Convention, wanting to know when it held its sessions and if it were possible for a stranger to gain entry to it.

She confessed later, and there is every reason to believe her statement, that it had been her intention to stab Marat in the hall of the Convention. The picture of the event in her imagination was of herself plunging a dagger through his heart before the assembled senate, as Brutus had immolated Caesar. Her persistent demand for a letter of introduction to Duperret can probably be traced to her belief that Duperret would be able to secure her the pass necessary to gain admission into the Convention, although it is not the least strange element in the ensuing drama that Charlotte Corday did doggedly continue to solicit the pension for Alexandrine de Forbin for which Duperret's letter was the pretext.

Pétion was in the room during this interview and he listened to the enigmatic young woman's questions with a sardonic smile. The day was very hot and she was dressed in muslin with a thin fichu, or shawl, to cover her bare shoulders. She carried a small paper fan in her hand. Her carriage, her low tone of voice, her polite address of that kind which ignorant people often suppose to be servility but which is, in fact, pride, all so impressed Pétion that he could no longer contain himself. He made a suggestive remark about "beautiful young aristocrats who are so interested in us Republicans."

Charlotte Corday turned to him coolly. "Citizen Pétion," she said, "today you judge me in ignorance. One day you will know who I am." The words were as close as she came to committing an indiscretion.

Barbaroux promised to have his letter delivered to her immediately. He wished her good luck on her journey and offhandedly asked her to send him an account of her trip. This she promised to do. Little can Barbaroux have imagined the circumstances in which she would keep that promise. She was to write her letter to him in prison, and he would read it after her death, published in every newspaper in France. With a deep curtsy she took her leave of him. "Adieu, then, my dear deputy," she said. "Tomorrow I go to Paris, where I shall meet your famous tyrants face to face." One wonders if Charlotte, who had an acute appreciation of irony, smiled as she delivered herself of this *double-entendre*.

That evening she wrote a letter to her father: "I am leaving without seeing you," she wrote, "because I am too full of grief. I am going to England. I don't believe that one can be happy or calm in France at this time. I am putting this letter in the post as I leave. When you receive it I shall no longer be in this country." The hardships of her childhood, the poverty endured with dignity by her parents came back to her. "Heaven has refused us the happiness of living together," she continued, "as it has denied us so many other blessings. Perhaps it will be more clement toward our country. Adieu, my dear father, embrace my sister for me and do not forget me."

With the sealing of this note she cut the last of the threads that bound her to life. Methodically she put her room in order, destroying all remaining papers that might compromise her aunt or friends. The books she loved, those companions that, more than living men, had formed her character, the well-thumbed Rousseau, the Corneille whose exalted stanzas she knew by heart, the copies of Plutarch and Raynal, she put on a shelf beside her bed. She would need them no more. They were part of her. One small significant object she left behind, a bit of silk on which she embroidered the phrase that had haunted her during her agony of indecision: *"Le ferai-je, ne le ferai-je pas?"* (Shall I or shall I not?) She put it beside her mirror, and for those who found it there that scrap of embroidered cloth succinctly told the story of those long summer evenings wrapped in silence and mystery, when the world of Charlotte's imagining finally became for her the world af action and of actuality.

Towards noon on the following day, she set out for the stagecoach offices. She embraced her aunt and told her that she was going to Argentan for a few days to visit her father. She had her sketchbook and pencils with her and said that before leaving she planned to go into the meadows near Caen to make sketches of the farmers taking in their hay. The casual air that thus surrounded her departure lulled her aunt's apprehensions. Without looking behind her, Charlotte took leave of the house where she had lived for two years. On the stairs leading into the courtyard she encountered little Louis Lunel, the son of the carpenter who rented Mme. de Bretteville's ground floor. She was fond of the child and had given him many of her sketches. "Look, Louis," she said, handing him her pencil box and portfolio, "these are for you. Always be good, and kiss me, because you will never see me again."

Louis Lunel died an old man. In telling the story in later years he always remembered that Charlotte Corday had been crying and that she had left her tears on his cheek as she kissed him.

16

THE TRIP from Caen to Paris, as she related in her letter to Barbaroux, was uneventful. "I traveled with good *Montagnards,* whom I allowed to chatter to their hearts' content. As their conversation was as stupid as their persons were disagreeable, I found it all the easier to go to sleep. I might almost say I woke up only on reaching Paris."

When she was interrogated in Paris about this trip, the President of the Tribunal expressed astonishment that a woman of condition such as herself should have been permitted by her aunt to travel on a stagecoach alone. To the judge's concern over the proprieties—an unexpected note in the midst of a revolution—Charlotte tartly replied that "when one is embarked on a mission such as mine one doesn't much worry about the conventions [*on ne tient point aux etiquettes*]." The handsome young woman of such unusual bearing was indeed, as her interrogator suggested, out of place in that public coach, and she attracted the curious stares of her fellow passengers. The night was spent at Lisieux, and at dawn on the following day she took an overnight coach straight through to Paris. A man tried to make her acquaintance on the night coach. "He said that I was the daughter of an old friend of his. He endowed me with a fortune which I did not possess, gave me a name I've never heard and in the end offered me his hand and worldly goods. 'This is a comedy we are playing,' I said when I began to grow tired of his attentions. 'It is a pity that so much talent as yours should not have an audience. I'm going to waken our fellow passengers so that they may share this entertainment.' He left me in a bad temper."

Charlotte's coach reached Paris at eleven o'clock the following morning, rolling into the cobbled courtyard of the booking office on the Place des Victoires. Composed though she might have been and wrapped in her secret purpose, she must have suffered a pang of apprehension as she stood there suddenly alone in a large and unfamiliar city. While her luggage was being unloaded she went into the office and asked if there was a hotel in the neighborhood. The booking agent gave her a card with the address "Hôtel de la Providence, rue des Vieux Augustins, 19" written on it. Above was inscribed the name of the proprietor, one Mme. Grollier. A porter (his name was Gilles Vivien—from this moment the details of the three days in Paris of this unknown provincial are available in the smallest particulars) hoisted her trunk onto his back and conducted her a few yards down the street to the Hôtel de la Providence.

Paris was in the middle of its annual heat wave, and though the day had just begun the city was already stifled under a humid blanket of heat. Mme. Grollier assigned a room on the second floor (Number 7) to the new arrival. Her trunk was taken upstairs. Charlotte remained at the desk to fill out the police form. When this had been completed and she had been conducted upstairs to her room, she requested that her bed be made up. The long trip and the heat of the day had exhausted her, and she planned to sleep for a few hours. A waiter, François Feuillard, came to make up her bed and she fell into conversation with him, asking a few discreet questions about what was thought of Marat in Paris. Feuillard replied that though aristocrats detested him, he was very much liked by the people (during her trial Feuillard deposed that "the woman smiled at these words"). The waiter went on to say that Marat had been seriously ill since the *coup d'état* of June 2 and was no longer able to go to the Convention.

Unknown to Feuillard this bit of information, which he casually passed on to her, had a most upsetting effect on the young woman, which her tranquil exterior in no way betrayed. Until now she had planned to assassinate Marat in the hall of the Convention or, that failing, during the ceremonies of the Festival of the Federation, which were scheduled to be held in the Champs-de-Mars on July 14. Feuillard's remark was the first hint she had received that Marat was an invalid. In the days that followed her decision to assassinate him she had pictured the Poussinesque scene of Marat's death in the hall of the senate with such fervor of imagination that every detail of it was lovingly fixed in her mind. The dreams of those who live in the world of the imagination die hard. One wonders what Charlotte would have done had she known, as many people in Paris already knew, that Marat was a dying man, and that in a few weeks, at most a few months, nature would have done what she was about to do. Fantasy and resolution had both fixed her attention on Marat; it is probable that she would have killed him anyway.

Reality was to intrude on her dreams more than once in the ensuing days. It is, in fact, this contrast between Charlotte's high-minded Corneillian posture that she never for a moment relinquished and the commonplace, inappropriate "props," reality's contribution to the stage, that cause the approaching drama to be bathed in so garish a light.

Feuillard's news caused her to abandon her plans for a nap. She suddenly declared that she had changed her mind and would not go to bed at once, since "she had some business to attend to." She sent him out to buy writing paper, ink and a pen for her. When he returned she asked him the way to rue St. Thomas du Louvre. This was the street where Barbaroux's friend Lauze Duperret lived. It was situated in a rabbit warren of old and narrow streets, long since demolished, directly behind the Tuileries and the Place du Carrousel. Half an hour later she left her hotel, setting out for the rue St. Thomas du Louvre on foot. That walk, a long one through the dust and confusion of an unfamiliar city, testifies to her strength of mind. She reached Duperret's residence shortly after one o'clock and was told that he was at the Convention. Duperret's daughter came to the door and Charlotte Corday left Barbaroux's package and letter with her, saying that she would return later in the day. She did not leave her name. She then returned to the hotel by fiacre and went upstairs to her room, where she remained closeted for the rest of the afternoon.

Towards five she again came downstairs and at the desk fell into a short conversation with Mme. Grollier, who enquired how things were at Caen. She replied that an army was being raised there to march on Paris, but laughingly dismissed the matter by saying that the "army" consisted of thirty men (she had told Feuillard earlier in the day that there were thirty thousand volunteers). She again set out for Duperret's house. She arrived there to find that the deputy was entertaining at dinner. She begged that he might see her for a moment, insisting that her business was of the greatest importance.

She was taken to his study, and a few minutes later Duperret appeared. Charlotte asked if he had received the communications from Barbaroux that she had left earlier in the day. He replied that he had, but that he had not yet had time to read them. She gave him news of Barbaroux and of the other Girondins whom she had seen at Caen.

She then explained her ostensible business in Paris and asked him for an introduction to the Minister of the Interior, in whose office Mlle. de Forbin's papers had been languishing for more than six months. Duperret offered to take her to the Minister himself and said he would stop at her hotel around noon of the following day. To make certain he would not forget the address and that he knew her name, she gave him the card of Mme. Grollier's hotel, which the porter at the booking office had given her when she had arrived in Paris that morning. On the front of the card she wrote the single word "Corday" in pencil. The card still exists, a curious souvenir, and is to be found pinned to a page in the dossier of Charlotte's trial, which gathers dust in the National Archives in Paris. The penciled signature, though somewhat faded, is firmly written and testifies to a steady hand.

This short interview over, Duperret returned to his guests. He could not give them his full attention, for he found that his mind wandered back to his mysterious visitor. There had been something about her that disturbed him and, as he later testified, constantly interrupted the train of his thoughts during the rest of the evening. Charlotte, meanwhile, returned directly to her hotel, where presumably she slept well after her long and fatiguing day. Sometime during those hours, however, she carefully rearranged the stage on which she would kill Marat. When she awoke in the morning she had a new plan in her mind.

17

STILL CURIOUS about his visitor of the night before, Duperret appeared at the Hôtel de la Providence shortly before noon. Although Duperret now no longer served any purpose in her scheme to assassinate Marat, Charlotte Corday was genuinely interested in helping her friend Mlle. de Forbin and went about this incidental business with the same resolution as, on the following day, she was to proceed with the real object of her trip to Paris. It does not seem to have crossed her mind that a recommendation from the murderess of Marat would be unlikely to further her friend's cause.

At the Ministry of the Interior, Duperret and his guest were informed that the Minister received deputies only in the evening. Duperret accordingly made an appointment for eight that evening. He brought Charlotte Corday back to her hotel, saying that he would return towards eight. In the course of their outing they did not discuss politics—such, at least, was to be the testimony of each of them at her trial. One must suspect that, on the contrary, their conversation inevitably turned to the plight of the Girondins at Caen and very probably to the man who had brought them to ruin. It is possible that Duperret confirmed what she had learned from the waiter at the Providence, that Marat was a sick man and no longer went to the Convention.

That afternoon Charlotte was surprised by an unexpected second visit from Duperret. The deputy appeared at her hotel in a state of great agitation and announced that the police had just put his house and papers under seal. He was a prudent and temperate man, but his association with the expelled Girondins—he was a deputy from the same department as Barbaroux—was too intimate to escape observation. The net was closing about Duperret, as it was about many of his friends. He told Charlotte Corday that in supporting her petition he would now do her more harm than good. He recommended that she give up any hope of helping Mlle. de Forbin at this time. The political situation in France was taking a turn for the worse. He then enquired when she planned to return to Caen.

She did not answer this question, but suddenly turned to him and in a low but earnest voice said, "Citizen Duperret, I have some advice to give you. Leave Paris at once and go to Caen."

An honorable man, Duperret replied that his post was in Paris and that he could not abandon it.

"That is very foolish of you," she said. "Once more I warn you—leave Paris. Leave before tomorrow evening."

Startled by the intensity of her warning, he promised that he would think the matter over and let her know what he had decided. There was nothing further that she could say to him without revealing her plans for the morrow. Their next meeting was to be in the courtroom of the Revolutionary Tribunal. Duperret did not heed her warning and was to pay for his generosity to her with his head.

After Duperret's departure she returned to her room, where she sat down and wrote what she called "An Address to the French People." This exhortation was found on her at the time of her arrest, as she intended that it should be. It was pinned to her bodice along with her baptismal certificate (the presence of that second paper suggests that she did not wish to die quite so anonymously as she later protested that she did). Her "Address" is a curious document, filled with echoes of Raynal, Rousseau and Corneille, self-consciously "written" and devoid of any life. It is testimony to the regrettable fact that intensity of feeling and nobility of purpose have little to do with the quality of an author's writing. "How long, oh, unhappy Frenchmen," she began, "are you to suffer this trouble and disunion? Too long have scheming men and scoundrels put their ambition ahead of public interest. Why, unhappy victim of these disturbances, do you tear out your heart and destroy yourself to establish this tyranny on the ruins of desolated France? . . . Oh, my country! Your misfortunes break my heart; I can only offer you my life, and I thank heaven that I have the freedom to dispose of it."

She wrote the truth perhaps, but she did not write it well. This address contrasts revealingly with her unaffected, observant and ironic letter to Barbaroux. She went on to justify her act—she at no time considered it as either murder or crime—by stating that Marat was condemned by the universe and that his bloody deeds had placed him outside the law. She concluded her testament with the statement that her relatives and friends were innocent of any knowledge of her enterprise. When she had finished this paper she folded it and put it on her bureau along with her birth certicate. She then blew out her candle and went to sleep. She planned to murder Marat in the morning.

The following day, July 13, was a Saturday. Provincial to the end, Charlotte Corday was up at an early hour—six o'clock to be precise —and made her way to the shopping arcades of the nearby Palais Royal. These arcades have changed little since that summer dawn when Charlotte Corday nervously paced them waiting for the late-rising city folk to wake and be about their business. Nowadays stamps and various uninteresting curios are sold there. During the Revolution, however, the Palais Royal was an animated market place and one could buy in its shops all manner of necessaries, ranging from vegetables to cutlery. It was a store specializing in the latter that attracted Charlotte's attention. At her trial she stated that she had walked up and down the arcades so often that morning that she could no longer remember the store she entered or even on which side of the garden it was located. The researches of G. Lenôtre place it with certainty on the side of the gardens along which runs the rue de Valois, behind the arcade that is still numbered 177. The name of the man who owned the shop was Badin.

Shortly after seven in the morning, the shutters of this *boutique* were removed, and a few minutes later M. Badin greeted his first customer of the day, a comely woman dressed in a brown striped piqué who wished to buy a kitchen knife. He showed her his wares, which she examined with interest, finally selecting one with an ebony handle. The blade was six inches long. A sheath of green cardboard came with it. She paid two francs for this object, and bidding M. Badin a polite good morning, slipped it into the pocket of her dress and departed.

In the gardens of the Palais Royal the fever of a new day had begun. Not far from Badin's shop a newsboy was shouting the latest bulletins, and Charlotte, realizing that it was too early to do what she planned next, bought a newspaper and seated herself on one of those benches between the arcades, which have since been removed. She opened her paper and began to read the news. What she read must have caused her hand to slip towards the knife that lay concealed in her pocket.

The outrageous Bourdon case had just come to its conclusion, and nine men, dressed in the red smocks of parricides, were being sent to the guillotine that afternoon for the murder of the deputy Leonard Bourdon. What made the case singular was the fact that the "murdered" man was very much alive and able to testify at the trial of his so-called murderers. Bourdon was, in fact, a typical "Maratist," a brutish, boastful individual whose sudden succession to absolute power in the city of Orléans had gone to his head quicker than the brandy to which he was addicted. A long and shameful record of brutality gave him good reason to suppose that many people might, indeed, have wished to murder him.

One evening a sentry who did not recognize Bourdon made the mistake of challenging him in front of the city hall of Orléans. Indignantly he lunged for his pistol and fired point-blank at the sentry. Since Bourdon, as usual, was so drunk that he could scarcely stand, the shot went wild and missed its intended victim. The sentry moved in with his bayonet and inflicted a slight wound on Bourdon's shoulder. This was what was called his "murder." The deputy, crazed with fear and suspicion, raised a loud cry that there was a plot afoot to assassinate him. Twenty citizens of Orléans, some of whom had never even heard of the man's name, were rounded up, placed under arrest and brought to Paris. They had been put on trial July 11, at the very hour Charlotte Corday had alighted from the coach from Caen. Nine had been sentenced to death, and were being taken to the guillotine on this same day when Charlotte, ablaze with indignation, read the account of their trial and sentence.

It was nearly nine o'clock when she rose and with quick steps walked to a hack stand on the Place des Victoires. She entered a cab and asked the driver to take her to the residence of Marat. She had not the slightest idea of where he lived, but she naïvely supposed that everyone in Paris would know. When her driver informed her that he did not know where the famous deputy lived she expressed surprise and asked him to find out if one of the other coachmen knew his address. After considerable consultation among his associates her driver returned with the information that Marat lived in the "Faubourg St. Germain near the beginning of the rue des Cordeliers." These words Charlotte scribbled in pencil on the back of a scrap of paper in her pocket. That paper too still exists, and one can still detect in her hurried hand the lurching motion of the hackney as it set forth towards Marat's residence, jogging over the cobbled streets.

Marat's residence, more precisely, was at 30 rue des Cordeliers, very near the rue de l'École de Médicine. It was torn down towards the end of the last century to make room for additions to the College of Medicine, but there are buildings nearby, and indeed all over this ancient quarter of Paris, which clearly suggest its appearance. Facing the street there was a narrow carriage entrance leading into a small cobbled courtyard in the center of which was the inevitable well. At the end of the court, set back from the street, was the house in which Marat had his apartment. It was on the first story above the ground floor and was approached by an outside staircase of stone with a plain iron banister. These houses, of commonplace and often squalid appearance in their time (they were usually of eighteenth-century construction), must startle today's visitor to Paris, for these are the rabbit warrens of the lower middle classes, so often referred to in commiserating tones by the writers of Revolutionary history. The twentieth-century student who nowadays could get so much as a room in one of them might count himself fortunate indeed.

Marat's first-floor apartment was sizable and consisted of seven or eight rooms, three of which had fireplaces with mantels of carved marble. But it was only partly furnished, and was dirty and uncared for. Simonne Evrard was a devoted mistress, but a poor housekeeper. Four people, moreover, shared the apartment, Simonne and her sister Catherine, Marat and his sister Albertine. A thick smell of bad cooking, rancid grease and human sweat hung like miasma over the hot, unventilated rooms. Everywhere, carelessly thrown about the narrow entranceway in the hall, in Marat's cluttered antechamber, were bales of newspaper and printers' equipment, along with all the material and paraphernalia necessary to the publication of his sheet.

Charlotte arrived at 30 rue des Cordeliers shortly before ten. Alighting from the carriage, she dismissed her coachman and made her way across the courtyard. Two women were in conversation in front of the porter's apartment. She was to learn later that these were Mme. Pain, the porter's wife, and Jeannette Maréchale, Marat's cook. Charlotte Corday politely enquired of them the way to Marat's apartment; one of the women indicated the door at the top of the stone stairs. They eyed the well-dressed caller with silent suspicion before continuing their shrill midmorning gossip. Charlotte ascended the stairs and pulled the bell chain. A moment later the door was opened by Catherine Evrard, who asked her business. Charlotte replied that she had secret and important information to give Marat and that she would like to speak with him. Catherine replied that it was not possible, that Marat was very ill and saw no one. Charlotte then asked if he might be well enough to receive her in three or four days. The woman replied that she was unable to say. Simonne Evrard now made her appearance at the door and said that Marat could make no appointments of any kind and cut short Charlotte's explanation with a few firm words; she then rudely closed the door in her face.

Discouraged by this reception, which was not part of her voluptuous imaginings of the scene, Charlotte descended the stairway and, again followed by the sharp eyes of the two women in the courtyard, made her way back to the street. There is some evidence that she may have returned again within half an hour. The evidence is that of Mme. Pain, who claimed to have spotted her at the foot of the stairs trying to sneak up to Marat's door a second time that morning. Charlotte's testimony does not confirm Mme. Pain's, however, and it is possible that the frightened concierge may have invented it to demonstrate her vigilance to the police who later questioned her. What is certain is that Charlotte returned to the Hôtel de la Providence at about noon and penned a short note to Marat. "I come from Caen," she wrote. "Your love for your country should make you curious to know the plots which are afoot there. I await your answer." To this missive she signed her name and gave the address of her hotel. She brought it downstairs to the desk for delivery, asking how long it would take to reach its destination. She was told it would take no more than an hour—an interesting detail to those who are the beneficiaries of postal service in certain present-day republics.

She returned to her room and waited for Marat's reply. As the afternoon waned and she received no answer, she began to consider other expedients. She asked Mme. Grollier to have a hairdresser sent in. Never before had Charlotte Corday, isolated in the world of her own elevated standards, had recourse to coquetry. The conquest of men had never been of interest to her. Fastidiously clean, she had never adorned her body. Now, as she waited for the hairdresser to arrive, she selected a fresh dress, "a spotted Indian muslin," from her small wardrobe, and to go with it a fichu of rose-colored gauze. She changed the ribbons on the tall, black, cockaded hat that she had worn in the morning from black to green. The hat had three or four black tassels dangling from its sides. It seems to have made a great impression on everybody. All artists who later depicted Charlotte Corday in Marat's bathroom are agreed about one detail—the hat. It is to be seen in every drawing, in every cheap, sensational gravure: tall and black with the tassels dangling at its sides.

The hairdresser arranged her long chestnut tresses in a more modish fashion, binding them at the back of her neck in a way that brought them cascading from her shoulders down to the waist. When this was finished he powdered them lightly in front, giving them the *blond cendré* cast that was then in vogue. "Judith," thus arrayed in all her beauty, was now prepared to go into the tent of "Holofernes." When the hairdresser had departed she wrote another note.

"I wrote you this morning, Marat," she said. "Did you receive my letter? Might I hope for a moment's interview with you if you received it? I hope you will not refuse me, because the matter is very interesting. My great unhappiness gives me a right to your protection." She did not sign this note, nor, as some historians have contended, did she mail it. She folded it and put it in her pocket. Her intention was to have one of the women of his household deliver it to him should they again try to turn her away from the door. Marat's curiosity aroused, he would then, she hoped, grant her that moment's interview which was necessary for the execution of her plan.

She put the final touches on her toilette, arranged the gauze fichu about her shoulders and pinned the "Address to the French People" and the birth certificate inside what the French delicately call the *corsage*. Along with the literature that went into her bodice she also slipped the knife, still in its sheath of green cardboard. She put on a pair of white gloves and, because the evening was breathless, she carried a fan. The fan was of green paper and matched the ribbons she had put in her hat. It was almost seven when, attired thus, the tall and icily composed young woman stepped from Room Number 7 of the Hôtel de la Providence and made her way to the hack stand in the Place des Victoires.

She arrived at Marat's residence at seven thirty and asked the cab to wait for her, probably foreseeing the possibility that she might again be turned from the door. For the second time that day she ascended the stone steps and with a gloved hand pulled the bell rope. One of the women whom she had seen gossiping in the courtyard that morning opened the door. It was Jeannette Maréchale, the cook. Within the flat Charlotte could glimpse the signs of considerable activity. This was always a busy hour of the evening in Marat's apartment. His newspaper was being prepared for distribution on the following morning. It was the hour when Marat saw his printers and managed the business of his enterprise. In the room adjoining the entrance hall the porter and his wife were folding papers, engaged in lively conversation with Catherine Evrard, who was grinding bits of clay in a preparation of almond water, a bizarre mixture that had been prescribed by Marat's doctor to quench his insatiable thirst. Simonne Evrard was at the moment with Marat in his bathroom, a small, damp cabinet to the right of the entrance hall, but separated from it by a dining room and an antechamber.

Annoyed to see this persistent visitor at the door once more, Jeannette Maréchale was about to have angry words with her when there were two more arrivals at the front door. One of these was a printer's assistant named Pillet, who had an invoice with him that required Marat's signature; the other was a street porter by the name of Laurent Bas, who was employed by Marat in the distribution of the newspaper. He had come this evening to pick up some copies for delivery to the War Office. The momentary distraction occasioned by their arrival permitted Charlotte Corday to step over the threshold into the hallway. Pillet, carrying his invoice, went directly to Marat's cabinet. He left the door slightly ajar so that the sounds of the altercation that had broken out in the hallway reached Marat's ear.

Catherine Evrard and Mme. Pain had now joined Jeannette Maréchale in refusing the woman admittance to Marat's bathroom. Charlotte asked them if Marat had received her letter of the morning. Jeannette Maréchale answered that Marat received many letters. It would be impossible to know if he had read hers. Charlotte insisted that she had many important matters to reveal, that it was urgent for her to see him, if but for a minute. Jeannette Maréchale replied that it was not possible, that Marat was too ill to see anybody and that, in any case, he could not be seen because he was in his bathtub at the moment. Carrying the invoice, Pillet hurried out of the bathroom and departed.

Marat had now become aware of the acrimonious discussion going on in his hall. He could hear the visitor persistently asking if he had received her letter. He had, in fact, received and read it, and his curiosity was aroused. The next issue of his paper was to be devoted to the disturbances at Caen. He turned to Simonne and gave orders that this woman who came from Calvados be admitted. Reluctantly, for as she later deposed, "she had a distinct sense of impending harm," Simonne complied. A moment later Charlotte Corday was in Marat's bathroom and saw before her, hideous in the terminal stages of his corruption, the man whom she had come to Paris to kill.

18

MARAT SAT in his bathtub, a curious portable contraption shaped like a stub-nosed, high-backed shoe. It covered his shriveled body to a line high above his waist. A bandana soaked in vinegar was wrapped around his forehead and a bathrobe slung over his shoulders. His chest was bare. A long board, on which were placed an ink bottle, a quill and some paper, lay across the front of the bathtub; here he was able to correct proof and compose copy.

"I killed him in cold blood," Charlotte later reported to Barbaroux. It must have taken considerable *sang-froid* indeed to face with equanimity the sight that greeted her eyes and to stiffen her hand to the task that lay ahead. Not by the flicker of an eyelash did she betray any sign of faltering nerves. She was to go through the chaotic events of the ensuing hours with a deathlike serenity. The profound calm of the somnambulist, of one wrapped in a dream too deep for the sounds of reality to penetrate, cushioned her from the blows of the outer world. She was disengaged from herself, yet some part of her remained in Marat's bathroom to observe and to act with precision.

Marat's astonishment must surely have equaled hers. No woman such as this had ever entered his apartment. Her sort, fine-boned and clear-complexioned, was familiar to him from his days of private practice on the fashionable rue de Bourgogne. Work, ill health, and his uncouth appearance had long placed such women beyond the pale of his experience. He had probably both hated and desired them. The tall beautiful creature with cold, blue eyes whom he suddenly saw looming before him, moving through the aquatic light of his bathroom, carrying a green fan in her gloved hand,

128

must have seemed to him, in the fleeting minutes that preceded his death, to have been the figment of some dream.

One hundred and seventy years later the historian must view the brief meeting of these two people, in appearance so different but beneath bound by a ruthless and exalted determination that made fanatics of them both, with an astonishment equivalent to their own. No scene in the Revolution is more peculiar. It flickers with a hundred obscure ironies and invites a hundred idle reflections that range from the aesthetic to the political.

Two crossed pistols hung on one wall, and beneath them, written on an enormous cardboard poster, were the sinister and significant words LA MORT. The room was lit by a single window directly behind Marat's bathtub, which shed an amber light over the aquarium-like chamber. The stage on which she found herself was far from any described in the dramas of her ancestor Corneille. Whatever her imagination may have pictured, it could not have pictured this.

Motioning towards a stool that was standing beside his bathtub, Marat politely asked his visitor to be seated, enquiring at the same time what he might do for her. She answered in a low, musical voice that contrasted strongly with the high-pitched voices of the women of his household. She said that she came from Caen and had some interesting information to give him about the uprising there. Marat immediately seized a piece of paper and dipped his quill in ink. The information of an eyewitness would be of invaluable help to him in the edition of his paper devoted to the uprisings in Caen. He asked her questions and as she answered he wrote. He asked her the names of the Girondins who were in Caen. She had just begun to list them when they were interrupted by Simonne Evrard.

Simonne had been disturbed by this unusual visitor. It seemed strange to her that a fashionably dressed woman, so conspicuously out of place in the Cordeliers' quarter of Paris, should have found her way to Marat's door. Jealousy no doubt excited her suspicions. She used as a pretext for interrupting Charlotte's interview the mixture of clay and almond water that Catherine had been grinding. Simonne asked him if there was too much clay in the mixture. He examined it and replied that it was satisfactory, but that some of the clay might be removed if they wished to do so.

Simonne noticed that the visitor had drawn the stool close to

Marat's bathtub and was now seated very near him. Before leaving the room Simonne went to the window behind Marat's back and from its sill removed a plate of veal rissoles and sweetbreads that she planned to serve for supper. She darted a few suspicious glances at the intruder and departed, closing the door behind her with a meaningful snap.

Charlotte continued from where they had been interrupted. She listed the names of the Girondins at Caen: Gaudet, Barbaroux, Pétion, Buzot. . . . Marat, delighted, dipped his quill in ink and copied the names down. The implacable scratch of his pen followed her voice. When she had finished he laid down his pen and with a grin said to her, "Excellent! In a few days' time I shall have them all guillotined in Paris."

The words were his death sentence. He probably did not see her hand go to her breast as she rose and came towards him, but if he had noticed it, the movement would have been too swift for him to realize its meaning. In a single sweeping motion she removed the knife from its sheath, raised her hand and drove it with full force downwards into Marat's chest. The blow, missing his ribs by the fraction of an inch, cut directly through a lung and penetrated the aorta. A student of anatomy could not have done better. She then withdrew the knife and let it fall on Marat's writing board. Without haste she started to leave the room. The event had taken place so quickly that Marat was already dying before he realized what had happened. In the instant that followed the knife's plunge he was able to utter one hoarse cry that was heard through the household: "À moi, ma chère amie; à moi!" (Help, dear friend; help!)

Screaming, "Oh, my God, they've killed him!" Simonne ran to Marat's cabinet. Charlotte Corday was just leaving the room as Simonne entered it, but Simonne's eyes saw only Marat, his life ebbing away with his blood. In despair, the distracted woman thrust her fist against the wound, hoping thus to staunch the great jets of blood that spurted from his open heart. Though his eyes were already glazed, Marat's tongue twitched convulsively as though he wished to speak.

Outside Marat's bathroom, in the antechamber where the four members of his household and Laurent Bas had been gossiping and folding newspapers, the wildest consternation had broken out. Some ran to get help from outside, while Laurent Bas, surely the most ignoble character in the drama, seized a chair and, his teeth chattering with a terror to which he was not ashamed later to admit, brought it crashing down on Charlotte Corday's head. With a sleepwalker's composure she had just left the cabinet and was crossing the floor of the antechamber towards the front door. In its boastful admission of both cowardice and cruelty the testimony of Laurent Bas before the Jacobin Club almost passes belief. His behavior must have confirmed Charlotte's contemptuous view of the cowards who composed Marat's following.

"Seeing the assassin approach," he related, "I seized a chair to stop her. The monster had reached the antechamber, so with a great blow of the chair I floored her. The creature struggled to rise. Defying her great strength I seized this monster by her two breasts, knocked her down again and struck at her. Holding her thus, I saw a citizen whom I didn't know—I later learned that it was Citizen Cuisinier—come into the room. I then cried out 'Help me, Citizen! Oh help me! Help!'"

Citizen Cuisinier's appearance on the scene coincided with a sudden rush of people into the house, first neighbors and then officials. As the news of Marat's death spread through the quarter, a great crowd began to assemble in the street below. "Marat has been killed by a woman of Calvados . . ."—the rumor spread like tongues of flame from door to door.

Marat's body was lifted from the bathtub and carried to his bedroom. Crazed with grief, Simonne thought that she heard him sigh as she and two of the neighbors laid him on his bed. His eyes were fixed on her, but they were lifeless. He was pronounced dead by a member of the nearby College of Medicine who arrived as Marat was being taken from his bathtub.

Accompanied by several soldiers of the National Guard, the district police commissioner arrived soon after. He found Charlotte Corday in the antechamber with Cuisinier and Laurent Bas holding her down as they tied her wrists. Simonne Evrard's shrieks from the bedroom filled the apartment and were clearly audible to the excited mob that had gathered in the street below. Jeannette Maréchale ran screaming hysterically from room to room brandishing the fatal knife for all to see. The police commissioner immediately dispatched notice of the crime to the Commune and to the Committee of Public Safety. He then ordered the prisoner to be taken to the salon, where, while waiting for the Committee's representatives to appear, he began a preliminary examination. Like everyone else that evening he was astonished by the woman's composure.

She stated very bluntly and at once that she had come to Paris in order to kill Marat. "Convinced that the flames of civil war were about to be ignited throughout France and certain that Marat was the principal author of these disasters, the prisoner testified that she wished to sacrifice her life for her country." She stated that she had never been to Paris before and that she knew no one in the city. She made no mention of Duperret in this first examination; only later did she discover that his name and address had been found in her room at the hotel. She then tried with truth, but in vain, to exonerate him of all knowledge of her plan. It was the purpose of this and of all subsequent interrogations to uncover a far-reaching Girondin plot behind Charlotte's knife thrust. The discovery of such a plot would give the Commune justification for the bloodshed it was planning.

"Would you have attempted to escape through the window?" the commissioner asked her.

"I never thought of that, but I would have certainly left by the door if I had not been stopped."

The prisoner was then searched. Her few possessions, among them a small gold watch and thimble, were laid on a table and inventoried. The commissioner sent his men out for refreshments, and while awaiting their return three representatives of the General Security Committee (the police branch of the Committee of Public Safety) made their appearance. These were Legendre, Drouet and Chabot, all of them coarse and violent men.

The most notorious of the three was Chabot, a foul-mouthed degenerate who had once been a monk of the Capuchin order. The renegade priests who achieved secondary positions of power during the Revolution were consistently a contemptible lot, ignorant and sadistic bullies who were almost without exception cowards too. They supply excellent evidence of the low state into which the Church had fallen before the Revolution. Chabot was one of the more conspicuous of their ignoble kind, a brutish, red-faced man whom Marat sarcastically called "the Turkey" because his warted, purple face resembled the wattle of that bird. He was a thief and even then was secretly involved in the swindle of the assets of the

East India Company, which was soon to cost him his head and cost the heads of his many corrupt associates. When he saw the beautiful woman who had murdered his colleague Marat, his eyes glittered with sudden interest. She sat on a chair with her wrists tightly bound behind her back, but that position in no way caused her to lose any of her composure. Her purity, the Norman freshness of her complexion, the cleanness of her body fascinated him. "She has every grace," he noted in his report to the Committee; "she is tall and of superb bearing. She seems to have the courage to undertake anything." To engage her in conversation he began to ask her a great many useless questions.

"There is very little to say," she finally stated. "And anyway I've already told it." She recognized Chabot. She had read his name many times in the newspapers and had seen his face among the gravures that were circulated in the provinces. His behavior now justified her prejudice. Chabot's interest in the prisoner was suddenly distracted by her little gold watch, which lay on the table. He reached out to take it. She followed his movement with ironic eyes.

"Have you forgotten that the Capuchins take a vow of poverty?" she asked.

This sarcastic reference to Chabot's past caused everyone in the room to chuckle. Chabot's weakness for other people's property was common knowledge. Disconcerted, the former monk hurriedly withdrew his hand from the watch. His attention returned to the woman. His bloodshot, angry eyes found their way to the expanse of white flesh just above her laced bodice. In her struggle with Bas the fichu which she had wrapped about herself had been torn and her shoulders were now more exposed than her modesty would, in ordinary circumstances, have permitted. Gazing hungrily at the fine breasts, whose shape was clearly distinguishable beneath her dress, Chabot suddenly noticed evidence of the papers which she had pinned there. With a triumphant howl he lunged forward. Outraged, Charlotte pulled back, but too late. Chabot's searching hand tore open the laces of her bodice.

For a moment the proud, fastidious girl found herself exposed to the ogling gaze of every man in the room. Quickly she lowered her head, letting her long hair fall forward to serve as a curtain. She asked the men near her to untie her wrists for a moment so that she might turn to the wall *pour réparer le désordre de sa toilette.* She was permitted this favor. There was some trace of decency in Chabot's associate Drouet and in a deputy named Harmand de la Meuse, who was also present. Harmand eagerly rushed forward to help her. "Charlotte Corday's movements breathed decency and grace," he gloatingly recalled in his memoirs, "and that which her misfortune permitted me to see was worthy of the chisels of Zeuxis and Praxiteles." The coy libertine seems to have taken full advantage of misfortune's unexpected offering.

Harmand's description of the evening's events does not omit reference to Charlotte's impressive self-command. "She gave us many astonishing examples of a really extraordinary memory and presence of mind. The whole of her interrogation was read over to her, and it was then proposed that each article be read separately one by one. She replied that this was unnecessary. She remembered that in the fifth interrogation a certain question had been asked her and although the recording of her reply had been generally accurate, one or two of her words had been omitted, thus slightly changing her sense. She requested that these words be replaced. She went on to observe that in the twelfth examination one word had been substituted for another. She was able to go through every interrogation by memory, the questions as well as the answers . . . a memory such as this is very rare, and particularly so in such circumstances as Mlle. Corday found herself.

"She was strongly built," continues the author; "her features were rather strong, her eyes were blue and penetrating, with a certain severity to their glance. Her nose was fine, her lips pretty, her hair of a chestnut color. . . ."

Marat's death led many excitable *Montagnards* to believe that they too might have been Charlotte Corday's victims. Such was the effect on the man Legendre, who hopefully asked her, "Weren't you the woman who called on me this morning claiming that you were a nun?"

Charlotte drew those "blue, penetrating eyes" across his face with contempt: "You deceive yourself, Citizen," she replied. "A man such as you is not big enough to be a tyrant. It would not be worth the trouble to kill you. I never had the intention of striking anyone but Marat."

Her answer caused another wave of suppressed laughter to ripple through the room. Legendre, like Chabot, was not popular among his associates. Henceforth her inquisitors measured their questions with care. Charlotte's low and cultivated voice masked a tongue more sarcastic than those of the shrill, termagant wives who awaited these *petits commissaires* at home.

Shortly after midnight the session in the salon ended and Charlotte was taken into the bedroom to identify Marat's body. All through her interrogation, surgeons from the medical college had been at work embalming his remains. The corrupt condition of Marat's body at the time of death and the suffocating heat of that July night had caused premature decomposition. The undertakers and surgeons had lit a small fire, in which they burned aromatic herbs, but neither this nor the Cologne water which they intermittently sprayed about the room could mask the unwholesome stench that pervaded the death chamber. On the street below an uneasy mob gazed up at the windows of Marat's bedroom, where from time to time they could see the shadows of the busy doctors as they passed before the flickering light of the torches. All this lent an air of mystery and additional horror to the occasion.

Charlotte's composure was for the first time visibly upset when she was confronted with the grey, shrunken body of her victim. She looked down at him lying on his bed, then quickly turned away. "Yes," she said. "It is I who killed him."

It is probable that the sobs of the bereft Simonne troubled her more than the sight of the dead Marat. These sobs were to bother her up to her own end. She had never imagined that someone might love Marat. But she was able to console herself with the justification that was Marat's and that was soon to be Robespierre's: to achieve one's end it is sometimes necessary to injure the innocent. Since she was convinced—as were Marat and Robespierre—that her end was a desirable one, she was able to sacrifice her compassion. All the same, the heart-rending grief of Simmone troubled her. She was glad when they led her from Marat's room.

Long after midnight the expectant crowd saw what it had been waiting for. The door to Marat's apartment was finally opened and, escorted by two national guardsmen and her inquisitors Legendre, Drouet and Chabot, the "Woman of Calvados," her wrists bound, her black hat knocked awry, slowly descended the stone steps that she had mounted nearly seven hours before. At the sight of her a great roar went up from the mob, which surged ominously forward. The hackney that had brought Charlotte still waited outside, presumably ordered by the police to do so. Escorted by her guard, Charlotte was able to reach the cab. Drouet gave orders, "To the Prison of the Abbaye," but the mob that filled the street was now screaming for immediate vengeance and would not make way. Expecting to be lynched on the spot, Charlotte fainted.

In a loud voice Drouet snapped orders that the coach be allowed to pass "in the name of the law." The mob, pampered by demagogues and accustomed to hearing itself lauded from the rostrum of the Convention, was startled by this unexpected tone of authority and obediently fell back. The carriage pulled away and clattered off to the Abbaye. Charlotte recovered a moment later, astonished to find herself still alive. She complimented the police on their courage.

It was almost dawn when they reached the prison and she was at last allowed to sink into sleep. "I have done my duty," she declared. "Now let others do theirs. . . ."

19

THE DETAILS of her trial belong to the history of the Revolutionary Tribunal, that organ of "justice" which was then just beginning to be the right arm of the Committee of Public Safety and through which the Committee was to achieve the dictatorship. The Revolutionary Tribunal had been established four months earlier. The trial of Charlotte Corday was the first of its many sensational trials and brought into prominence the name and appearance of that grim public servant, the State Prosecutor, Fouquier-Tinville.

Throughout her imprisonment and trial Charlotte remained serenely certain of one thing: that she had brought peace back to France and put an end to insurrection. The two letters that she wrote from her cell testify to this sublime delusion. The first was to her father, a short note of explanation and farewell, written the day before her trial.

"Forgive me, dear Papa, for having disposed of my life without your permission. I have avenged many innocent victims and I have prevented many future disasters. The people will one day be disabused and be glad to have been delivered of a tyrant. I tried to persuade you that I had gone to England because I hoped to keep my incognito. I soon realized the impossibility of this . . . a deed such as mine admits of no defense, but one must go through the forms. Adieu, my dear Papa. I beg you to forget me or rather to be glad of my ending—its cause was good. I embrace my sister, whom I love with all my heart, as I do all my family. Don't forget this line of Corneille: *"Le crime fait la honte et non pas l'échafaud."*

Her other letter was to Barbaroux. It is difficult to realize that this small masterpiece, filled with description and ironic humor, was written only hours before her death on the public scaffold. It is dated "on the second day of the preparation for Peace"—the second day, in other words, after the death of Marat. "You asked me, Citizen, to send you an account of my trip. I shan't bore you with anecdotes." She gave him a few details of her journey to Paris, then moved on to matters that were of more concern. Barbaroux's friend Duperret was much on her mind: "I confess that I was very much afraid they would find out that I had spoken to him. I regretted having been in touch with him when it was too late. I tried to make up for that mistake by making him promise to join you. But he was too strong-willed to make any such promise. Knowing that he and everybody else were innocent, I decided to go ahead with my plan anyway.

"Can you believe it, the Abbé Fauchet [the juring Bishop of Calvados] is in prison for being my accomplice. Fauchet, who doesn't even know of my existence! But these people here don't like having only an insignificant woman to offer up to the shade of their great man. Forgive me, men, the word is an insult to all your sex. Marat was a ravening monster who would have devoured the whole of France through civil war. But now . . . *Vive la Paix!* . . . I shall not give you any details about the great event. The newspapers will tell you all about that. I confess I made use of a treacherous trick to induce him to receive me; but in such circumstances the end justifies the means.

"When I left Caen I had counted on sacrificing him on the summit of the Mountain, but he was no longer attending the Convention. People in Paris are such good Republicans that they can't believe that a mere woman, who would not have been of any use no matter how long she lived, could have sacrificed herself in order to save her country. I was expecting to be killed at any moment, but brave men who are really above all praise saved me from the excusable rage of those whom I had made unhappy. Since I killed him in cold blood the crying of certain women upset me. But if one saves one's country one must not think of the price that has to be paid. May Peace be established as quickly as I hope it will be. A great step has been taken in that direction without which we never should have had it. . . ." She went on to speak of friends and relatives who might be persecuted on account of their association with her. In this appeal she betrays her naïve conviction that Barbaroux and his party were soon to be restored to positions of power: "I beg of you, Citizen, that you and your colleagues take up cudgels on behalf of my family and friends, whose memory I shall keep in my heart. I have hated only one man in all my life and I have demonstrated the strength of my hatred. But there are thousands whom I have loved far more than I hated him. An ardent imagination and a tender heart gave promise of a stormy life, and I beg those who may possibly regret me to remember this and to rejoice in seeing me at rest in the Elysian Fields with Brutus and the other heroes of old ... in any event the Mountain will not rule France; you may take my word for that. ..."

She was in the middle of this letter when she was interrupted by officials of the prison who had come to transfer her from the Abbaye to the prison of the Conciergerie for her trial. During the Revolution all trials took place at the Palais de Justice and all prisoners brought up for trial were taken to the Conciergerie, which adjoined it. The Conciergerie, with good reason, became known as "Death's antechamber"; nearly all who entered that fortress left it only to go to the guillotine. The officials scrutinized her letter to Barbaroux with interest. They were still hopeful of unearthing a widespread plot or, failing that, of netting a few important accomplices. They assured her that her letter to Barbaroux would be delivered to him and encouraged her to continue it in her cell at the Conciergerie. They had no intention of delivering it to him, but they made the mistake of reading it aloud at her trial—thus making its contents known to the public and to irresponsible journalists who distorted its meaning. To prevent this possibly dangerous abuse of the truth it was decided to release the letter for publication. And thus, in the newspapers, did the astonished Barbaroux finally read it.

At the Conciergerie Charlotte Corday calmly continued her letter. "I must have a defense counsel. It is the rule here. I thought of asking for Robespierre or Chabot," she wrote with an ironic grimace. "My trial begins tomorrow morning at eight. Probably by noon of tomorrow 'I shall have lived,' as the Latin expression goes. I have no idea how my last moments will be spent. It is the end that crowns the achievement. I don't have to feign indifference to my fate, for up until now I haven't felt the slightest fear of death. I have never had the slightest regard for life except as a means of being useful. ...

"I hope that you will continue to take an interest in Mlle. Forbin's business. Tell her that I love her with all my heart. Farewell, Citizen! I commend myself to the momory of the friends of Peace. The prisoners in the Conciergerie, far from insulting me as the people in the streets did, look on me with sympathy. Misfortune arouses compassion. This is my last reflection." She signed the letter "Corday."

The day before her trial Charlotte was subjected to a preliminary examination conducted by Montané, President of the Tribunal, and the Public Prosecutor, Fouquier-Tinville. Her blunt answers disconcerted her inquisitors as much as, at her trial, they were to amaze all spectators.

"What was the purpose of your trip to Paris?"

"To kill Marat."

"What motive determined you to do so terrible a thing?"

"His crimes."

"For what crimes do you reproach him?"

"The desolation of France and the civil war he kindled throughout the kingdom."

"On what do you base this answer?"

"The man's past crimes were an index of his present ones. He was responsible for the September Massacres. In order to become dictator he lit the fires of civil war. He violated the sovereignty of the people this past June by causing members of the Convention to be expelled and arrested."

They enquired into the details of her three-day sojourn in Paris and of her murder of Marat. Her answers were direct and clear.

"How did you kill him?"

"With a knife that I bought at the Palais Royal. I drove it through his chest."

"Did you believe that in doing this you would kill him?"

"That was assuredly my intention."

Eager to find accomplices, they asked the next question: "So atrocious a deed could not have been committed by a woman your age. Someone must have incited you to it."

"I told my plans to no one. I was not killing a man, but a wild beast that was devouring the French people."

They asked her many questions, but always they returned to this point—accomplices. Over and again her inquisitors expressed their astonishment that a single woman such as herself could have committed a cold-blooded act of murder: "It is inconceivable that a person of your age and sex could have planned such an act. You must have been inspired by other people, whom you are unwilling to identify, namely Barbaroux, Duperret and others who are publicly known to have been Marat's enemies."

"You do not understand the human heart," she replied. "It is far easier to execute a plan such as this when one is inspired by one's own hatred than when one is inspired by the hatred of others."

Charlotte's trial, which took place on July 17, the day after this interrogation, was one of the most sensational events witnessed so far in the Revolution. The public, avid for excitement, was to have more than its fill of excitements before another year had passed—the Queen, Mme. Roland, Mme. du Barry, Hébert, Danton, Camille Desmoulins and finally Robespierre himself, were one by one to take the path Charlotte Corday was now taking. But in the summer of 1793 appetites were still sharp.

Marat's funeral, which had taken place the day before Charlotte Corday's trial, provided a suitable overture for the real drama. The funeral, an almost incredible ceremony, had been organized and designed by the wretched David, one of the more violent Extremists, a man who in Danton's contemptuous phrase "had the soul of a lackey," but who also happened to be one of the great artists of his century. In a few years his genius was to be fawningly laid before the satin slippers of the Emperor Napoleon, and posterity was to be made the richer, thanks to David's magnificent canvases of imperial grandeur. In 1793, however, his services were at the disposal of less exalted masters and he was appointed director of the obsequies of his friend and hero, Marat.

Marat's body—neither surgery nor cosmetics could conceal the fact that his face in death was uglier than it had been in life—was extended on a sort of couch raised on steps and drawn by twelve men. Around the funeral car, young girls, dressed in white, carried wands and branches of cypress in their hands; the whole of the Convention followed. Next came the municipal authorities and then "the People," disposing themselves beneath the banners of their Sections. Revolutionary hymns and patriotic airs were chanted and, surrounded by all the paraphernalia—urns of incense, symbolic pyramids, cardboard trees and mountains—that were the indispensable properties of Republican ceremony during the Revolution, Marat's body was carried to its temporary tomb in the garden of the Cordeliers' Club.

The crowd that attended these elaborate obsequies seems to have been close to delirium. Many people fell to their knees and through their sobs began to chant the blasphemous prayer, "Oh heart of Jesus! Oh sacred heart of Marat!"—in its way as much a defilement of Marat's militant atheism as assuredly it was of the faith that France had abjured. Marat's heart was placed in a porphyry urn that was suspended from the ceiling of the Cordeliers' Club. "That heart," in the words of Lenôtre, "which had remained inaccessible to any feelings save hatred, now seemed to communicate its rancor, its fury and its fanaticism to all members of the Club."

So hysterical a worship of the dead man's remains was far from agreeable to certain of Marat's envious colleagues at the Jacobin Club. Robespierre, who had scarcely been able to mask his delight that a rival was dead, could not conceal his jealousy of the adulation that Marat's remains were receiving. The speech which he gave that night at the Jacobin Club revealed the envy that devoured him.

"If I speak this evening," he cried from the rostrum, "it is because I have a right to do so! Everybody is talking about daggers. Well, daggers are waiting for me too. I have merited them just as much as Marat, and it is only luck that Marat was struck down before me. I am therefore in a position to advise that we should not be thinking about all this vain pomp. The best way of avenging Marat is to track down his enemies without mercy."

Robespierre's own dagger thrust lay in the last sentence; he was determined that the Girondin party, leaders and followers, should go to the guillotine. Marat's death provided him with that pretext which in every situation he was always so resourceful at finding.

Charlotte Corday's trial began at eight in the morning before an audience that filled the hall of the Tribunal to its capacity. Her youth, her dignity, her unexpected beauty caused a murmur of appreciation to ripple through the galleries. The sensation-seekers began to make hurried rendezvous with one another to meet at the guillotine later that day. The "Woman of Calvados" exceeded the most hopeful expectations. From the moment of her entrance into the courtroom she captured the undivided attention of every spectator. No catcalls interrupted that trial; she was heard throughout in the dead silence of astonishment. Her answers were as precise and unaffected as they had been during her preliminary examinations. Only the sight of Simmone Evrard seemed to disturb her. She winced and turned away when she was confronted again with the woman's grief.

"Who inspired you with so much hatred of Marat?" the President asked.

"I had no need of the hatred of others. I had plenty of my own."

"What did you hope to gain by killing him?"

"Peace for my country," she answered simply.

"But do you believe that in killing him you have killed all the Marats?" the President asked her.

"This one dead—the others perhaps will be afraid."

The President reproached her for having used subterfuges in order to gain access to Marat. She admitted readily that such methods were not worthy, but she said that "anything was justified for the salvation of her country."

"How could you regard Marat as a monster when he generously gave you an interview after you wrote to him that you were persecuted?"

"What could his humanity to me matter if he had been a monster for so many other people? . . . It is only in Paris that people have been hypnotized by the man. In the provinces he has always been regarded as a monster."

"The newspapers which you read must have caused you to believe that Marat was an anarchist."

"Yes. I knew that he was perverting France. I killed one man in order to save a hundred thousand. . . . I was a Republican long before the Revolution, and I have never lacked energy."

"What do you mean by 'energy'?"

Her answer to this evoked a murmur of respect from the fascinated gallery: "That resolution which is given to people who put their private interests aside and who know how to sacrifice themselves bravely for their country."

The knife was now brought to her for identification. She considered it for a moment, then said, "Yes. That is the knife. I recognize it." According to the comment of a court stenographer, a tremor in her voice here betrayed a certain agitation that was not present in the words. Fouquier-Tinville pointed out that the blow had been skillfully dealt. If her stroke had not been delivered at that exact angle, Marat might well have survived it. "You seem to be very well practiced in this sort of crime," he said sarcastically.

Her answer to this insinuation struck the courtroom like a thunderbolt. Its echoes have reverberated into history: "Good heavens!" she cried indignantly. "He takes me for an assassin!"

During Charlotte's exchanges with the judge and the Public Prosecutor she happened to notice an officer of the National Guard who was making a sketch of her. She smiled at him encouragingly and shifted her chair slightly so that he might have a better view of her face. The name of this guardsman was Hauer, and after her condemnation she was able to arrange for him to come to her cell in the last few hours that preceded her execution to finish the sketch. Facts persistently belie Charlotte's assertion that she wished only anonymity. She was entirely aware of the effect she was making in the courtroom; there is evidence that she had one eye turned towards posterity as well.

Fouquier-Tinville now rose to demand her head. He wasted no words, since there was little doubt of his being awarded that prize.

Charlotte Corday's lawyer was placed in a more difficult position. The man chosen for this hopeless task was Chauveau-Lagarde, a brave and honorable lawyer who was also to defend Marie Antoinette and other persons of prominence during those early days of the Terror when the pretense of a trial was still accorded the condemned. Chauveau-Lagarde was not concerned with trying to save Charlotte Corday. That, of course, would not have been possible. But in making his speech for the defense, he was confronted with a matter of tact which was almost as difficult. During the trial a note had been delivered to him from the President of the Tribunal ordering him to plead insanity. This plea, which would not have saved his client's life, was intended to humiliate her and to divest her act of the aura of patriotism that surrounded it and that had made such an impression on the courtroom. Chauveau-Lagarde himself was profoundly impressed by the young woman whom he had been drafted to defend. Chivalry and an innate respect for her standards prompted him to make a short, dignified and skillful speech. The matter of insanity was touched on delicately—enough to satisfy Montané, but so lightly that it could not hurt Charlotte: "This incredible calm," he said, "this entire dedication of self which shows no signs of remorse even in the presence of death itself, this complete tranquility and abnegation which in their way are sublime, are not natural. They can only be explained by that exaltation which is born of political fanaticism and which put the dagger in her hand. It is for you citizens of the jury to judge how much weight to give this moral consideration in the scales of justice. I rely on your discretion." As he sat down, Chauveau-Lagarde was conscious of Charlotte's look of relief and gratitude.

The jury retired and soon after returned. The legal formalities that attended the reading of her sentence appeared to bore her. She heard the sentence itself with complete indifference, but as she was being led from the courtroom she turned to Chauveau-Lagarde. "Monsieur," she said. "You defended me in a manner worthy of yourself and of me. I am very grateful. My property, alas, has been confiscated, but I am able to offer you a greater proof of my gratitude. I ask you to pay the few debts which I leave behind me in Paris." The delicacy of this compliment from a lady of the *ancien régime* to a gentleman was not lost on Chauveau-Lagarde, who duly savored it—and paid her debts.

She returned to her cell in a state of happiness that was clouded by only one fact—she had expected to be dead by noon of that day. It was now after one o'clock, and her execution was to take place at five. A small legal difficulty delayed it still another hour, so that it was close to six when they finally came for her. She passed the time chatting with the guardsman Hauer. She discussed her crime with him, speaking contentedly of the days of peace that, thanks to her, lay ahead for France. Now and again she interrupted herself to suggest some improvement or change in his composition. An oil painting that is now in the Museum at Versailles was later made of this sketch. Her appearance is very much what the story of her life would cause one to anticipate: that of a handsome, resolute and distant Norman gentlewoman with the poetry of youth and courage in her clear gaze.

Her session with Hauer was finally interrupted by Samson the executioner, who came to prepare what was called her "toilette." The long locks were shorn from the back of her neck. She was permitted to cut two of them with her own hands. One of these she gave to Richard, the concierge of the prison, and the other to Hauer. With her own hands too she put on the red chemise that murderers were obliged to wear to the scaffold. She modestly covered her shoulders with the same pink fichu that she had worn on the evening she had called on Marat. Samson, an expert in these matters, later declared that in the whole course of the Terror he never witnessed such unaffected indifference. Towards six she was led out of the prison and, her hands tied behind her back, helped into the wooden cart that was to take her down the rue St. Honoré to the Place de la Révolution (now Place de la Concorde), where the guillotine was installed.

An enormous, jeering crowd waited for her outside the gates of the Palais de Justice. She viewed them with mild momentary interest, but her glance indicated neither contempt nor compassion. She declined Samson's offer of a stool, indicating that she preferred to stand. The crowd grew thicker as the cart turned into the rue St. Honoré; insults were hurled at her like mud. As the cart jolted onwards, a sudden and violent thundershower broke over the city, putting an end to the heat wave that had hung over Paris since her arrival there, but driving away few of the spectators. The rain soaked her dress, outlining the voluptuous lines of her body, much to the delight of the onlookers. She turned her glance upward and away from them, and from that moment until her death appeared to have left them behind.

She could not have distinguished in the confused crowd certain faces that gazed at her with an ecstatic adoration worthy of her own pure but intemperate passions: André Chenier, whose heart burned at the sight of her; Adam Lux, who was so overwhelmed by her transfigured beauty that he resolved to die as she was now dying. His soul brimmed over with that sublime and half-erotic yearning that in other times had sent brave men proudly off to war—and in the Revolution had put a bread knife into the hand of Charlotte Corday.

In the tumbrel Samson turned to his passenger. "It seems like a long trip, doesn't it?" he said chattily.

"We're certain to get there eventually," she replied with characteristic irony. When the cart finally turned into the rue Royale and made its way towards the waiting guillotine, Samson compassionately stood in front of her so that she would not have to see the grim instrument. She asked him to step aside.

"I've never seen one of them before," she said. "In my situation I'm

146

naturally curious."

She examined it with interest and a few moments later with unruffled composure mounted the steps of the platform on which it was placed. She made some slight objection when they removed the fichu that covered her bare shoulders, but doubtless consoled herself with the reflection that her modesty would be of little value in a few seconds' time. She embraced the plank on which they bound her "almost with joy." The plank was then thrown forward and an instant later the executioner released the knife. A great roar went up from the crowd. This applause now inspired the executioner's assistant (a man named Legros, who had been hired for the day) to do an unpleasant thing. Samson, who was occupied with unbinding the bleeding body from the plank, had turned his back for a moment. His assistant eagerly fished into the wicker basket where the head had fallen, picked it up by the hair to show it to the delighted mob and then dealt it a savage slap across the cheek. The spectators, aghast, claimed later to have seen it blush. Legros was severely reprimanded by Samson—as later he was by the authorities —for this needless act of brutality.

Immediately after the execution Charlotte's body was sent to a nearby hospital, where a committee of surgeons under the observation of a government committee headed by David, performed an autopsy. It was discovered, despite rumors and gossip to the contrary, that the deceased had been a virgin. David's committee submitted a grudging report to this effect. The body was then buried in a common trench in the cemetery behind the Madeleine together with the others who had been put to death on the Place de la Révolution. There is evidence, however, that her head was never interred. Until recently a skull reported to be that of Charlotte Corday was in possession of the psychoanalyst Princess Marie Bonaparte. The history of this curious object (it is "of a dirty ivory yellow, glistening and smooth, indicating beyond question that it was never buried") is convincing. It is clearly a woman's skull, but there is a section of it in the forehead just above the nose that has caused authorities to call it "atypical," or partly masculine. One must suppose that in the Elysian Fields Charlotte Corday would not have been displeased by that diagnosis.

• • •

Her act must be measured on several scales. It was conceived and took place in that shadowy area of things where private standards come into collision with public morality. Against moral considerations she armed herself with the tenet that an end can justify the means. Exaltation and the transports of youthful idealism prevented her from recognizing the fact that Marat and Robespierre, too, girded themselves with the same argument.

In confused times, in a country where the government is in flux and one does not know who is about to seize power, it is as difficult as it is unwise to take a firm position. The heroes of one day are very likely to be the villains of the next. Such rapid changes, taking place when the relationship between "Might" and "Right" is highly ambiguous, pose as awkward a dilemma to today's historians as they did to the men and women who acted in the drama.

Those who in their hearts still honored the inflexible teachings of France's abjured faith had no difficulty in passing judgment on her. Her friend Mme. de Pontécoulant, the former Abbess of the Abbaye-aux-Dames, never mentioned her name again. Nor did the nun Alexandrine de Forbin, whose affairs had occupied Charlotte's mind up to the end of her life. In their eyes she was nothing more than a murderess. Such too were apparently the views of her father.

When the police came to interrogate him in his house at Argentan, they confirmed his worst fears, for he had already heard the rumor that a "woman of Calvados" named Corday had killed Marat in his bathtub. He lowered his head in his arms and wept unashamedly. The police had the discretion to leave him alone with his thoughts for a few hours. When the interrogation was over he never spoke of his daughter again. At the end of the Terror he left France and went to Barcelona, where he finally died in the obscurity he desired.

Her deed, in the end, must be measured by its effectiveness, for as the shrewd French saying has it, "Success can hide many errors." Had her act of sacrifice—and courage—brought peace back to France, as she was convinced that it had, or had it in any way deflected the onrush of the Terror, which was about to overwhelm that unhappy country, certain of her severe critics might have found means to adjust their high moral standards to suit this different circumstance. It is to be noted that no important street in France honors her name —always an indication of officialdom's view of France's historical personages; nor are many more, in fact, dedicated to Robespierre. The two have it in common that both failed in their purpose. Bonaparte, on the other hand, a man who was as much a usurper of power as Robespierre, has lent his name to the public squares and boulevards of half the towns in France.

Charlotte's act was ineffective because she was ignorant of the real nature of the events into which she intruded. Her scanty information about public affairs came from rumor and from inflammatory newspapers and pamphlets. She was unable to see that the *Montagnards,* despicable as many of them were individually, had the rude strength that was needed to repel invasion from abroad. Having seized the prize of power from the incompetent hands of the divided and quarreling Girondins, the *Montagnards,* dominated by—and dominating—the Commune of Paris, did not intend to lose that power through civil war. It is in the natural order of things that in times of violence the strong should devour and enslave the weak. The Girondins, because they were weak, and because they indulged themselves in the weak man's luxury of substituting good intentions for resolute deeds, were doomed long before that fatal day of June 2. Charlotte's firm hand could not possibly have reinstated them.

A chain of events, far too intricately linked for her to perceive its beginning, its end or any of the connections, was being forged by men she knew little of and in circumstances that she could not have understood. "If only she had consulted us!" lamented Louvet, a Girondin. "It would not have been against Marat that we would have directed her blow." The alternative of her killing Robespierre presents fascinating but fruitless possibilities on which to speculate.

Her private life commands interest because it was characteristic of a rather large and unnoticed segment of French society, the silent, faceless class of the poor but honorable *petite noblesse*—people who played no role in the witty chronicles of high life before the Revolution and who played even less a part during the excesses of the Terror. Marat's death and the subsequent events that were inseparable from it ("She has killed us," pronounced Vergniaud on behalf of his fellow Girondins, "but she has taught us how to die") weave her story into the pattern of that larger tapestry, the Terror itself.

Across the stage left empty by Marat, the inscrutable green eyes of Robespierre cautiously appraised the stature of his rival Danton.

II. THE TRIAL OF DANTON

APRIL 1794

20

THE EXPULSION of the Girondin deputies from the Convention, that scene of turbulence which had taken place in the Palace of the Tuileries on June 2, 1793, and which in the hallucinated eyes of Charlotte Corday transformed a kitchen knife into the dagger of Brutus, was also a crucial event in the affairs of the Revolution's most famous leader of men, Georges-Jacques Danton. For it marks the opening of Danton's fatal struggle with Robespierre, a contest that was to conclude nine months after Charlotte's execution with the execution of Danton on the Place de la Révolution. The struggle between these two men informs the background of the first part of the Reign of Terror.

The facts of the drama, the endless *coups d'état,* the popular uprisings, the ever-shifting ideologies, the welter of dates, the confused and hurried scramblings to seize the fallen crown of power, are complex and not always easy to follow. There is no leisurely unfolding of events during the Revolution. The happenings of a century are compressed into months and even weeks.

But this "second fit of the Revolution," as it has been called, cannot be understood without some appreciation of those facts that, forged link upon link in close and fatal sequence, culminated in the struggle between Danton and Robespierre. They are essential to any understanding of the French Revolution on its political level. Political significance apart, however, in the short tempestuous life of Danton one is brought face to face with the Revolution on its human level. Danton's rise to power, his happy marriage brought suddenly to its tragic end, his quarrel with Mme. Roland, his remorse over the fate of the Girondins, and his second marriage were

153

events of a personal kind that may be counted among the forces that have altered history.

Significantly, the antagonism between Danton and Robespierre has been bequeathed to today's historians of the Revolution, between whom rage animosities that time has in no way tempered. The historian Mathiez, a passionate partisan of Robespierre, once became so enraged by a defense of Danton that fears were expressed for his life. Those who find themselves on Danton's "side" are hardly more temperate. So firm and final is the line which divides these two famous men of the Revolution that it is not possible to view their quarrel without oneself taking a position in it. Sooner or later one's own instinctive antipathies become aroused by either one or the other of these disparate personalities. One is thus led to reflect that while history may not repeat itself, it is possible that certain human "types" —the cats and the dogs among men—do have a continuity that may impress its influence on the times. Although the costumes have changed and the language may be different, the Dantons and the Robespierres remain with us today.

Georges-Jacques Danton was born in October 1759. He was thus thirty years of age when the Revolution began and thirty-four when his life concluded on the scaffold. He was born in the village of Arcis-sur-Aube, a town situated in the flat and chalky country of the Champagne Pouilleuse, some hundred miles from Paris. Not far away, on the slopes behind Rheims, are grown those grapes from which the celebrated wines of the district are made. Despite what its name might suggest, Champagne is not the most beautiful province of France, and to a Norman the countryside surrounding the town of Arcis would seem monotonous and barren and the land a poor investment, for the soil is shallow and its woodland sparse.

But to one born there, such as Danton, it had its own beauty, and for him this corner of Champagne was forever France, just as Calvados was France for Charlotte Corday. The gentle river Aube, lined by poplars, flowed cool and deep through the little town and was an invitation to swimming and fishing through the long summer afternoons of boyhood. To the end of his brief, violent life Danton retained a taste for those two agreeable pastimes. In his early years in Paris, when he was an obscure student of law, he would often plunge into the Seine as though it were the Aube—a bit of recklessness that eventually put him to bed with a case of typhoid fever.

Danton was passionately attached to the countryside of his birth. Through the fury and fever of his political life the picture of that quiet community set by the banks of a river never left him. Time and again he returned to Arcis, buying a house and land there, always planting and improving his growing property—not for purposes of investment, but because he was a man to whom the cultivation of the soil was a primary nourishment to his being. These trips to Arcis would heal his wounds and restore his exhausted vitality; towards the end of his life they began to correspond in their frequency with his loosening grip on the reins of power. He was at Arcis—and most unwisely—when the Girondins were condemned to death, a moment when Robespierre's star had begun to rise in the Committee of Public Safety.

This attachment to the soil, so considerable an element in Danton's character, contrasts significantly with the views about land of that other provincial, Maximilien Robespierre. To Robespierre, devoted disciple of Rousseau, the land was an ennobling abstraction called Nature, the mother of the Virtues, an elevating concept to be honored at public festivals with symbolic sheaves of wheat and cornucopias filled with agricultural produce: a thing to be admired, not handled.

Danton, a well-read man, was never among the admirers of Rousseau. Nature for him was a reality, a river to swim in, a pile of muck to plant in, a good farm well stocked with chicken and geese. The sight of his livestock coupling, that diverting spectacle which is the amusement of simple country folk, would bring from him roars of Rabelaisian laughter. Because he was close to animals the large component of appetite that humans have in common with cattle never surprised or offended him. There was a broad strain in his character that was coarse and brutish. It was one day to give dangerous offense to more genteel spirits than himself who considered humans, and in particular themselves, to be a notch or two higher on the social scale than cows and bulls.

Although it is not at present the vogue to grant much importance to the influences of ancestry, ancestry nonetheless explains much that was in Danton's character. His grandparents and their forebears had been peasants, and Danton's acquisitive love of the soil surely owed itself to some inheritance of memory from this unbroken line of men and women sprung from the land. The word "peasant" conventionally evokes a picture of black poverty and receives the generous compassion of twentieth-century Americans so fortunate as to be domiciled in apartment houses or real estate developments. In the circumstances of the Danton family, however, there was little to invite tears. They were a tough, hard-working breed, strong physically and vigorous intellectually. By the time of Danton's birth they were no longer peasants, but citizens of that class known as *petit bourgeois,* people who made their livelihood through their acumen in trade and their cunning in negotiation. The harsh law of nature which insists that the inept shall sink and the competent rise often transcends the more complicated laws of men that are designed to oppose nature's law. At Caen the ineffectual Cordays slipped slowly downwards; at Arcis the energetic Dantons began to rise in the world.

There exists a likeness of Danton's mother that was painted in her old age, and this little portrait reveals much about Danton's background. Beneath an enormous frilled bonnet the wizened old woman peers out on a world that she views with the suspicious scepticism of one who has met a few cheats in her time. Bright as shoe buttons, the eyes seem to be fixed on some panorama of recollection unfolding itself in the middle foreground. The lips are parted in cynical, affectionate amusement at what she sees. It is a face entirely French, the prototype of countless mothers who have raised families in provincial towns and who, though not usually dishonest themselves, are alert to the small trickeries of others. Shrewdness, opportunism and a harshly realistic view of life are qualities that circumstance has necessarily bred in this class of people. The *Champenois,* the men of Champagne, have always had them to a fault.

Danton's often careless manner, his reckless and blustery way of speech, concealed a native cunning that an adversary would have been unwise to overlook. Though his emotions sometimes carried him away, he never, in the negotiations of ordinary life, wandered too far from what he believed to be his own interests. But the passions unleashed in him by the Revolution were beyond his control and in the end they overwhelmed him. He had never been trained in the aristocratic school of self-discipline, in that icy and unyielding command of the emotions which was to carry such men as Talleyrand and the priestly Fouché successfully through the disturbances of the Revolution, the Directory, the Consulate and the Empire. But until he was overcome by the dangerous and vulgar dictates of personal feeling, Danton managed affairs of state as he managed his own affairs—with the rude view of the realist and the calculating shrewdness of the opportunist. It is not so much to be deplored that he was often motivated by self-interest but rather that such interests, when they intruded on his vision, were of a mean and unworthy order. Large in so many things, he remained small in matters of money. The far-visioned and energetic leader was too frequently the grasping grandson of peasants. The statesman could never quite separate himself from the wardheeler.

It is probable that Danton stole money from the ministry of which he was head. "Delicate food, exquisite wine, women one dreams of—that is the prize of acquired power." Danton was heard making this statement at a moment when he himself held the prize of power. "The Revolution is a battle," he once declared. "Shall it not be followed like all battles by a division of the spoils among the conquerors?" It would not have been in his heart to condone overt pillage any more than it would have been in Danton's nature to hold up men at gunpoint or to rob women of their jewelry. But the Treasury, vast and impersonal, presented opportunities for a little self-enrichment that were less disturbing to the bourgeois conscience. For this kind of pillage words may be found that are not so blunt as "theft," though it is to Danton's credit that if he stole money he would have admitted the fact to himself. Self-deceit was not among his weaknesses.

His dishonesty will always present a problem to those historians who are his admirers. Some of them have attempted to disparage the evidence that accuses him—and that evidence, though very suggestive, is by no means conclusive. Others have had recourse to the same reasons and excuses that dishonest people themselves are usually able to find in order to justify their thefts. It is as difficult to believe the first group as it is to accept the justifications of the second. It is wisest to view Danton with his own realist's eyes, admitting that he probably was a thief, giving him the small allowance that his thefts were of public rather than private money, and reflecting on the mitigating fact that in the final accounting his peculations cost France far less than did the rectitude of certain of his puritanical adversaries. History is not wanting in examples of opportunists, and even of dishonest ones, who have served their country better than well-intentioned idealists who do not understand the human heart and who, in consquence, misapprehend the nature of power.

When he was a child of two, Danton, while sucking on the udder of a cow—such was the custom of the *Champenois* country—was attacked by an angry bull who ripped open his face with a horn. The attack disfigured him for life and gave him that cast of feature, his upper lip twisted in a permanent sneer, his nose smashed against his face, that terrified his enemies. A few years after the bull's attack he was knocked over by a herd of pigs and trampled upon; his face was further disfigured. His family's barnyard appears to have been as agitated a place as the city of Paris during the Terror: when he was seventeen Danton was attacked by another bull and again kicked in the face. Before he was ten, smallpox had added its pits and seams to his badly scarred countenance. The extreme ugliness that was the outcome of these accidents lent a certain power to the appearance of Danton the man. "My ugliness is my strength," Mirabeau once boasted. Danton, known as "the Mirabeau of the lower classes," might well have echoed these words. The stocky boy grew into a bull-necked, barrel-chested man. Every gesture of his enormous hands, every toss of that huge and broken head expressed the presence in him of vast reservoirs of vitality. Big in so many things, his ugliness was cast in rude, large strokes, like the massive and unfinished marbles of Michaelangelo, and enhanced the size of him. He was not unattractive to women.

From an early age Danton resisted all attempts to curb his naturally rebellious spirit. When he was thirteen his parents enrolled him in a school at Troyes, capital of Champagne, which was run by the Oratorian priests. The Jesuits had been expelled from France during the reign of Mme. de Pompadour, and since that time the Oratorians had been in charge of most Catholic education in France. The Oratorian priests in all ways comprised an open-minded and admirable order. The scientific discoveries of the century (many of which the Jesuits would have considered as inducements to heresy) captured their imagination and interest. By the time Danton was enrolled with them, their curriculum had acquired a strong scientific flavor and included such unusual courses as cosmography, anatomy and physics. More than one of their graduates left school inflamed with theories that were to bring destruction down on the Oratorians during the Revolution. Danton always kept a soft spot for them in his heart and, when he was able to do so, he saved their lives.

Danton's record as a student suggestively parallels his approaching life as a politician. He was lazy and brilliant, one of those pupils whose sudden interest in a subject can carry him far beyond the limits of the curriculum, but who is bored by method or discipline. Flashes of inspiration would suddenly illuminate long stretches of unfinished work. Literature particularly captured his interest. The classics, with their Republican overtones, thrilled him. Those passages of Corneille that elevated the virgin soul of Charlotte Corday excited Danton with a ruder enthusiasm. "Corneille," he once proclaimed, "was a thorough Republican." Danton's taste for reading lead him to such Gallic writers as Rabelais and Molière, masters of comedy who were not popular among his more earnest contemporaries. Rabelais, who would have bored Charlotte Corday and shocked Robespierre, was a particular favorite of Danton. The Rabelaisian was a substantial component in his character.

Danton graduated from school in 1780. Following the custom of their kind, his family held a meeting at which his future was discussed. It is said that one of his uncles wished him to become a priest, a suggestion that was fortunately dismissed. Danton himself wanted to be a lawyer, to which his family finally agreed. Not at all uneasy about the difficulties and hazards that he might face in a great city where he knew no one, the vigorous grandson of peasants was determined to seek his fortune in Paris rather than in Rheims or Troyes, the cities of his province.

And so it came to be that with not a sou in his pocket, but full of confidence and vitality, Georges-Jacques Danton set out one summer morning of 1780 on the post road to Paris and to the great adventure in which he was to be so spectacular a participant.

21

PARIS HAD THEN (as indeed it has now) a number of restaurants, hotels and lodging houses that catered to the various provinces of France. A visitor to the capital could choose a place where he would be most likely to meet fellow travelers from his own country. The Cheval Noir on the Right Bank, directly across the bridge from the Île St. Louis, was patronized by the men of Champagne, and here Danton stayed while he looked for a lawyer who would be willing to give him a job and training in his profession. Unqualified though Danton conspicuously was for the legal calling—careless, fitful and wanting in attention to detail—he soon found a patron. The lawyer, one Maître Vinot, was impressed by that quality in Danton which was to carry him into history and with which, in history, his name is associated: *l'audace,* or daring and assurance. "In our profession," Maître Vinot is reported to have said, "assurance is a needed quality." So, despite his illegible handwriting and his inability to add a column of figures, Danton was given the job and established himself in Paris.

The eighteenth-century Paris of aristocratic brilliance and of the famous salons has captured the fascinated attention of posterity. So, too, for students of a more earnest disposition has the Paris of the slums and reeking tenements. Less interest has been shown in the respectable lower middle class, in the nameless men and women who, like Danton, were gainfully if drably employed, and who made up by far the larger part of the city's population. Exciting neither the envy nor the admiration that is aroused by the rich nor the compassion that is awakened by the poor, the *petite bourgeoisie,* the clerical classes, have trudged unnoticed through most of history, inviting the sympathy or the contempt of no one. The chroniclers of the day, Restif de la Bretonne and Mercier, have given us occasional glimpses of these classes.

The impression we have been left with is far from depressing. One has a sense (too often wanting in the more elaborate distractions of our own time) of pleasure. The theatres were cheap and many. They were also of the highest degree of excellence. There were many fairs or public festivals that one could attend free of charge. Nor were the working classes all starving. Their gastronomic standards appear, in fact, to be higher than today's—if we are to believe an account of Restif, who tells of a restaurant near the rue des Mauvais Garçons that catered to workers (a class well below Danton's on the economic scale). For the price of six sous one was given the choice of a main course of roast veal, roast lamb, grilled chicken or *boeuf à la mode*. The main course was served with lentils and bacon and followed by a salad and cheese. A carafe of red wine was included in the price of the meal. This excellent establishment (one wishes it were still there) served over 150 customers an hour. Loitering, that Parisian pleasure, was not permitted. But cafés of every conceivable political or artistic complexion were plentiful, and in them a considerable part of most men's day was spent in idle and animated conversation, which, when it turned to politics, often became violent.

In this obscure but lively world Danton, a naturally convivial man, made many friends. He was a great frequenter of the cafés and spent more time in them than perhaps would be permitted him by a modern employer. Many hours were idled away at the Procope over dominoes and over the interminable political discussions which raged in that particular café, once the favorite of Voltaire. Towards the end of 1787 another café, the Parnasse, which was located on the Right Bank just over the Pont Neuf, began to receive his patronage. At the Parnasse he had met and fallen in love with the woman who was to become his wife. She was the daughter of the owner, a man named Charpentier, and every day she was to be found sitting beside her mother on a high stool in front of the cashier's desk. David painted a portrait of Gabrielle Charpentier when she was Mme. Danton, just before her premature death. The painting discloses to us a familiar Parisienne of the buxom rather than the frail variety. Her broad face is set in a rather stilted and severe expression, not natural to her. A cheerful grin is so clearly her normal expression that one senses the constraint imposed on her by so important an experience as having her portrait painted. Amiable, merry and decent, she was clearly the ideal wife for the big and volatile Danton.

There were many people alive after the Revolution who remembered with pleasure this Charpentier who became Danton's father-in-law. "We imagine that we see him still," one recalled; "the master of the house with his little round wig, his grey coat and his napkin tucked under his arm. He was full of kind attention for his customers, and he was treated by them with cordial respect. The daughter of the proprietor, a respectable girl who was as charming as she was obliging, served at the counter. . . ." Over the years Charpentier's café had flourished, and with the proceeds he had realized from the Parnasse, "the master of the house" had bought himself a lucrative position as a collector of taxes. By the time Danton was courting his daughter, the buxom beauty who sat enthroned on the cashier's stool had become something of an heiress. The figures, indeed, are revealing. For purposes of sale the café was appraised at a sum close to $40,000 today, but out of the earnings of the café and as a tax farmer M. Charpentier had salted away the very tidy sum of another $100,000—no mean nest egg by anybody's measurement. Assuredly the Café Parnasse and its thrifty proprietor had little in common with that wretched wine shop run by the Defarge family that Dickens depicted in *A Tale of Two Cities*.

The comely heiress did not want for suitors, among whom, and the most assiduous, was Danton. For her part Gabrielle appears to have had eyes for no other man. A small difficulty, but one that was overcome with the help of M. Charpentier's fortune, stood in the way of this marriage. Danton, though he had been awarded his certificate permitting him to practice law, was without employment and, worse still, without much hope of it. To secure himself a few clients and an income with which to support his wife, it was necessary, in accordance with the custom of the day, to buy himself a post. By putting up $20,000 of his wife's dowry and by raising another $30,000, which he was able to borrow from M. Charpentier and his own family at Arcis, Danton finally bought himself the office and appointment to the courts of a Maître Huet, which were for sale at $78,000. M. Huet agreed to accept the remainder of his price in annual installments. Danton's practice was thus purchased with no outlay from his own pocket. The entire negotiation was effected by credit—hardly a solid foundation on which to build one's house. The figures in the exchange have been carefully examined by historians, for they represent a considerable subtraction from Danton's future earnings, and in conjunction with certain other factors hint strongly at a large and unexplained source of income during the Revolution.

Two days after the purchase of his practice Danton and Gabrielle were married. His family came to Paris for the wedding and it has been related that they nearly burst with pride when they saw their son so handsomely established in the great world. The position *avocat és counseils,* which came with his office, brought him into contact with officials at Versailles. It is for this reason, perhaps, that pretentiously he began to sign his name as "d'Anton," an unjustified use of the nobiliary *de* that evokes derisive comment from historians of Monarchist (or Robespierrist) leanings. M. Charpentier, who had paid for the better part of these honors, was as satisfied as everyone else. From rich café proprietor to poor barrister represented a large advancement up the social ladder of that time.

The bride and groom set up household in the Cour du Commerce in the Cordeliers' District on the Left Bank (not far from the corner on the rue des Cordeliers where Marat was soon to live). Though their house has vanished—it was demolished when the Boulevard St. Germain was pierced through this ancient quarter of Paris—a segment of the Cour du Commerce still stands. To visit it is to enter the still living world of Danton, Marat and Camille Desmoulins. Heard on a summer's evening, the hurrying footsteps of today's students become the footsteps of the past and of the Revolutionary crowds that once gathered in this old passageway.

Like most Frenchmen of his class, Danton was a man of strong domestic inclination. He said many times, and thus offended Robespierre, that he could not live without women. By "women" he had in mind the delights of the hearthside, a good table, and the congenial comforts of home that only a wife or a well-established mistress can bestow. Gabrielle was an excellent housekeeper. A plump chicken always simmered in its juice at the back of her stove and there were bread and wine enough in her well-provisioned larder for any number of her husband's friends who might drop in for supper. And in the atmosphere of so convivial a household a great many friends did indeed come and go. The result was that between the years 1787 and 1789 Danton became a well-known and popular figure in his quarter, an important factor in his rise to eminence during the eventful year of 1789.

22

THE CORDELIERS' DISTRICT, which played so important a rôle both in the history of the Revolution and in the life of its two famous residents, Danton and Marat, was situated in that part of Paris which today includes the Odéon, the Medical School, and—on the river —the Hôtel de la Monnaie. At the time of the Revolution it was inhabited by an assertive, self-reliant population whose unsteady employment tended to be in the arts and whose interests were of a vaguely intellectual character. The Théâtre Français was situated on the edge of the district, and many people attached to this institution, actors and playwrights, counted themselves as Cordeliers. Among them, soon to be conspicuous, were the unemployed Collot d'Herbois and Fabre d'Églantine. A great many writers, itinerant journalists and men who had caught the fever of political philosophy that then raged in France, had come to roost in this quarter, where they found congenial friends and neighbors. Among these were Camille Desmoulins and—soon after the outbreak of the Revolution—the terrible Marat.

It was a quarter, too, in which lived the printers, typesetters and journalistic handymen associated with the publisher's trade. Students abounded here then, as they do now, and though the flavor of the quarter has been diluted by time, its character today, in the mysterious way of these old Paris quarters, remains strangely similar. A great many printers, apprentices, unemployed actors and unpublished writers continue to live there. The conversation one hears on street corners or in cafés tends to be more fluent, more opinionated, more political than in the rest of Paris. Because of the reputation it was to acquire during the Revolution, one might suppose that that roaming wolf pack, the famous mob, was recruited from this district. In reality the mob came largely from the poor quarter of the Faubourg St. Antoine, whence, in times of trouble, it continues to come even today. The Cordeliers, though poor, were far from being among the dispossessed.

"I never move about its territory," Camille Desmoulins once wrote of the beloved district, "without experiencing a religious feeling . . . and on all its streets I read but one inscription, that of a Roman street, the Via Sacra."

A fierce and defiant loyalty to the quarter burned in the hearts of all its denizens. The day was at hand when the city of Paris would arrogate to itself the right to govern France. The Cordeliers, from the opening days of the Revolution, never doubted that it was their right to govern Paris. The other fifty-nine Districts into which Paris was then divided were either defied or ignored by the Cordeliers, who had established their own aggressive self-government. From their headquarters in a confiscated monastery the Cordeliers began to issue every kind of order about matters that were not within their authority. They presumed to regulate the flow of grain and provisions through Paris, to give instructions about the minting of money, to assume powers and prerogatives that belonged to the government of the city of Paris and not at all to the Cordeliers.

In permitting the Cordeliers to establish within Paris a kind of independent republic defiantly separate from the rest of the city, the Municipality exhibited in minuscule that same weakness which at the top was destroying the entire kingdom. As the established government fell into pieces, it became apparent to certain small but well-organized interests that there no longer existed any effective government in France. Psychologically speaking, the situation was analogous to a household in which parental authority has been delegated to some elderly and well-intentioned but ineffectual baby sitter. The children, naturally resentful of authority, test the ground to see if they can get away with the first forbidden step and, finding that they can, take the second, third and fourth steps with increasing confidence. By the time open rebellion has broken out it is often too late to restore the household to its former condition.

Bailly, the mayor of Paris, was a weak man. It was disagreeable to him to enter into combat with the belligerent Cordeliers. He let himself (and the government of Paris) be carried along by events, and the Cordeliers, with Danton at their head, greedily seized every prerogative that was not contested. The Cordeliers' District at last came into open conflict with the Paris municipality over the matter of the delegates whom the Municipality had ordered all its districts to send to the Hôtel de Ville, in order to draw up a plan for a new city government. The plan was designed to clip the wings of the Cordeliers, who, on Danton's advice, refused to present themselves at these sessions. In the ensuing dispute, Bailly, for once, stood his ground, and the district suddenly found itself in open rebellion not merely against the Municipality of Paris, but against the National Assembly—the government of France—which had hurried to the aid of its sister. The Municipality thus won that round, but not before the pugnacious and cocksure young lawyer, the "Commandant of the Cordeliers," had made a name for himself. Everywhere in Paris people had begun to discuss the latest demagogue whose voice had been heard in the land.

During the winter of 1790, some six or seven months after the fall of the Bastille and the outbreak of the Revolution, the Cordeliers' District (and Danton) again found themselves at the center of a local rebellion. This fresh upheaval began over Marat, for whose arrest Bailly and Lafayette had issued a warrant. The inflammatory pamphleteer fled to the heart of the Cordeliers' District where he sought what he believed would be safe asylum. From his refuge he continued his seditious attacks on the government and in particular on the mayor and Lafayette, Commander-in-Chief of the National Guard, two officials more conspicuous for their conceit than for their ability. Their easily injured vanity, indeed, had become as offensive to the Court as it was to the Extremists—which probably explains the curious alliance that took place at this stage of the Revolution between the Crown and the Extremists.

The day finally dawned when Lafayette could no longer tolerate Marat's libelous attacks, and an army of three thousand men was dispatched into the Cordeliers' District with orders to arrest and bring back the rabble-rousing Marat.

At this violation of what they believed to be their sovereignty, the citizens of the District let out a great cry of outrage. The matter was even spoken of as "an invasion by foreign troops." Danton, as leader of the Cordeliers, was present to greet the officers of the invading army. With great skill he questioned the legality of their warrant and threw up a smoke screen of quibbles and prevarications that distracted Lafayette's delegates—and gave Marat time to escape through a back door. In the course of these discussions, Danton, in a moment of anger, spoke some indiscreet words. He gestured contemptuously in the direction of the National Guard and declared in a loud voice, "What good are these troops of yours? We need only ring the tocsin and we would soon have the whole mob of the Faubourg St. Antoine with us, twenty thousand strong."

With this treasonable threat Danton put his finger on the strength of all the insurgents who in the approaching months would, one by one, try to seize the government. He put his finger too on the fundamental weakness in the position of the National Assembly. The Paris mob (often neither so seething nor so large as it appeared to frightened observers), acting in combination with various cunning leaders, was eventually to present an overpowering front of defiance to the government. Danton's ill-advised words spread through Paris and soon reached the shocked ears of the National Assembly. The "Marat affair" was suddenly forgotten. It became the "Danton affair." Investigation was indignantly demanded. Challenges and justifications were hurled in every direction.

To the accusations of sedition that were thrown at him Danton blandly evoked "freedom of speech," that smokescreen behind which many another agitator has safely retired in moral rectitude. The "affair" dragged on for some months and finally terminated in a vague compromise, the only decisive element in which was the emergence of Danton as a local power to be reckoned with. He had managed matters throughout with the skill and energy of a born revolutionary, taking full advantage of his opponents' weaknesses and using their high-minded laws and precepts as ammunition for his own guns. On his part he finally concluded the affair with a vulgar and satirical pamphlet, privately printed, that ridiculed the government and caused many people who were indifferent to both parties in the quarrel to laugh. Well-aimed ridicule has never been the least powerful of an energetic agitator's weapons.

Shortly after the conclusion of these excitements, Gabrielle gave birth to a son, whom the idolizing District hailed as "the Dauphin of the Cordeliers." The time that Danton gave to his political activities was subtracted from his law practice, yet, with no visible source of income to meet his increasing expenses, he had begun to spend money like a rich man. He bought a sizable property at Arcis, in which he installed his mother and relatives. He soon bought a small estate near Paris. These places were well furnished, and the apartment in the Cour du Commerce was stocked with the finest vintages. All this was observed by sharp eyes and Rumor, trumpet in hand, walked side by side with Fame. It was whispered that Danton was in the pay of the scheming Duc d'Orléans, who aspired to the throne. It was whispered too that he was in the pay of the Court, who hated the Moderates far more than they feared the Extremists.

Mystery still surrounds these intrigues hatched in an atmosphere in which the dangers had begun to grow in proportion to the value of the prizes. But there does survive for posterity to read and for Danton's biographers to think about, a letter from Mirabeau to the undercover representative of the Court asking for "an additional 6,000 livres to be used on bribes." Mirabeau, the hero of 1789 who was now playing his own double game, goes on to state that "while these 6,000 livres may be wasted, at least they will be thrown away more innocently than the 30,000 that we have given to Danton." (The value of a livre at that time was approximately the value of today's dollar.) A letter from the French Ambassador in London written in 1789 (a date when Danton's name would not have been known to the ambassador and consequently was not used for purposes of defamation) states flatly that "two individuals named Danton and Paré are believed to be in the pay of the English government." Paré was the name of Danton's secretary. The English government in the initial stages of the Revolution, and for its own shortsighted purposes, was inciting the disturbances in France. Whatever the answer may be to these suggestive riddles, by 1790 Danton had become a man of some affluence.

Like the storms of nature, the Revolution was punctuated by brief periods of deceptive calm during which the greater fury of the next violent phase silently gathered itself. One such lull took place between the summer of 1790 and the spring of 1791 when the Moderates Bailly and Lafayette appeared to have won the day. The Municipality of Paris was formed into a new organization called a "Commune." Danton and the radical portion of the Cordeliers were not represented in this body. Among the first acts of the new Commune was a revision of Paris "Districts." Under the old Municipality the city had been divided into sixty Districts. The Commune redivided Paris, reducing the number of Districts to forty-eight. These new divisions were called Sections, each of which came to have its own "Revolutionary Committee," its own "mob," or unofficial army, and its own system of surveillance over the lives of its residents.

Acting separately, these Sections may have presented no great threat to the government. Acting as one, however, they became something more serious. The unifying element among them was that far-reaching and Argus-eyed octopus, the Jacobin Club.

As the Revolution advanced, the appetite of this extraordinary organization grew by what it fed on and its power grew proportionately. Through its affiliates in the provinces, the Jacobins were able to institute throughout France Revolutionary Committees with Jacobin agents at their head. In Paris the leaders of the Sections, ignorant and illiterate thugs for the most part, were all members in good standing of the Jacobin Club and took their orders from its officials. The Jacobins thus had at their command a reservoir of brute force that, skillfully used, might make them the real though unofficial rulers of France.

The Assembly itself was divided into members and nonmembers of the Jacobin Club. The men who controlled the intricate piece of machinery that was the Club would have command of a weapon of incalculable power. During the apparent lull in the Revolution between 1790 and 1791, the casual observer would not have been aware of the activity that was taking place within the precincts of the Club. Here, during those days, the machine was being put together, cog upon wheel.

When the Commune redivided Paris, the old Cordeliers' District was absorbed into another, larger Section, which was called the "Section of the Théâtre Français"; the old District consequently vanished from the map of Paris. The loyal patriots of the District immediately formed themselves into a club, modeled on the pattern of the Jacobins. The Cordeliers' Club, which described itself as being "the elixir of Jacobinism," was not always the rival or competitor of its fearsome elder brother. Jealousy arose only when it fell under the control of certain of Robespierre's enemies at a time when Robespierre had command of the Jacobins.

In considering these famous and often confusing institutions of the Revolution—the Jacobin Club, the Cordeliers' Club, the Commune, etc.—one must be careful always to remember that the char-

170

acter informing each institution was in a constant condition of change. Resembling the shell of a hermit crab, these institutions were occupied by one interest at one time and by another at the next.

The Jacobin spirit during the Terror was diametrically opposed to what it had been during the early days of the Revolution, when the Vicomte de Noailles and the Duc de Biron had been among the men who occupied its President's chair. The Cordeliers' Club, founded by Danton, was one day to become the bitterest of Danton's enemies. The Commune, which in the beginning had been at the command of Bailly and Lafayette, was taken possession of by Danton, by Marat, and finally by Robespierre.

Political labels and party names are often taken at their face value by uninformed people. They thus have provided excellent screens behind which politicians can practice the deceptions necessary to their craft.

Between the summer of 1790 and August 1792, when he was to emerge as one of the great leaders of the Revolution and a figure of national importance, Danton lived in semiobscurity, by no means retired from the theatre of affairs, but restricted in his movements to that small part of the stage which was the city of Paris, where preparations were being made for the next onslaught of the storm.

23

DANTON'S PLAN to overthrow the monarchy owed itself in part to a frustration that took place during the winter and spring of 1792. The first Assembly, having completed the Constitution it had promised to give France, disbanded itself in 1791 and proposed elections to a new Assembly, to be called the Legislative Assembly. To his unconcealed disappointment Danton was not elected to this body. He did manage to capture a position in the Commune, a foothold that was to be of use to him in the approaching August, for the Commune was the agency through which he was able to dethrone Louis XVI.

In the new Assembly the party of the Girondins had begun to form itself about the policies of the man Jacques-Pierre Brissot and —unfortunately for Danton and for herself—about the person of Mme. Roland. Along with certain characteristics common to the Girondins, such as the muslin bows that they wore as cravats and an exalted idealism whose source was the writings of Plutarch, these men shared with Brissot the conviction that France should embark upon a war; not, they made it clear, a vulgar old-fashioned war of conquest, but a war to elevate the character of the French people.

"I have persuaded myself that a people which has won freedom after ten centuries of slavery needs a war"; so argued Brissot before the new Assembly. "This people needs a war to consolidate them; it needs a war to purge away the vice of despotism; it needs a war to drive out the men who corrupt them."

Dulce et decorum est pro patria mori. Idealists of a certain stamp have always found something thrilling in the sacrifice of life, usually not their own, that war demands. Patriotism after the austere Roman fashion can express itself most nobly in a good war. There is no reason to question the sincerity of Brissot's sentiments: that is what makes his patriotic exhortations so peculiarly horrible.

Condorcet, another Girondin and a disciple of Brissot, contributed his wisdom to the discussion with the peculiar statement that the French nation, "though forced to go to war, would fight without any desire of conquest"—a bit of sophistry that was greeted with "great applause." Despite such high-minded assurances about Europe in general, there were some observers of the political arena in Paris who detected in the Girondins' agitation for war a calculated maneuver by that party to make itself indispensable to the government and to secure for its adherents certain desirable positions in the cabinet.

Robespierre, ever suspicious of the motives of others, became from this moment a bitter enemy of Brissot and the Girondins. Words of a personal kind were publicly exchanged between himself and certain representatives of that party, which he could neither forgive nor forget. He awaited the day of his vengeance and in the meanwhile incited Marat and others to those overt threats and acts of hostility that he himself did not have the courage to carry out.

The war with Austria, which began in April 1792 (the war with England began a year later, in 1793), was to continue on and off until 1815 and was to outlast the lives of most of the politicians who had begun it. It is bound in the closest way to the events of the Terror and is a background which, either intrusive or receding, is always present in the intricate sequence of cause and effect that informs the Terror.

The Girondins who so blithely embarked on it discovered too late that they had set France asail on a sea of dissension and disaster. A firmer hand then theirs was soon needed to navigate the stormy waters that lay ahead. But the first and immediate effect of the war was that which Robespierre feared and which the Girondins hopefully foresaw: the Girondins came into power as a party. The important prerogative of appointing a cabinet fell into Girondin hands in March 1792 in the middle of preparation for war (and one month before its outbreak). The King assigned General Dumouriez, a friend of Danton, the task of appointing new ministers. Dumouriez turned to Brissot, leader of the Girondin party (which was in fact called the "Brissotin" party at that time), for advice in the matter. The rumor went abroad—and soon reached Danton's delighted ear—that Danton was to be given the choice portfolio of the Ministry of the Interior.

His hopes had been fully aroused—when it was announced that J. M. Roland, a bald-pated and insignificant *protégé* of Brissot who had been working in the Correspondence Committee of the Jacobin Club, had been accorded the ministry that Danton had anticipated as his own. It has been said, and perhaps with reason, that Danton's rage over this disappointment planted in him the seed that was to bear fruit five months later when he organized the invasion of the Tuileries and overthrew the throne and its portly occupant. He blamed Louis XVI as much as he blamed Brissot.

Many historians, recalling Mirabeau's observation that "a Jacobin who is appointed to the Ministry is not always a Jacobin minister," feel that the King made an error by not advocating Danton's appointment. Time and again Danton, when he was in power, proved himself a moderate. He was not scrupulous about the means he used to acquire power—the events of August were shortly to demonstrate that—and he did not hesitate to ally himself with the most violent of the Extremists to achieve power; but once "elected" to a position of responsibility, he usually showed himself temperate and amenable to compromise.

He and the King might well have found a meeting place of mutual sympathy with one another. Temperamentally they had much in common, for Louis, like Danton, was at heart a *bon bourgeois*. As for the Queen, she was, when she chose to be, a woman of great charm. Danton would not have been the first revolutionary she had fascinated into the Royalist camp. The effect that she had had on Mirabeau after a brief, secret meeting with that venal politician, who in so many ways resembled Danton, was such as might have altered the course of the Revolution had not the exhausted Mirabeau died in 1791 with the prescient regret on his lips: "I am overwhelmed by the thought that all I have done is help bring about a terrible destruction. . . ."

Had Danton been appointed to the Girondin ministry and consequently been brought into close and personal touch with the King and Queen, he might, even at that late hour, have continued Mirabeau's work and by saving the constitutional monarchy, have prevented France from plunging into the abyss before which she now was poised. Circumstances and his thwarted ambition drove him into precisely the opposite camp. It was Danton's great weakness, and finally his ruin, that he too frequently permitted emotions of the moment to overcome the deeper counsels of prudence. Anger, affection, gratitude and defiance boiled forth from him unrestrained and undisguised. Sudden violent gusts of passion would destroy in a second the carefully laid plans of months. It was this impetuousness which gave to his speeches that quality which distinguished them from the too literary, too flowery harangues of Robespierre or certain of the Girondins.

When Danton spoke before the Assembly or the Jacobin Club his words belched forth like lava. No one who heard him ever forgot the huge ugly head tossing this way and that in rage or exhortation, the rude and massive gesture of his arms or the phrases that hurled themselves in great uncut chunks out of the crater of the volcano. In the easily ignited atmosphere of the time his speeches were invariably greeted with an applause that was close to hysterical. Danton rarely decorated his speech with those Greek or Latin embellishments which were then considered indispensable. He bluntly said what he wanted to say. Transported by the emotions of the instant, what he had to say was frequently indiscreet or unwise. Continually he found himself "driven," thanks to those indiscretions, into a camp opposed to his best interests and not congenial to his temperament. After Roland's appointment to the Interior, Danton found himself making uneasy common cause with Robespierre, an ill-advised *rapprochement* with the man who was to kill him.

To understand the most important of the influences that drove Danton into Robespierre's welcoming arms it is necessary to introduce the woman who is as closely tied to the chaotic condition of France that precipitated Danton's *coup d'état* of August 11, 1792, as she is to the petty but fatal animosity between herself and Danton that followed that event. For it was not really Roland who had been awarded the Ministry of the Interior. It was his wife.

24

Mme. roland's is a name, like that of Charlotte Corday, identified by many people with some vague heroine of the Revolution who was "sent to the guillotine." The name is familiar, but the woman herself, the position she occupied and all her works have, for the average spectator of history, almost faded out of sight. This is a condition of things that would not at all have pleased Mme. Roland. She was thirty-eight years of age when she came into collision with Danton, an event that also marks her brief emergence into history. She was guillotined the following year. She was born in Paris (one of the few Revolutionary figures who were) on the second floor of that beautiful house of red brick facing the quai de l'Horloge which forms the apex of a triangle in the middle of the Pont Neuf. Her maternal grandfather had been chef in the household of the Prince de Créqui and he disputes with the Vicomte de Béchemel the honor of having created that culinary masterpiece *potage à la jambe de bois,* which has made life supportable for those who enjoy an imaginatively prepared marrow.

Of this distinguished forebear, however, Mme. Roland never boasted; a fact in which there are to be found intimations of a weakness that was central in her character. Mme. Roland was a snob. This snobbery, expressing itself in an envy of those who were her betters and a contempt for those who were her equals, distorted her judgment of people and consequently her total view of life. Her father was a master engraver, a jovial, blunt-spoken fellow who was content in the station of life in which he earned his livelihood, but which caused his sensitive daughter shame. Mme. Roland herself, in her astonishing *Memoirs,* which she wrote in prison shortly before her execution, has related all these things with a frankness that was inspired by the *Confessions* of Rousseau. Even in her *Memoirs,* however, even at the threshold of the tomb, snobbery in its most fundamental expression—blunt social snobbery—makes its appearance. To discriminating sensibilities her justifications are often more disconcerting than the unworthy weaknesses to which she is not ashamed to admit.

When she was a girl of twelve—it is she who relates this anecdote —she was taken by her grandmother to visit an aged noblewoman in whose household her grandmother had once been employed in the capacity of governess. The girl, dressed up in her Sunday best, was shocked by the rouged and arrogant old harridan, a relic of the Regency.

"Come right over here, little one, and sit down beside me," ordered the old woman. "You look to me as if you'd have a lucky hand in drawing lottery tickets. Have you ever drawn one?"

"Never, madame," responded the girl. "I do not approve of games of chance."

"She has a sweet voice, but she seems so serious! Are you sure you're not a bit priggish, little one?"

"I know my duties, madame, and I shall always endeavor properly to fulfill them." That is a sentiment which can only be uttered with the eyes cast down and with the hands primly folded in the lap.

"You sound as if you want to be a nun."

"I am indifferent to my destiny, madame. At present I do not seek to decide it."

"Your granddaughter must read a great deal!" exclaimed the astonished old woman.

"Reading is her greatest pleasure, madame," answered the grandmother with pride. "She spends much of every day in reading."

This little scene reveals much not only about self-righteous little Manon Phlipon, but about the Mme. Roland she was to become. It was the first of several unfortunate meetings with the *noblesse,* a class she bitterly resented. When she was twenty there occurred a more significant exposure to their world. Through friends she was invited to stay a few days at the Palace of Versailles. She and her mother were lodged in a servant's room high in the eaves of that rabbit warren. For two unhappy days she burned with resentment at the glittering spectacle that surrounded her. When her mother asked her how she was enjoying their visit, Manon angrily snapped,

"I am glad that we are soon leaving. Another day of this and I should hate these people so much that I wouldn't know what to do with all my hatred. . . ."

"What have they done to hurt you?" asked her mother.

"They make me feel injustice and they force me to look at their childish absurdities all day long," replied the future Mme. Roland. Manon had the courage to admit that she was mortified by the scornful glances that she and her unrouged, too respectable mother attracted in the gilded corridors. None among that sycophant throng could have imagined that the hand of the sullen-faced, mousy young woman at whom they sneered would be instrumental in pulling down the edifice that supported them. This was the first year of the reign of Louis XVI, and Manon saw the young Queen pass by in her youth and radiance. For Marie Antoinette Mme. Roland always cherished a hatred that was personal and unrelenting. It probably owed itself to some fancied slight that took place during Manon's unhappy visit to the royal château.

Her dislike of the upper classes was balanced by no noticeable affection for the lower. Many suitors made their appearance at Phlipon's door to court this superior young lady, among them a well-to-do young butcher of the neighborhood. Manon haughtily discouraged all overtures of marriage from men of this station. "I could never ally myself with a man of the commonalty," she told her father with an indignant sniff. "I despise merchants who make their fortunes by overcharging people in the market." To herself she brooded: "Should I have lived with Plutarch and with the philosophers only to unite with a common shopkeeper . . . ?" Manon Phlipon was an intellectual snob as well as a social snob.

"You are up in the clouds," her father once said during a family discussion. "It's all very well to be up there, but you'll find it isn't so easy to stay up. Just remember that I'd like some grandchildren before I'm too old." M. Phlipon appears to have been a sensible man. His bluestocking daughter was well into her twenties, however, before she decided to marry. The object of her affections was a traveling inspector of the Office of Commerce, a man who was twenty years older than herself. His name was Roland de La Platière. The territorial qualification at the end of his name "may," in the tart words of Lenôtre, "have deluded a few peasants into thinking that he was of noble birth."

Roland was a pedant and a bore of such proportions that even to read about him 170 years after his death is enough to deplete the room of its air. His specialty in the Commerce office was memoranda. No subject ever daunted that dry, meticulous pen: the raising of sheep, the manufacture of cotton velvet, the culture of wool—all were grist for a mill that ground out statistics with a merciless persistence and an undoubted accuracy. "Quakerish" was the admiring adjective most often used by his contemporaries to describe his appearance. His suits were always of a plain sober color, black or snuff-colored brown, unembellished by ornament. A black hat shaped like a dish accentuated the gravity of his demeanor. Beneath the hat his balding egg-shaped dome was covered by a few grey hairs, as sparse as himself, which were always neatly combed.

Bearing a letter of introduction from a mutual friend, he came to call on Manon during one of his visits to Paris. She was fascinated by him. His erudition, more than a match for her own, the extraordinary scope of his information, which ranged from the theories of the Abbé Raynal to certain technical considerations about sheep's-wool, impressed her profoundly. Hour after hour she would listen to his pompous, opinionated, probably nasal monotone and hang with respect on each portentous clearing of the throat. Roland was a man who was so convinced of his own superiority that the opinions of others were of interest to him only to the extent that they gave him an opportunity to demonstrate his own erudition by disagreeing. "I listen to his reasoning," Manon reported of one of their conversations, "and stick to my own opinions until I find better ones . . . but I talk very little."

Their courtship lasted four years. Traveling through the provinces, Roland ground out his interminable memoranda. Betweentimes he wrote letters to the earnest young lady in Paris, and she, in return, wrote to him. They were both addicts of the pen. Roland always kept a notebook handy to jot down any passing ideas or impressions that might some day be useful to him, while Manon spent a good part of each day engaged in the writing of her diary and correspondence. It was a weakness that was to do them great harm when history summoned them into the theatre of political dispute. To the end they felt that there was no situation that could not be dealt with by a good long letter. Nor were they averse to publishing their observations: *The Raising of Sheep* and *Letters from Italy* testify to the diversity of their interests. The letters of their courtship were published after their deaths under the title *Correspondance amoureuse,* and of all such *correspondances* ever published theirs are surely the dullest. "My task shall ever be to satisfy you," writes Manon in one billet-doux, "and to add unceasingly to your satisfaction . . . prepare now our dwelling; it will be the abode of fidelity and happiness."

Marriage brought these effusions to an end. The "abode of happiness" was fixed in Amiens, where Manon snubbed her bourgeois neighbors by secluding herself with the works of Tasso and Winckelmann. She gave birth to a daughter named Eudora, who was raised according to the questionable dicta of Jean-Jacques Rousseau. The little girl occupied her attention for a time. She found herself studying such matters as colic, milk and medicine. Roland contributed a few memoranda on those subjects. But in a few years' time the scales, not about herself, but about her husband and her marriage, had slipped from her eyes. She soon saw him as the inept but self-satisfied old man that he was. From this awareness the personality of Mme. Roland known to the Revolution began to emerge: an energetic, ambitious and strong-willed woman whose character overpowered that of her husband.

In 1784 "on behalf of Roland" she went to Paris to solicit those patents of nobility for which her soul secretly thirsted. It must have been a torture to her pride to do so, for in petitioning for so rude a prize she knew that she was betraying the very things she had always protested that she stood for—simplicity, Republicanism and the superiority of the intellectual over the vulgar, worldly life.

In Paris she received a disagreeable shock when she learned that Roland, far from being eligible for any title, stood in momentary danger of being dismissed from his job. His smug, meddlesome reports had offended a great many prickly spirits at the home office, for he never troubled to conceal his opinion that his superiors were less qualified to occupy their positions than himself. Manon, a tactful woman with a genuine talent, just then awakening, for small social intrigue, was able to smooth the ruffled feathers of officialdom. She did not return with a title, but she managed, at least, to have her husband transferred out of Amiens to Lyons, a larger and more lively city where Roland had relatives of a certain consequence. From this moment one begins to detect her capable hand behind the management of her husband's affairs. She took it upon herself to "help" him with his reports and correspondence and ended up writing the better part of them. "We are too honest to succeed," she once complained in a letter to her husband. Her use of "we" betrays the fundamental orientation of her thinking. She managed everything; his failure thus became her failure, just as, when the day of prosperity finally dawned, his success was to become hers too.

Lyons inevitably proved as dull to her as Amiens. "I would rather squash the caterpillars in my garden than mix with these people here," she wrote to a friend. But the year was 1787 and the misery of her insignificance was about to end. With the outbreak of the Revolution Roland was elected to the Municipality of Lyons, where his self-righteousness quickly alienated him from most of his associates. It was one of Roland's several weaknesses that whenever he was appointed to any committee or to a position of responsibility he would immediately demand to see the account books. He would then closely scrutinize them in the hope of finding evidence of sloppy bookkeeping or dishonesty that might enhance his own reputation for rectitude and efficiency.

Mme. Roland began archly to speak of him as "Cato," and of herself as "Cato's wife." The fashion for Greek or Latin euphuisms was embraced by her with as much enthusiasm as by the other future Girondins. "I am very much annoyed at being a woman," she once confided to a friend. "I ought to have lived in another century. I ought to have been born a Roman or a Spartan woman—or at least a French *man* . . ."—words that strongly recall the lament from Caen of that other Roman *manquée,* Charlotte Corday.

With Cato ensconced in the Lyons City Hall his wife began drawing up a program for the regeneration of the French character and for the establishment of the Republic that she felt was on its way. The theatres were to be restrained from presenting frivolous plays. Dramas with titles like *Cataline* or *The Death of Caesar* and the masterpieces of Corneille were to replace the frothy and popular nonsense that for too long had been enervating the French people and encouraging their propensity towards superficiality. The stern precepts of antiquity were to be instilled in children at an early age, while among the Elders who were appointed to administer this paradise—erudite and sober men who could write good clear memoranda, and women of sentiment who had been educated in the

181

classics—deportment was to be grave at all times. Recreation was not specifically considered by Mme. Roland, but one is left with the impression that an occasional folk dance would not be looked upon askance. *Potage à la jambe de bois* appears, alas, to have had no place in this Utopia. One supposes that wine and cheese, though no mean fare if they come from Lyons and Beaujolais, were to make up the staple of diet.

Such ideas as these and many others with a more immediate application to current events were committed to paper and sent off to Paris as letters, where they were circulated among Manon's admiring friends. One of these, a man named Bosc, was a friend of Brissot, about whom the Girondin party was soon to compose itself. Brissot, who was still an obscure lawyer, had just founded his newssheet *Le Patriote Français*. He wrote Mme. Roland inviting her to contribute an occasional article to his revue. The invitation was accepted with alacrity. Under the byline "Letters from a Roman Lady," Mme. Roland became the Lyons correspondent of a Paris newspaper. Her letters from Lyons began to acquire a tone of importance disproportionate to the modest position in life that she still occupied. She had plans about the army, plans about a "federated" France—a France divided into more or less autonomous states that were to be represented at the Assembly in Paris by their deputies and by their own armies. Such weighty matters were hoisted onto her shoulders with so firm a hand that an uninformed reader of these letters might suppose that she was already of some consequence in the management of the French government.

Unfortunately she was still at Lyons, many miles distant from the events that were disturbing Paris and determining the course of history. The letters to Bosc and Brissot began to increase in number, and a nagging note of frustration became audible in them when she started begging for news from the capital. She lost interest in Tasso and her vegetable plot, those faithful consolations for thwarted talents and a dull marriage.

The autumn of 1790 found her pacing restlessly about the terrace of her mist-shrouded garden, waiting for some stroke of good fortune that might recall her to Paris. It came finally in November. The Municipality of Lyons decided to send Roland to Paris to solicit funds from the Assembly to pay off a city debt that had been incurred there under the *ancien régime*. The matter was complicated and promised to be long in resolving. Cato's wife, along with their daughter Eudora and a nursemaid, set out for Paris in January 1791. In less than three years Mme. Roland would be dead, decapitated on the scaffold of the Place de la Révolution; and Roland, a wandering fugitive from the hounds of the Robespierre-dominated Committee of Public Safety, would one day lie down beneath the sheltering chestnut trees of a Norman pasture and drive a knife through his heart.

The Hôtel Brittanique, where the Rolands set up lodging in Paris, was on the rue Guénégaud, not far from the red house on the Pont Neuf where Manon had spent her childhood. Scarcely had she and her husband unpacked their luggage when she got in touch with Brissot. Brissot, who had never met this woman with whom he had been corresponding, immediately hurried to the Hôtel Brittanique to pay his respects. He was charmed by her. She was bright, responsive and vivacious in a way that contrasted interestingly with the earnestness of her outlook. Nor, as she took pains to explain to posterity, was she ill favored physically.

"My complexion is vivid rather than clear," she writes in her *Memoirs,* "and it is of a dazzling color. My mouth is a bit large, but it would be difficult to find a smile that is sweeter or more engaging than mine. Though my hand is not small, it is very elegant because of its long slender fingers, which indicate cleverness and grace. My teeth are white and well placed and I enjoy the fullness of excellent health. Such," she concludes, "are the treasures with which nature has endowed me."

And such were the treasures that charmed Brissot and the coterie of friends whom Brissot gradually introduced to the Circe from Lyons. The delegates to the National Assembly were a serious-minded group of men who concerned themselves with political theory and the constitution that they had been elected to draw up. No woman such as Julie de Lespinasse or Mme. Geoffrin who had graced the salons of yesteryear had yet emerged to establish a gathering place for these sober, shabby young men. Brissot's friends belonged to that faction of the Assembly which was called "the Left" because they sat on the left side of the President's desk and as a group voted almost consistently against measures that were proposed by the Monarchists, who sat on the right of the President's desk. The canaille, led by Marat, as yet had no representation in the Assembly.

The unexpected appearance of Brissot's charming friend from the provinces answered a need of some of these men of the Left who had been looking for a place to meet where they might discuss politics in an informal and friendly atmosphere. The Jacobin Club, originally designed for this purpose, had grown too big and had already become too rent by political dissension. It lacked, furthermore, that air of ease and comfort which a woman's tactfully directing presence can lend to a gathering. Most of these men, Brissot among them, had wives, but they were women too occupied with small domestic duties to have any time for running a salon. They may have known where to buy a kilo or two of fresh fish at the cheapest price, but, unlike the meddlesome, ambitious women of the vanished nobility, they were not interested in the abstractions of political theory.

Mme. Roland was different. Her erudition, her considerable reading in the classics and those philosophic speculations to which her years of boredom and frustration had driven her, gave her the appearance, entirely false, of having a "man's mind." Her outlook usually coincided with that of Brissot and his circle (now, indeed, Mme. Roland's circle). Where it did not, she was tactful enough to restrain herself from disagreement, a discipline that she had doubtless developed during her years of marriage with the opinionated Roland.

"It was arranged," she writes, "that the deputies who were accustomed to meet and confer together should come to my house four times a week after the session at the Assembly and before that of the Jacobin Club. I would . . . write letters . . . because that made me appear more of a stranger to the matters which were being discussed, but permitted me all the same to listen. With the exception of the customary compliments on the arrival and departure of these gentlemen, I did not permit myself to utter a word, although I was often obliged to bite my lips to prevent myself from doing so."

Self-effacing, unobtrusively hospitable, the Egeria of the Girondins must have had to pinch herself as, scratching away at her letters, she eavesdropped on the epoch-making conversation of the men who gathered four times a week in her little salon. Only a few months before she had been hilling melons, a nobody, in her garden in Lyons; now she was at the center of a group of men who planned to change history. Pétion came there and Buzot and Clavière. Robespierre, too, made his appearance. Mme. Roland has left a tart description of this last visitor, but it must be remembered that she was in prison when she wrote it and very soon, thanks to the rancor of Robespierre, to be put to death. "The conduct of Robespierre during the discussions which took place at my house was remarkable. He spoke little, sniggered a great deal, uttered a few sarcasms and never gave an opinion. But on the morrow of these discussions he took care to appear in the Tribune of the Assembly and turn what he had heard his friends say at my house to his own advantage."

For Mme. Roland, occupied with her salon, the year 1791 passed quickly. She was in Paris and at the center of things at the time of the King's flight to Varennes. She was also in Paris when, a few weeks later, a petition for the deposing of the monarch came to its violent conclusion with the "Massacre of the Champs-de-Mars." But none of these happenings had yet brought her into touch with the famous hero of the Cordeliers, Danton.

Danton at this moment was a friend of Brissot and may probably have been invited by him to stop by at the Hôtel Brittanique for a glass of sugar water (such was the refreshment served there) and a little conversation.

The society of bluestockings was not congenial to the Rabelaisian Danton, who at this time had irons in a hotter fire than that which burned on the fifth floor of the Hôtel Brittanique. After the riots on the Champs-de-Mars he retired from Paris for a few months, not having met Brissot's hospitable friend from Lyons. As for Mme. Roland, with her fatal inability to distinguish fundamental from superficial expressions of character, she mentally placed Danton, whom she had heard speak at the Jacobin Club, among such lawless rabble-rousers as Marat and the filthy-tongued Hébert, who, along with others of their kind, had emerged from the obscurity of the gutter and cast so dark a shadow over the bright promise of the Revolution.

The Girondins, though professing otherwise, had in reality no great love for the so-called "People." "Verminous insects rising from the slime," "coarse and filthy creatures," "imbeciles,"—such are the descriptive phrases that fill the correspondence and memoirs of the Girondins when speaking of the "People." So boisterous and rough-spoken a man as Danton could only fill Cato's refined wife with repugnance. She could not have supposed, as she daintily sipped the weak tea of Rousseau and nibbled on the leftover crumbs

185

of the classics, that he was, in fact, far better educated than either herself or Roland and, despite the crudeness of his manner, was a genuine intellectual. It is the fault of many self-centered people that they are often incapable of estimating others beyond the framework of their own limits or of recognizing the existence anywhere of talents that are not their own.

The new Assembly gathered in the autumn of that year, and shortly afterwards Roland, his work in Paris completed, returned to Lyons. A few months later, probably on the instigation of his restless wife, he decided to resign from his position in Lyons and go back to Paris. To do so, however, it was necessary to find some employment; the Rolands had little money. The salon, modest though it was, had eaten into their small savings.

When the Rolands finally returned to Paris they found that the wheel of fortune had brought many of their old friends there into positions of prominence. Pétion was now mayor of Paris and Mme. Pétion, puffed up as much as her husband by self-importance, found it difficult to remember where it had been that she and Pétion had met the Rolands some months earlier. No one now paid much attention to them. Discretion masked the bitter pangs of jealousy that Mme. Roland must have suffered on finding that the spoils of power had once again eluded her husband's fumbling grasp. For people of Mme. Roland's temperament it is bad enough to see anyone wearing the diadem of authority, but to see one's friends wearing it, and especially friends who have forgotten one, is insupportable.

Brissot, fortunately, remained loyal, and Brissot, leader of the "Left wing" in the new Assembly and a person of consequence in the Jacobin Club, was then a man of importance. An abortive petition for the dethronement of the King on the Champs-de-Mars had torn the Jacobin Club asunder. Half of its membership had resigned to form the Feuillants, a new club of a more conservative complexion. Certain Monarchists hopefully supposed that for want of membership the Jacobins now might wither away and vanish. Brissot and Robespierre were appointed to recruit new members. Because he was occupied with affairs at the Assembly, Brissot, most unwisely, delegated his share of this task to Robespierre, who filled the club with his admirers or those whom he knew would be loyal to him in "times of trouble," which, with such foresight, he always felt to be imminent. Brissot, nonetheless, was still a man of weight at the Jacobin Club, and his friends and followers, the Girondins, were at that moment the dominant influence there. He was thus able to secure Roland an appointment as head of the Jacobins' Correspondence Committee.

Roland's job, relative to the plums that had fallen into the hands of certain of his friends, was perhaps not the most important in France, but it had potentialities that were readily appreciated by his wife. Through its Correspondence Committee, through its directives and letters written in Paris, the Jacobin Club was able to exercise an authority and influence that spread like a net over most of France. By applying pressure on its provincial affiliates, the Jacobins were able to control the election of deputies sent up to Paris, and by the dispersion of well-aimed propaganda the Jacobins were able to direct the provinces towards a civic fervor that was in line with the interests of the head office.

Soon after Roland's appointment, the brochures and directives sent out by the Jacobin Club to its provincial affiliates began to reflect the private enthusiasms of Mme. Roland—a "federated" army to be sent to Paris, a good cleansing war with Austria ("In times of Revolution one needs to burn away the fever . . .") and other such projects advocated by associates of herself and Brissot. "I put into Roland's writings," she declared, "that mixture of strength and sweetness, of authority and reason which only belongs to a sensitive woman endowed with a clear head."

All this was observed by the ever-watchful Robespierre. The drums of war had begun to beat loud and clear, and Robespierre, who had already quarreled openly with Brissot over the war issue, watched the activities of Brissot's "agents," the Roland couple, with suspicion and rancor. Suspicion and rancor blazed into fear and hate when in March the King (who had only five more months to reign) decided to appoint a Girondin or "Leftist" ministry. The King (like many people who are only casually informed about this period of French history) did not realize that the Left was an ever-changing entity and was already divided within itself into factions as bitterly hostile one towards the other as ever the Royalists had been towards the Republicans. The King's appointment of a "Girondin Ministry" served temporarily to unite the squabbling fragments of the Extreme Left: Danton, disappointed in his hopes of being awarded the Ministry of the Interior; Robespierre, devoured by jealousy of Brissot; and Marat, who hated them all.

The appointment of Roland to the Interior was a surprise to everyone, including the Rolands. The insignificant head of the Correspondence Committee was chosen for the position because a rule that disqualified deputies from holding Cabinet posts had left so few other candidates. Danton, who was not a deputy either, was probably passed over because of the position he had taken against the war program.

Mme. Roland has left no description of that March morning in 1792 when she quit her modest lodgings in the Hôtel Brittanique (where she and Roland had got themselves a "rate" by accepting fifth-floor rooms inside the court) for the magnificent *hôtel particulier* of Calonne, the Ministry of the Interior, one of the most beautiful buildings in Paris. This immense establishment had several chapels, winter and summer apartments and stabling for sixty horses. One can only surmise the sensations of the former Manon Phlipon as her carriage lumbered through the portals of that palace and, escorted by liveried footmen—for "officials" such things still existed in Paris—she entered her new home. Scarcely was she installed there (this she does discuss with posterity) when she began to draw up a program of behavior for herself. Tactfully she determined that the dignity of her official position should be maintained at all times. The footmen were immediately informed that observance of the old etiquette was to be continued and that they were to open both halves of the gilded doors that led to her salon only for persons of sufficient rank.

All women, and especially women who might come soliciting favors for their husbands, were banned from that precinct of the palace occupied by her. Mme. Roland had had some experience with that sort of distraction and she wisely decided at the beginning that she was not going to be embarrassed or compromised by the close presence of any women such as she herself had recently been. Tastefully, she realized that it would be foolish of her to affect the airs of a great lady of the *ancien régime*. Her private life was therefore carefully distinguished from her official existence. Her dress remained neat and simple. Frivolity of all kind was banned from those frescoed halls, where, too recklessly, laughter and wit had once run riot. Her manner was at all times grave, austere and proper.

Roland continued to wear the black, dish-shaped hat. His unbuckled shoes, his dun-colored garb, his thin lips set in a self-satisfied but unsmiling line, expressed his indifference to those fading and useless fripperies of the past—the VanLoo portraits in the salon, the portrait of Louis XIV being crowned by Victory set in a sculptured wainscoting that was one of the marvels of its age—that surrounded him. His practical, common-sense demeanor managed to transform the Hôtel de Calonne on the rue Neuve des Petits Champs into a philosopher's cabin by the banks of the Susquehanna.

Unimpressed by the Hôtel de Calonne and its flaking appurtenances of past grandeur, Roland was less stolid when he was finally ushered into the presence of Louis XVI. Apart from a few second-rate officials who had once been his superiors and the parvenu clerks and lawyers who, like himself, now comprised the government of France, Roland had never before met anyone of importance. He was therefore astonished to find that the King was an affable, unaffected and even intelligent human being (the King's "intelligence" especially impressed him, since Roland had the self-satisfied conviction, common to many of his associates, that, as a class, they alone were "intelligent"). Louis XVI, who appears to have exerted for Roland's benefit the charm that he might more profitably have used on someone like Danton, submitted patiently to the patronizing lectures given him by that garrulous bore. The unhappy monarch probably viewed these conferences with Roland as one more station on his Calvary.

Roland hurried home to his wife with many enthusiastic reports about the King's condescension and sympathetic manner. Mme. Roland, who had not been invited to the Cabinet meetings (she had unsuccessfully tried to have them held at her house), and who had not, therefore, been exposed to the King's celebrated charms, was filled with angry contempt for her husband's naïveté. She warned him that the King was playing a double game and that his friendly manner concealed ulterior motives—a surmise in which she was correct. From the *petits cabinets* of the Hôtel de Calonne she began dictating demands to the King that became more and more extravagant. Obediently, and as though they were his own, Roland would belligerently advance his wife's proposals to Louis. The King's initial affability rapidly diminished. He found his new ministers, and Roland, in particular, exasperating.

It was not only Roland whom his wife now dominated. In the sanctuary of her new salon at the Hôtel de Calonne she became a central figure, the unifying element in the Girondin party. Here, at evening receptions given twice a week at a table "served with taste but without profusion," the Romans of the new Assembly, men congenial in their views to herself, to Brissot and to one another, gathered and acquired identity. All-seeing and all-hearing, their tactful little hostess directed the train of their thoughts and clarified for them the trend of the policies that took shape at the Hôtel de Calonne. Thus, at last, she came into her own, the mistress of an important salon, the Egeria of a dominant political party, a force to be reckoned with among the several forces that at this moment in the Revolution were shaping the outline of a new France.

Unfortunate Mme. Roland! In the flush of excitement that followed her unexpected elevation in the world of affairs, she forgot the existence in others of those too human emotions that formed so significant a part of her own character: envy and spite. Those meals she speaks of, "served with taste but without profusion," seemed profuse indeed to the despicable Hébert, who still remained in his garret in the rue St. Antoine, and to the readers of his scandal-mongering newssheet. Marat, who loathed Roland, Brissot and all their associates, and who in a year was to hound them to their deaths, glared at the tasteful little salon with the hot angry eyes of a ferret. Robespierre, who was once condescendingly invited to partake of supper at the Hôtel de l'Interieur, indignantly refused—and broadcast his jealousy in more discreet and deadly doses than did the shrieking journalists Hébert and Marat.

The price of prominence in a rapidly changing social order such as that in France during the Revolution comes high indeed. Mme. Roland and her friends, who had so meanly calumniated others in order to establish themselves in power, were now obliged to taste a dose of their own poison—just as those who now attacked Mme. Roland would in a short time be given a still more bitter dose. "It is to be feared that the Revolution, like Saturn, will end by devouring its own children." This simple statement, spoken by the golden-tongued Vergniaud, surely stands out in history as the most memorable utterance of the Girondin party.

Mme. Roland's unfortunate influence upon her husband and upon the men of his party was a major factor in bringing about the dismissal of the Ministry. The rock on which it sank was that issue, always close to Mme. Roland's enthusiastic heart, of a "federated France," a France whose provincial units were to be more or less independent of the authority of Paris. Mme. Roland was convinced that the provinces should be represented in Paris by their own army, who would protect the provincial deputies from the mobs of Paris that were evoked from the gutter by such agitators as Marat. This program of a federated France (and of a federated army), which in the less volatile atmosphere of the earlier phase of the Revolution might indeed have prevented many ills, was in 1792 an ill-conceived theory.

The war, of which Mme. Roland and her friends had been the most spirited advocates, had changed everything. With revolt and dissension raging within its borders, France now faced invasion from abroad. Unity, central and firm, had become essential not merely to the salvation of "the Revolution"—however one might wish to interpret that concept—but to the existence of France herself. The dreaded word "dictator" began to be heard in the land. Unwittingly and with the best of motives, the Girondins—Mme. Roland foremost among them—had brought to pass a situation that was finally to destroy them. A federated France was the last form of government that was needed in the chaotic spring and summer of 1792.

Blindly, Mme. Roland furthered her theories, stubbornly insisting on the summoning to Paris of a federated army to protect the tottering Ministry from the menace of Marat and Hébert. The King, who felt that Paris was already sufficiently disturbed without introducing another army within its limits, refused to sanction the decree, which Roland belligerently presented to him. In a rage—women of her kind rarely learn that first lesson of statesmanship and of good manners: the control of one's temper—Mme. Roland penned an insulting letter to the King, which was dutifully signed by Roland. The letter was too much, even for the patient King. He dismissed the Girondin Ministry. It was one of the last official acts of his reign.

In a fury at this defiance of her wishes, Mme. Roland, through her friend Pétion at the Commune, incited her party to a short-lived alliance with the gutter element of Paris. On June 11 an invasion of the Tuileries was staged, during which the King and his family were subjected to indignities by a pike-carrying mob. The Girondins never hesitated to use for their own purposes the same methods of violence that they deplored in others. It is this fact which alienates them from the full sympathy of posterity.

"They were satisfied with the power which they had won," writes M. Gaxotte of the Girondins, "and they cherished the hopeful belief that they could emancipate themselves from the mob violence which carried them to office . . . but they bristled with rage at the thought that those auxiliaries of yesterday were the masters of today. The law became sacred in their eyes now that it was they who made it. They said, as Lafayette had said before them: 'The Revolution is now at an end. The Revolution stops at the point where we now stand.' "

After the invasion of the Tuileries, the army of *fédérés* that played so prominent a part in Mme. Roland's schemes began to pour into Paris. The Girondins were startled when, too late, they beheld the latest evil they had inadvertently released from Pandora's box. For the most conspicuous element among the army of the *fédérés* were the fearsome *Marseillais*. This "scum of crime vomited out of the prisons of Genoa and Sicily" had no intention of defending the dainty salon of Cato's wife, where meals were "served with taste but without profusion" and the theories of Rousseau were earnestly discussed after an inadequate repast. The hearty amusements, traditional in history, of all occupying armies—rape, pillage and bloodshed—were what interested these lusty fellows from the south. During July they marched into Paris, a city scarcely able to feed itself even before their arrival, in terrifying numbers. Marat and his colleagues were already planning the massacres of the approaching September, to which the *Marseillais* were to lend their helpful arm. Prominent among the victims scheduled by Marat for death were Brissot and the two Rolands.

The war in which the Girondins had embroiled France during their brief ministry had begun to go very badly indeed for the French. Hurling dire threats, the German allies were assembling at the frontier during the month of July and making appointments to meet one another in the gardens of the Palais Royal in a few months' time. Paris, rent by political dissension, divided into frightened, squabbling fragments, was in no condition to defend itself. The single point of possible unity, the King, was an object of such suspicion that his immediate dethronement was demanded.

The Assembly, crippled by scruples that were never to trouble its successor the Convention, refused to dethrone the King, because to do so would be contrary to the Constitution it had been elected to uphold. Chaos and fear, in which the seeds of dictatorship best germinate, characterized the Paris of July 1792. Screaming in his newspaper, Marat demanded bloodshed. Danton, from the Cordeliers' Club, demanded dethronement. Brissot and Mme. Roland in well-bred voices that were scarcely audible above the din, recommended suspension of the King and the convoking of another Assembly. On August 3, in the midst of this cacophony, the threatening contents of the Brunswick Manifesto became known. Seven days later Danton overthrew the monarchy. On August 10, the great storm broke over Paris, a whirlwind of violence that tore through the Tuileries and swept the King from his throne—and the Assembly out of existence.

On the morning of August 11 Mme. Roland, like the rest of Paris, awoke to view with astonished eyes the new France that had been born during the storm. The hour of the Republic had come at last. Roland was given back his ministry, a beginning to the new order of things that must have seemed auspicious to his wife. But if Mme. Roland supposed that the removal of that irritating authority, the King, was to open paths of unrestricted ambition to Cato and herself, she was soon to find that she was sorely mistaken. For the presiding genius of the new Cabinet, now called the Executive Council, was the powerful and resolute hero of the hour, the man who had organized the uprising of August 10, Georges-Jacques Danton. Mme. Roland, who at first had mistrusted him, soon found reasons to loathe him.

25

DANTON, in overthrowing the monarchy, had, with characteristic clarity of vision, gone directly to the root of the matter and struck his initial blow at the Paris Commune. By seizing control of the city government he seized command of the Paris militia, a critical factor in all such upheavals, and of the ammunition that was stored under the city's jurisdiction. For some weeks the Sections had been presenting themselves before the Assembly, demanding the dethronement of the King and threatening to take matters into their own rude hands if the Assembly did not act.

Terrified (many deputies hid like frightened hares during the ensuing disturbance), the Assembly nonetheless refused to submit to the arrogant demands of a few demagogues, who by threatening to call forth a mob hoped to violate the Constitution and to appoint themselves as dictators to the government. The Commune, as it was constitutionally obliged to do, had every intention of protecting the monarch. The Paris militia, in command of a man named Mandat, put the Tuileries under arms and organized the palace to resist attack. It is believed by many historians that the Tuileries might well have withstood the assault of August 10 if the militia had remained loyal. But, as at every moment of crisis during the Revolution, the ambiguous nature of loyalty cast a fog over men's minds that was favorable to the insurrectionists. To whom should the militia have remained loyal? In such situations as pertained to civil riot in Paris, it took its orders from the Paris Commune.

But the Commune, as it had been legally elected and constituted, existed no more. For on the night of August 9, just before the outbreak that was scheduled for dawn on the following day, the leaders of the Sections of Paris, who in turn were supported by their local mobs, entered the Hôtel de Ville and at pistol point demanded the resignation of the key officials of the Commune. Very sensibly, only those men who might obstruct Danton's plans were ordered to retire. The body of the Commune, headed by Pétion, the mayor of Paris, a weak but ambitious man who had long since sold himself to Danton, remained intact. A certain superficial appearance of legality was thus retained. So far as the head of the militia, Mandat, was concerned, Danton was obliged to have recourse to ruder methods. Nothing can soften the surface appearance of murder.

Mandat was at the Tuileries making last-minute preparations for the defense of that citadel of the monarchy when, unknown to him or to anyone else at the palace, Danton's Insurrectionary Commune was established. Mandat was surprised but not suspicious when he received orders to report at once to the Hôtel de Ville. Here he was met by Danton's grinning henchmen, who forthwith demanded his resignation. Mandat's answer was that he would take no orders from this "self-appointed Commune" and that he owed an account of his behavior only to "that Commune which is composed of honest men." The Section leaders thereupon denounced him as a traitor, dismissed him from his command (which was handed over to Santerre of the Faubourg St. Antoine) and ordered him to be placed under arrest. As he turned to descend the steps of the Hôtel de Ville he was shot through the back of the head. His body was dragged away and thrown into the river.

Shorn of its defenses, the Tuileries could no longer hope to resist the uprising that was scheduled for the morrow. The "popular movement" that might have been contained as a civil riot became, in fact, a revolution within the Revolution. The old Commune had courage enough to protest this brutal violation of its legal power. The answer of the Insurrectionary Commune deserves inscription in the front page of every history of the French Revolution. "When the People puts itself into a state of insurrection," came the blunt reply, "it withdraws all powers [from others] and takes them to itself." The words may well have been Danton's. "Thus," comments the historian Madelin, "may a handful of agitators give the law to a nation numbering thirty millions of men."

Scuffling through the new-fallen leaves of that hot August morning, the King and his family abandoned the doomed palace and sought refuge in the nearby meeting place of the Assembly. Not even here, however, were they safe from the authority of the Commune, who demanded jurisdiction over them. Instead of sending them to the Palace of the Luxembourg, as the Assembly had decreed, they were imprisoned in the Temple Tower, as the Commune wished it.

The rôle of the Girondins, those sticklers over the fine points of constitutional law, remains ambiguous in the *coup d'état* of August 10. Some writers have claimed that certain members of the Girondin party actively conspired with Danton to establish this new order of things that appeared to them to be to their advantage. Some have even claimed that Mme. Roland cherished the illusion that she, not Danton, had been the animating force behind the overthrow of the throne. In any case, no outcry of indignation was heard from their collective throat. Roland and certain of his colleagues were given back their portfolios. None of them seems at this point to have been troubled by any awareness that command of the Revolution had now been seized by the city of Paris. Preparations for the September Massacres, a holocaust that was only three weeks away, were already secretly afoot.

Early in the morning of August 11, Danton, asleep in his apartment in the Cour du Commerce, was awakened by his friends Camille Desmoulins and Fabre d'Églantine. "You are a minister!" they cried.

Exhausted by his exertions of the day before and still half asleep, he gazed at them in disbelief. "Are you quite certain that I have been appointed a minister?" he asked.

"Yes! Yes!" answered his friends. They informed him too that as Minister of Justice he had been appointed to lead the whole Executive Council. He had been elected first and by the most votes. He was the hero of the hour.

"You must make me Secretary of the Seals," declared Fabre.

"And I," added Camille, "must be your private secretary."

It was one of Danton's humanly admirable but politically inexpedient traits that in prosperity he always remained faithful to his friends. The awkward but necessary business, which every newly elected politician must face, of tactfully disembarrassing himself of friends who have not prospered never disturbed Danton. He handed out appointments and largesse to this needy horde with reckless generosity. It was a trait in him that contrasts significantly with Robespierre's firm management of the same problem. Robespierre killed most of his friends and former associates.

Flanked by Camille Desmoulins and Fabre d'Églantine, Danton rose from his bed and went to the Assembly to take over his new office. Fabre, as he had demanded, was then entrusted—fatal error—with the State Seals, and Camille was appointed "secretary" to the new Minister of Justice.

These two men, minor but interesting figures on the teeming canvas of the Revolution, were for varied reasons to have a deplorable influence on Danton and his reputation in history. Fabre d'Églantine had been born more plainly under the name of Philippe Fabre. In his youth he had won the prize, a crown of *églantine,* from one of those poetic societies that, in Macaulay's phrase, "turned men who might have been thriving attorneys or useful apothecaries into small wits and bad poets." He believed himself, as did so many characters in the Revolution, to be a man of letters. The number of not very good writers who played some rôle, often ignominious, in the Revolution is remarkable. Fabre d'Églantine, Marat, the Rolands, St. Just, Brissot, Desmoulins were but a few of the many of that time with literary pretensions. Each looked resentfully on the talents of the others. The personal animosities that raged between them more often had their source in a jealousy of one another's literary output than in any differences of political belief. Eloquence in the tribune was but one of the strings with which Robespierre fancied his lyre to be strung. After its delivery his public utterance was generally published and distributed through the provinces by the affiliates of the Jacobin Society.

Fabre was the author of a tragedy in blank verse called *Philinte,* whose opening lines, *"Le théâtre, n'est-il qu'un passe-temps frivole?"* depressingly augur the hours that are to follow. He was a man of very dubious character, of shallow insight and of limited talent; one of those persons, too, who excuse their dishonesty with the observation "Others do it, why shouldn't I?" Unfortunately, in making such excuses to their conscience they forget that embezzlement is not merely a moral wrong but a civil crime. After his appointment by Danton, Fabre began to traffic in army stores and to thrust his hands into the riches of the East India Company. He got caught and in the end he fatally compromised his whole group. There are many who believe that the large sums for which Danton was unable to account and for which he has been held responsible may have found their way to Fabre's secret trove. If *Philinte* earned him no money, Fabre's unmerited position as secretary to the Custodian of the Seals amply indemnified him. He was more energetic than most in his adulation of "Liberty" and the first to denounce the wealth of others. He was not a man to be trusted.

Camille Desmoulins, Danton's other colleague, was a man of different character. In speaking of him his contemporaries always used his first name. Posterity takes the same liberty. He came of respectable parents in Guise and he was what might be called a "father's boy." He was thirty-two years old at the time of his association with Danton, but the letters that he wrote home to his father, boastfully reporting every detail of his rise in the world, suggest more a boy of sixteen than a man. These embarrassing letters cast a curious light on the Revolution in its human expression. "The cause of Liberty has triumphed!" crowed Camille to his father on the day that followed Danton's *coup* of August 10. "And here I am lodged in the palace of Maupeou and Lamoignon! So, in spite of all your predictions that I should never amount to anything, here I now am at the top of the ladder! How the people of Guise, so full of envy, will burst with jealousy today!"

Camille's father, who disliked his son's political opinions, was never quite so astonished as his excitable son would have liked him to be at the unexpected eminence to which the boy had risen. Camille's craving to impress his father expressed itself away from home in a hero worship of older men. It was always necessary for him to be attached to some older man. First there had been Mirabeau, then Robespierre—an unsatisfactory liaison—and finally Danton.

"Mirabeau and I have become close friends," he wrote to his father at the beginning of the Revolution. "Anyway he calls me his very good friend. He is always gripping me by the hand or giving me a friendly punch or two with his big fist. . . ." Those friendly man-to-boy punches, those hand grips accompanied by a few rough embraces about the shoulder, gratified a deep need in this eternal adolescent. Until the middle of the Revolution poor Camille was dependent on his father's reluctant charity. The breathless boastings about Mirabeau are interspersed with demands for money: "I have a big reputation here in Paris. I am consulted on important matters. I am asked out everywhere to dine. All I lack is a lodging. I implore you to help me. Send me six louis or a bed."

He had led something of a Bohemian life in Paris before the Revolution. Ostensibly employed as a barrister, he drifted from job to job with no fixed course before him. When his allowance from home was cut off, he would pick up money by copying legal documents. When he grew weary of dirty lodgings and back rooms in Paris he would return to his family in Guise for a few months' rest and some good home cooking. No one there took him or his "new ideas" very seriously. His great day came on July 14, 1789, when in the gardens of the Palais Royal he leapt onto a table and exhorted the crowd gathered there to storm the Bastille.

"The people were struck by my enthusiasm and by my eager bearing. They surrounded me and urged me to mount a table. In a moment I had six thousand people around me." The story is curious because Camille was afflicted with a bad stammer and in ordinary circumstances found it an ordeal to speak in public. It was his stammer, indeed, that probably directed the talents of the public speaker *manqué* towards journalism. His natural gift for that calling was considerable. One can read Camille's editorials today with ease and even, at times, with pleasure. He wrote without wit but with clarity and a skillful use of invective that contrasts pleasantly with the hatchet blows of Hébert's journal or the hysterical pages of *L'Ami du Peuple*.

Success acted on Camille like an intoxicant. His pen flew out of control. The irresponsible boy grew into a spoiled adolescent, delighted with his unexpected celebrity. He was without conscience as an artist. Sensation and success were more important to him than the responsible use of his talents. Mischievous boys do not age well. Camille's impish laughter became shrill invective; light mockery turned into cold and vulgar cruelty. The excitements of the age finally destroyed him, as they destroyed so many others. Goaded by Robespierre, he used his reckless pen to provide the Revolutionary Tribunal with the "evidence" it needed, a tissue of slander and invective, to send the Girondins to the guillotine. His rivalry with Brissot had been "literary." He did not realize until it was too late that he was no longer playing games in the realm of literature. Brissot and many other men with whom he had been friends were sentenced to death before his eyes and Camille fled the courtroom blinded by tears of remorse. His pen was soon after that to bring the knife down on his own and Danton's head.

But the final years of his short life illuminated the Revolution by a warmer glow of light than his writings, for he met and married the charming Lucile Duplessis. In the darkness of the Terror the happiness of these married lovers is radiant still. "I have waited so long for happiness," he wrote his father on the day when his proposal of marriage to her was accepted, "but it has come to me at last, and today I am as happy as any man can ever be on this earth. Lucile, about whom I have written so often and whom I have loved for eight years, has promised to marry me and her parents have at last consented! A moment ago her mother came, crying with joy to tell me the good news. . . . She led me into her daughter's room and I threw myself on my knees before Lucile. I heard her laugh and I raised my eyes in surprise. But, like mine, her eyes were filled with tears of happiness and she was crying at the same time as she laughed. Never have I seen anything so beautiful. . . ."

They set up household in the Cordeliers' District, not far from the apartment in the Cour du Commerce where their friends Danton and Gabrielle lived. A son named Horace arrived to fill Camille's cup to overflowing ("I have a son!" he wrote home. "My only wish is that one day he will love me as much as I love my father.") On Sundays this contented family of bourgeois would go to nearby Bourg-la-Reine, where Lucile's parents maintained a small *rustique*. Camille's father-in-law, like Danton's, was a "man of means" and Lucile brought Camille, along with happiness, a fat dowry, which the venomous Hébert could not forget. Lucile sweetened Camille's bilious temper and she might even have quieted his impetuous pen had he not set out that August morning, at Danton's side, for the offices of the Ministry of Justice.

Tragedy for all of them was about to begin.

26

WHEN SHE LEARNED that Danton had been appointed Minister of Justice, Mme. Roland was distressed. She had heard the man speak at the Jacobin Club; she knew him too by his reputation. He seemed to her to be "ferocious in face and probably in heart." The brutality of his countenance, the violence of his gestures and the coarseness of his oaths seemed to her to be incompatible with the refined austerity of the Republic of which she dreamed. There was an insolence about his manner and a daring that spoke to her of self-seeking and self-indulgence. "I could not apply the idea of a good man to that face," she confessed in her memoirs. Far-sighted friends warned her that it would be better to have Danton on her side than to have to fight against him. She did not listen.

All the same she resolved in her own mind not to pass final judgment on him until she had had a chance to "examine his personality" more closely. The self-important complacency of this can only astonish the reader of Mme. Roland's confessions. She makes it difficult to remember that officially, at least, she was only the wife of a none-too-important figure in the new Ministry. But like so many other figures of the time, Mme. Roland had the impression that the Revolution was her personal property and that where it differed from her it went awry. "At heart," states the historian Aulard, "she believed that nothing good could come to the Revolution save from her."

It is a tribute to Danton that in the chaotic weeks between the insurrection of August 10 and the massacres that began on September 2 he was able to find time to go to the Ministry of the Interior and try to ingratiate himself with the sensitive wife of Roland, whom he knew to be hostile to him. He did so because at this juncture in the Revolution he knew, as no other man did, the necessity for national unity. The personal animosities, the quarrels and dissensions that divided the country into so many small and quarrelsome fragments, were in his eyes a grave menace to a France that was at war and on the verge of invasion.

From the moment of Danton's appointment as leader of the Executive Council, his foremost purpose became to unite Frenchmen. To help achieve this goal he began to go at the lunch hour to the Ministry of the Interior where he would ask the Minister's wife for a bowl of soup. Mme. Roland exercised sway over the opinions of an admiring coterie of the younger Girondins, Brissot, Barbaroux, Buzot, Pétion and others, all of whom were men of importance at this moment in the Revolution. Danton saw her good will as a stone in the foundation of national unity.

The first few weeks of his effort seemed to bear fruit. Without actually approving of the man, Mme. Roland with well-guarded respect began archly to refer to him as "our burly patriot," as "Cyclops," and even on one occasion as "the sturdy Danton." Perhaps he reminded her of the butcher who many years before had courted the priggish little Manon Phlipon. Repelled but fascinated, she was unable to resist, as perhaps she would have liked to do, the advances of the powerful and interesting man who was her latest suitor. She may have been more of a woman than she wished to believe, for there is something about the intensity of her many feelings towards Danton that suggests a smouldering sexuality. Her final loathing of him, indeed, seems to have been informed by passions not unlike those of lust.

A series of minor irritants, all magnified to a size disproportionate to their importance by these two passionate individuals, soon brought about the final and deplorable rupture. Beneath everything lay Manon's jealousy of Danton as leader of the Executive Council. She thought that Roland ought to occupy that position and from the first she had been unable to swallow her disappointment.

Not only had Danton been elected to the position, but psychologically he seized it. The other ministers on the Council were men much like Roland, red-tape theorists whose practical contributions to the problems of the hour consisted in perfecting office routine. Danton rose above them like a giant. Beneath him he saw the forest, not the trees. He strode with sublime and arrogant indifference across the little fences each had put up about the prerogatives of his office. He was not interested in memoranda. Neither, for that matter, was he very much interested in the minutiae of constitutional law. But he recognized the danger in which France then stood, and with a resolution and vigor that has placed him among the great leaders of history, he lifted the sagging spirits of his countrymen to his own height. It was his finest hour. The boundaries of party affiliation and even of private interest seemed for a moment to collapse, and at the sound of his stentorian voice all men became Frenchmen.

"We must dare, and dare again, and dare forever, and France will thus be saved!" The words ring still with the audacity of the speaker.

They did not ring with quite so thrilling a timbre in the ears of the ruffled Rolands. Danton's highhanded indifference to ministerial prerogatives soon caused Roland's thin lips to quiver with indignation. Mme. Roland smouldered with rage at the increasing boldness of the man who hustled people about, rushed his business through and arrogated to himself a larger authority than constitutionally had been granted him. It infuriated her, for instance, that the meetings of the Executive Council were always held at the Ministry of Justice, "Danton's house." She was a woman who set great store by meetings and the place where meetings were held. The same concern had manifested itself during Roland's brief ministry under the King, when Mme. Roland had tried to have certain of the conferences held under her roof at the Ministry of the Interior. Through Roland she now advanced the proposal that all meetings of the Executive Council take place at the Tuileries. That would diminish Danton's importance in the public eye. Incited by his wife, Roland also proposed that each minister in turn act as titulary president, and preside over these meetings for a week. The niceties of parliamentary procedure were always a matter of great concern to the Rolands. Occupied with the immensity of his task, Danton paid little attention to these initial attacks by the gnats.

Danton and Madame Roland finally came into direct collision over the business of the so-called Bureau de l'Esprit Publique, the government's office for the dissemination of "educational material," or, put in today's language, "propaganda." The education of the public was especially close to Mme. Roland's heart. With her literary propensities and her vigorous political convictions, the management of this department of her husband's office was a task that she anticipated with pleasure. The Assembly had voted the sum of 100,000 livres to be spent on the publication and distribution of "useful pamphlets." Mme. Roland's program for the expenditure of that sum was already prepared when Danton, on one of his visits to the Ministry of the Interior, asked her whether her husband had any particular scheme in mind for publishing this literature and if he knew of any good writers and editors who were available.

The question alone must have piqued the former correspondent from Lyons, the author of *Letters from a Roman Lady,* who not only knew a great many writers, but who certainly counted herself among their number. Waspishly she informed Danton that she had had a great deal of personal experience with this sort of thing and indeed had already drawn up a scheme for the management of the Bureau de l'Esprit Publique. This she outlined to Danton. She then told him that she was planning to hold a few informal meetings in her salon at the Hôtel de l'Interieur, where these matters would be discussed by the writers and editors who were to be employed. Danton suggested that Camille Desmoulins might be a suitable candidate for the administration of her plan. Mme. Roland, who had no love for the sarcastic Camille, replied stiffly that Roland would be glad to accord him an interview should Camille be interested in the position.

Camille was indeed interested, but he never came for an interview. Danton's ministry simply seized the funds that had been allocated for the program and, following Mme. Roland's outline, set up its own journal. The effect on Mme. Roland, who believed— and properly so—that the Bureau de l'Esprit Publique fell under her husband's jurisdiction, may be imagined. Camille was probably more at fault than Danton in the tactless handling of this negotiation. Neither he nor Fabre d'Églantine gave much thought to the easily wounded sensibilities of the bluestocking of the Hôtel de l'Interieur.

It was decided by the Executive Council that commissioners should be sent into the departments to explain to the Provinces the events of August 10 and the approaching elections. This matter, too, fell under the jurisdiction of the Ministry of the Interior. But Roland was one of those men who must have time "to think things out," and he asked for a day's time to submit his list of candidates.

To this request Danton highhandedly replied, "Oh, well. Don't bother. We're in a hurry. I'll see to it. There are plenty of excellent patriots in the Commune." The next day he returned with a list of thirty commissioners for Roland to sign. This contretemps was doubly disagreeable because Mme. Roland feared and hated the new Commune, from whose numbers Danton had selected his candidates.

One day during that critical August, Fabre d'Églantine made a chance remark to her that confirmed her growing suspicions about Danton. Prussian troops had just crossed the French frontiers and were making an unobstructed march towards the capital. Never had the situation been more grave. The Executive Council was meeting twice a day, and between meetings Danton, with inexhaustible vitality, rushed about Paris exhorting the people and organizing a defense. Fabre and Mme. Roland fell into a discussion of the serious turn that events had taken. It is curious that nowhere in her *Memoirs* or in her other writings does Mme. Roland ever convey the impression that she was really aware of the seriousness of that moment for France; her attention seems to have been so occupied by affairs within the Assembly that she had little thought left for the dangerous situation on the frontier. Perhaps she did not care to dwell on a crisis for which she and her party were largely responsible. It was she, not Danton, who had advocated the war that was now taking such an unforeseen and unfortunate turn. In the course of conversation Fabre suddenly made a remark that chilled her blood.

"All this talking is very well," he declared, "but the head of the Executive Council ought to be given dictatorial powers. That's the only way we will be able to get the quick decisions that will save France."

A dictator! Mme. Roland reeled back, appalled. And nothing from that moment on could convince her that Danton's secret scheme was other than a seizure of the supreme power. The rankling jealousy of Danton's exceptional executive abilities that ate at her heart was now converted into patriotic indignation. The bold manner with which he dismissed the prerogatives of his associates, the arrogant way in which he directed other people's business—these things were all now explained. He aspired to the dictatorship! The rough geniality, offensive anyway to her ladylike sensibilities, now revolted her. The heartiness of his speech, his blustering, excessive gestures, the too confident swagger, became in her eyes parts of a mask that concealed the face of a scheming hypocrite. She had always flattered herself on the accuracy of her insight. Instinct, prompted by a jealousy to which she would never have admitted, told her these things about Danton. She stuck by her instincts as obstinately as did Robespierre by his principles. The stubbornness of that stand, as events were soon to demonstrate to the readers of history (though never to herself), brought death to Mme. Roland and Danton and destruction of the one barrier that might have stood between France and the dictatorship of Robespierre.

The September Massacres began a few days after Mme. Roland's unfortunate flash of insight. Like Charlotte Corday at Caen, like all civilized people in France, she was prostrate with grief and horror. "All Paris let this happen," she cried out. "All Paris is accursed in my eyes, and I no longer hope that Liberty may be established among cowards, cold spectators to crimes that the courage of fifty men might have prevented." Mme. Roland had come to the parting of the ways. The fire with which she and her friends had irresponsibly played had now became a conflagration raging out of control.

It is a curious fact that from this moment the conceited and spiteful little bourgeoise begins to grow attractive, and indeed even admirable. She never had the courage to admit that she had been wrong, but she had the courage to face the terrible outcome of her mistakes. She viewed the catastrophes that were to follow the September Massacres with the unflinching stoicism of the Roman matron of her imagination. As it was to do to so many other participants in the Revolution, misfortune made her a bigger person than she otherwise might have been.

Sometime during the days that followed the massacres, she even fell in love. Whether she had the satisfaction of actually cuckolding Roland is still a mystery. Buzot, the man she loved, was young and attractive, an admirer of the writings of Rousseau and an ardent Girondin. Their letters were accidentally discovered over seventy years after their deaths, tucked away in a secondhand bookstore. They contrast significantly with the stifling exchanges between herself and Roland published in the *Correspondance amoureuse*. Though there is no phrase in the letters to suggest anything so down-to-earth as sexual intercourse, they are vibrant with feeling. Such passionate friendships in that day, when the novels of Rousseau still found admirers, were often more explosive in their effect than the lustier expressions of affection to which later-day novelists have incited their readers. Just before she died Mme. Roland began at last to live.

Blinded by her hatred of Danton, she inevitably saw him as the villian behind the September Massacres. "Danton," she pronounced, "is the secret chief behind the horde."

Were her accusations correct, Danton's name would have to be placed with Marat's among the pariahs of history. Though the organization of the massacres came directly from the Paris Commune, and though the Commune had been established by Danton's hand, the blame for the atrocities cannot be placed so squarely on Danton's shoulders as Mme. Roland would have liked her readers to believe. Scarcely had the gunsmoke of August 10 lifted, scarcely had the din of insurrection died down and the new order of things been established, when Marat crept out of the sewers where he had been hiding and made his way to the Hôtel de Ville. The uncontested ease with which the odious journalist installed himself at the council tables of the Commune strongly hints at some furtive collusion between himself and Danton. It may be that the services of "The People's Friend" had in some way been necessary to the furtherance of Danton's *coup* of August 10.

Such pacts with the Devil are usually more costly than the needy parties to them realize at the moment of signature. Danton's concern with the organization of French defense distracted his attention from the affairs of the Commune. Marat's grip on the Commune's crucial Committee of Surveillance grew tighter. Only Charlotte Corday's dagger was to release his hold on the machine that was soon to paralyze Paris with fear. Marat was the animating spirit of the Committee of Surveillance. Marat, not Danton, was the "secret chief of the horde," and, in the words of Charlotte Corday, "all France knew it."

Nonetheless, Danton's complicity in the massacres cannot be doubted. The instances, cited by his admirers, of men whom Danton saved from Marat's murderers are proof not only of his compassion, but of his guilt, too. If he had the foresight (and influence) to save a few friends from arrest, he then had foreknowledge of the fate from which he saved them. He sat at the meetings of the Committee of Surveillance and was present when Marat proposed the massacre of the whole Girondin party and half the Assembly. Danton's power in the Committee of Surveillance was enough to override that suggestion.

Carnage was never repugnant to Danton's fierce nature, but he was not a Marat, driven by a feverish thirst for vengeance that could only be slaked by the flow of human blood. He would have given orders for bloodshed if he thought it necessary or expedient. He was certainly well informed of the schemes of the Commune and he certainly gave his tacit consent to them. The stain of this fact lies dark on his memory.

But the cost of his complicity in the September Massacres was far dearer and more immediate for Danton than merely his good name in history. His rôle in the massacres was used by his enemies to separate him forever from that alliance with the party of respectable and moderate men that as early as the opening session of the new Convention he saw to be vital for the salvation of France, of the Revolution, and of himself.

27

THE SEPTEMBER MASSACRES had the effect on the elections to the new Convention that the agitators of the Commune intended them to have. Paris had shown its fangs, and the delegates from "that city stained with blood, lust and lies" (the phrase is Mme. Roland's) were all men of the Extreme Left. Marat was elected a deputy, as were Robespierre and Danton. Paris, indeed, sent no representative to the Convention whose name was not linked with the Commune. Behind these delegates stood the faceless and terrifying horde that Marat and the local Revolutionary Committees had evoked from the prisons and the gutters. The provinces remained more "conservative" in their choices. But the political disposition of these men, who arrived in a city still stunned by the horrors of a few weeks earlier, was soon determined by either fear or opportunism. The better portion of them, though secretly fearing the city of Paris and the forces of violence and anarchy emanating from it, remained neutral in the great battles that were approaching. They were, in the words of one of them, "upright men who remained motionless during evil deliberations." Another, when asked after the Terror what he had done during the Revolution, made the laconic reply, "I survived."

Noncommittally, they watched their neighbors of the Right and the Left tear one another to pieces. Of the 750 members of the Convention such men were by far the greater number. They voted where it was safest to vote, and they followed, with as little danger to themselves as possible, the flow of the greatest power. As the Extremists seized more and more prerogatives, as deputy after deputy vanished from the Convention and was dispatched by the guillotine, they naturally voted without protest for the very measures that further restricted their freedom and their safety. This amorphous party was known as the Plain. Many of its members were to survive the Revolution, finally betray the Convention to Napoleon, and to become barons, counts and marquises of the Empire.

Roland, Brissot, Vergniaud, and the bulk of the party which was now popularly called the Gironde, were all returned to the Convention by their provincial constituencies. The leadership of this group was in the hands of those twenty-two men whom in eight months' time Marat was to order expelled from the Convention. The historian Aulard believes that the sympathy of some 165 more men in the Convention was actively with them. Those who were not leaders of the party, such as the obscure Duperret, on whom Charlotte Corday paid a visit, were generally prudent in the declaration of their convictions. They did not, like Vergniaud or Louvet, race up to the Tribune to make public denunciations or declarations. Many of them thus escaped the death that awaited their more voluble associates. At the first session of the Convention (September 28) the Girondins, sitting on the Right, glared across the Plain at the Extremists on the Left who called themselves the Mountain. Taken in its general —and superficial—view, the battle between them was to be between the city of Paris—the men of the Commune—and the country of France. A narrower and closer examination reveals the real heart of the contention: the actual struggle was between ambitious and inimical personalities. The theories over which they struggled masked but poorly the bitter private resentments, the envy, fear and antipathy that divided not parties in general but personalities in particular. After the September Massacres the Girondin party hated and feared the city of Paris. But Mme. Roland hated it with an especial venom because, as she believed, it was dominated by her enemy Danton.

Her own private antipathy prevented her from seeing the equally bitter antipathies that divided the men of the Mountain. Robespierre, the most deadly adversary of them all, had crept from the shadows where he had hidden during the *coup* of August 10 and the September Massacres. Robespierre's envy and dislike of Danton smouldered visibly after August 10; it was matched in its warmth by Danton's contempt for Robespierre. The two *Montagnards* had in common only their contempt for their ragged colleague Marat, and both wished that their association with him, once expedient but now embarrassing, were dissolved. One of Danton's first peace offerings to the Gironde was, in fact, a public disavowal of "that man Marat and all his writings." Marat was too occupied with dreams of mass destruction and large-scale massacre to concern himself with such small bickerings. Among his colleagues, Marat was indeed singular in that his rancor was directed at the whole of organized society rather than at individuals. Had he lived long enough, he would certainly have found himself among Robespierre's victims.

What makes the quarrel between Mme. Roland and Danton so deplorable is that their dispute, whose outcome was public catastrophe, need, on a private level, never have taken place. They had much in common. Both were "French" to the marrow of their bones. Danton disliked bluestockings, it is true, but Mme. Roland, her political enthusiasms apart, was an excellent housekeeper. She darned her husband's socks, managed her household expenditures with thrift and could cook as well as any French bourgeoise. One may be certain that the bowl of soup that Danton begged of her during the early days of his attempts at *rapprochement* was both nourishing and tasty. Danton's dislike of bluestockings was as nothing beside his hatred of the hideous harpies, the shrill-voiced belligerent females who composed the Paris mob. His masculinity was revolted by them, and on several occasions he risked his popularity by suggesting to the Convention that they be ordered back to their husbands' firesides and to their looms. In this dislike he and Mme. Roland shared another view in common. Both were strong and vigorous personalities, both were persons of moral and physical courage, a quality that they admired in others.

Their similarities apart, their very differences would have made an alliance between them a matter of consequence in the history of the Revolution. Each would have rectified a deficiency in the other. To Danton's grasp of the difficulties of statecraft Mme. Roland might have added the warm and softening influence of her undeniable talents as a "hostess"; and to his impetuous violence she might have applied the tactful brake of caution. Danton's far-sighted but always realistic vision of men and affairs would have modified some of Mme. Roland's theories to their advantage. Together these two leaders might have presented a formidable front indeed to the ambitions of Robespierre. Apart, they were ruined. Danton knew this; Mme. Roland did not. Perhaps the failure of his hopes is to be traced to Mme. Roland's snobbishness which dominated her life.

The *petite bourgeoise* of Paris could not bear to see the *petit bourgeois* of Arcis walk off with the crown of power.

The opening meeting of the Convention was distinguished by a curious and suggestive speech by Danton. "Let us abjure all ideas of exaggeration," declared the man whose hands were still black from the gunpowder of August 10; "let us declare that all ownership, whether territorial, individual or industrial, be maintained by or·der." This proposal, the essence of conservative thought, fetched a round of applause. The Right looked at him with astonishment and interest. The Left, from whose benches he spoke, remained silent. Over and again in the following weeks Danton was to maintain this unexpected attitude. "France," he declared in a subsequent public session, "would be completely upset by a too hasty application of certain philosophical principles which may be dear to me personally, but for which the People, and particularly the People in the country districts, are not yet ripe."

Only Danton could have uttered a sentiment such as that before the Convention of 1792 and gotten away with it. The evils of religious persecution—the inevitable accompaniment to a government threatened by anarchy—were already abroad in the land. From the desecration of sacristies to the murder of priests, ministers or rabbis is but a short step. Danton's words on these matters are curious indeed. "When a man who has nothing sees a rich man gratifying his tastes, his consolation becomes the other world. He should be left in this error. The man of the soil regards the Man of Consolation as a saint, because to Him he owed a few happy moments in his youth, his early manhood and his old age." The grandson of peasants, though an unbeliever himself, knew more about human nature than the atheistic abbés and the *philosophes* of the vanished Parisian salons.

Two interests informed Danton's overtures to the moderate portion of the Convention. He was now a man of property himself. Many hectares of land had been added to the farm in Arcis. New orchards had been planted, the woodland increased. His land at Arcis drew him away from Paris with a pull that was irresistible. Fishing in the waters of the sleepy Aube, hunting in the autumn with his friend the local curé, drinking the *marc* of the country before a warming fire and talking endlessly with his friends the farmers and small officials of the town—the cares which weighed upon his shoulders in Paris slipped away. The pleasures of country life in France are many for persons of a certain temperament. They would not have been attractive to Marat or Robespierre. Danton's attachment to the land necessarily affected his outlook. Despite Marat's admonitions, Danton did not see his friend the curé as an enemy of the human race whose heart should be devoured. He did not, in accordance with Robespierre's theories, find his neighbors at Arcis imbued with any Rousseauesque virtue. Mme. Roland, city-bred and choked with philosophy though she was, at least knew how to hill leeks and tend a lettuce patch, and had come into touch with the reality of the soil. The farm at Arcis was the fruit of Danton's questionable labors in Paris. He had no intention of being dispossessed from it by such wild theorists as Marat and his radical cohorts, who had never milked a cow or pruned a vine in their lives. Taste and private interest thus conspired to make him "conservative." By September 1792 the Revolution, in his eyes, had come to its natural and desirable conclusion. This was the point at which he believed it should be stopped and the *status quo* maintained.

His private interests apart, however, Danton seems to have glimpsed more clearly than any other leader of the time the dangers that France then faced. The precarious union that the threat of foreign invasion had momentarily imposed on Paris dissolved with the victory of the French on the battlefield of Valmy. The Germans were repelled from French soil; the French could now go back to their own quarrels. Danton foresaw with accuracy the inevitable outcome of this dissension: anarchy. The men who sat on the Mountain hated one another with an intensity that only their common hatred of the Girondins now kept under restraint. To the left of Robespierre, to the left even of Marat, loomed the obscure and fearsome faces of the criminally insane, creatures such as Hébert, or Carrier who in a paroxysm of blood lust once raced about the room, foaming at the mouth and screaming, "Kill!! Kill!!" Danton's beloved precinct, the Cordeliers', was already invaded by creatures of this stripe. The dissolution of the Assembly had brought them out of their lairs. They waited now in the shadows for the end of the Gironde, the last barrier between themselves and anarchy. More and more boldly they began to appear in the hall of the Convention, accompanied by their followers, to make exorbitant demands. Buzot, Mme. Roland's "friend," left a telling description of these deputations: "It seemed as if their leaders had sought in all the slums of Paris and Europe for everything that was most hideous and polluted. With dreadful earthen faces black or copper-colored, with eyes half sunken in their sockets, they gave vent with fetid breath to the coarsest insults and the shrill screams of hungry animals. Their leaders were worthy of such a following: men whose frightful appearance gave evidence of crime and wretchedness, women whose shameless air exposed the foulest debauchery. When all these, with feet, hands, and voices, made their horrible din one would have supposed oneself to be in an assembly of demons."

As a man of property, as a politician of acumen, but as a patriot too and as a Frenchman, Danton looked on these auguries with alarm. He did not care at all for the society on the left in which he found himself isolated. His *coup d'état* of August 10 and the consequent elections had completely altered the political disposition of France. The Girondins, considered only a few months before to be dangerous radicals, had now become the leaders of the party of conservatism. A realist always, Danton was not one to be distracted by such words as "Left" or "Right." He attached himself to the party that best promised to serve his own interests. The label describing a party was in his mind of only incidental interest. Within their "party" the Girondins were almost as divided as the Mountain. The coterie of Mme. Roland was not on good terms with that of Vergniaud. Mme. Roland disliked Vergniaud's mistress Mme. Dodun. Vergniaud was (as was Danton) a friend of General Dumouriez, the hero of Valmy, whom Mme. Roland could not abide. Such trivia weighed heavily in the scales on which men were about to be measured and alliances apportioned.

Vergniaud was, with reservations, an admirer of Danton. He and his friends were favorably impressed by Danton's unexpected overtures to their party. "The hopes of thoughtful men," wrote one of them, "pointed to Danton as the person through whose intervention the genius which was to organize the new Republic might hold converse with the past which had given it birth." Condorcet patronizingly spoke of Danton as "a man who might easily become attached to good principles."

Mme. Roland's circle simmered with rage at the thought of any *rapprochement* with the sinister man of August 10 who now flagrantly flaunted his opportunism. They assembled their ammunition and prepared for battle. Had Mme. Roland been a weaker woman it is possible that the Girondin party might have broken apart on this rock and Vergniaud and his friends have taken another path arm in arm with Danton towards a different destiny from that which awaited them.

Four days after the opening of the Convention (and Danton's peace offering) the Roland party opened fire. A man named Lasource, one of Mme. Roland's favorites, rose in the Convention and made a scathing denunciation of the city of Paris, declaring that it should be reduced at once to its proper share of influence in the country, an eighty-third part of the whole. A Paris deputy, one Osselin, immediately protested, and the quarrel began—not, it is to be noticed, directly between Roland and Danton, but between surrogates of their points of view. The discussion was at its warmest when another obscure *Rolandiste* seized the Tribune and made the bold statement that "a certain faction" using the Commune of Paris as its instrument was endeavoring to set up a dictatorship. The words "a certain faction" were accompanied by many significant glances in the direction of Danton, who had thus far sat in silence through the agitated session. He knew precisely at whom this last thrust was leveled and whose hand aimed it. Quick-tempered and passionate in his responses though he usually was, he rose now and with admirable temperance made a conciliatory speech:

"The day that brings about a fraternal understanding between us all will be a great day for France," he declared mildly. He again publicly separated himself from the association with Marat that Mme. Roland's party imputed to him. He then went into the matter of "Federalism," the political theory that separated the Girondins from himself—though he must have known that wilder passions than those aroused by theories were at the root of Mme. Roland's differences with him. "As for myself," he continued, "I do not belong to Paris. I was born in a department to which my eyes will always turn back with pleasure. But none of us belongs exclusively to this or to that province. We now belong to all of France." Over and again in this speech he returned to the great need of the moment, that aim which possessed his whole attention: the unity of Frenchmen, the expedient shelving of personal and factional dispute. "The Austrians," he concluded, "will not hear of our new harmony without a shudder. And then, I swear to you, our enemies will be dead indeed."

Danton's answer to the *Rolandiste* charges was greeted by a great round of applause, only Mme. Roland's friends and Robespierre withholding their enthusiasm. Robespierre viewed the possibility of an understanding between Danton and the Gironde with an anxiety he was not able to dissimulate. Dissension between those stronger than himself, the skillful pitting of one rival against another with the consequent weakening of both, was the "trick" that was basic in Robespierre's accession to power. A *rapprochement* between the two dominant parties of the Convention, both of whom disliked him, was the last thing he wished to see. He cautiously fanned the flames of animosity and behind their backs incited each party to act against the other. Danton, in his attempts to come to an agreement with the Gironde, was thus working against more formidable and more sinister forces than Mme. Roland's open hatred of him. Time has long since covered most of Robespierre's traces. Such quarrels are more effectively stirred up by the tongue than by the pen, and so the record of them is not to be found in the archives of written history; but the extent of his subterranean activity cannot be doubted. Sometime during those days he began to keep a notebook. The details of Danton's overtures to the Girondins were assiduously jotted down. One of the charges against Danton at his trial was that he had tried to achieve an understanding with the "Federalists." Robespierre provided the evidence needed to support this accusation.

The sitting concluded with what the Rolands fancied to be a master stroke on their part. Roland arose and with much fanfare announced that he was going to resign his ministerial post. The purpose behind this maneuver was lost on no one. In the Convention, as in the Assembly, no deputy was legally allowed to hold a ministerial post. Both Danton and Roland were deputies. National emergency had temporarily justified their retention of both appointments. By submitting his own resignation Roland imagined that his public example would force Danton to retire too. And with Danton's resignation would come the moment for which Roland, the bookkeeper, thirsted—the submitting of the accounts of the Ministry of Justice. Both Roland and his wife suspected that Danton was a thief; they knew with certainty that he was slovenly and unmethodical. His books would contrast tellingly with Roland's neat columns, in which every penny was, precisely and without erasure, accounted for. Danton's books would publicly unmask him.

Unfortunately, Roland's example did not have its anticipated effect. The boss of the Executive Council showed himself to be in no hurry to resign either his post as Minister or his position as deputy. Outraged, Roland refused to attend further meetings of the Executive Council. A few days later, at another disturbed sitting of the Convention, Buzot proposed that Roland be persuaded to retain his Ministry but relinquish his position as deputy. This move regained Roland the portfolio that he had too hastily resigned, and stressed again the conflict that was Danton's as much as it was Roland's. All the followers of Mme. Roland and Buzot turned around to stare at Danton. And this time Danton lost some of his admirable patience, probably because he knew by now of the Rolands' plans respecting his accounts. He rose to answer Buzot with what is described as "a surly countenance."

"If you make this proposal to Roland," he declared, "then you had better make it to Mme. Roland too, because everybody knows that Roland does not work alone in his department."

At these insolent words Mme. Roland's friends and even some of those deputies who were not members of her circle, gasped in indignation. While returning to his seat, Danton was overheard grumbling that "the nation needs ministers who can make decisions without being led by their wives." His rude words confirmed the suspicion of many deputies that Danton was little better than Marat. The Girondin press expressed its outrage in an editorial, while Mme. Roland's coterie now resolved to speed the matter of the accounts to a public meeting.

Roland resumed his position at the Ministry of the Interior on October 1, and submitted his resignation as deputy. Any embarrassment that this hurried change of face might have caused him was well concealed behind a barrage of patriotic protest. In a letter to the *Moniteur* he explained that he was returning to an office that he did not want and that he was now well weary of, only as "a duty to the country which needs me" and because he had been persuaded to do so by a deputation of responsible citizens. Poor Roland's expressions of reluctance may not have been quite so false as they sounded. The hounds Marat and Hébert were now in full pursuit of the hare.

The attacks by the rabid *L'Ami du Peuple* on Roland and his wife were as scandalous as they were frightening. She was referred to as "a toothless hag," "a whore," and even "a pervert." A fragment of one sentence from Hébert's journal *Père Duchesne* amply suggests the general tone of these daily libels, which, horrified, Mme. Roland forced herself to read. "It was past midnight and the 'virtuous' Roland slut was relaxing in the arms of the nigger Lathenas from those pleasures which her bald old husband has to procure for her. . . ." Such was the literature that, at Caen, Charlotte Corday had begun to read with hot indignation.

Fortunately for Mme. Roland, neither Marat nor Hébert had any inkling of the real storms that had begun to gather over the domesticity of the Hôtel de Calonne, but poor Roland already suspected what his wife was soon to tell him. She and Buzot had begun to exchange sighs. His private life in a turmoil, his public life shadowed by menace, Roland lost his will to struggle against the forces that had destroyed the dreams he once had shared with Manon, and which now threatened to destroy his life. The events of September had aged him beyond his years. He returned to his office a sick old man whose shuffling steps betrayed his broken spirit.

His wife was not so yielding before adversity. Hatred is as powerful a force as love. Mme. Roland was ready and able to face the battle. Anger blurred the clarity of her vision. In her confused sight, Danton, Marat and Robespierre became one man, a single, three-headed beast that should be destroyed. In the hall of the Convention they were spoken of as a "triumvirate," an ill-chosen word of Mme. Roland's inspiration that only served to unify the opposition, whom the Girondins, had they been statesmen, would have attempted to divide. The great mistake of the Girondins was not fixing on one man of the "triumvirate" and concentrating their attack on him. Instead they dispersed their ammunition and their energy, flying at Danton in one session and at Robespierre in the next. They used shot rather than a single well-aimed bullet. The result was precisely what the waiting Robespierre wanted: inch by reluctant inch Danton was driven back to the Mountain.

The atmosphere in the Convention grew frenzied as wilder and wilder charges were hurled across the Plain from the Mountain to the Gironde and back again. At one of these, Marat, screaming epithets of the most extraordinary kind, pulled out a pistol and threatened to shoot himself. Robespierre, trembling alternately with fear and rage, hissed from his bench or shrilly screamed from the rostrum. Insults like "pig" and "imbecile" flew about the hall. In the galleries Marat's blood-curdling horde, those "men of copper faces and sunken eyes," joined in the melee, brandishing pikestaffs and bawling obscenities. Chaos within the Convention reflected too clearly the chaos of the country. Anarchy was at hand.

One ray of good news illuminated this darkness. The armies of the young Republic were at last triumphant abroad. The country was no longer in danger. Bearing the message that General Dumouriez would soon be in Brussels and that the old dream of the French monarchy—a French Rhine and French Alps—was shortly to be realized, Danton finally submitted his resignation from the Ministry of Justice. His timing was characteristically opportune. With a flourish he handed over his resignation. Wrapped in parchment and tied in ribbon, Belgium and the Rhine appeared to go with it. The leader of the Executive Council retired from his seat as Minister and assumed his seat as deputy in a blaze of carefully ignited glory. The light of it did not blind the Rolands, who waited impatiently to examine his accounts. Danton, who crossed all his bridges with a sure foot, submitted these almost immediately after his resignation. What the Rolands now saw exceeded their fondest hopes!

Each minister had been granted the sum of 100,000 livres "for expenses." This sum Danton had accounted for, though carelessly. Certain of the expenditures were peculiar in the extreme. To Santerre, the mob leader of the Faubourg St. Antoine, had been allocated the sum of 30,000 livres "for the making of pikestaffs," an enterprise that could in no way be construed as part of the business of the Minister of Justice. Prudence restrained any objections that may have been felt about that sinister and too suggestive disbursement.

But the 100,000 livres allocated to him as Minister of Justice was the least of the sums for which Danton was actually responsible. To the Executive Council as a whole had been granted the additional sum of 500,000 livres for "extraordinary expenditures"; and of this sum more than half had passed through Danton's hands and vanished without explanation. Three drafts of 100,000 livres each had been drawn by the Minister of Justice against this deposit. More than that, by wheedling and grabbing, he had taken for himself a good share of the other ministers' portions. His seizure of the funds allocated to Mme. Roland's Bûreau de l'Esprit Publique was typical. Of the use he had made of these enormous sums he offered no account at all. He simply stated that the nature of the expenditure was "a secret," and from this position, in the ensuing attacks on him by the Right, he refused to budge.

"There are certain items of expenditure that cannot be mentioned here," he declared. "There are certain agents the revelation of whose identity would at this moment be impolitic and unjust. There are certain revolutionary missions which demand a great sacrifice of money. . . ." The Convention listened in stony silence. The employment of spies and *agents provocateurs,* the disbursement of bribes and the purchase of treason, were functions of government with which the idealistic Girondins were not in sympathy. No one in October could remember the emergencies of September that Danton had met with daring and dispatch. "When the enemy took Verdun," he reminded them, "and dismay spread among the best and bravest of citizens, the Assembly told the Executive Council to spare nothing, and if necessary to fling money away in order to win back confidence and stimulate the whole of France! Well, that is what we did! We had to make extraordinary disbursements, and I freely admit that for most of them we have no proper receipts. Everything was done in haste, everything happened precipitately. You wished the ministers to act. Well, we did. Our success is the account that we present you."

The Rolands could not have cared for Danton's carefree use of "we" in this explanation. The upright Minister of the Interior hurried to dissociate himself from the corrupt hero of the Executive Council. With thin lips stretched in a smug unsmiling line, Roland now submitted the books of his particular ministry. Every column testified to the efficiency and the rectitude of the Quaker from Lyons. The Convention voted not to insist on the figures of the "extraordinary expenditures," but demanded proof of the fact that the Council as a whole had checked on them. Roland, who had been absent from many Council meetings, stubbornly refused to give any such proof. During this session the word "embezzler" was spoken aloud. Danton kept his anger under control, but the battle which was only to end with the expulsion of the Girondins from the Convention was on. All through that autumn and into the winter, the Girondin party returned to the matter of the accounts. Whenever Danton spoke from the rostrum, on no matter what subject, his speech would be interrupted by hecklers of the Right who would call for "the accounts." On October 26 a furious session centered about the accounts. On November 8 there was another. As late as April 1793, less than two months before the expulsion of the Girondins from the Convention, the men of the Right continued to raise the question of the accounts, goading the bull from anger to blind rage. Danton began contemptuously to speak of the Girondins as being "as trifling as the silly woman who inspires them." Regret that they would not accept him (and his regret must have been acute, for he saw clearly the abyss that was opening before his feet) changed into fury as step by reluctant step he was driven back to the Mountain.

During that October a small but significant happening divided Danton even further from the party of Mme. Roland. General Dumouriez, hero of Valmy, returned to Paris for a short and triumphant visit. This ambiguous personage, who in four months' time was to defect to the Austrians, was momentarily the jewel in the Girondin crown. His military victories became their political victories, and they, who had embroiled France in the war, found their program, thanks to Dumouriez, amply justified—indeed, for scrupulous souls, a little too well justified. For the Girondins, who had smugly renounced all intentions of "conquest," found France in possession of Belgium and its riches. The embarrassment inherent in this situation was concealed by the customary device of plebiscites and a "popular vote" for union with France.

Gratifying though Dumouriez's victories may have been to the Girondins, they filled such souls as Marat and Robespierre with consternation and envy. Marat, far more interested in his rage and in fanning up the fury of others than he was in any amelioration of the conditions against which he ranted, was nonplused by Dumouriez's victories. An excuse for another massacre such as that of September was taken from him. He refused adamantly to believe that there had been any victory at Valmy, and in his newspapers he said so, accusing the Girondins of having invented the story. It was during this visit of Dumouriez to Paris that he appeared in the salon of Talma and denounced the guests there as "a flock of whores and counter-revolutionaries." Robespierre feared Dumouriez because he suspected the General of planning to put his fame to good use and, armed with more glorious victories even than Valmy or the conquest of Belgium, march his army into Paris, overthrow the Convention and the Jacobin Club, and establish a reign of order superintended by himself—a curious prefiguring of the scheme that Bonaparte under more propitious circumstances was to realize. If there was to be a dictatorship in France, Robespierre was determined that it should be his. He watched General Dumouriez's activities in Paris with suspicious, malevolent eyes.

Among the many people who disliked the victorious General was Mme. Roland. She considered him arrogant and she disliked the vulgar women with whom he kept company. He also happened to be a friend of Danton, a fact that by itself would have been enough to prejudice her. The small dapper general and the bull-voiced leader of the Cordeliers had it in common that they were both voluptuaries. They may also, as Robespierre was later to contend, have shared certain political aspirations. In any case, they were friends, and remained so until Dumouriez's flight across the Austrian lines.

Soon after his arrival in Paris that October, Dumouriez paid a polite and official call on the Rolands. He brought gifts for Madame and compliments for the Minister. Like Danton, he was aware of Mme. Roland's influence on a segment of the Girondin party. He hoped to propitiate her or even to win her good opinion. The Girondin party was split in half over its opinion of Dumouriez. Many of them did not share Mme. Roland's hostile view of him. In a burst of good spirits, induced no doubt by the wine of which he was known to be too fond, Dumouriez at the end of his call suggested that the Rolands repair with him to the opera. Mme. Roland stiffly declined. She felt it would be "indiscreet" to be seen in public with so disreputable a figure as Dumouriez. She pleaded a headache and the General departed.

After he had gone she turned to Vergniaud, who had been present during her reception of Dumouriez, and suggested that he accompany her to the opera. Vergniaud accepted her invitation and they drove off, taking her daughter Eudora. (Mme. Roland was a mother who concerned herself about exposing her child to "cultivating influences"—the day when such amusements as the opera were considered a pleasure rather than a civic duty was fast drawing to its close.) Mme. Roland was astonished when she and her guest arrived at the opera house to be told that the box of the Ministry of the Interior was already occupied. She replied that this was impossible and insisted on being conducted to her usual seats. Protesting, the usher opened the box and revealed to Mme. Roland's outraged sight the figures of Danton, Dumouriez and "two women of bad appearance" lolling within. They did not see her, and she hurriedly ordered the door to be closed and departed, boiling with righteous anger.

The "two women of bad appearance" whom she noticed happened to be Danton's wife and mother, both as respectable as Mme. Roland, though not like herself well read in the works of Winckelmann and Tasso. These women whom she supposed to be off the street appear to have excited Mme. Roland's imagination. Danton is singular in that he stands forth among the figures of the Revolution as a man who is recognizably of the male sex. The hysterical humors of Marat, the feline malice of Robespierre, the undisguised physical cowardice of themselves and of their minions, contrast conspicuously with the virile and direct character of Danton. He was a man, and his masculinity was sexual in its effect on the women around him.

Rousseau had introduced a strong strain of puritanism into French life, which the Revolution, employing the word "Virtue," had begun vigorously to enforce. The burgess class, from which such people as Robespierre and Mme. Roland sprang, tends to disapprove of those appetites—for delicate foods, strong spirits or sexual congress—that might distract attention from man's major purpose in life: the acquisition and saving of money. The asperities of puritanism, indeed, became so ascendant during this period of the Revolution that the Reign of Terror acquired the character of some stern preceptress, a grim and disapproving *gouvernante* armed not with the birch rod of Rousseau's Mlle. Lambercier but with Robespierre's guillotine. It was the day of the cold theoretician and of the spinster, not of the male.

Danton, with his massive gestures, his bold, vigorous stride, his broken muzzle of a face, was inevitably the object of suspicious attention in such a society. Among women his prowess was whispered to be something exceptional. His very appearance excited speculation and inspired stories of various kinds. Here, perhaps, is to be

223

found an obscure but important source of Robespierre's antipathy for him. The spinster's dislike of rampant masculinity, the cat's dislike of the dog, made more hateful by the fact that in this instance the spinster happened herself to be a male, the fantasies of the virgin about a libertine, are all betrayed in Robespierre's ultimate and death-dealing denunciation of Danton before the Convention. Lurking somewhere about the dim frontier that separates conscious from unconscious motive, one senses in Robespierre's and Mme. Roland's antipathy to Danton a muffled sexuality of a kind better understood by Freud than Rousseau.

Because her fevered imagination could not comprehend such a possibility, it would not have crossed Mme. Roland's mind that Danton might take his mother and his wife rather than a prostitute to an evening at the opera. Danton's private life was not up to his interesting reputation among the prudes. He was in love with his wife and she with him. He had little need to seek diversion away from his hearthside. Danton himself has treated posterity to an unexpected glimpse of the contentment of his private life. One day during an argument with Robespierre he became exasperated by Robespierre's repeated references to Virtue. In a sudden gust of anger he turned to him and in a loud voice that could be heard by everyone in the room he said, "I'll tell you what this virtue you speak of is—it's what I do to my wife every night!" The expression on the face of the prim authoritarian of the Committee of Public Safety can only be imagined, but the words were carefully recorded in Robespierre's notebook. The impolitic phrase reveals in one bright flash a difference between Danton and Robespierre far more significant than any of the political theories that apparently divided them.

But the wife to whom Danton referred when he made this statement was no longer his beloved Gabrielle. Gabrielle died in February 1793, scarcely six months after her husband's appointment to the Ministry of Justice. And in the circumstances surrounding this fact may be found much that probably altered the course of the Revolution.

28

THE SEPTEMBER MASSACRES had cast a cold shadow over the once happy apartment in the Cour du Commerce. The Girondins, led by Mme. Roland, never let Danton forget that they held him responsible for that bloodshed. The awful accusation *Septembriseur!* was hurled at him in the Convention as frequently as the challenge "The accounts!" Appalled by the horrors with which her husband's name was associated, the once merry Gabrielle began to withdraw from the society of her friends and neighbors. In the person of this bewildered woman we catch a glimpse of the myriad obscure, decent people—by far the greater portion of the city—who were the helpless victims of a holocaust unleashed by ambitious and desperate men. Law-abiding and by nature incapable of comprehending those abstractions that concealed the private lusts and rancors over which men murdered one another, such gentle citizens as Gabrielle Danton found themselves lost in the convulsed city of Paris as though in a nightmare. Too often after September did the chicken bubble in its pot untasted. Dedicated to the huge task of forging a new France, Danton did not always come home. During October his efforts in the political arena to bring the Girondins to his side occupied much of his time and energy.

The jovial household of the leader of the Cordeliers was not as it used to be—though Camille Desmoulins and his Lucile still came to share a meal. In the market place, in all the streets of her quarter, Gabrielle felt the contemptuous glances of other women, respectable citizens like herself, who did not dare utter the epithet *Septembriseur* that openly followed her husband. Like many of her kind she still honored the spirit of France's abjured faith. The genteel atheism of the Girondins prefigured the sacrilege and blasphemy of

Hébert and his followers. The murder of priests that took place during the September Massacres in the gardens of the Carmes opened this chapter of the Revolution. Gabrielle has been described as "recoiling in horror" from the rumor of things that the doors of her apartment could not shut away. Danton himself—and Robespierre too—was soon to look with disgust at the orgies of blasphemy inspired by Hébert and held by Chaumette and Collot d'Herbois in the once sanctified precincts of France's ancient faith. But Gabrielle, by then, was dead.

She died in February 1793. In the three months preceding her death we are witness to a succession of upheavals that seem to have culminated in a breakdown of Danton's stamina. The war effort took him from Paris to Dumouriez's winter headquarters in Belgium. Though success appeared to have crowned the General's brow, beneath the surface all was far from well in Brussels. Marat and his minions in the Commune had insinuated their influence into the Ministry of War. The War Minister, a man named Pache, had assiduously curried favor with the Girondins in order to be given his appointment. Once he received the coveted post he turned his back on his benefactors and offered his services to Marat. He turned the Ministry into "an indecent tavern in which four hundred clerks and a number of women affecting a filthy appearance and a most impudent cynicism did nothing and rushed about. . . ." Marat hated the war and hated the victories that Dumouriez had been sending home to the Girondins, which entrenched them even further in the power Marat was trying to wrest from them.

Through the War Minister Pache, Marat engaged in a program of deliberate sabotage of the war effort. Communication between the Ministry of War and the General broke down completely. Dumouriez's messages went unanswered for weeks. When their tone grew first frantic and finally furious, they were taken to the Convention and exhibited as examples of the arrogance of military men and as evidence of Dumouriez's secret designs. Worse than this for Dumouriez, the source of military supplies was cut off. Shoes and warm clothing, urgently needed by the Republican armies wintering in Belgium, never reached their destination. Enormous quantities of arms and ammunition, without which France would be unable to maintain its position, were diverted at their source.

Desperate at first, then enraged, Dumouriez demanded an explanation. When it was discovered that Pache, instigated by Marat, had handed over to the Paris Commune arms intended for the French army in Belgium, there was an outcry of indignation from Dumouriez and his supporters. Called upon to explain the matter, Pache boastfully admitted his guilt, stating that "patriots at home" had need of arms too. The "patriots at home" happened to be Marat's mob, now well armed, who in a few months' time were to expel the Girondins from the Convention. Pache's bold statement, uttered publicly, was greeted by a great round of applause from Marat's horde in the galleries.

Nothing could better illustrate the direct collision of interest between the Paris Commune and the rest of France than this episode. And it illustrates, too, the confusion of purpose within the Commune. The Commune, which had begun as Danton's creation, was now at Marat's beck and call and was the instrument of its master's dreams of sedition and insurrection. Marat, perhaps because he was not French, had not the slightest interest in National Glory, nor in that wider vision of France's new identity that had begun to capture Danton's attention. He was willing and able to sacrifice the grandiose dreams of the Convention to his own somber view of what the Republic should be. The needs of the Commune seemed to him to be more important than the needs of France.

The Girondins were justified in their suspicion of the Commune. But it was their mistake that they confused the whole city of Paris with Marat's Commune. The two were distinctly different, as Danton might well have explained to them. Their fault was the fault of many theorists who cannot see beyond the label to the human identity that informs it. Though personal rancors and private jealousies rent their own party asunder, they were unable to recognize the small, often ignoble, but human passions that lie behind the façade of most institutions. And so, fatal error, they attacked the machine rather than the man who worked it. Danton, a patriot in the large sense of that word, viewed the seditious activities of Marat's Commune with a dislike as acute as their own; and ironically, that dislike deepened as his hopes of an understanding with the leaders of the Gironde diminished.

Pache's sabotage was but one of the problems with which Danton had to contend during those dark months of March and April. Representatives of the Jacobin Club, *agents provocateurs* dispatched to Belgium by the Club's central office in Paris, had begun to do their mischief in the territory occupied by Dumouriez's troops. Just as Danton had lost control of the Commune to Marat, so, during that October, had the Girondins lost control of the Jacobin Club to Robespierre. For in the midst of their attacks on Danton, the Girondins had unwisely turned on Robespierre too. A fearful scene had taken place in the Convention when someone had risen and accused Robespierre of scheming to establish a dictatorship.

Robespierre indignantly demanded to know the name of the persons who dared accuse him of such an ambition. Louvet, a Girondin, then ascended the rostrum and with the words "I accuse you, Robespierre . . ." uttered in low, level tones, unloosed a terrible denunciation. According to most accounts Robespierre shriveled in terror at the words, and "his eyes began to shift wildly every which way." Characteristically he did not immediately answer Louvet's charges, but requested a few days' time in which to prepare his response.

Time so weakened the force of Louvet's accusation that when Robespierre finally came to the rostrum he was able to refute it in an atmosphere more favorable to himself. The seismograph of the Jacobin Club quickly registered this particular earthquake in the Convention. All members of the Club who were associated with Louvet and the Girondins were expelled. The Jacobins fell under the control of Robespierre—and the activities of that society in Belgium became another thorn in Dumouriez's side.

Public sentiment among the Belgians had at first been in favor of the French, and Belgium's vote for union with the French Republic might have been given voluntarily had not the Jacobins behaved so brutally. The Belgians quickly realized that the glowing promises uttered by the Girondins in the Convention were nothing more than words. The occupation of Belgium was accompanied by all those horrors, familiar to the readers of history, that have always attended foreign occupation. Women were raped, property was stolen and men put to the sword. Dumouriez, who had entered Brussels with fine phrases on his lips ("I do not ask for the keys of your city"), stood by in helpless rage as he saw his work reduced to nothing by greedy, inept and brutal men.

What upset him particularly was the pillaging of churches. The Belgians, piety apart, were proud of their ancient attachment to the

Holy Roman Empire, with the Dukes of Burgundy and that division of Christendom once known as Brabant. Reliquaries of superb craftsmanship, crucifixes of gold, "monuments to superstition" possibly, but irreplaceable works of art certainly, were ripped from altars and torn from sacristies to be melted into ingots of gold that were sent back to Paris in cartloads and caravans. Jewels were picked from their settings and stolen by Jacobin commissioners of minor rank. Posterity can lament these pillages as much as General Dumouriez, for it is said that many of the paintings of the Van Eycks and other early Flemish masters were wantonly destroyed.

The indignation of the Belgians was matched by the anger of General Dumouriez. His letters to the Convention grew indiscreet. The Convention in its turn began to fear and mistrust Dumouriez. Tension increased by the hour. In December, his own struggle in the Convention not yet resolved, Danton went to Belgium as a representative of the Convention to try to placate Dumouriez and unravel the snarls that had developed there.

Another committee, the Defense Committee, was formed to attempt (as the Executive Council had done) to impose some authority on the rapidly disintegrating unity of French purpose. It was as the head of this committee that Danton arrived in Belgium and tried to patch up the quarrel between the Convention, Dumouriez and the Belgian people. His friendship with Dumouriez, his grasp of political realities and his unflagging energy made him an ideal candidate for this assignment. He went to Brussels for ten days, returned to Paris and then, his task still unfinished, returned again to Brussels. Several of his letters to Gabrielle may still be read: "Kiss my little boy for me a thousand times. Tell him that his Papa will try not to be away much longer. . . . I hope to kiss you on New Year's Day after having spent a day or two at Arcis. . . ." But he was not back in Paris on New Year's Day. He remained abroad until January 16, 1793. An event of great significance took place in Paris during those early January weeks and Danton, with calculated intention, absented himself from the city, where with great publicity the trial of Louis XVI had begun.

The King came up for sentence on January 16. On that day Danton returned from Belgium. Danton's real feelings about the King's trial and death remain a mystery. Many things suggest that his vote, uttered publicly and vehemently for unconditional death, did not at all reflect his private opinion. A secret interview that he had with Théodore de Lameth in October 1792—his overtures to the Girondins were then in progress—is suggestive of the difference between Danton's public and private attitudes. Lameth, a onetime revolutionary (of the Lafayette order) was now a proscribed man. He stole into Paris under the cloak of night in order to solicit mercy for the King from Danton. Louis' trial had not yet begun, but the political climate in Paris during that October accurately forecast its approach.

"Save the King!" said Lameth. "You will leave a great name behind you if you do."

"It is the King's own fault that he has come to this pass," declared Danton.

Lameth invoked the Constitution. "How can you judge a man whose person is held to be inviolable by the constituted will of the people?"

"Nonsense!" replied Danton. "What is a Constitution to men who choose to do a thing and who have the power to do it? Was the trial of Charles I a legal proceeding? . . . The Convention will sentence him to death because few men care to endanger their own lives in order to save someone else's."

"Is there nothing you can do?" pressed Lameth.

"I don't know what I can do. But I will not pretend to be any better or worse than I really am. I think it wise that the King should be delivered out of his present situation. To effect this I will do all I can that is bold but at the same time prudent. If I see any chance of success I will even endanger my own safety, but I warn you that I don't plan to risk my neck with his if there should be no chance of saving him. I will then vote for his death."

Danton at that moment was waiting to see the outcome of his overtures to the Girondins. His position regarding the King depended of necessity on his relationship with the Girondins. Together they might have saved the life of the King; their division doomed the unfortunate monarch. The King's trial, as the men of the Mountain knew it would, drove a wedge through the Girondins' party, splintering that already divided group still further and forcing Danton closer towards the waiting arms of Robespierre and Marat. Danton's absence from Paris throughout the unsettled days that preceded and culminated in the King's trial hints at that ambiguity of attitude that Lameth's report openly describes.

Just as Danton feared, the King's execution provided England with the justification it needed to enter the continental war against France. Slowly the stage was being set for the appearance of France's future Emperor. Danton, just before he returned to Belgium, expressed precisely the policy that one day was to become Napoleon's: "The boundaries of the Republic are marked out by nature. We shall attain them all at the four corners of our horizon; on the banks of the Rhine, at the Alps and by the shores of the ocean. The limits of our Republic end there and no power on earth will stop us from obtaining them." Stirring words to the ears of a nationalist! They excited many dreams and gave to Frenchmen the community of purpose and identity that was fundamental to the outlook of the patriot Danton. But they coincided with a severe nervous collapse or moral breakdown on the part of their author.

Danton's second visit to Belgium was marked by a frenzied indulgence of the most brutal part of his nature. The accounts of it are vague, but in all of them one is left with the impression of a man seeking oblivion in an orgy of self-destruction. The prudes and scandalmongers among his colleagues in Paris were finally given the scandals which only imagination and fantasy had heretofore provided. Rumors of the darkest kind reached the capital—among them the report of a caravan filled with loot that Danton had sent under private guard to Paris, and that was embarrassingly intercepted at Arras. The caravan was said to contain "fine linen and plate formerly belonging to an Archduchess."

Robespierre took careful note of this episode, which a year later was to be among the charges leveled against Danton at his trial. At the same time another rumor reached Paris that Danton was spending his nights "eating and drinking with loose women." Debauchery and the despair that was probably at the root of Danton's collapse led to an outbreak of savagery. He appears to have hardened his heart against that pity and magnanimity which were as natural a part of his character as the unfortunate streak of brutality. Too susceptible to the promptings of his passions, he seems in these chaotic weeks to have permitted them to carry him towards the borderline of madness.

And then, just as the frenzy began to subside, just as he was preparing to leave Belgium, the news reached him that Gabrielle, his wife, was dead. Some intimation of this terrible blow and a consequent remorse or some inadmissible despair may well have been at the source of Danton's behavior in Belgium. What now happened suggests a spirit as much overwhelmed by guilt as by grief.

Danton hurried back to Paris, going directly to his apartment in the Cour du Commerce. The flat, once the scene of hospitality and warmth, was now cold and deserted. Danton's two sons, "our little Dantons," had gone to their grandparents. Gabrielle had been dead and buried for nearly a week. The bereft husband uttered a wild and terrible cry that was heard with horror throughout the quarter. He became a man demented. A paroxysm of uncontrollable anguish drew from his body the sounds of an animal that has lost its mate. He went to the cemetery, found his wife's grave and, bellowing and sobbing, ordered that her body be disinterred. Appalled, the grave-diggers at first refused. But the man who gave them orders was Danton, and few men would have dared defy his commands. The grave was opened, the coffin lifted to the surface and its lid unsealed. Uttering passionate phrases, Danton leaped forward and seized the dead woman in his arms. Clasping her to his breast, he covered her decaying flesh with kisses. He then ordered a cast made of her features. A pupil of Pajou, Deseine, was summoned to execute this macabre commission. The poor woman, over whose remains a priest had only six days earlier uttered the words *requiescat in pace,* was then returned to her grave.

Danton was a man who made little separation between his public and private life. The turbulence that disturbed his day at the Convention had been carried back to Gabrielle's once serene fireside. The domestic anxieties that clouded the apartment after the September Massacres expressed themselves with virulence in Belgium. Gabrielle's death inevitably had its effect on Danton's political life. For the proud and passionate man who had neither religion nor philosophy to support him in the hour of his trial, remorse and grief quickly converted themselves into blind hatred of any person he might deem responsible for his bereavement. There were many unscrupulous persons who were ready to make political hay out of this situation, and these now hurried to direct Danton's anger towards the Girondins.

"The Girondins," pronounced Collot d'Herbois in the Jacobin Club, "have caused the death of a citizeness who is much regretted and for whom we all weep. . . . Her husband was away. Roland

and his cowardly partisans leaped on the opportunity afforded them by Danton's absence. They represented him as having drawn up the list of victims whose throats were cut during the second and third of September! When she read this infamous libel in the newspapers his wife was dealt the blow that killed her. . . ."

From Robespierre came a strange letter. One wonders what Danton's thoughts must have been as he read this honeyed missive of condolence from the man who in a year's time was to call him "a rotten idol, putrid with corruption." "If the certainty of having a tender and devoted friend could bring you any consolation, I offer that to you. I love you more than ever and will love you until death. From this time on I am one with you. Don't close your heart to an affection that shares your suffering. Let us weep together. *And let us make the tyrants who are the cause of our public misfortunes and private woes feel sharply the effects of our deep grief. . . .*"

If Gabrielle's body found no rest in its grave, her spirit found no repose on earth. Every faction was determined to put her death and Danton's grief to its own use. For two weeks Danton immured himself with his sorrow and made no appearance before the Convention. But when, in the beginning of March, he appeared again in public, his scar-torn face was swollen with fury and his jaw fixed in a line that wrote for all who wished to read it the news of his approaching alliance with those who plotted the destruction of the Girondins.

29

THE REVOLUTIONARY TRIBUNAL, that agency of bloodstained name which was to become the right arm of the Terror, was established on March 10, 1793, shortly after Danton's emergence from seclusion. The death of his wife and the bitterness that darkened his spirit during his weeks of mourning undoubtedly contributed to the institution of the Tribunal. It was on Danton's proposal that the machine which was to kill him a year later was established.

The situation of the army in Belgium had now become desperate. It was indicative of the breakdown of confidence between the politicians of Paris and the headquarters of the Republican army in Brussels that General Dumouriez was not informed that England was at war with France until ten days after the declaration of hostilities. Without men, without guns, ammunition or clothing, the army kept a precarious hold on Belgium. The Belgians, who only a few months earlier had welcomed the French as deliverers from Austrian oppression, now looked back with longing eyes at their former oppressors, who were preparing to recapture the land they had lost to the French. The Austrians returned to battle better equipped than they had departed. Dumouriez began to retreat. Beside himself with chagrin, the General wrote another scalding letter to the Convention, bluntly blaming the political disputes in Paris for the military defeats in Belgium.

In an atmosphere ominously similar to that of the previous September, Danton, his heart heavy with private grief, ascended the rostrum of the Convention and made another of his ringing appeals to all Frenchmen.

"We have found before now that the temper of the French people needs danger to discover its full energy. Well, the moment of danger

234

is here again! If Dumouriez is enveloped, if his troops are obliged to lay down their arms, we cannot calculate the misery entailed by such a surrender. . . . We promised the army in Belgium 30,000 men on the first of February; none have reached them. I demand that commissioners now be named to raise a fighting force in the forty-eight Sections of Paris . . . remember I was at this same post when the enemy last August invaded France. I said then to our so-called patriots: your discussions are compromising to the success of liberty; your quarrels are despicable; you are traitors. Let us beat the enemy and then continue our own disputes. What is it to me that my name should perish, so long as France be free! I am content to be called a drinker of blood! Let us drink the blood of the enemies of humanity, but let Europe be free!"

The references to blood, his open defiance of the Girondin accusation that he was a *buveur de sang,* did not dampen the Convention's enthusiastic reception of this trumpet call. But the ghosts of September returned to haunt the hall of the Convention in a second speech that Danton gave that evening. It was then that he demanded the institution of the Revolutionary Tribunal.

Throughout those early days of March, Robespierre and Marat had been spreading stories of "treason among our generals." "We must sweep away the traitors, we must suspend the sword of justice over powerful conspirators and perfidious generals," Robespierre declared. The so-called "common people," Marat's hooligans from the Sections, formed themselves into deputations and appeared before the Convention to demand the permanent installation of the guillotine and of a court designed to try persons who might be accused of "crimes against the Republic," a vague charge that comprehended anything from treason or speculation in currency to an insufficiency of civic enthusiasm.

The potentialities of so fearsome a weapon in the hands of the state was not lost on the moderate portion of the Convention. The Convention had been able to resist Marat's demands without difficulty, but on the evening of March 10, just as the sitting was about to break up, Danton rushed to the rostrum and in a stentorian voice called out, "I call on all of you to remain seated!" So peremptory was this order and so pregnant with significance that all deputies remained in their seats as though frozen.

"When Dumouriez may well be surrounded do you dare leave this assembly without having taken firm measures against the internal enemies we have among us? Let us snatch them ourselves from the popular vengeance!"

In the moment of silence that followed this grim proposal—when the full meaning of it had become clear—a single but terrible word was heard from the back of the room. *"Septembre!"* It was hurled at Danton by Lanjuinais, a Girondin, and it struck its mark. For a moment Danton faltered, then recovering himself he said in a "thunderous tone": "Since some one here has dared to recall those bloody days over which every good citizen has groaned, I say that if a Revolutionary Tribunal had then existed, the people who have been so cruelly reproached for those days would not have stained them with blood. Let us profit by the mistakes of our predecessors. Let us be terrible so that we can prevent the People from being terrible!"

He then asked for the organization of a Tribunal and of an executive power with greater authority than the feeble Defense Committee on which he himself impatiently sat. In vain did Vergniaud and his colleagues point out that in establishing a Revolutionary Tribunal the Convention would be "laying the foundations of an Inquisition a thousand times more terrible than that of Spain." In vain did Buzot go to the rostrum and depict such a tribunal as the instrument of despotism. That very evening amid wild applause the Convention decreed the establishment of the Tribunal, which from that hour until July of the following year was to paralyze it with terror and before which many of those who now enthusiastically applauded would themselves be hailed.

To make the conditions for the Reign of Terror complete, all that was now needed was a man or a group of men who had control of this machine that dispensed life and death. The Committee of Public Safety was duly instituted four weeks after the Revolutionary Tribunal. Its establishment was inevitable; the need for some power greater than that invested in the various Executive Councils, Defense Committees and other such agencies of weak or uncertain authority was made evident by the bad news that reached Paris from the military fronts—the direct outcome of dissension, of inefficiency, and a shameless placing of private political passions over the needs of the young Republic. Behind bitter political dispute lay spiteful personal differences. The records of the sittings of the Convention at this period are shameful. They remind one of the screams of fish-wives or of children in a tantrum: to such a pass had come that senate of grave and Roman appearance imagined by Mme. Roland, the Abbé Raynal and Charlotte Corday.

In the middle of this discord, on April 4 came the announcement that General Dumouriez, after making a separate and secret negotiation with the enemy, had deserted to the Austrians. The atmosphere generated in Paris by this news was such that the Committee of Public Safety was recklessly granted "exceptional powers." To resist the demands of its partisans at such a juncture would have been to open oneself to the accusation of treason. Even the Girondins, who had no representation on the new Committee, were compelled to accept it without protest. The intimate association of their objectives (and of their name) with Dumouriez had already brought ruin on them. They could hardly protest at the remedy that was prescribed for the ill for which they were held responsible. The situation was one that sent Marat into a fever of joy, and Robespierre into a paroxysm of vindictive rage.

The Committee of Public Safety was instituted with a membership of nine men (soon to be enlarged to twelve). Danton was at its head. The Convention's understandable fear of too strong an executive body manifested itself in a variety of small hedges, the most important of which was a reservation that the Committee should be reappointed once a month and its membership then reaffirmed or renewed by the Convention.

But the monster was now born. It quickly and skillfully used the powers it had been granted in order to acquire more powers. During Danton's brief dominion it limited itself more or less to the size in which it had been constituted, but after July when Danton was replaced on the Committee by Robespierre, dictatorial powers were craftily wheedled or extorted from the Convention. The rule that membership on the Committee had to be reaffirmed every month was soon forgotten, and at so early a date as September, hardly five months after the Committee's establishment, the sinister motion was proposed to the Convention that all who questioned the Committee of Public Safety be considered among the voices of dissent—and thus "suspect." Behind such proposals loomed the menacing shape of the Revolutionary Tribunal and the guillotine.

Dumouriez's defection was the spark that ignited the many resentments by which—accumulated, like bundles of brush about an executioner's stake—the Girondins were now surrounded. It was the signal for an open attack on them by every faction. Among the first acts of the Committee of Public Safety was an order to impound the papers of the Roland couple. Roland was visited at night and his files peremptorily seized. Since little of a treasonable nature was found among these papers, the Jacobins had recourse to a favorite expedient: they invented charges. Their calumny appeared as a pamphlet called *L'histoire des Brissotins,* in which the Girondins were accused, among other things, of intriguing with the English and the Duc d'Orléans. This tissue of lies was represented as being "based on the papers seized at Roland's flat." Its author was Camille Desmoulins. His assault was venomously personal as well as recklessly general. One short passage conveys an idea of the whole. Litterateur always, he stung the Rolands in the spot where he knew it would hurt most: "Roland," he declared, "was so miserable a writer that when he was a member of our Correspondence Committee he never wrote a passable letter. It was always necessary to correct his letters in several places, both on account of the poverty of their ideas and the vulgarity of their style. . . ." Camille knew full well that Mme. Roland wrote the better part of these letters.

In writing his denunciation of the Girondins, Camille did not work alone. *L'Histoire des Brissotins* was inspired by a more fiery hatred than Camille's malicious literary rivalry with Brissot. Behind Desmoulins can be distinguished the guiding hand of that guileful calumniator Robespierre. Camille provided the words; Robespierre provided the charges. The accusations that Camille penned with such skill and malice were almost identical to those uttered by Robespierre from the rostrum of the Convention. There can be no doubt of collusion between Robespierre and Desmoulins in the writing of this disgraceful pamphlet, though the exact interests that may have brought the two men together remain unclear. Robespierre probably excited Camille's literary vanity and stirred up his easily aroused jealousy. The pamphlet concluded with words that might have done credit to Marat. Camille exhorted the Convention "to vomit the Girondins from its belly." Meanwhile from the rostrum Robespierre demanded that the leaders of the Brissot–Girondin party be hailed before the Revolutionary Tribunal and be made to answer for their guilt.

Inept to the end, the Girondins refused to clutch at the remaining straw that might have kept them afloat. Danton, ignoring the Roland circle, turned to Vergniaud and once more, and for the final time, made overtures of peace. "Let bygones be bygones," he is reported to have said at a private conference with certain Girondin leaders.

"We will grant everything but immunity for cutthroats and their accomplices," answered Gaudet defiantly. "Let it be war and let one side perish!"

"You want war, Gaudet?" replied Danton. "Then you shall have death."

Danton was, in fact, more deeply implicated than the Girondins in the Dumouriez affair. When the hour was propitious and the Girondins were all safely in their graves, Danton's friendship with Dumouriez was to be the main basis of the charges leveled against him by Robespierre. By standing together in this hour of their mutual embarrassment, Danton and the Girondins might have saved one another from an accusation that was to kill them both. But far from showing themselves amenable to any understanding with Danton, they publicly and belligerently accused him of the crime of which they stood accused: complicity in the intrigues of Dumouriez. They tried to shift blame onto Danton's shoulders at a meeting of the Convention held on April 1. By all accounts it must have been one of the more agitated sessions of that senate. Lasource, a creature of Mme. Roland, opened fire by stating that Dumouriez had intended "to restore royalty after he had dissolved the National Convention."

To this accusation Danton made no answer. "He sat," according to a witness of the scene, "without movement on his bench, his lips curled in that expression of contempt that was peculiar to him. He inspired a sort of terror: his glance expressed both disdain and rage." Lasource's accusation brought other Girondins to their feet. One of them, a man named Birotteau, declared that "Danton hoped to make himself King." With a howl of anger Danton rushed to the rostrum, resolved now to crush his adversaries completely.

"These people are wretches!" he declared to the men of the Mountain. "They are trying to blame us for their crimes!" Then he spoke. He spoke for nearly an hour, but the opening sentences of his speech told the Mountain what it had been waiting many months to hear—his complete disavowal of the party of moderation, and the admission of his error in attempting to align himself with it.

"Citizens of the Mountain," he declared. "I must begin by paying you homage. You are the true friends of the welfare of the people. Your judgment has been clearer than mine!" At these words the men of the Mountain burst into frenzied applause.

"His great voice resounded in the midst of the assembly like the alarm gun that summons soldiers to the breach." So recalled one deputy who was present. Danton continued in scorching phrases and stentorian tones: "I once believed that it was my duty, despite my natural impetuosity, to employ the moderation for which the difficult duties of my mission and current events seemed to call. But I was wrong. . . . I now abandon the system of moderation, because prudence has its limits. When I see myself attacked by the very men who ought to be congratulating themselves on my circumspection I feel free to attack in my own turn and to step beyond the limits of patience. . . ."

Delighted by the denunciation of the Girondins that followed these words, Marat from his bench on the top of the Mountain called down: "Tell everybody about the little supper parties they used to have!"

And Danton, Dumouriez's former supper companion and confidant, brazenly answered, "Yes! They are the only men who dined in secret with Dumouriez when he was in Paris last fall."

"Lasource was one of them!" cried Marat. "He was one of them! I'm going to denounce them all as traitors!"

"And they dare accuse *me!*" Danton lifted his great fist and shook it in the direction of those benches on the right that were soon to be empty. "No more terms with them! I have returned now to the fortress of Reason. I will have it armed with the artillery of Truth in order to pulverize these enemies!"

And having spoken thus, he descended from the rostrum, and was carried on a wave of applause, back to his seat on the Mountain, where he was embraced by the real victor of the hour, Robespierre.

Without representation on the Committee of Public Safety, expelled from the Jacobin Club, and with no authority at the Commune, the Girondins were from this moment doomed. The only man who might have helped them, Danton, had publicly joined sides with the forces dedicated to their destruction. Some small power remained with them in the Convention and they cherished the illusion that the cowards and opportunists who composed the Plain would come to their support. They forgot that the Convention had already handed over much of its sovereignty to the Committee of Public Safety.

Marat and his horde of cutthroats at the Commune were the actual instruments of their destruction. That scene that took place at the Tuileries on June 2, 1793, when Marat's "army" expelled the Girondin deputies from the Convention, silenced forever the protesting vote of such squeamish deputies of the Plain as may still have believed that government must be based on a mutual respect for the Constitution by the people and their representatives.

The events of June 2, which at Caen exalted Charlotte Corday with the calm passions of the classic theatre, mark a turning in the road that is critical in the history of the Revolution. Marat's murder, the immediate outcome of those events, brought a hurried strengthening of authority in the Committee of Public Safety. With Marat's death anarchy ceased and the period of dictatorship began.

On July 10 Charlotte Corday was speeding towards Paris. On that same day Danton lost his position in the Committee of Public Safety. In the monthly renewal of confidence that was still required from the Convention, neither he nor his auxiliaries on the Committee were returned to their seats.

Little more than two weeks later, on July 26, Robespierre quietly took Danton's place on the Committee.

30

DANTON'S DISMISSAL from the Committee of Public Safety did not seem to him to be so serious an event as it now appears to his biographers. For at the time when Danton left it, the Committee had not yet been forged into the instrument of dictatorship that potentially it was. Under Danton's leadership the Committee had made free use of the considerable powers that the Convention had granted it, but it had never used them in order to acquire more. Indeed, it had been Danton's publicly expressed hope—and there is no reason to question his sincerity—that the Committee of Public Safety would be dissolved at the earliest possible moment. From its beginning he had viewed it as a temporary expedient, an emergency measure, never as a permanent institution. And such, during the three months of his influence it had remained. He was not, therefore, aware of any serious menace to himself when he found himself ousted from it in July. Indeed for private reasons he may have viewed his dismissal more with relief than with apprehension.

His downfall is an event of crucial significance in the history of the Revolution. Danton, who had helped establish both the Revolutionary Tribunal and the Committee of Public Safety, was now obliged to surrender to Robespierre and the Jacobin Club those institutions of such dangerous potential. From the moment of Robespierre's entry into it, the Committee of Public Safety becomes the focal point of the Revolution. In exact proportion as the power of the Committee waxed, that of the National Convention, still technically the governing body of France, waned. Robespierre's Committee was to last exactly one year. This is the Committee of Public Safety of sinister name that appears in historical fiction. Danton's short-lived Committee is generally ignored or forgotten.

The reasons for Danton's overthrow are both political and personal. Danton had in him the makings of a genuine statesman. Unlike the shortsighted Robespierre, who never lost his provincial suspicion of foreigners, Danton viewed the French Republic in its larger, European context. As head of the Committee of Public Safety, he examined the chessboard of Europe and realized that either the war on which France had so recklessly embarked would have to be brought to an end or the allies who fought against France would have to be divided.

Peace overtures, cautiously advanced, were among the first fruits of Danton's work in the Committee of Public Safety. At the same time that he proffered the olive branch, Danton, with skill and duplicity, began to insert the wedge of dissension between France's enemies, bargaining with one hand, enticing with the other. Between Prussia and Austria, those old natural enemies, there lay an uneasy suspension of historic antipathies that had been brought about only by their common horror of Revolutionary excesses in France. A split between these allies was not beyond the realm of likelihood even so late as April 1793. During the few months he held office, Danton even envisioned the possibility of England's withdrawal from the ranks of France's enemies. There still remained a group of Liberals in England to whom the French Revolution, though badly stained by the September Massacres, was not yet anathema. With these men, Danton, who admired English law and spoke English, hoped to communicate. As leader of the Committee of Public Safety he aspired to make himself the spokesman of a sane and moderate Revolution.

As Richelieu had done before him (and Talleyrand was to do after), Danton set about to attract certain of Europe's smaller powers —governments such as Sweden, Denmark, Naples and Venice—who were jealous of their larger neighbors and ripe for alliances that might do Prussia, Austria or England an injury. Obscurity hangs over the complex and secret diplomatic maneuvers that Danton at this time began. The study of them presents a perennially fascinating problem to those scholars whose patience and curiosity draws them to the forgotten corners of Europe's archives. But fundamental to all of Danton's schemes lay one single condition that was critical in the balance of their success or failure: the stability of the government in whose name he proffered his secret enticements.

The monarchies of Europe, delighted though they had been in the opening days of the Revolution to see the once arrogant French crown humiliated and the conceited and fashionable coxcombs of the French Court brought low, had been shocked by the September Massacres and appalled by the execution of Louis XVI. The rantings of Marat were heard in the chancelleries and throne rooms of Europe with incredulity and horror. There could be no traffic with a government run by maniacs and supported by murder. It became, then, a vital factor in Danton's negotiations abroad that France be represented as a power with which the customary bargainings of diplomacy might be transacted, and not as a nation of drunken cannibals. To gain desirable ends for their governments, the statesmen of this world have smilingly swallowed many a bitter pill and dipped their fine hands into deep pools of mud. But there is a point beyond which none of them has ever sensibly gone. To deal with rational gangsters or with sensible thieves is one thing; to deal with madmen is quite another.

In its efforts to present to Europe a façade of moderation, Danton's Committee of Public Safety was compromised and finally ruined by the demands of the Paris mob and its ambitious leaders. Incited by Marat, the men of the Commune howled for extravagant measures. At the Jacobin Club Robespierre, in control of the intricate machinery which dispensed insinuation and slander, denounced in a hundred subtle and deadly ways the moderation of the Committee of Public Safety. Although most of these libels were aimed at Danton personally, their intent was usually disguised by a thin veneer of discretion that made them appear to be a general attack on the Committee rather than specifically on Danton. At other times direct charges were made—references for instance to the old rumors of venality; but this poison was always sweetened by a sugar-coating of social concern (*"Some* people say that Danton is in the pay of the English and that the money which supports the pleasures to which he is addicted is drawn from the veins of patriots . . . gossip such as this, *if it is idle,* does not do credit to the people of our great Republic.")

Robespierre was too cautious at this delicate juncture in his political life to spread his slander in any way that might make it traceable to himself. Just as he had incited Camille Desmoulins to write *L'Histoire des Brissotins,* so now he incited others to slander Danton and undermine his position in the Committee of Public Safety. The war, of which Robespierre had been the bitterest opponent during the Girondin ministry of the previous spring, had now become in his eyes a holy obligation, an inseperable part of the Revolution. The possibility that Danton might successfully negotiate peace with Europe, thereby capturing the laurels of popular acclaim, sickened him. Robespierre's every utterance at this time betrays both his apprehension and his envy. He became the most vehement advocate of total war.

An immediate outcome of the insurrection of June 2, to which Danton had lent his spirit if not his name, was the outbreak throughout France of civil war. Lyons burst into flames and a great convulsion shook the Vendée. At Caen, with the arrival there of Barbaroux and other proscribed cohorts, Normandy too gathered its forces to join the revolt of the provinces against the illicit dictatorship of Paris. The political climate of Paris in June 1793 was scarcely propitious for the establishment of that moderate Revolution of which Danton hoped to be the leader.

The Revolutionary Tribunal, which was three months old, had heretofore reaped only a small harvest of heads (judges and jury wept together when they sent their first victim, a man named des Maulans, to his fate). The guillotine was first installed where the Place du Carrousel now is, not far from the Tuileries. It was soon moved to the Place de la Révolution (formerly Place Louis XV and now Place de la Concorde); in that ample public square designed by Gabriel, the multitude could be both edified and fascinated by its operation. In the early days of the Terror, the victims were usually brought there in batches of two or three. An execution was still a sufficiently novel entertainment to arouse interest among the curiosity-seekers and the sensation-hunters of the city. Refreshments, lemonade and *petits pains* were sold in the courtroom of the Tribunal, as they were at the foot of the guillotine. The time when forty, fifty and sixty victims were to be dispatched daily was not yet foreseen.

The provincial uprisings occasioned by the overthrow of the Girondins put the machinery of the Terror into second gear. Charlotte Corday's was the first of the Tribunal's sensational trials. Marat's murder provided Robespierre and his Committee with all the evidence it needed of a widespread and sinister Girondin conspiracy. Charlotte Corday, who died believing that she had put an end to the Terror, had in actuality helped precipitate it. The Girondins and many men and women who were only innocently associated with them were doomed from the moment of Marat's death.

And Danton, who might have saved them, no longer held power.

Confronted with civil war on one hand and foreign war on the other, engaged abroad in negotiations that he believed necessary to France's survival, but beset at home by exigencies in direct opposition to these international needs, Danton was caught between contradictory demands that he was not able to reconcile. The attacks on him by Robespierre and the Extremists in the Commune grew more and more vehement. He was accused of "pampering the enemy within and indulging the enemy abroad"—two vague charges from which the subsequent rumor of "treason" was to be manufactured.

Danton's old club, the Cordeliers', was now infested by the so-called Hébertists, the most extreme men of the Revolution. Danton was denounced from the rostrum of the Club that he had founded. It is to be observed that, while the tenor of Robespierre's accusations against him (none of which at this time ever emanated in any direct or compromising way from Robespierre himself) centered about financial dishonesty and "corruption," those launched by the Cordeliers cautiously avoided any reference to this delicate subject. For the hands of the ex-priest Chabot (that same Chabot who interrogated Charlotte Corday) were, along with those of certain of his fellow clubmen at the Cordeliers, already plunged deep into the coffers of the *Compagnie des Indes*.

The Cordeliers therefore contented themselves with denunciations of Danton's lack of Revolutionary ardor. It was pointed out that he rarely came to the Club any more. One member peevishly deposed that "once Danton turned his back on me in order to talk to a general." Danton finally made an appearance before the Cordeliers and explained that all his time and energy now went into the Committee, while he assured the members of the Jacobin Club, Robespierre's bailiwick, that he would never lag behind them in Revolutionary zeal.

At this particular meeting Robespierre rose and made a little speech that was characteristic of him. He praised the Committee at great length and pointed out that, *"though it might err occasion-*

ally," so far as he, Robespierre, was *personally* concerned, it appeared to have the welfare of the People genuinely at heart.

This statement, uttered in forbearing tones that prompted everyone to admire the speaker's tolerance, left no one in doubt that in Robespierre's opinion the Committee as it was constituted would have to go.

In June 1793, a month before his dismissal from the Committee, an event of importance took place in Danton's private life. His marriage to Louise Gély was probably among the influences contributing to his downfall. Just as grief and bitterness over the death of Gabrielle had poisoned his political outlook in the early spring of that same year, so in the summer, happiness and love insinuated their relaxing influences into his work. The moderation that was publicly expedient welled from a private source. Danton was a happy man. The circumstances surrounding his second marriage and the effect it had on the "Cyclops" of the Revolution constitute one of the most curious passages in the human drama of the Revolution.

Louise Gély was sixteen years of age when she married Danton. He was thirty-three. She was the daughter of a clerk employed in the Admiralty, a man whom Danton had known back in the days when he practiced law in the "Republic of the Cordeliers." Gabrielle too had been a friend of her parents. It is believed that Gabrielle on her deathbed had expressed a wish that Danton marry Louise Gély. Louise, like Gabrielle, was a woman educated in the spirit of religious principles, a bourgeoise without the intellectual pretensions of Mme. Roland, an uncomplicated creature whose behavior was governed by the concerns traditional to most respectable French housewives: family, God and domestic economy. The existence in Paris throughout the Revolution of this mute majority is too frequently forgotten or overlooked. The historian's attention is captured by the screaming fishwives who formed the female portion of the mob or by the so-called *tricoteuses,* the idle women, sadistically inclined, who stationed themselves about the guillotine to watch the heads fall.

Like any large city of that time, or of this, Paris had its drifting population of the vicious, the perverted or the insane. In times of trouble, when the restraints of law are no longer imposed on it, the lunatic fraction of a city's citizenry inevitably emerges to indulge in lusts and crimes that are as much forbidden by the civilized conscience as they are by the laws of the civilized state. It was Robespierre's gravest error that in speaking of the "People"—a word he always uttered in an unctuous tone of voice—he embraced this vociferous and dangerous element of the population. Like many another sentimentalist he equated the ownership of property with dishonesty and immorality. In his simple creed poverty made a man virtuous and wealth made him vicious. The poor were thus all lumped together, the depraved along with the decent, the dishonest along with the honorable, while the large class of people from which such women as Gabrielle Danton and Louise Gély and their families sprang was as ignored by Robespierre as it has been by posterity. For the most part the Parisian bourgeoisie viewed the advanced stages of the Revolution with the same attitude as their provincial counterparts—at first with enthusiasm and then, as it began to impinge on their own lives, with horror.

Louise Gély, like her friend Gabrielle Danton, honored the spirit of France's abjured faith. More than this, however, Louise and her family had remained practicing Catholics throughout the religious persecutions that had begun with Marat's ascendancy to power. This means that they made their confession to and received the sacraments from the hands of a priest who had not sworn an oath to the Constitution. Such men were of course outlaws, as were the men and women who received their ministrations, and all were liable to the death penalty. Great secrecy naturally surrounded these clandestine celebrations of the Mass. The priest and his congregation usually assembled in such places of concealment as subcellars or attics. An abbé named Kerenavent attended to the spiritual needs of the family into which Danton married in June 1793. And the Abbé Kerenavent was astonished indeed when one day during the first part of June he found himself alone and face to face with the fearsome Danton and heard, from those twisted lips that struck terror into the hearts of his opponents, the extraordinary words, "Bless me, Father, for I have sinned. . . ."

The fact seems incredible, yet it is verified not only by the Abbé Kerenavent (who survived the Revolution) but by the Gély family as well: just before his marriage to Louise, Danton made his confession to this priest. It was the price of Louise Gély's hand, for she desired that they be married in the Church. "Of all the startling spectacles that the chronicle of the Revolution has bequeathed to posterity, Danton's confession is assuredly one of the most unexpected"; so writes that student of *petite histoire,* G. Lenôtre. The Abbé Kerenavent in his memoirs recalled this meeting with the Revolutionary leader. "His face was pitted with smallpox. There was a wrinkle denoting bad temper between his eyebrows. The crease of good nature was at the corner of his mouth. He had thick lips, big teeth, a hand like that of a street porter, and a piercing eye." When the Abbé recognized his visitor, he blanched!

The scene, as Lenôtre has declared, is assuredly "unexpected." Yet if one examines it in the light of Danton's background and character, it is not so startling perhaps as it might first appear. The conventional observances of religion had been as much a part of his early life as they were of his young wife's. The women of his family were neither bluestockings such as Mme. Roland nor fishwives such as flocked around the atheistic Hébert. It is probable that Mme. Danton *mère,* still alive at Arcis, continued to honor, as Gabrielle had done, the faith of her birth. The Catholic faith was an old and familiar part of Danton's life, and if he believed, as did many Frenchmen of his time and class, that that faith was a superstition, he saw no good reason to substitute another superstition in its place. The pasteboard deities of the Girondins had no more attraction for him than did the Rousseauesque divinity of Robespierre's invention. He looked on the militant atheism of Hébert with undisguised loathing. The blasphemy and sacrilege indulged in by the lunatic fringe of Paris seemed, in the eyes of this man who had been educated by the Oratorian fathers and who was known to have saved the lives of several Oratorian priests during the September Massacres, to be the desecration of a heritage that was inseparably woven into the lives of ordinary French people. Such outrages not only insulted the peasant who "worshiped the Man of Consolation because to Him he owed a few happy moments in his youth, his manhood and his old age," but they offended Danton personally because they seemed to strike at the memory of his dead wife and to debase the innocent faith of the woman he loved. That curious strain of conservatism which was so profound an element in his character disposed him towards a sympathetic view of France's traditional faith.

But how deeply, one wonders, did the spirit of that faith affect Danton's life in the ten months that remained to him after his confession to Abbé Kerenavent? Did he receive the sacraments without heart or conviction, only to gain the hand of a desirable young wife? Or did he in some part of his being accept with contrition the precepts in which he had been instructed as a boy?

A consideration of such questions is essential to any understanding of Danton's character, but no answer is ever likely to be found among the letters, diaries or confidences of recorded history. Posterity can only examine Danton's behavior during the ten months between his second marriage and his death and hope to find there some reflection of his deeper self. There can be no doubt that beginning with the month of June 1793, when he married Louise Gély, we are witness to certain changes in his character that suggests the impetus of some inner experience.

Certainly his marriage itself contributed much towards the making of this "new" Danton. He was an unembarrassed sensualist but at the same time a *bon bourgeois*. The extravagance and promiscuity of France's vanished monarchs and nobility in no way allured Danton. His private life is more redolent of nightshirts and bedroom slippers than of those love couches of the *ancien régime* that were bedizened with ostrich plumes and whose mattresses were stuffed with the down of swans. The stink of body sweat reminiscent of the barnyard at Arcis, rather than the essences of flower water with which the roués of the old order used to scent their couches, clings to his brief idyll with Louise Gély. Passionately in love with his young bride and warmed by the glow which she brought back to the dead ashes of his fireside, it is no wonder that Danton's revolutionary fervor began to lag. Revolutions are best made by restless or unhappy people who privately anticipate some amelioration of their own inner discontent in that general amelioration which they strive to effect on the society in which they live.

Danton's attendance at the meetings of the Cordeliers or Jacobin Club fell off sharply after his marriage to Louise Gély. He could not view those nightly sessions, often extending until late hours and dedicated to a dissection of the minutiae of ideology, with the same enthusiasm as Robespierre, who had no effective life outside the Convention or the Jacobin Club. Men of Robespierre's disposition who are in charge of clubs or group gatherings too often have the irritating habit of summoning special or emergency meetings or of needlessly prolonging ordinary meetings. In this way they are able to thwart the desires of men happier than themselves who have a private life and who wish to go home to enjoy it. To protest or to grow visibly restive under such restraints betrays to suspicious eyes an insufficiency of enthusiasm. With Robespierre's accession to the Committee of Public Safety, the day dawned in France when a "bad attitude" was sufficient to bring one before the Revolutionary Tribunal. To prefer oneself or one's family to the ideological abstractions propounded at the Jacobin Club was to give the Tribunal enough material to concoct a death sentence. Indeed absence of civic fervor was no mean accusation even when Danton sat on the Committee. It is to be noticed that Danton quickly tore himself from the distractions of his hearth in order to answer the charges, probably spread by Robespierre, that he no longer attended club meetings. Danton answered that accusation by stating that the business of the Committee of Public Safety now occupied most of his time; but in saying this he was not telling the full truth. Louise Gély, too, occupied a good part of the time that he no longer gave to the Jacobins or to the Cordeliers.

More significantly, Louise began to consume much of the time that during the critical months of June and July Danton should have devoted to the Committee of Public Safety. The maintenance therein of those two mutually hostile attitudes—moderation on one hand and severity on the other—demanded a legerdemain that would have taxed the abilities of the most energetic of politicians. Relaxed by love to the point of fatigue, Danton's grip on affairs of state began to loosen. Love had opened his eyes to the sweetness of living and he now wanted to leave the arena of political debate where those sterile substitutes for happiness, ideology and intrigue, occupied the time and drained the vitality of men who had nothing else to live for.

It is curious that one by one the men and women of the Revolution were almost all to be overcome by this same weariness now infecting Danton. "Where are my fields of Guise?" cried Camille. "Where can I hide from this world and be alone with my wife and child?" And Mme. Roland's *cri de coeur* is no less poignant: "I should like to see my trees again and my garden after so many fools." One by one—Robespierre in his turn, too—the leaders of the Revolution were to be struck down by this disgust, this fatal lassitude that, at the very moment when struggle was most urgent, seemed to paralyze their wills.

To attribute Danton's deepening compulsion to escape the rigors of political combat to some sudden accession within him of the precepts of the Catholic faith would be to extend assumption too far. Nonetheless, at about the time (November 1793) when Danton began openly to struggle with Robespierre, it is difficult to escape the impression that alongside the drama unfolding in the political theatre we are witness in the person of Danton to another drama of an inner but no less powerful kind.

The eighteenth century had lost its appetite for tragedy, but in its closing years it was given several tragedies that might have excited the interest of the Greek dramatists. In its basic elements the story of Marie Antoinette is worthy of the invention of Euripides. The concluding months of Danton's life, too, appear to have been informed by those powerful forces which are elemental to the great religions of mankind and in consequence to its great dramas: crime or sin; guilt or remorse; retribution or expiation—the label varies according to the faith of the theologian or the philosopher examining the concept. For Danton the "crime" that altered the remainder of his days was assuredly the September Massacres. Link upon fatal link, the connection between his rôle in the massacres and his own destruction was forged in a direct line and, as is necessary in true tragedy, the gods used their victim himself to forge the links.

Viewed on a political level, Danton's rôle in the September Massacres might be described in the words Fouché was one day to use in deploring the murder of the Duc d'Enghien: "It was worse than a crime, it was a blunder." The massacres alienated him from those colleagues in the Convention who might have supported and finally saved him, and they were maliciously used by such personal enemies as Mme. Roland and Robespierre (each of whom in making such a use unknowingly forged another link in their own fatal chain) in order to divide the Girondins still further from Danton.

The massacres brought shame upon him and clouded the final days of his wife with terror and grief. Danton's dissipation in Belgium in the weeks that preceded her death suggest that his part in the massacres may have seemed to him something worse than a crime and even worse than a blunder: reflected in the dying eyes of the woman he loved, he may have glimpsed some intimation of his sin. The death of Gabrielle in its turn drove him to a second association in crime with Marat that the effects of the first had made necessary.

The expulsion of the Girondins from the Convention, that event so fraught with consequence for so many people, was the cornerstone on which Robespierre was to build his dictatorship. At the Convention, in the weeks and months that followed the expulsion of the Girondins, Danton was to gaze with increasing regret at the empty benches of the men who might have been his allies. His retirement from the Committee of Public Safety and Robespierre's ascendancy foreshadowed the proscription and death of the Girondin leaders—men who, whatever the political differences that may have divided them, had been his friends. Their execution filled him with a remorse that is reflected everywhere in his behavior during the final months of his life. It weighed heavily among the forces that drove him from retirement in Arcis back to Paris to fight Robespierre and put an end to the Terror.

Orthodox Catholic or Christian he may or may not have been, but in almost precise proportion to the decline of his political fortune Danton begins to emerge as an admirable human being, a man susceptible to the influence of those concepts: mercy, love—and courage, too—that inform the spirit if not always the word of many of mankind's creeds. This much is believed to be true: on the day that Danton died, the Abbé Kerenavent followed his tumbrel from the Palais de Justice to the place of execution. Somewhere along the way, probably on the rue St. Honoré rather than at the foot of the guillotine, the eyes of the two men met and, according to the Abbeé Kerenavent, Danton bowed his head for a moment while the fugitive priest gave him conditional absolution. When he recalled that extraordinary exchange, the Abbé was always understandably proud.

But for those like Danton himself, who incline to measure men more by the inner grace than by the ritual sign, the real suggestion of his redemption is perhaps to be found in the story of the mission of mercy that brought him face to face with Robespierre and soon after to the scaffold.

31

ROBESPIERRE ENTERED the Committee on ground that had been carefully prepared for him in advance by two men who had been members of the Committee under Danton and who were, in fact, Danton's enemies. Their names were Couthon and St. Just, and in the
month preceding Danton's downfall they had assiduously reported
to Robespierre all that took place in the secret meetings of the Committee. He was, therefore, well informed of its workings and of the
private animosities dividing its membership.

Characteristically, he entered by the back door. One of the members, an obscure delegate named Gasparin, conveniently resigned his
place on the Committee "for reasons of health." Without fanfare,
Robespierre was appointed to replace him on the following day. One
would give much to know the arrangements and preparations that
may have contributed to Gasparin's "ill health." On that small pivot
swung the history of France. Robespierre was industriously at work
within the Committee two full days before he was, in fact, officially
appointed. He seems to have had no doubts about the security of his
position there. Only fifteen days after his appointment he appeared
before the Jacobin Club with a bitter denunciation of certain of his
associates on the Committee. Typically, no names were given in this
diatribe. Insinuation was as characteristic of Robespierre's workings
as were the quarrels and dissensions that continually gathered and
broke around him.

"Called to the Committee of Public Safety against my wishes," he
declared, "I have seen things there which I would not have believed.
On one side I have seen patriotic members who work for the good
of their country, and on the other side I have seen traitors who conspire against the interests of the People within the very bosom of the

Committee. Since I have seen the government at close range, I have become aware of the crimes which are committed by it every day. . . ."

No member of the Committee rose to protest these slanderous words that surely must have filled many of them with indignation. They knew, as we today cannot, the full power of the forces that had introduced Robespierre to their midst. Their silence is proof, more convincing than any conceivable document, of the ascendancy over them of their new colleague. Almost from its beginning, the character of the new Committee, soon known as the "Robespierre Committee," began to take on the outline and color of that institution of infamous name familiar to the readers of Revolutionary memoirs and Victorian fiction.

The Law of Suspects was passed during the first week of September. This bit of legislation defined in vague and allusive terms those who were to be considered suspect and therefore liable to arrest—"persons who, by their conduct or language either written or spoken, have shown themselves to be partisans of tyranny or Federalism [a knife thrust at the Girondins] and enemies of Liberty." The number of fish that might be scooped up in this net left nothing to be desired by the Revolutionary Tribunal or its energetic prosecutor, Fouquier-Tinville. Also suspect were those citizens "who could not give a satisfactory account of their means of support or their discharge of civic obligations since the preceding March 21."

The third article in this list was particularly odious. It stated that persons who had not received "good citizenship certificates" from their local Section leader were also to be considered suspect. The Vigilance Committees of each Section—to whom the unhappy resident of Paris had to apply in order to obtain his certificate—were, in Taine's words, "composed of social outcasts and perverts of every known sort, subordinates full of hate and envy, vagabonds off the street and idlers who lived in drinking shops . . . many of whom adopted the Revolutionary faith only because it offered them means to sate their appetites and fill their pockets." The power given by their prerogatives to issue "good citizenship certificates" was an open invitation to these people to fill their pockets: "The Vigilance Committees were very profitable. The men who sat on them trafficked in certificates of civism and warrants of arrest. People paid them not to be included in the list of suspects; they paid to be released; they paid to have their records mislaid. The only way to save oneself was to pay one's potential executioners by gradual installments, to pay them like wet nurses by the month, on a scale proportionate to the activity of the guillotine."

The Law of Suspects cast a cold shadow over all of France. The psychology of the Terror seems to have reflected on a national scale the private persecution complex of Robespierre. After the law was passed the public utterances of that naturally suspicious man began to acquire a fear-ridden tone that is suggestive of paranoia. He saw conspirators everywhere. Every speech, every thought that was confided to his notebook or published by the Jacobin Club, has some reference to "plots," to "secret enemies," to conspiracy or treason.

Scarcely had Robespierre entered the Committee when preparations were begun to bring the Girondins to trial. This was a project especially close to Robespierre's heart, for he felt for Brissot a hatred so implacable that Brissot's execution in November in no way diminished it. The source of this hatred, which, on a superficial level, may be traced to a series of public slights inflicted on him by Brissot during the weeks that preceded France's entry into war, lay in reality at a profounder depth that has been best described by that other Girondin Buzot. "Robespierre never forgave his friends the injuries which he had done them, nor the kindnesses that he had received from them, nor the talents some of them possessed which he did not have. . . ."

When the news reached Danton that the Girondins were to be brought to trial he was visibly stricken. His friend Garat relates that "great tears fell down that face that would have served as model for a Tartar." "I shall not be able to save them," he declared. And the tone of his voice was "expressive of great sorrow." The news undoubtedly contributed to his decision to leave Paris, to go away from the scene of the approaching slaughter and avert his attention from thoughts that were too oppressive to bear.

During the first week of August a further piece of news indicated the direction in which the winds were blowing. The widowed Queen was transferred from her prison in the Temple Tower to the prison of the Conciergerie to await trail. Danton's attitude towards the royal family has always remained ambiguous.

There is evidence that during the beginning of the Revolution he may have been in the pay of the Court. At so late a date in the

Revolution as August of 1792 when Danton was about to lend his arm to the overthrow of the monarchy, Mme. Elizabeth, the King's sister, was heard to make the curious remark, "We are quite at ease about all of this because we can count on M. Danton." His views on the trial and execution of the King have been described by de Lameth—he would have preferred that the King did not come up for trial, and might have been party to an attempt to help Louis escape if the hazards of the game permitted. Should the King be arraigned, however, as Danton assured de Lameth, he would vote for his death without hesitation; to do otherwise wou'd be to risk his own head. Such views probably reflected no private sympathy for the person of Louis XVI. They expressed, rather, the attitude of a political realist who foresaw in the King's execution the domestic and foreign complications which were indeed to be its outcome.

By the time that Marie Antoinette was brought to the Conciergerie, six months after the King's death, the character of the Revolution and the disposition of power within France had undergone alterations that were critical for all who were engaged in the struggle. During Danton's short tenure of office in the Committee, when he was attempting to make agreements in favor of France with the rest of Europe, the Queen had been a high card indeed in the hand that he held. As a Hapsburg Archduchess her fate was of interest not only to the Austrian Emperor, but to her sisters in Naples and Parma and to her many relatives who occupied thrones or positions of influence in Europe. More than this, the unfortunate woman's plight had captured the sympathy of such bastions of middle-class respectability as England, where public opinion was not without influence.

Political expediency apart, Danton, who in his rough way was not an unchivalrous man, may well have viewed the Queen's situation with the compassion that would be natural to a normal man who sees a woman of beauty and dignity, the mother of two children, at the mercy of bullies and cowards. There are historians who believe that through intermediaries Danton may have entered into some sort of correspondence with her—though all traces of any such communication have long since disappeared, if they ever existed at all. At Danton's trial a "document" was shown to the jury in the privacy of its chamber, a document about which we know nothing except that it was introduced at the last minute, when the Committee of Public Safety had reason to fear that the jury might render an acquittal.

That evidence, whatever it may have been, quickly brought any waverers among the jury to heel. Was it, as certain historians suspect, something to do with the Queen that was not in the interest of the Committee of Public Safety to release to public view?

In any case, Marie Antoinette's last hope vanished with Danton's retirement from the Committee of Public Safety. At the time of her transfer to the Conciergerie, Danton expressed his views without ambiguity. "The men who are leading Antoinette to the scaffold," he declared, "are destroying all hope of our ever coming to terms with Europe."

Danton stayed in Paris through the remainder of that summer of 1793, watching the Committee gather power. He made a halfhearted attempt to align himself with the Extremists, the party of Hébert, whose excesses were becoming offensive to Robespierre. But the Hébertists who now dominated the Cordeliers' Club and described themselves as "the heirs of Marat" distrusted Danton as a Moderate and rejected his advances.

In September, borrowing Robespierre's well-developed technique, Danton incited several of his acquaintances to make an attack on the Committee at a session of the Convention. Robespierre, recognizing the direction from which the blow really came, deflected the thrust with a threatening insinuation. "Those who denounce us today will be denounced in their turn," he declared. "Those who are our accusers now will one day become the accused." Already Robespierre had at his command that strange ability which in the ensuing months was to narcotize the Convention and to generate around him an atmosphere of menace and fear. When he sensed that the moment was propitious he assumed a martyr's stance and said, "If you do not believe in the Committee's zeal, then dissolve it! I propose that a new Committee of Public Safety be elected!" A dutiful cry of "No! No!" was heard throughout the hall.

The scene should have given Danton—who probably had far more partisans among the cowardly deputies than did Robespierre—conssiderable material on which to brood.

The loss of Toulouse during September gave the Committee an excuse to make "Terror the order of the day." In November a fiery speech by Billaud-Varennes, one of the committee members, frightened the Convention into abdicating still more of its powers in favor of the Committee.

"No inviolability for anyone at all!" demanded Billaud-Varennes. "No deputy in the Convention is to be inviolable if he obstructs the public will! Let us prove to the world that we are not anarchists. Let us show the world that by our own free will we have substituted severe Revolutionary law for the oscillations of interest and passion which tears us apart. . . ."

It was then agreed that no further elections were to be held: "When the Revolutionary machinery is still rolling, you injure the People by entrusting them with the election of public functionaries. . . ." The Committee of Public Safety was given the power to replace those deputies whom "the People" had elected but who had since been removed from their seats by "popular insurrection" or by the guillotine.

France was about to be delivered to the most dictatorial government it had ever known. On the Place de la Révolution the guillotine began to go about its business in earnest.

One evening, probably in late September of that year, Danton and his friend Camille were returning from a meeting of the Convention. It was the hour of sunset and, as they crossed the Pont Neuf, the crimson light of the sky was reflected in the river below. The two men paused to gaze at the strange glow. Suddenly Danton turned to his friend and cried out, "Look! The river seems to be running blood! Look, how much blood! You must take up your pen again, Camille. You must write and demand clemency. I will support you."

But Danton's nerves had begun to fail. A friend went to see him in the house near Paris where he had immured himself with Louise after his unsuccessful bout with Robespierre. Danton seemed to fall asleep in the very middle of their talk. "What is happening to Danton?" cried his friend.

"Danton is very tired," answered the weary man. "He fell asleep . . . one day he will wake again."

Others who saw him at this time heard him complain repeatedly of "suffocation." Over and again he spoke of a need to "get away from men, to escape to the country so that he would be able to breathe again." All at once he fell ill. We do not know the nature of his illness though surely it was "psychological" in origin. At last, on October 13 he dispatched a letter to the Convention. "Delivered from a serious illness," he wrote, "my doctors have informed me that to shorten

259

the period of my convalescence I must retire to the country and breathe my native air: accordingly I request permission from the Convention to proceed to Arcis sur l'Aube. I need hardly protest that I shall return with haste to my post as soon as my strength permits me to share the Convention's labors."

A few hours later he was off, taking with him his wife and his two sons. He arrived at Arcis on October 15 (Marie Antoinette was guillotined in Paris on the following day), and like one preparing to retire to bed, he drew the curtain of silence about his life.

At Arcis he contented himself with the company of old friends, the former parish priest, the village mayor, the many friends of his childhood with whom he had grown up. When the Paris papers arrived, the news in them was already several days old; Danton scarcely scanned them. When conversation among his friends turned to politics, Danton firmly directed its course in another direction. He was more interested in the black mares in his stable and in the wild sow which he kept in his hogpen than he was in the theories and futilities that caused such bitter contention in the Convention. The Danton of fierce visage and stentorian voice, the Titan of the Revolution engraved in history, was not at all the man who was seen that autumn by his neighbors at Arcis. "Often," relates one of them, "I used to glimpse him at his window or standing before his doorway, wearing a nightcap. . . ."

In the first days of his convalescence he stayed at home. Then, as the healing influence of his native air began to have its effect, he went hunting with his friends. Some days he would spend a whole afternoon drifting on his boat in the Aube with a net and fishing rod. He pruned his trees and tended his garden. He introduced his young sons to the pleasures and responsibilities of country life and to the land that they were to inherit. During his stay at Arcis, indeed, he bought more land, adding a hectare of woodland and another pasture or two to his already extensive holdings. Far from the Paris whirlwind, "breathing the pure air and enjoying the tranquility and repose of Arcis" (so recorded his friend the curé), Danton quickly grew strong again.

One day—it must have been on November 2 or 3—he was walking in his garden with one of his neighbors when a friend came running towards him, excitedly waving a newspaper.

"Good news, Danton!" he cried.

"What news?"

"The Girondins were sentenced to death and have all been executed."

The color drained from Danton's face. "You call that good news? Ah, no——."

"But they were a factious lot, after all," protested his friend.

"Factious! Factious? Which of us cannot be called factious? We all deserve to be guillotined as much as they. We will all of us share their fate, one after the other. These men in Paris will guillotine the whole Republic."

Twenty-one Girondins had been decapitated in a single batch. One of them, Valazé, was already dead when taken to the scaffold. Brissot, Vergniaud, Gensonné . . . all of them were men whom Danton had known well. It is said that they died singing the "Marseillaise," a chorus that diminished in volume as, one by one, their heads were taken off and their blood-soaked torsos thrown into a straw-lined cart beside the platform. Mme. Roland was not among them. Her turn came on November 8, and whatever the differences may have been that had once divided them, Danton cannot have heard the news with any pleasure.

She died bravely, after the Roman fashion. Perhaps she had Charlotte Corday in mind. Mme. Roland had been in prison when the steely assassin of Marat went to her death, but she had had the event described to her. Mme. Roland's comment on Charlotte Corday expresses perfectly her disgust with the Revolution and her contempt for the persons who now dominated it: "Charlotte Corday was a heroine worthy of a better time. I no longer wish to leave this prison except to die." The night before she died she penned the last sentence of those memoirs that she had been writing secretly in prison. "Nature, open your arms," she wrote. "God of justice, receive me! At the age of thirty-nine!" Rousseau thus exerted his influence upon her to the end. But in that final apostrophe, in the heart cry of a dying woman who believed herself to be still young, there is something more moving than may be found in the lachrymose musings of the masochist from Geneva.

For Danton, the death of the Girondins cast a deep gloom over the autumn landscape at Arcis. The season of mist—Brumaire, as the new calendar now called it—wore on and the weather grew raw. Danton stayed on at Arcis, unable to tear himself from the peace he would never know again. Then one day, just as he was leaving his house to join a hunting party that was to gather in the nearby village, a messenger from Paris unexpectedly made his appearance. He handed Danton a letter.

"Your friends implore you!" he announced. "You must come back to Paris at once. Robespierre and his party are preparing to destroy you."

Only a few moments earlier Danton had informed the village priest and a few close friends that he had at last decided to turn his back on politics, that he would stay on at Arcis forever, that he would raise his sons there, that he would live out the remainder of his life "in his native air, surrounded by his family and the friends he cared for." His face glowed as he spoke and a great weight seemed to have been lifted from his heart.

"There is no time to be lost, Danton," the courier insisted. "You must return to Paris immediately."

"What is it they want?" asked Danton. "Is it my head that Robespierre is after? He would never dare."

"You are optimistic. Come back! There is no time to be lost."

"Very well!" declared Danton with vehemence. "Go back to Paris then and tell Robespierre that I shall return and that when I arrive I will crush him!"

And so Danton left Arcis. Accompanied by his family and two servants he set out for Paris on November 17. He arrived there on the afternoon of the nineteenth, in time to attend an evening session at the Convention. He discovered then that during the period of his absence many sinister changes had taken place in the capital.

32

No PASSAGE in the Revolution offers more eloquent testimony to the power of those human and personal forces which shape or alter history than does the struggle between Danton and Robespierre. The difference between the two men was almost entirely one of temperament. In matters of ideology or politics their views were in many ways similar. Neither was in sympathy with the theory of Federalism, which on a political level brought the Girondins to ruin. Both were shocked by the excesses of the Extremist Hébert, who soon after Robespierre's succession to the Committee had emerged as the leader of the party of anarchy and atheism. Both men hoped to have the Republic of their dreams based on a system of law and civic order. And each supported what each believed to be in the best interest of the People.

But for Danton the Republic was to be a happy state, a product of all that his own background and temperament had contributed to his picture of a pleasant life. A chicken bubbled in every pot of his Utopia and a full bottle of *vin rouge* sat on every table. Danton was a materialist in a not unpleasant sense of the word. His own life reflects his full bodied enjoyment of *la bonne chère*: good food, good books (his library was of remarkable scope and size), good company and good talk enjoyed before the warming glow of a cheery hearthside. These were the components to him of the happy life in which all citizens of the Republic should share. He belonged in the admirable tradition of many of his fellow countrymen who feel that a well-prepared soup is as important an adjunct to human felicity as the discussion of philosophy or of art. He did not separate the pleasures of the flesh from those of the mind. His Republic therefore does not seem unattractive, though a refined spirit might wonder on whose tables the great vintages of Bordeaux and Burgundy were to be discovered and when, if ever, the chicken-in-the-pot might become *poulet à la Nève*. The citizens of Danton's state laughed heartily and went about their business in an atmosphere of joviality and freedom that approached laxity. The moral restraints which it was Robespierre's ambition to impose on France in no way interested Danton.

In his simplicity (and, sexually speaking, he appears to have been a direct and uncomplicated human male) Danton was unable to conceive of the nightmarish places to which ungoverned passion might lead another sort of man than himself. "I dreamed of a republic which all the world would have adored," lamented Camille Desmoulins, whose words echoed Danton's. "I could not have believed that men were so savage. . . ." Too late did Danton learn that all men were not like himself, content within the bosom of their families and that, by no means, did all the world wish to be happy. The orgy of blood-lust, the satanic frenzy of sadism to which Hébert invited the psychopaths of Paris, opened his eyes too late to the fact that there are men and women in this world who like to torture, to maim and to kill other men and women.

Just as Danton's Republic was an expression of his individual temperament, so too was Robespierre's. It is impossible to understand this strange man, about whom there are still so many differing opinions, without some glimpse into his past. Robespierre was born at Arras in 1758, four months after the marriage of his mother and father. He was therefore thirty-five years of age when (in November 1793) Danton returned from Arcis "to crush him"; he was thirty-six when he himself was finally guillotined in July 1794. Robespierre's mother died in childbirth when he was six, and not long after that grief Robespierre's father left Arras and vanished forever from the sight of his family. It has never been known either why he abandoned his children or where he went. Maximilien, his brother Augustin and his two sisters were brought up by their grandfather, their mother's parent, and by two maiden aunts.

They were people whose small revenues came from a brewery and their situation in life contrasts revealingly with the bumptious, up-and-coming peasant stock from which Danton came. They were stiff and respectable small bourgeois and had been such for many years. Before the Revolution Robespierre signed his name with the nobiliary particle, but any claim to noble birth had passed out of the hands of his remote ancestors. At the time when Robespierre lived there, Arras was a sleepy provincial capital without the dark medieval undertones that lent distinction and interest to such a city as Caen. It was a town of notaries, small businessmen, lawyers and modest *rentiers* where neither the rich nor the poor made their presence conspicuous. Arras lies some 150 miles northeast of Paris, not distant from the Channel. Its atmosphere is northern in quality. The light there is curiously redolent of the pallid greens and clear cold blues that are characteristic of certain early Flemish paintings.

Maximilien the boy prefigured Robespierre the Revolutionary. From an early age he appears to have been of an unnaturally serious disposition, rarely smiling, never joining in the games of his schoolmates. He preferred the company of his own thoughts to the friendship of other boys, and he viewed the more boisterous of his fellow pupils with disdain. To the end of his days he was to recoil from close contact with people. He worshiped the People with the fervor of a *dévot* worshiping God, but he shrank in distaste from all familiarity with a particular person. Among Danton's qualities that must have particularly irritated him were that leader's careless camaraderie and loud, hearty voice.

It is tempting to attribute such sensibility to the irregularity of his birth (of which he was well aware) or to the embarrassment that a fatherless boy might understandably suffer in so provincial a society as Arras—one may be certain that the neighbors discussed the "situation" of the Robespierre household with curiosity and pleasure. But one is left in the end with the conviction that he was born, as many persons are, deficient in humor and with an unnaturally acute consciousness of himself. The slights he imagined that he received from his schoolmates were consequently more magnified by him than they would have been by someone less self-centered, such as Danton.

Robespierre was a good student, although nature endowed him with no exceptional intelligence. He worked with application and method, always acceptable substitutes for those intermittent flashes of insight or originality that are too often the only recommendation of the pupil who is brilliant but lazy. His conduct at school was exemplary to a fault; he was considered something of a "goody-goody" by his fellow students. Prudent pupils such as he, who are priggishly obedient to school rules, are apt to be resentful of bolder school-mates who break regulations and they are especially resentful of those schoolmates who get away with it. They tend, in one way or another, to be tattletales.

This prudence, so conspicuous an element in Robespierre's character, was inborn and is the key to much that seems inconsistent in his political life. He was a Monarchist when it was unsafe to be otherwise; he became a Republican when it was inexpedient to remain a Monarchist. Such changes of attitude in no way bothered him, because he was one of those men who are able to justify any behavior to themselves by the invocation of vague moral or philosophic principles. Cowardice and jealousy prompted Robespierre to his view of many situations, but he never recognized such motives at work in himself. He seems to have been totally blind to the workings of his own character. He cannot be called a hypocrite. He lied to himself; he was able therefore to speak what he believed to be the truth to others. Mirabeau, a close observer of human nature, recognized this trait in Robespierre. "That man will go far," he declared. "He believes what he says."

When Robespierre was eleven his industry came to the attention of the Archbishop of Arras, who awarded him a twelve-year scholarship to the famous college of Louis-le-Grand in Paris. Here he remained until he was twenty-three years old, returning for his vacations to Arras and to the maiden aunts who were his guardians. "Everything went into his studies," recalls the Abbé Proyart, who was one of his teachers at Louis-le-Grand. "Stubbornly preoccupied with developing his mind, he seemed to forget that he had a heart, too, to consider. His study was his God."

It was at Louis-le-Grand, probably towards his fifteenth year, that he made his fatal acquaintance with the writings of Rousseau. The effect on him was no less than apocalyptic. "Divine man!" wrote Robespierre in his diary at the time of the States-General, addressing his dead hero. "It was you who taught me to know myself. When I was young you brought me to appreciate the true dignity of my nature and to reflect on the great principles which govern the social order. . . . I saw you in your last days and for me the recollection of that time will always be a source of proud joy. I contemplated your august features and saw there the imprint of those dark griefs which the injustice of men inflicted on you."

During his maturity Robespierre addressed only two entities in the *tu* form—the second person singular that in polite French is reserved for God and one's family: the People and Jean-Jacques Rousseau. There were times when he appears to have believed himself to be in direct communication with Rousseau's spirit and the agency on earth of the master's will. He himself stated, and publicly, that it was only the writings of Rousseau that gave him the strength to continue his work. He read the *Contrat Social* as other zealots have read the works of Karl Marx or the Bible. A copy of the *Contrat Social* was always by his bedside. It was a book that transformed a self-centered but commonplace young man into a fanatic.

In examining Robespierre's passionate idolatry of Rousseau one cannot but be struck by the close correspondence between these two men of certain faults of character. Whether Robespierre became an admirer of Rousseau's writings because he unconsciously recognized these similarities, or whether he caught, as it were, a disease to which he was susceptible, is an idle speculation. With both men, jealousy and suspicion were the offspring of an overweening egotism, and in both cases jealousy grew to pathological proportions.

It would be to misapprehend the nature of Robespierre's jealousy to picture him lying awake at night in Arras devoured by his envy of the French nobility and scheming a revolution to overthrow it. His was not the kind of envy that is awakened by some privileged but distant class of people. It was rather of the sort that is excited by those who are near. Robespierre's jealousy was always personal and specific. He did not care to see men whom he knew receiving more attention than himself. Marat's elaborate obsequies, for instance, filled him with jealousy. Danton's acclaim after the *coup d'état* of August 11 provoked his resentment—as did Danton's friendship with Camille Desmoulins, who had once been his, Robespierre's, friend. He was jealous of Vergniaud's Rousseauesque oratory just as he was jealous of Brissot's literary flair. His suspicion and jealousy of all who came near his beloved People was unnatural in its intensity. In that particular jealousy and in Robespierre's ill-advised idealization of the ignorant and debased mob to whom he pandered are to be found the source of many of the misfortunes that overwhelmed France during his tenure of power.

Suspicion, the twin sister of jealousy, clouded Robespierre's final days, as they did Rousseau's, with paranoid delusions of plots against his person, of conspiracies against him among his associates and hidden snares laid everywhere for his destruction. Retreating from men as they are in actuality, he drew closer to men as Rousseau had imagined that they ought to be. The People grew more precious to him, and his public utterance, in consequence, grew repetitive with references to "Virtue," that obsession of Rousseau which fascinated so many other Revolutionaries but which fell from Robespierre's thin lips with so singular and sinister a ring. Intelligent only in a narrow sense of the word, pedantic, literal, and unalterably provincial, Robespierre in his own mind ultimately divided human society into two classes, the virtuous and the vicious.

"Virtues are simple," he once declared. "They are modest and poor . . . they are the appanage of misfortune and the patrimony of the People. Vices, on the other hand, are rich. They are adorned by the love of pleasure and the snares of perfidy; they are escorted by all the dangerous talents; they are escorted by Crime." The punishment of the vicious—those, in other words, who had an appetite for pleasure or who were endowed with "dangerous" talents—became an obsession with him. In exact proportion to their references to Virtue, Robespierre's speeches became tinctured with allusions to "pollution," to "impure blood," to guilt and to the cleansing benefits of bloodshed.

It is thus through Robespierre that Rousseau most powerfully exerted his posthumous influence on the French Revolution. As is often the case when the philosophy of a prophet is interpreted by a too ardent disciple, the resemblance between Rousseau's dream and Robespierre's translation of it into reality is faint indeed. The Master would have been astonished could he have seen the varied effect of his writings on such dissimilar personalities as Charlotte Corday, Mme. Roland and Robespierre. Just as they interpreted the Revolution according to the promptings of their own tastes, so did these enthusiasts interpret the philosophy of Jean-Jacques Rousseau.

Robespierre returned to Arras in 1781. He was twenty-three years old; the Revolution was eight years away. He established himself as a lawyer in his native city, where, according to his biographer Gérard Walter, his practice was far from busy. The little material that remains to shed light on this period of Robespierre's life leaves one with the impression of a young man well armored in self-righteousness. There are hints of quarrels, of perfidious friends, of cases lost because of intrigue. The provincial cities of France, so seemingly placid to the passing eye, are often hotbeds of envy, dispute and malicious gossip. It is more than likely that the prim and humorless young lawyer, uncompromising in his narrow principles, may have aroused the rancor of his neighbors and colleagues, one of whom recalled him at this period as having "a weak, simpering face." His aunts and his sister Charlotte kept house for him. "We surrounded him with all those little attentions of which women alone are capable," recalled Charlotte. But the watchful ministrations of those adoring women did not always lighten the weight that seemed to hang upon the young lawyer's shoulders. "My aunts and I would sometimes scold him for seeming preoccupied when we were together of an evening. Whenever we played cards or chatted about small or insignificant things he would retire to a corner of the room, seat himself on a sofa and deliver himself to thought as though he were alone."

He rose every morning at six and devoted an hour or so to dressing. Neatness of person was a conspicuous expression of his character. All who knew him commented on this trait, which during the days of the Terror lent him the appearance of a dandy in contrast to the ragged and filthy horde that surrounded him. He went to court at ten, returned home for an early dinner at three, after which he took a walk; he spent the remaining hours of the afternoon either in his "study" or in the company of Charlotte and his aunts. His day was regulated by an undeviating schedule. The women of the household shielded him from any small intrusions that might have upset this ordered pattern. His life in Paris in the household of the Duplay family, where he lived during the Terror, was to be much the same. Routine in the disposition of his day, method in his work, tidiness in his dress were habits of life that were sympathetic to his temperament.

Not all of the early period is grey. In 1785 Robespierre was invited to join a local club called the "Society of the Rosati," an innocent Bacchic group among whom "roses, wine and poetry were honored." Such little associations were much in vogue just before the Revolution, and every provincial capital had its version of the one Robespierre joined. The Rosati held their meetings by the banks of a nearby river under an arbor of roses. The rules were boyish and charming. On entering the society, the candidate plucked a rose, inhaled its fragrance three times and then, after proposing a toast to all present, quaffed a bowl of rose-colored wine on which rose petals floated. He was handed a diploma on rose-colored paper sealed with a wax rose and perfumed with rose water. The initiate then read a poem of his own composition. Robespierre's, though suitably pastoral, casts an inadvertent light on his character. One stanza began with the lines:

> Je vois l'épine avec la rose
> dans les bouquets que vous m'offrez. . . .

> I see the thorn that's with the rose
> in these bouquets you offer me. . . .

One wonders if the recollection of that summer's afternoon beneath a rose arbor set by the banks of a peaceful French river ever returned to him during the turmoil of the days that were to come. Our glimpse of the event is fleeting, but it is so charming an expression of the age Robespierre was to help destroy that it contrasts irresistibly with the violence of his future. "To indulge in unaffected amusement, to laugh at ambition and all such thousand nullities—that is the chief aim of the Rosati." Such was the insouciant slogan of the pastoral academy at Arras. It is a pity that certain of its initiates did not regulate their lives according to its precepts.

The honor that attached to the invitation to join this group can have been but poor compensation to Robespierre for a slight he received at the hands of another local society. At about the time that Robespierre joined the Rosati, the president of the Court of the Province of Artois established an informal dining club at Arras. The purpose of this society was to discuss possible ameliorations in the administration of laws in the province. More than twenty lawyers, young men who were recommended to the President as being the "most able and learned" of the bar at Arras, were invited to join the group. Robespierre was not asked. The wound inflicted on his self-esteem appears to have been deep, and especially so because his practice was at this time going into a decline. He handled only ten cases in 1788. The figure contrasts revealingly with the number of cases awarded two fellow lawyers who were the same age as Robespierre. One of these (a "mediocre" man named Geoffroy) had fifty-two cases while another (Blanquet, who was two years younger than Robespierre) had seventy-seven.

Shortly after the snub administered by the Court of Artois, Robespierre published a justificatory pamphlet entitled *A Letter from a Lawyer in Arras to a Lawyer in Douai*. In it he observed that although his exclusion from the club had filled him with chagrin he consoled himself with the reflection that membership in it had been more determined by personal feelings and intrigue than by merit. "Everyone proposed the candidates that they liked, reserving the black ball for those they didn't like. There are always jealous people around who aim to destroy your happiness and who secretly plot your ruin. I have had more than one sad experience with this fact." The pamphlet continued in this strain: "Woe betide those aspiring lawyers who don't exert themselves to flatter their superiors or who are unwilling to lie. No matter how talented they might be, no matter how hard they work, they will be doomed to vegetate without cases. Arras is the worst city of all. . . ."

One senses that in 1788, when Robespierre was thirty, his future as an attorney was no longer promising. Resentment, or *rancune*—the word in French has overtones of spite and bitterness that its English translation does not quite convey—is a noun that figures prominently in Robespierre's vocabulary. He attributed to others, and probably with some justice, many of the emotions to which he himself was most susceptible. Balzac has unforgettably depicted the mean but all-too-human passions of the provincial bourgeoisie of France in *La Comédie Humaine;* Daumier has drawn their vulpine faces. Such neighbors may well have done Robespierre an injury. He knew the workings of the middle-class provincial mind because he himself was a conspicuous example of its kind. His skill in the use of calumny and slander, the craft with which he sowed the seeds of dissension, the instinct that prompted him to arouse in others, and then to use, the envy or the animosity that were his own, were the heritages of his environment. They were to be effective weapons in the arena of political dispute.

What was the path that led this spinsterish lawyer of fading promise out of the obscurity of his mediocre condition to such a position of power that for a short time he was able to impose on the laughter-loving French people his famous Reign of Virtue and of Terror? Many books have been written to answer that question; few of them are in agreement. The details of his rise to power necessarily belong to that department of history which specializes in the Revolution as a political phenomenon. Within the broader picture of the Revolution as a human drama one is nonetheless able to see the outline of the larger steps by which he ascended to the presidency of a dictatorship. The facts are probably less interesting (and less revealing) than the psychology of the man himself. Events presented themselves. He knew how to use them. Robespierre's temperament is an indispensable key to the examination of his political fortunes.

He knew instinctively how to profit from those private jealousies and resentments that almost from the moment of its inception divided the National Assembly. Dissension among his rivals was the rock on which he built his house. "I never saw anything but ruses and *astuce* in the man," wrote a member of the Convention when Robespierre was safely dead. "His single and most conspicuous talent was his Machiavellian skill in dividing men and sowing differences among them, of enticing others to go ahead of him and then either abandoning them or supporting them according to his ambitions or political opinion. . . ." Though the description is written by an enemy, all the facts of Robespierre's political life testify to the accuracy of its insight. Pitting party against party, he weakened each to his own advantage. He watched the Girondins destroy the Monarchists and profited by that. He watched Danton and Marat destroy the Girondins and he profited by that. He watched the dissension between Hébert and Danton and he profited by that. Dissension characterizes his relations not only with political parties but with individuals. Jealousy and quarreling seem to have been inevitable in any association with him. So had it been with Rousseau.

There grew in him the conviction that he was the incarnation of Rousseau's Virtue and that it was his mission to introduce the Reign of Virtue to France. Of this creed he believed himself to be both prophet and pontiff. Dead prophets are like dead lovers; they can be moulded without resistance into the ideal image desired by their admirers. "He is a hateful being," wrote Mme. Roland, "who lies to his own conscience." That was not true of Robespierre. It was in his conscience, indeed, where was born the conviction of the sanctity of his mission. He never lied to his conscience; he obeyed it. His conscience was the agency that gave him the moral translation of the mean and commonplace motives that were at work in the unconscious part of his nature. He never looked beyond his conscience. In positions of power such men can be very dangerous. Robespierre, with the assistance of his conscience, was able to view all those who were not of his own opinion and all men whom he didn't like, not as personal enemies, but as enemies of Virtue and of the state. "Heretics" during the Reign of Terror were called "Aristocrats"— a description of most victims of the Terror that the *ci-devant* College of Heraldry would vigorously have disputed. The epithets may vary but the outcome for the suspected and the convicted, whether under Torquemada or Robespierre, was the same.

Robespierre has not gone without his defenders, among them such historians of distinction as Mathiez and Hamel. And it cannot be denied that odious though the man may seem to biographers of one temperament, he was not wanting in qualities that other men might find admirable. He was incorruptible. Among his partisans his nickname was, in fact, *l'Incorruptible,* a compliment which, when pronounced in French and with a Parisian stress upon the *r,* has a singularly disagreeable sound to the ear.

Neither money nor the things that money can buy were of the slightest interest to him. Incorruptible himself, he kept a watchful eye on those of his associates who he suspected were more susceptible than he to certain temptations. Along with despising hypocrites and opportunists, he abhorred the kind of man who might use the Revolution for his own financial gain. And in this it is difficult to resist a certain sympathy with Robespierre. Under the Incorruptible's bilious eye those advocates of change who hoped to enrich themselves out of the confiscated goods of the former rich were obliged to move with trembling and caution. It was only after Robespierre's downfall that the great town houses of Paris gradually began to be occupied by their new tenants—successful speculators in currency, politicians who sold army contracts and officials of the government who had profited from the misfortunes of their country. During Robespierre's reign the progenitor of the princely house of Murat still curried horses at his hostelry near Pau and that vigorous Jacobin, Cambacérès, the future Duke of Parma, still fulminated against other people's titles of nobility from the austerity of his Republican garret.

Gross manners, vulgar show, the loud or overbearing behavior of those whom the French call *nouveaux riches* were all offensive to him and incompatible with the character of the Republic he envisioned.

Robespierre was chaste. But his chastity was not of the kind that depends upon any exercise of the will. He had no taste for the pleasures of sexual or psychic intimacy. Everything in his life, on the contrary, hints at a distinct distaste for that desire which is popularly believed to motivate the greater portion of the male sex. The testimony of certain of our present-day novelists to the contrary, it is difficult to resist the conclusion that some men are more driven by ambition and envy than they are by a desire for sexual intercourse. Beyond doubt Robespierre's chastity was a very significant component in his character, both a symptom of deeper motives and the cause of those more superficially expressed. From this distance in time it cannot be susceptible to Freudian diagnosis. It was probably at the source of Robespierre's antipathy for Danton.

Danton's virility both repelled and fascinated this male spinster. Danton's vulgar remark to him that "the best virtue is the virtue that I practice with my wife every night," and another remark that Danton once made to him that Camille Desmoulins practiced a certain "shameful and secret vice" were carefully recorded in Robespierre's private notebook, from which he distilled the poison of future calumny. Danton's masculinity must have been a constant conscious and unconscious humiliation to him. Beside Danton, Robespierre's shrill voice seemed to grow shriller and his small stature smaller. He suspected what others knew—that in the privacy of his circle of friends Danton laughingly dismissed him as a "eunuch."

Robespierre doubtless suspected too what Danton could scarcely have concealed, that Danton considered his cherished dreams of a Republic of Virtue, the outcome of his mystical communion with the *Contrat Social* and with Rousseau, as "a lot of nonsense."

This Republic of Robespierre's dreams was very clearly defined by him only a few weeks before Danton's death. He presented it to the Assembly from the offices of the Committee of Public Safety. Like its author it has not gone without its admirers. But to such cynical Frenchmen as Danton it can only have appeared ludicrous in its naïve and ignorant suppositions about human nature. And to those lovers of life's warm and colorful inessentials, it is a bleak and sterile prospect indeed that Robespierre proudly proffered to France: a world of pompous, impossible virtues, a world devoid of beauty and pleasure or even the promise of them—and consequently devoid of life.

"The only ambition in our Republic," he stated, "will be the desire to be worthy of glory and to serve the nation. Souls will grow larger as they exchange Republican sentiments with one another. The arts will embellish Liberty, which in turn will ennoble the arts. Commerce will become the source of public riches, not of the monstrous opulence of a few families. We wish to substitute morality for egotism in our country, rectitude for empty honors; principle for habits, duty for etiquette, the love of glory for the love of money, merit for intrigue, talent for superficial wit, the delights of contentment for the weariness of self-indulgence [*volupté*]. . . ."

Thus were "the happy-go-lucky, frivolous and miserable French people" to become "magnanimous, powerful and happy," and the virtues of the Republic to replace "all the vices and puerilities of the monarchy." Among these vices and puerilities, alas, were the paintings of Fragonard and Boucher, for which Robespierre had no taste; the letters of Mme. du Deffand, which he had not read; the soft paste porcelains of Sèvres, whose spirit he could not have understood, and all the other useless frivolities that composed the famous *douceur de vivre* of the *ancien régime*. The arts have rarely been at their ease in expressing the ideals of dictatorial political theorists and, Robespierre's contention to the contrary, they seem to have been far more at home embellishing the Duc de Penthièvre's pleasure pavilion at Sceaux than they were "embellishing Liberty."

It is often the deficiency of social reformers that, overly earnest themselves, they are incapable of understanding the appetite for pleasure that makes life supportable for all classes of men. It does not seem to have occurred to Robespierre that the poor, too, might have enjoyed those vices and voluptuous pleasures that he deplored in the rich (who at the time of the Revolution, ironically, were practicing the austerities recommended by Rousseau; they wept in the solitude of their hermitages and went on diets). Were there many people, one wonders, in the France of reality, the flesh-and-blood republic of living men over which Robespierre presided, who really wished "to substitute the love of glory for the love of money" or the delights of domestic contentment for the fatigue of *volupté*? Had Robespierre looked carefully into his own heart he might have discovered that "morality" is not so easily substituted for "egotism" as he wished to believe; nor, for that matter, is "merit" for "intrigue." Had such been the case Maximilien Robespierre might have remained an undistinguished country lawyer.

Robespierre's personal appearance seems to have rather suggestively reflected his character. Many descriptions of his appearance remain to us, and although most are tinctured by the strong feeling of those who describe him, there are certain elements consistent in all of them. Taking these descriptions in conjunction with several excellent portraits done by such artists as Moreau le Jeune and David, we are able to evoke a distinct impression of Robespierre's appearance. Admirers and critics are in accord when they speak of his face as being "catlike." All his portraits confirm this. His narrow sloping skull, wide-set, slightly slanting eyes, tiny nose and prim, simpering lips were feline in character. His eyes were green and, because he was short-sighted, he often wore spectacles whose lenses were tinted green. The neatness of his person and his self-sufficiency augmented the catlike quality of his face. His complexion is described variously as being "green," "pasty," "sickly" and "bilious." He is known to have suffered from bad digestion, and as a specific for this he would suck on three or four oranges a day. His bones were delicate and fine, but his hands were marred by his habit of nail-chewing. He was short of stature and wore high-heeled shoes. "His features were mean, his complexion pallid and his veins were of a greenish hue," pronounced Mme. de Staël, who had met him in 1789. A man named Fievée has left what is perhaps the most telling description of him. Fievée heard Robespierre addressing the Jacobin Club in 1793 and never forgot the scene.

"Robespierre came slowly forward. He was one of the few men who at this time still wore the costume in vogue before the Revolution. His hair was dressed and powdered in the old style. He resembled a tailor of the *ancien régime* more than anything else. He wore spectacles which probably served to conceal the twitchings of his pallid face. His delivery was slow and measured. His phrases were so long that every time he stopped to raise his spectacles one thought that he had nothing more to say, but after looking slowly and searchingly over the audience in every quarter of the room he would readjust his glasses and then add some more phrases to his sentences which were already of inordinate length."

There is something about this description of Robespierre pausing in his speech and lifting his spectacles that rings very true. That myopic, searching glance was to make men's blood freeze in the three months that preceded his overthrow.

Robespierre left Arras in May 1789, one of eight deputies who had been elected to represent Artois at the States-General. Neglected by the Assembly, he devoted his attention to the Jacobin Club, gradually shaping it into the dangerous instrument that it became—a kind of political holding company which, through its members who sat in the Assembly, was able to direct the votes of that governing body, and through its representatives in the Commune was able, when needed, to call forth the rude mob power of the Sections. Putting the events of the Revolution to use, Robespierre entrenched himself in the Jacobin Club and at the same time extended the power of the Jacobins throughout France. It was through Jacobin influence that he was to establish himself in the Committee of Public Safety. And through the Committee of Public Safety he worked towards the dictatorship. He moved with speed but with caution, wheedling greater powers for the Committee out of the Convention with one hand and extorting them by menaces with the other. The mass execution of the Girondin deputies at the end of October had sent a shudder through the Convention and had demoralized the weak and ineffectual Plain even further.

By November 1793, when Danton returned to Paris from his vacation at Arcis, Robespierre had progressed far in his ascent. But between himself and the summit that cautious politician saw two obstacles looming before him. One was Hébert, representing the forces that were to the left of him; the other was Danton, representing those that were to the right. The party of the Mountain, having successively destroyed all its opponents, was now, like a pack of sharks, ready to turn upon itself.

33

THE HÉBERTISTS had been a thorn in Robespierre's side since his entry into the Committee of Public Safety. They had taken over Danton's old club, the Cordeliers', and they had insinuated themselves into positions of power at the Commune. The vilest dregs of the populace composed their party. They were a vociferous remnant of Marat's anarchistic activities. In Marat's time they had served Robespierre's purpose well, but now that Robespierre was in the Committee they were a nuisance. With their antireligious antics and their coarse and lewd behavior they became in Robespierre's eyes a menace to the state.

The man who lent his name to this party, Hébert, was one of those personalities common during the Revolution, whose private life contrasted strangely with their public appearance. On the title page of his salacious newssheet *Père Duchesne* he was represented as being a gruff, pipe-smoking old sage; in actuality he was a small dandified man with fluttery white hands and a "fussy, effeminate manner." For filth and invective his newspaper was without a rival during the Revolution. Compared to it, *L'Ami du Peuple* reads like the London *Times.* Yet no coarse or vulgar word was ever spoken in the sanctuary of Hébert's comfortable apartment, which he shared with his wife, an ex-nun. Hébert was the man who, during her trial, accused Marie Antoinette of having sexually abused her son. In doing so he brought the wrath of Robespierre down on him. "That fool!" Robespierre declared. "It's not enough that Antoinette should be a Messalina. That idiot must make her an Agrippina." Yet Hébert himself was a tender and thoughtful father. A few weeks after the Marie Antoinette episode Robespierre was given further reason to resent Hébert's interference with the working of the government.

On November 10, incited by the Commune (of which Hébert was leader), the rabble of the Paris Sections held a "Festival of Reason" within the precincts of Notre Dame. The cathedral was stripped of its religious embellishments and a Greek temple made of cardboard was constructed in the nave. An actress from the opera impersonated the Goddess of Reason while the crowd sang the "Ça Ira" as she was enthroned. A few days earlier the Constitutional Bishop of Paris had been ordered by the Hébertists to publicly abjure the Catholic faith. "If you do not do this you are a dead man," they warned him. The Bishop obediently presented himself before the Convention and casting aside the insignia of his office, declared that there should be no other worship in France but that of Liberty and Equality.

Bishop Gobel's abjurance and the so-called Festival of Reason were signals for an outbreak of blasphemous scenes. Mercier, a witness of them, has described "the infuriated populace dancing before the sanctuary and howling the Carmagnole. The men wore no breeches; the necks and busts of the women were bare. In their wild whirling they imitated those whirlwinds, the forerunners of tempests, that ravage and destroy all that is in their path. In the darkness of the sacristy they indulged in the abominable desires that had been kindled in them during the day. . . ." One such group appeared before the Convention to demand that the worship of Virtue be substituted for that of "that Jew slave" and his mother, "the adulterous woman of Galilee." The Convention listened to this proposal in silence and nervously referred it to the Committee of Instruction. A Hébertist named Clootz, whose militant atheism was informed by the psychotic intensity of acute religious mania, declared to the Jacobins that "a religious man is a depraved beast. He resembles those animals that are kept to be shorn and roasted for the benefit of merchants and butchers."

Robespierre looked on these scenes with a disapproving eye. It shocked him to see drunken blasphemers and prostitutes representing themselves as the worshipers of Virtue and Reason. Offensive as these exhibitions were to his taste, he had still further reason to deplore them, for he recognized in them a threat to the authority of the Committee on Public Safety. Hébert and his Commune were arrogating to themselves a right that they did not have: to decide for France its form of worship. The Hébertists were behaving as though Marat were still alive. Now that he was on the Committee, Robespierre could say as those who had gone before him had said: "The Revolution stops with me." In Hébert's anti-Christian manifestations Robespierre recognized the overture to more of those "popular" uprisings which had swept his predecessors out of office. He was determined that this would not happen again. On November 21, a few days after Danton's return to the capital, Robespierre gave a sharp warning to the Hébertists in a speech against atheism.

"Under the pretense of destroying superstition there are men among us who would make a kind of religion out of atheism itself. Any individual may have on that matter whatever opinion he pleases . . . but the legislator would be mad to accept such a doctrine. The National Convention is not a writer of books. It is a political and popular body charged with protecting not only the rights but the *character* of the French people. . . . atheism is aristocratic; the idea of a Great Being that watches over oppressed innocence and punishes crime is altogether popular. . . ." These pronouncements were greeted with a gratifying round of applause, which put the Hébertists out of countenance. Then, after having given a warning, Robespierre suddenly struck: "There is an army of foreign spies among us, of paid wretches who insinuate themselves everywhere, even into the heart of popular societies. I demand then that this society purge itself of this criminal horde! I demand that Dubuisson be driven from the society and with him those two other intriguers, Desfieux and Pereira. I demand that a purifying scrutiny be held at this tribune to unmask all agents of foreign powers who may be among us."

Dubuisson, Desfieux and Pereira, all Hébertists, were duly expelled from the Club—a disgrace that usually presaged arrest and the death sentence. A "purifying scrutiny" was then held. This ceremony, which involved a great deal of breast-beating, confession, "virtuous denunciation" and challenge, was (and still is) a form of self-exposure greatly relished by people of Robespierre-like mentality. Under the guise of patriotism and in the name of civic duty friend can accuse friend, the seeds of suspicion be sown and the fruit of dissension harvested. Robespierre presided over this *épuration* or "cleansing" of the society, which lasted for several weeks. In the course of it several more Hébertists fell victim to the scrutiny of their Jacobin colleagues.

Danton had even less taste than Robespierre for what he called the "religious masquerades" of the Hébertists. He appeared before the Convention on November 26, soon after his return to Paris, and made a scathing denunciation of the Hébertists. "Why does the Convention waste its time on these people? The People are sick of them." Then, with greater temerity, he spoke against the Terror itself. "Perhaps the Terror once served a certain purpose," he declared, "but it ought not to strike at innocent people. No one wishes to see an individual treated as a guilty person because he doesn't happen to have sufficient revolutionary vigor."

On December 1 Danton again spoke before the Convention, this time openly attacking the Hébertists. He demanded the recall of the Hébertist commissioners who had been sent by the Convention to the Vendée, where they were disgracing themselves and the Republic by their acts of gross cruelty. Although Danton's remarks were directed at the Hébertists, Robespierre's sensitive ear detected in them an oblique thrust at the Committee of Public Safety. The Hébertists answered Danton with an attack of their own at the Jacobin Club two days later. Danton went to the rostrum of the Club and made an emotional appeal. "Am I no longer the man whom you have so often embraced as your friend and with whom you swore to die in the same dangers? . . . I defy malice to furnish any proof against me."

The Jacobin Club was still in the midst of the "purifying scrutiny" of its members. The mood was therefore propitious for an examination of Danton. Affecting to take Danton's plea for "proofs" *au pied de la lettre,* Robespierre scampered to the rostrum.

"If Danton demands an investigation into his conduct and thinks it will be serviceable to him I, for one, do not object to complying with his request. *If he wishes the crimes with which he has been charged to be specified, I shall now enumerate them . . .*" an appropriate beginning to one of the most skillfully malicious speeches Robespierre was ever to make. By affecting to defend Danton, Robespierre was able to calumniate him. Robespierre now enumerated the rumors about Danton that had been circulating during his absence, adding a few to boot. "Danton, you are accused of having emigrated, of having gone to Switzerland laden with the spoils of your corruption. Some people even say that you were at the head of a conspiracy to enthrone Louis XVII [The Dauphin imprisoned in the Tower] with the understanding that you were to be the Regent." Robespierre then turned and spoke to his fellow members of the Jacobin Club, giving Danton an ambiguous testimonial that more resembled the kiss of death than the defense it purported to be. "I may be mistaken about Danton, but I have seen him in his family circle; his conduct there deserves nothing but praise. In his political attitudes too I have observed him very closely. It is true that he was slow to hate Brissot and to suspect Dumouriez, but if I did not always agree with him, who am I to conclude that he has betrayed his country? He has always *seemed* to be serving it zealously.

"Danton wishes to be put on trial here. He is right. Let me be put on trial too. Let all those people who have anything to say against Danton now come forward."

This masterpiece of unction and malice has been singled out by some historians as an example of Robespierre's forbearance and pointed to as evidence of the man's generous impartiality! Not even Maximilien wished to have it accepted in quite so literal a manner, as his response to the first issue of Camille's *Vieux Cordelier* clearly suggests. "After that tremendous speech of Robespierre's," wrote Camille in his paper, "it is now impossible for any man to raise his voice against Danton without giving a public receipt, as it were, for the guineas of Pitt." This was not at all the sense in which Robespierre had wished his words to be taken. Camille's dithyrambic and deliberate misinterpretation alerted Robespierre to the latest menace to his Committee of Public Safety—the *Vieux Cordelier*.

That newspaper had been inspired by Danton's plea to Camille— "Take up your pen and plead for clemency; I will support you." Its title suggested the difference between the old Cordeliers—Danton, Camille and their friends—and the new club, which had now become the citadel of the Hébertists. The paper was, in fact, a vehicle of the "Dantonist" party. Its purpose, discreetly masked in the first two issues, was to advance Danton, the "Old Cordelier," as Robespierre's rival and Danton's policy of clemency as an alternative to that of Robespierre's Reign of Terror. Camille prudently submitted the first two numbers to Robespierre's inspection, tying his hands with an ingratiating dedication and placing the sheet under the protection of both Danton and Robespierre, "his two great friends." This gratuitous coupling of his name with Danton's can hardly have pleased Robespierre. "Victory is ours!" pronounced Camille. "In the midst of so many fallen reputations, that of Robespierre still stands because he has held out his hand in friendship to his rival in patriotism, to our eternal President of the Old Cordeliers, Danton. . . ."

Robespierre had in fact done no such thing, nor can he have cared for the statement (even if it were true) that the reason his reputation still stood high was because he had held out his hand in friendship to Danton. He grimaced, but he lent his halfhearted support to Camille's enterprise because he saw in the paper a means of destroying the troublesome Hébertists. He had used Camille's talents before, to calumniate the Girondins.

The journal enjoyed an immediate success. The first issue was sold out within hours. Paris eagerly awaited the second, which appeared five days later. On the surface both issues were savage assaults on the Extremists, yet in them Robespierre's alert nose scented criticism of the Terror and of the Committee itself. "Open the prisons," Camille implored, "and release the two hundred thousand suspects who are in them! In the Declaration of Man's Rights there is no house of suspicion. There are only houses of arrest."

The second issue of the *Vieux Cordelier* created an even greater sensation than the first. Camille's program of clemency excited a wide popular response. Its unexpected success caused Robespierre to stir uneasily, first with jealousy and then with alarm. From the rostrum of the Convention Danton preached what Camille wrote: "Open the prisons!" And the Convention, heretofore paralyzed by the Law of Suspects, by the Revolutionary Tribunal and the guillotine, suddenly began to take heart. On December 12, two days after the publication of the second issue of the *Vieux Cordelier,* an audacious deputy, Bourdon de l'Oise, who was a friend of Danton rose in the Convention and proposed that the members of the Committee of Public Safety be subject to re-election. "Although the majority of the Committee enjoys the confidence of the Convention," he stated, "there are several members on it who do not."

The significance of these words was not lost on Robespierre. He was able to defer the election issue, but he knew that the time had now come for him to act. The Dantonists were said to have already drawn up their list of candidates for the new Committee. A great wave of hope passed over the choked prisons of the city.

Just as Danton had a devoted follower and agent in the person of Camille Desmoulins, so did Robespierre have a disciple in the person of that strange and terrible young man, Louis-Antoine de St. Just. Described by those who saw him as being as "beautiful as an angel," St. Just has been better known under the sobriquet "the Angel of Death." Chiseled as finely as the statues of Periclean Athens, his white features aptly suggested the medium of sculpture. He was as cold as marble and as inaccessible as stone to all the warm passions of the living.

The son of respectable people from Blérancourt, he had developed during the final years of the *ancien régime* into one of those cruel and conscienceless young men who are the despair of their parents and of society. He had finally been placed under the restraint of a *lettre de cachet* by his widowed mother for the theft of her jewels and her money. During his incarceration he wrote a dull pornographic poem called *Organt*. Like so many Revolutionaries he was convinced that he possessed exceptional literary talents. In 1792 he was elected to the Convention by the *Nivernais*. He was an impassioned admirer of Robespierre and finally made his acquaintance after a series of letters to him in one of which he stated that "I know you as I know God, Robespierre." Through Jacobin influence he had been appointed to the Committee of Public Safety. His appointment preceded Robespierre's by a month and this enabled St. Just to prepare the ground for him. He was more skilled than Robespierre at public speaking and far more audacious. Robespierre therefore availed himself of St. Just's services when he did not care to expose himself to a situation that might be dangerous or compromising.

Like his master, St. Just was a fanatic. For all Robespierre's faults —indeed *because* of his all too human faults—Robespierre belongs well within the pale of recognizable humankind. St. Just does not. There is a frigidity about him, an inhumanity, a profound strangeness that makes him seem as alien as some species of reptile or insect. Unlike Robespierre he appears to have been bloodthirsty. His speeches are choked with blood-drenched imagery. "The vessel of the Revolution can arrive in port only on a sea reddened with torrents of blood," he once declared to the Convention. Such references to blood and immolation, voluptuous in their repetition, are common to all St. Just's public utterance. His "Virtue" was even more austere than Robespierre's. No temptation ever seduced this cold paragon into stepping from his pedestal. His proposals for the regenerated France of the future reflect his almost total alienation from humankind: all boys over five years of age were to be taken by the state to be raised in battalions, either as farmers or as soldiers. At sixteen the male citizens of St. Just's Utopia who were not soldiers were to become "workers." Rulers and citizens alike were to wear coarse cloth and to sleep on straw mats. Since he did not recognize the existence of women, he has given us no picture of their lot in his Spartan Republic, but we may assume that it would not have been to the taste of many of today's examples of their sex. "He who does not conform must be driven from the gates of the city," pronounced St. Just (the quotation was taken from Rousseau) in summation. In the meanwhile, of the real France, the France of Robespierre's emergent Committee, St. Just stated, "We must not only punish traitors, but all people who are not enthusiastic. There are only two kinds of citizens: the good and the bad. The Republic owes the good its protection. To the bad it owes only death."

At the time of Danton's return from Arcis-sur-Aube this stern young visionary was on a mission to Strasbourg, where under circumstances that might have seduced a stronger man "he displayed at all times the spirit of a Scipio." Robespierre, taking alarm at the rising wave of popular sympathy for Danton's program of clemency (in which Robespierre correctly saw a move by Danton's party to overthrow Robespierre's Committee), sent an urgent message to St. Just summoning him back to Paris. The two men put their heads together and examined the field on which they were about to do battle.

The great danger to Robespierre's party (or to "the Committee," as he and St. Just probably preferred to call it) was that the two warring factions, the Dantonists and the Hébertists, might unite against it. Because they estimated—and correctly—that of these two factions the Dantonists would be by far the more difficult to destroy, St. Just and Robespierre decided to eliminate the Hébertists first, letting Camille drive an ever-deepening wedge between Danton and Hébert with his vitriolic attacks in the *Vieux Cordelier* and so isolate each party from the possibility of *rapprochement* with the other.

In the meanwhile, with caution and through the agency of the

Jacobin Club, Robespierre began to nibble at the edges of the Hé-bertist party, arresting one here, "cleansing" the Club of another there. This was the purpose behind those soul-searching sessions at the Jacobin Club. Robespierre by this means incited the Jacobins to do under the guise of group indignation the work that he did not yet dare to do—to accuse and make liable for arrest those Extremists who might come to the support of Hébert when Hébert's hour for expulsion came round. In his management of this difficult matter, Robespierre's tactics were, as usual, admirably astute. It was not for nothing that his enemies called him the *chat-tigre*. The wheels of the approaching juggernaut were, as always, well greased with moral unction and civic righteousness.

Unknown still to all but a few of those who were about to be in-volved in the battle, Robespierre held a card of high value con-cealed in his hand. The matter of the embezzlement of the East India Company funds had finally come to his notice. Certain Hébert-ists and Dantonists were involved together in this swindle. The love of money like that of women often transcends those small doctrinal differences that are the preoccupation of political or religious zealots. Though the ex-monk Chabot was a Hébertist and though Fabre d'Églantine was a follower of Danton, a community of interest that they discovered in the tempting coffers of the East India Company brought the two men together. This complicated affair, which in-volved the falsification of state documents and forgery of certain sig-natures, depended for its ultimate success on the kind of mutual trust which is not uncommon among experienced thieves but which these too greedy revolutionaries did not have. Sometime during October (while Danton was still at Arcis) Fabre suddenly took fright and decided to protect himself by denouncing Chabot and his other asso-ciates in the East India embezzlement to Robespierre. In order to dis-tract Robespierre's attention from himself and from the real crime, Fabre wove an intricate tale, most of it untrue, about a far-reaching foreign conspiracy being hatched in Paris.

Few men were more disposed to a suspicious view of foreigners and to a fear of conspiracy than Robespierre. Fabre's strange tale was filled with an assembly of motley characters such as have always made the flesh of men like Robespierre creep—foreign financiers, defrocked priests, Jewish speculators, men with suspicious-sounding, un-French names like Gunzman and Pereira. The German court even appeared to be involved in this plot, for the Frei brothers, whose sister was married to Chabot, were discovered to have been ennobled in Prussia under the name of Schönfeld. For a fee (and for a marriage settlement that ran into the hundreds of thousands), Chabot advanced the interests of his brothers-in-law behind the mask of patriotism. It is a difficult matter to determine where truth ends and fiction begins in this murky affair. But there can be no doubt that Chabot, Fabre d'Églantine and the Frei brothers were thieves. There is little evidence of any organized "foreign plot."

With mingled emotions of relief and terror, Robespierre seized the card that Fabre had unexpectedly handed him. Relief, because he now had at hand the means to destroy the Hébertist party; terror, because to the last detail he believed all that Fabre had told him.

So at the Jacobin Club there began a fresh series of arrests and expulsions. Robespierre began to make many cryptic references to "foreigners." He warned the Sections about granting certificates of good citizenship too easily. "The foreigner who creeps among you," he declared, "disguised in a red bonnet in order to plunge a dagger into your back, is no less dangerous than the Austrian slave who plunges his murderous bayonet into the breast of a defender of freedom!"

Chabot, sensing danger, now hurried to Robespierre to make his own denunciations. Thus were St. Just and Robespierre handed the evidence they needed of Fabre's dishonesty. And Fabre was said to be Danton's "right-hand man." If the hand was gangrened, who could not be made to believe that the body too was unhealthy?

On December 15 Camille published the famous third number of his *Vieux Cordelier*. He did not submit this issue to Robespierre's prepublication scrutiny as he had the other two. That fact alone would have been enough to prejudice Robespierre's view of it. Made bold by the success of the first two issues and by the surge of public sentiment in favor of Danton, Camille apparently felt that he no longer needed to put himself under Robespierre's protection.

Robespierre would in any case never have given his approval to this particular issue of the *Vieux Cordelier,* for it was an impassioned attack on the Law of Suspects, the very cornerstone on which Robespierre's government had been built. Purporting to be a translation of Tacitus, Camille's third number portrayed Roman life under Caligula and Nero, when suspicion drove men wild and all talents and distinction were leveled by the sword of an envious despot. The insinuation behind this apt but unwise comparison was not lost on Robespierre. Camille concluded the sensational third issue of his journal with another exhortation to open the prisons of the Republic. "Do you really think," he asked, openly addressing the Committee of Public Safety, "that these helpless women, these old men, these poor laggards of the Revolution whom you have shut up are dangerous?"

Copies of the sheet were snapped up by an avid public the instant they appeared on the stands. Within hours the entire edition had been sold out. Emboldened by Camille's cry for clemency, a great crowd appeared before the Convention to demand the release of suspects. And from the rostrum of the Convention Danton continued to say what Camille wrote but in even bolder and more outspoken words. The Terror, he declared, was no longer necessary. The victories that the Republican armies were now enjoying proved that. From all over France and from abroad came nothing but good news. Toulon had been recaptured in the first part of December. The civil war in the Vendée, the insurrections at Lyons and Marseilles had been put down. There was thus no longer any excuse for the Terror. The Committee of Public Safety, which had used these disturbances to acquire dictatorial powers for itself, should therefore resign these powers. In the beginning Danton advanced this argument through a surrogate named Philippeaux, a personal friend whom the Committee had removed from a position of authority in the Vendée. Philippeaux returned to Paris with a horrifying report of Hébertist excesses in the Vendée, which he made public before the Convention in early December.

The activities of the men whom Philippeaux denounced, such creatures as Carrier in Brittany, Lebon at Arras and Collot d'Herbois at Lyons, pass all belief. Carrier, a man subject to fits during which he would fall to the floor howling and snapping like an animal, appears to have been a madman. His closest associates, cutthroats themselves, feared to approach him. He talked incessantly of killing and while doing so would often slash his sword through the air in the gesture of a man cutting off heads. The details of the massacres in Brittany for which he was responsible surpass in horror anything that took place in Paris during the Terror. The man had a peculiar hatred of children. "They are all little whelps," he declared, "and they must be butchered without mercy." Five hundred peasant boys and girls were driven into a field outside Nantes and upon Carrier's orders shot down and then clubbed to death. The famous *noyades,* or wholesale drownings in the Loire, were his invention. Great rafts were filled with the men and women who were Carrier's victims (nothing resembling a trial preceded these massacres), and in the middle of the river a plug was removed from the bottom of the raft and all on board went to their deaths. Women still clutching their babies, old peasants, invalid men and adolescent boys and girls too young to comprehend the "crimes" of which they were accused, made up the cargo of these vessels of death. The number of victims who perished in the *noyades* has never been established. One member of Carrier's committee placed it at over six thousand. To amuse himself Carrier would often cause men and women to be stripped naked before him and then bound together as couples before being thrown into the river. *"On attachait deux à deux les personnes de l'un et l'autre sexe, toutes nues et tournées comme pour s'accoupler."* These were known as "Republican marriages."

Another such madman named Lebon at Arras (and his wife, a former nun) left a record of atrocities behind them second only to Carrier's. Lebon preferred the leisurely guillotine to the swift methods of mass extermination used by Carrier at Nantes or by Collot d'Herbois and Fouché at Lyons. The guillotinings at Arras were accompanied by orgiastic frenzies. Lebon and his wife, like Asiatic despots, would watch the daily executions from the balcony of their house, which overlooked the public square. Their victims were taken indiscriminately from all walks of life, Republicans and Royalists alike, although the rich were the first to be dispatched, so that the Lebon couple and their equerries could take possession of their houses, furniture and wine cellars. "The Criminal Tribunal established at Arras will first pass revolutionary judgment on those who are distinguished by their wealth or by their talents . . .": such was the policy pronounced by Lebon upon his arrival in the unfortunate city over whose ruin he was appointed to preside.

The horrors at Lyons began on December 4, the day before Camille published his first number of the *Vieux Cordelier.* Lyons had capitulated to the army of the Convention some weeks earlier and an appalling vengeance was about to be wrought on the rebellious city. The executions began with a mass shooting. Some two hundred men were tied together and mowed down with grapeshot in a meadow outside the city walls. Robespierre's agent Achard, in a mood of patriotic exaltation, reported the matter to Paris— "What delights you would have tasted could you have seen national justice wrought on 209 scoundrels! Oh, what majesty! What a lofty tone! It was thrilling to see all those wretches chew the dust. What a cement this is going to be for our Republic." Achard was witness to but the beginning of these appalling scenes at Lyons, which another witness, apparently a disciple of Rousseau, extolled because they were held out-of-doors "under Nature's beautiful vault."

Such men as these, though they were beyond political affiliation (their kind may be found in all violent periods of history, associated with every side. Royalist or Republican, Fascist or Communist; whatever the label may be, they bring disgrace upon any group with which they are allied), were attached to the party of Hébert because that party condoned and encouraged their pillage and savagery.

Philippeaux, in his report on these excesses, not only denounced the Hébertist commissioners responsible for them, but also introduced a strong hint that the Committee of Public Safety was to be criticized for tolerating them. He implied, indeed, that the Committee had used the disturbances in the Vendée to keep itself in power.

Danton seized on Philippeaux's report with glee and advanced its views everywhere. In January he grew reckless. One day he turned to the assembled members of the General Security Committee (the police committee of the Convention) and said tauntingly, "You ought to read Philippeaux's memoranda about how to end the war in the Vendée which you have perpetuated for the sake of making yourselves indispensable." In making such a statement Danton committed a major tactical error. His indiscriminate hostility towards all members of the General Security Committee and the Committee of Public Safety only succeeded in bringing the ill-assorted individuals composing these bodies together at a time when it would have been to his profit to have kept them divided. As the Girondins had done before him, he too began to scatter his shots, firing in all directions towards Hébertists and the Committee alike, wounding some but killing none.

The Committee of Public Safety was, in fact, already rent by those bitter personal dissensions that were to manifest themselves after Danton's execution. But however violent these differences may have been, the members of the Committee (along with the members of the

Security Committee) had it in common that they were "in power," as Danton bluntly phrased it, and for reasons of self-preservation, they now drew together.

With the publication of the third number of the *Vieux Cordelier* —and five days later of the fourth, which was an even bolder assertion of Danton's hostility towards the Committee—Robespierre became seriously alarmed. "Love of country cannot exist," wrote Camille in an unmistakable allusion to Robespierre, "where there is neither pity nor love for one's fellow countrymen, but only a soul dried up and withered by self-love . . ." The time had come for Robespierre to begin his counterattack on the Dantonists.

Because of his great public reputation, Danton himself was still inviolable. Robespierre and St. Just decided therefore to attack him as they had been attacking Hébert—by isolating him from his followers and by removing, one by one, his allies and possible supporters. When he was alone and the ground beneath him sufficiently tunneled, Danton, that "rotten idol," as Robespierre was soon to call him, could be safely toppled. Camille Desmoulins, Fabre d'Églantine and a man named Hérault de Séchelles, who was Danton's only "friend" still sitting on Robespierre's Committee of Public Safety, were the three main targets of this attack. Circumstances brought Camille first into the line of fire.

34

Soon after the publication of the fourth number of the *Vieux Cordelier* Camille heard Nicolas, a juror on the Revolutionary Tribunal and the official printer of government publications, make a sinister remark. "Camille," he declared in a loud voice, "is skirting very close to the guillotine!" Barère, a member of the Committee of Public Safety, made another chilling remark in the Convention when he referred to "certain writers" who were reviving hope among the aristocrats. "The man who complains about everything that happens during a Revolution," declared Barère, "is a suspect."

These warnings appear to have had a sobering effect on the effervescent young journalist, for in the succeeding number he turned from the Committee and directed his castigations at Hébert, the original object of his attack. From this moment Robespierre need have had no fear that the Dantonists and the Hébertists would ever join forces against the Committee. Camille did his work only too well. With the publication of the fifth number of the journal, Hébert and Camille fell into a violent quarrel and began to scream personal insults at each other.

"You who now live like a Sybarite, the friend of counts and marquises," sneered Hébert in the pages of *Père Duchesne,* "no longer remember your days of poverty. You are ashamed to remember the Hôtel de la Frugalité, where we used to meet side by side with honest masons and poor workmen who were worth more than you or I." Hébert went so far as to mention the "rich dowry" Camille had received at the time of his marriage to the wealthy Lucile.

"My marriage has been so happy," retorted Camille, "and I have been so fortunate in my private life, that I once grew afraid that my heaven was to be here on this earth. Your revolting attack on me and

your cowardly calumny have restored me to my former views. . . ."
Then, after making a sarcastic reference to the days when Hébert
was a menial in a theatre, Camille flew at him: "Do you not know,
Hébert, that when the tyrants of Europe wish to make their people
believe that France is now darkened by barbarism and that Paris,
once the city of Attic glory and taste, is peopled with Vandals, they
insert fragments of your writings in their newspapers . . . as if your
speech were the speech of the Committee of Public Safety; as if your
filthiness were the nation's; as if the sewers of Paris were the Seine."

Camille's reference to the Committee is significant. The rumor
that he was to be arrested clearly put him on his guard. At the end
of his attack on Hébert, having openly called him a thief, Camille
made a statement that was intended for Robespierre's eye. "Note," he
declared, "that I have never advocated exaggerated clemency, only
the clemency which sorts the guilty from those who are merely led
astray." Camille was frightened; too late he began to make compromises, to explain, to backtrack.

The quarrel between Camille and Hébert came to a head a few
days later in the Jacobin Club, that theatre in which was enacted
most of the crucial political dramas of the Revolution. They went at
each other's throat over Camille's accusation that Hébert was a thief.
Robespierre suggested that explanations and a frank "purifying scrutiny" were now called for. This was exactly the kind of situation on
which Robespierre thrived. Affecting to be a dispassionate judge, he
would be able to pass judgment on the two quarreling factions, both
of which were a danger to him. On January 7 Robespierre went to
the rostrum of the Jacobin Club and in a paternal tone of voice called
on Camille to "abjure his errors."

"Camille," he declared in words that betray his rankling envy of
Desmoulins's success, "who sits there all puffed up over the prodigious sale of his newspaper and by the perfidious praise which the
aristocrats have showered on him, has not left the path of error. His
writings are dangerous. They give hope to our enemies and they stir
up public malignity. . . . Camille's writings," he continued, "are to
be condemned, but we must distinguish between the person and his
works. Camille is a spoiled child who once had good inclinations,
but *who is now led astray by bad companions*. We must use severity
towards his paper, which even Brissot would not have dared ac-
knowledge; yet we must keep Camille among us." Having delivered

himself of the shaft at Danton and the envenomed reference to Brissot, Robespierre lifted his spectacles in that gesture described by Fievée and gazed about the room with the long, searching stare that is said to have paralyzed the will of his auditors. His glasses came down again as he returned to his theme. "I demand," he concluded, "that the offensive issues of this journal be burned in the hall of the Society!"

Provoked at first by Robespierre's patronizing tone, then angered beyond control by his demand for book burning (a characteristically gross violation of the principles of freedom), Camille's too quick tongue ran away with him. His answer came with the speed of a rapier and it struck Robespierre in a spot where he was most vulnerable.

"Brûler," replied Camille, *"n'est pas répondre."* They were the famous words of Rousseau, used by him when *Émile* had been condemned to the fire by the magistrates of the *ancien régime:* "To burn is not to answer." Camille's audacious identification of himself with Rousseau (and Robespierre with tyranny) left Robespierre momentarily speechless. His green face is said to have suddenly turned red.

"Now know this, Camille," he replied with menace. "If you were not Camille, the amount of indulgence shown you here would be unthinkable. Your attitude proves to me that your intentions are dishonest." Robespierre, in effect, pronounced Camille's death sentence that night at the Jacobin Club. "I retract my motion, therefore. If Camille wishes it so, then let him be covered with ignominy. . . . A man who so stubbornly defends such perfidious writings is worse perhaps than a mere laggard."

Too late, Camille realized where his reckless tongue had led him. He blanched. Danton noticed his fear-ridden expression and spoke a few comforting words, exhorting him not to be frightened. But Danton, himself, if we are to believe a frantic letter written after this session by Lucile Desmoulins, had now begun to lose confidence.

"Come back, Fréron," she wrote to one of Camille's old friends; "come back quickly! You have no time to lose. Bring all the old Cordeliers that you can find with you. We have great need of them. . . . Robespierre has denounced Camille to the Jacobins! No one listens to Manlius [i.e. Danton] any more. He is losing his courage and vigor. D'Églantine has been arrested on very grave charges. . . . I can no longer think. I no longer play the piano. I see no one and never go out now. I meet Camille's eyes with a serene look and try to appear courageous, so that he will not lose his courage. . . ." A fear-stricken hush, the atmosphere of impending disaster, had fallen over Camille's home.

Fabre was arrested on January 14 for complicity in the East India Company swindle. Robespierre had never been able to abide the man. The words preceding his denunciation of Fabre to the Jacobins hint at the character of his hostility: "I demand that this man who always walks around with a lorgnette in his hand, and who is so skillful at writing about intrigues for the theatre, now explain himself to us." Robespierre hated that lorgnette, which added mockery to Fabre's supercilious expression. The lorgnette made Robespierre suspect that Fabre might be harboring sarcastic thoughts. Robespierre's hypersensitivity made him abnormally conscious of the expressions on people's faces—and Fabre's face he did not like. Furthermore the man was a playwright, "overly assiduous in the pursuit of fame" and often flippant or glib in his conversation. Robespierre, having no sense of humor himself, always considered any manifestation of levity in others to be some sort of vague reflection on himself. Lightness of tone or manner invariably aroused his ire and suspicion.

On the day of Fabre's arrest, Billaud-Varennes, one of Robespierre's more sanguinary colleagues on the Committee of Public Safety and a bitter enemy of Danton, made a sinister remark: "Woe be to the man," he declared, "who ever sat at Fabre's side and is still his dupe!" The remark reached the ear of Lucile's friend Fréron, who, instead of answering Lucile's plea to hurry to Camille's help, wrote another friend in Paris and asked him the meaning of Billaud-Varennes' suggestive words. "Did Billaud-Varennes mean Danton by this? Is Danton by any chance compromised?" Fréron enquired cautiously.

As Danton's followers were publicly struck down, his former friends, taking worried measure of the situation, began to abandon the tottering idol. Danton, aware of this, began to lose heart. The lassitude from which he had recovered at Arcis now returned to paralyze his movements. "Can power be worth these efforts to obtain it that I see all about me?" he mused to a friend. And to another acquaintance, a colleague from Arcis, he declared that "these people have given me such a hatred of the present that I sometimes regret the days when the whole of my weekly income depended on a bottle of ink." It was an ill-chosen hour for Danton to become philosophical. Now was the moment when that resolution and vigor, for which he was celebrated, was most urgently needed. Yet everything testifies to the fact that in January his nerve had begun to fail. Behind the cloak of the Committee of Public Safety Robespierre had started assiduously to dig Danton's grave.

Hérault de Séchelles was arrested on January 17, on charges of "conspiracy"; Philippeaux was removed soon after. Danton tried to speak in the hall of the Convention. He had the impression that no one heard him. "This hall," he bellowed, "is worse than a violin mute. Nobody without the lungs of a Stentor could make himself heard in it!" The Convention may have listened to him more attentively than he supposed. Aware of an impending crisis, that cowardly body had begun to stir nervously. Danton's pleas for clemency undoubtedly appealed to the majority of its members, but that majority was immobilized by fear. No one had thought to organize the trembling individuals who comprised its membership. Had Danton made some pact with the ambiguous Plain, he might have won his battle. Fouché, a far more skillful intriguer than Danton, recognized this fact when three months after Danton's death his turn came to meet Robespierre in the arena. And Fouché won.

To his friends Danton expressed his weariness. But he made the mistake, on the other hand, of threatening his enemies with wild, immoderate, but empty words. One day while leaving the Convention, he saw Vadier, a member of the General Security Committee, point to him and say in a gloating tone of voice, "We're going to gut that fat porpoise." In a fury Danton replied, "Somebody tell that villain over there that if ever I have reason to fear for my life I'll become worse than a cannibal: I'll eat his brains and dishonor his skull!" On another occasion he said of Robespierre, "If I thought that man was plotting my ruin, I'd eat his entrails." He talked, but he didn't act. Barras, who would have been a willing ally in the struggle against Robespierre if he had seen any chance of winning, was aware of Danton's weakness. Barras warned a friend, "We must be careful of Danton. He is using threats instead of striking."

Too often would he escape to the country—not to Arcis, which was now too far away, but to the woods near Sèvres, where he had a house—where he could breathe fresh air and try to forget the anxieties which oppressed him in the city. Spring came early that year and was of exceptional beauty, "as though Nature consoled the world for the crimes that were being committed by Society," commented an observer. At Sèvres Danton was able to watch his fruit trees burst into blossom and to revive his failing spirits with the fragrance of the stirring earth. But he seems to have known that he would not live to see the arrival of summer. A friend who visited him at Sèvres during the weeks that preceded his arrest found him to be "a sick man who had renounced the world because he senses that he is about to leave it." Alternately melancholy and truculent, languid frequently and discouraged always, Danton was in no condition to offer resolute resistance to the open attack that was about to be made on him.

The Committee struck down Hébert during the night of March 15. He and his remaining followers were rounded up and placed under arrest. This event, which on the surface might have seemed a triumph for the cause of Danton and Camille, was in actuality little more than a rehearsal of their own arrest two weeks later. Like Danton, Hébert had seen the shadow of the invisible meshes that silently and swiftly were being drawn about him. He took fright and a few days before his arrest made a desperate attempt to escape his fate. He turned to the Commune and to the Paris Sections, hoping to exhort the mob to come to his rescue. Hébert moved too late.

Fear of the Committee had caused the once redoubtable Commune to disintegrate into its weak and human components, a handful of frightened men, some of whom were themselves on Robespierre's list, who cautiously measured their chances of success against so formidable an adversary as Robespierre, who not only had the Committee behind him, but the Jacobin Club too. The Commune abandoned Hébert's party to its fate. Hébert's two supporters on the Committee, the bloodthirsty Collot d'Herbois and Billaud-Varennes, were persuaded to do the same. Their colleagues on the Committee promised them Danton's head in exchange for Hébert's.

The so-called Hébertists, twenty strangely assorted individuals, went to the guillotine nine days after their arrest. An enormous and high-spirited crowd turned out on the Place de la Révolution for that show. Hébert's screams were said to have been louder than those of poor Mme. du Barry, who had been executed in December. This vile man, who had sent so many others to their deaths with foul-mouthed imprecation and insult, was himself a coward of the worst kind. The mob to whom he had been so enthusiastic a panderer answered his cries with contemptuous howls and watched the fluttering of his dainty little hands with ribald amusement. Joining in the festive mood of the occasion, the executioner let the knife dance for a few moments on the screaming creature's neck before he finally dispatched him. The mob went wild with joy.

Hébert's arrest gave Camille and Danton a brief resurgent hope. Danton appeared before the Convention on March 19 and made a dramatic speech ("Let us now put all resentment behind us. Let us judge men only by their actions . . ."), which was so warmly received that Robespierre took alarm and realized that if his Committee were to save itself it would have to strike its next blow quickly. Danton's appearance before the Convention on March 19 was, in fact, his last. He had less than a month to live.

Several weeks before Hébert's execution, Danton, upon the suggestion of well-meaning friends, had gone to Robespierre's rooms at the Duplay house and tried to come to an understanding with him. Robespierre accepted these overtures with cold disdain. It was Danton, not himself, who now had need of an alliance. Their conversation became acrimonious when Danton referred to the Terror and deplored the fact that the innocent were being carelessly confused with the guilty. Robespierre turned on him and angrily demanded, "And whoever told you that a single innocent person has perished?"

Danton was so taken aback by this haughty disregard for truth that he turned to the others in the room and in his most sarcastic tone of voice said, "And he says no innocent person has perished!" He stormed away, leaving Robespierre more rancorous than he found him.

On March 22 Danton made another attempt at reconciliation. This time he came to Robespierre as a desperate man, as one who has almost lost the game—as a petitioner. And Robespierre knew it. Danton is said to have grown highly emotional at this meeting. He implored Robespierre not to listen to the voices of his enemies Collot d'Herbois and Billaud-Varennes. "Let us forget our differences," he entreated, "and look at nothing but our country and her needs. Once the Republic is respected outside our borders she will become beloved within them, even by men who now show their enmity against her."

Robespierre's answer is revealing. "With your principles and your morals," he replied tartly, "nobody would ever find any criminals to punish."

"And would you regret that?" cried Danton indignantly. "Would you be sorry not to find any criminals to punish?"

During their meeting Danton pleaded for the release of seventy-three deputies of the Right who had been arrested. Robespierre was implacable. "The only way to establish liberty is to cut off the heads of such criminals," he retorted angrily. Danton suddenly burst into tears. Rage as well as despair must have informed them. They in no way melted Robespierre's heart. On the contrary, they repelled his cold and puritanical spirit. One of the charges in Robespierre's "Notes" clearly indicates this. "Danton," he wrote, "made himself ridiculous by his theatrical gestures, producing tears in the tribune and at Robespierre's house." Tears only made him despise the big blustery man who was now at his mercy. Before taking his departure, Danton is said to have warned Robespierre that so violent a system as the Terror could not last for long because it was antipathetic to the French temperament. When he left he tried to embrace Robespierre, but his adversary pulled away in icy astonishment and remained "as cold as marble."

During the week that preceded Danton's arrest Robespierre cautiously moved his agents into the vacancies at the Commune that had been left by the vanished Hébertists. With Fleuriot appointed mayor and with other key positions occupied by equally loyal Jacobins, Robespierre eliminated any chance of a popular uprising in Danton's favor. All sides of the trap were carefully tested before it was sprung. There was to be no possibility that the prey might escape.

In the solitude of his room in the Duplay house, Robespierre now began to concoct the charges with which he was to secure Danton's head. Unfortunately for Robespierre's reputation, these repellent "Notes" still survive. They condemn Robespierre in the judgment of posterity as effectively as they condemned Danton before the Revolutionary Tribunal. "Danton," he wrote indignantly in one characteristic paragraph, "surrounded himself with rascals and he openly tolerated immoral living. . . ." At no place in his list of "charges" does Robespierre manifest any understanding of the difference between what may have been—to him—morally reprehensible and what, by a court of law, might have been construed as an act of treason. The dictator and the puritanical spinster speak together in every line of this extraordinary accusation.

The fourth of the charges—they are neatly catalogued—is interesting, since it inadvertently reveals the role of malicious tattletale that Robespierre played at the critical time when Danton had tried to come to an understanding with the Girondins. "When Robespierre informed Danton of the campaign of slander that was being prosecuted against him by the Roland couple and the Brissotins, Danton said to him, 'What do I care? Public opinion is a whore and posterity is nonsense!'" It is a pity that Mme. Roland could not have heard this sensible reply to the spiteful little talebearer—who very probably hurried from Danton's presence to the sanctuary of the Girondins carrying with him a distorted version of Danton's statement about them.

Quivering with indignation, Robespierre remembered Danton's remark about that "Virtue" which he practiced with his wife every night. "Danton laughs at the word Virtue as though it were a joke," he declared. *"How could a man so alien to every idea of morality ever be a champion of freedom?"*

Every word of this denunciation breathes a long-established private hatred. Danton, incapable of nursing such profound rancor, could not have suspected that all through the years of their "friendship" the man was silently, relentlessly, storing up his grievances, noting down for possible future use everything that might condemn him, the petty with the large. It was enough for Robespierre that "Danton never spoke energetically except about himself. His silence during serious discussions can only be explained by his big size and by his excessive love life. . . ." His size alone would have condemned him in Robespierre's mind.

When he had finished his "Notes," Robespierre handed them to St. Just, the Angel of Death, whose function it was to prepare the material in such a way that Robespierre would not appear to be directly responsible for it. In the ensuing days Robespierre hugged the shadows, coming forward only when the feet of his allies seemed to lag or when his vindictive nature overcame the counsels of prudence—when spite, in other words, transcended cowardice.

Danton and Robespierre saw each other from afar a few days be-

fore St. Just demanded Danton's arrest. The occasion was a performance of the tragedy *Epicharis and Nero* at the Théâtre Français. A
witness of the scene that took place there between the two adversaries has left this description of it: "Robespierre was in a box; Danton
was in the orchestra and behind him were many of his friends.
Hardly had the words 'Death to the tyrant!' been pronounced on
the stage when Danton's friends burst into wild applause and standing up and turning towards Robespierre shook their fists with a
threatening gesture. Robespierre, pale and nervous, thrust his little
clerk's face forward and then pulled it back in the way that a snake
does. He waved his little hand in a gesture that expressed both fright
and menace."

After that episode Danton's partisans urged him either to take
flight or to strike back. To the first suggestion, in a resonantly patriotic phrase that was characteristic of him, he replied, "One does not
carry one's country on the soles of one's feet." To the suggestion
that he prepare a counterattack he replied sorrowfully, "It would
only mean the shedding of more blood. There has been enough. It is
better to be guillotined than to guillotine." The will to live seems to
have left him. He was like a fly that has been paralyzed by the
spider's poison. Passively he let himself be trussed in the cocoon that
the spider had begun to spin about him. Without resistance he
waited now for the moment when they would come to arrest him.

They came in the night of March 30-31. Earlier that evening Robespierre had called the Committee of Public Safety and the General
Security Committee together in an emergency session. In such important cases as Danton's it was customary to have the order for arrest drawn up by both committees. St. Just read out Robespierre's
accusations, which had been polished and edited by his fine hand.
He demanded the arrest of Danton and Camille Desmoulins. Of the
twenty men present at this meeting only two refused their signatures
to the warrant: Lindet, a member of the Committee of Public Safety,
who declared, "I am here to feed citizens [he was in charge of Sup-
plies] not to put patriots to death," and an elderly Alsatian, Rühl,
who remained faithful to his old friendship with Danton. The others signed the document (which still exists) with a bold flourish
that betrays their zeal. Robespierre's small, cold signature betrays
nothing. He prudently signed his name towards the bottom of the

page wedged in between two others and near a corner. One would suppose from looking at it that he was not responsible for the order to which it was appended.

Carnot, the level-headed military advisor of the Committee, is said to have given his associates a warning before he signed the document. "Think long before you do this," he admonished. "A head such as Danton's will drag many others to their fall."

Before the order was given to the Commune, a discussion ensued about the manner in which Danton should be apprehended. St. Just was determined to have him seized publicly in the hall of the Convention after he, St. Just, had read out his accusations to the assembled deputies. In such a situation the triumph of the younger man over the older would be more dramatic and gratifying. St. Just had no known friends; Danton had always been surrounded by them. By demanding Danton's arrest in the hall of the Senate, St. Just could give the Convention an illuminating lesson in the value of friendship.

Other men in the inner circle of the two committees were less vain of themselves than the Angel of Death and consequently less confident of their hold on the Convention. Events were shortly to prove these doubts to have been well founded. Had the Committee attempted to have Danton arrested in the Convention it is very possible that the Convention, led by a few courageous men, might have seized the opportunity to tear itself from the stranglehold of the Committee and of Robespierre, and the Terror would have ended in March 1794 instead of in July. One of Danton's enemies on the General Security Committee recognized the danger and said to Robespierre (who was inclined to support St. Just), "If we do not arrest him immediately, we will run the risk of being arrested ourselves." This was the logic that governed the whole of the Terror. In his prison cell Danton was soon to sing that sad refrain himself when he spoke of the Girondins. "Brissot would have had me guillotined just as readily as Robespierre."

Robespierre, a coward in all risky situations, retreated before this remorseless argument and gave orders for the immediate arrest of the victims. When he heard this decision, the Angel of Death, the thwarted boy with the dreaming eyes, threw a tantrum. He is said to have stamped his feet in rage and to have thrown his hat into the fire before rushing out of the room and slamming the door behind him.

The order for Danton's arrest was then dispatched to the mayor.

Danton's friend Rühl instantly sent a messenger to the Cour du Commerce to warn Danton. He found him in an armchair sitting before a fire. Danton expressed no emotion at the news. Listlessly he continued to stir the dying embers while he waited for the police to come for him. He did not want to be arrested in bed. At last he heard the sound of a patrol on the street below. He rose abruptly and went to his wife.

"They are coming to arrest me," he said.

Weeping, Louise threw her arms around him. He kissed her gently on the forehead.

"You mustn't be frightened," he said. "They will not dare to do it." And so, with no attempt at resistance, he followed the police downstairs and into the street. They took him to the prison of the Luxembourg, which was nearby.

Camille was arrested at the same time as Danton. Beside herself with grief, Lucile clung to him up until the last possible moment. He seems to have borne himself bravely enough before his wife and young son, but as soon as he was in his prison cell he collapsed in a wild paroxysm of grief. Writer to the end, he seized paper and pen and wrote Lucile a series of passionate letters that have gone into history as part of the literature of the Revolution. From his prison window at the Luxembourg he could see the gardens where he had passed eight happy years walking with Lucile. "It brings back to me so many recollections of our love . . . then I throw myself on my knees, I stretch out my arms to embrace you . . ."; a tear is still visible on the paper where it fell on this sentence.

"I sleep," he cries, in another letter to his wife, "and Heaven has pity on me, for in sleep one is free again. Just a moment ago I saw you in a dream and held you in my arms again. You and our little Horace and Daronne [Lucile's mother], who had come to visit us. But our little boy had lost an eye and my grief awoke me. . . . I married a wife who was heavenly in her virtues. I have been a good husband and a good son. I would have been a good father. . . ." The love of this childlike man for his family did not distract his eye from his position in posterity. "I carry with me the esteem and the regrets of all true Republicans. I have walked for five years over the precipices of the Revolution without falling into them. I rest my head calmly upon the pillow of my writings, which all breathe the same philanthropy and the same desire to make my fellow citizens happy and free."

Camille's writings, examined in the cold light of fact, breathe no such thing. They were clever, but often bitter and malicious and irresponsible. But, for all their faults, there will always be something about them that invites the charity of posterity. Perhaps it is because the man who wrote them was a human being, compounded of familiar flesh and blood. "Oh, my beloved Lucile!" he cried in one of his letters from prison, "I was born to write poetry, to defend the unfortunate and to make you happy." The sentence is worthy of the pen of Rafael Sabatini or Baroness Orczy. It expresses the Camille that one would prefer to remember.

At the end he had no doubt of his approaching fate. "The shores of life are receding from me! I see you still, my Lucile, my beloved! My bound hands embrace you and my head as it falls into the basket will rest its dying eyes upon you!"

35

Paris and the Convention were stupefied by the news of the arrest of Danton and Camille, which they heard the next morning. Danton and Desmoulins were two of the Revolution's most celebrated figures. Camille was the hero of July 14, 1789, the man who five years before in the gardens of the Palais Royal had exhorted the mob to march on the Bastille. Danton was the man of August 10, the "Titan of the Revolution" from whose person seemed to emanate so much of the passion, for better or for worse, that had carried men into that great whirlwind. Of all men in the Revolution, Danton was undoubtedly the most admired by the public. To the people of Paris his was a familiar figure, but one that was invested too with that quality of legend which is often inseparable from great public leaders. That such men as these could be overthrown by the Committee of Public Safety, by the ruses and the guile of the schoolmarmish Robespierre, was a fact that now filled the Convention with consternation. No one henceforth could feel safe.

Cowardly and frightened though it was, the Convention did not succumb without a protest. Danton's friend, the butcher Legendre, went to the rostrum. "Citizens," he cried out, "last night certain members of this assembly were arrested. Danton was one of them. I demand that the arrested members of the Convention be brought before the bar of this assembly to be accused or absolved by us. I am convinced that Danton is as pure as myself." Legendre, with audacity, went so far as to declare that Danton was the victim of certain "private hatreds."

The Convention received his protest in a mood that suggests that if there had been any organized opposition, Robespierre's Committee might have been overthrown that morning. Danton's violent and almost successful struggle at his trial gives one reason to believe that he might have left the Convention a free man had he been present to defend himself there. Scattered cries of "Down with the dictatorship!" were heard in the hall after Legendre's protest. Tallien, a friend of Danton (or more accurately an enemy of Robespierre) was president of the Convention that day. He was about to put Legendre's motion to a vote when Robespierre entered the hall and hurried to the rostrum. Menace, like a shadow, suddenly fell over the room. M. Madelin has convincingly described the peculiar power, almost hypnotic, which seems to have been at the command of this man of insignificant appearance—"his political power had its root in the inexplicable confusion into which his very appearance at the rostrum threw his opponents." In some curious way he seems to have filled others with the paranoid terrors that were his own. When he mounted the tribune now he considered his audience for a moment through those green-tinted spectacles, "letting his eye rest for the space of two heartbeats on those whom he mistrusted." A deathly stillness settled upon the room.

"Legendre," he began, "has mentioned Danton. He seems to believe that some privilege attaches to this name. But has Danton any claim to privilege? Is he in any respect better than the rest of his fellow citizens? No! We will have no more privileges here! And we will have no more idols either! We shall see today whether the Convention will know how to break *a false and rotten idol* or whether that idol in its fall is to crush the Convention and the people of France. . . ." Robespierre's spectacles went up. He turned and fixed his cold, myopic stare on the trembling Legendre. "The man who trembles at my words," he accused, "is guilty. Innocence has never feared public scrutiny." At these words Legendre went white and with a stammered apology hurriedly abandoned his friend.

"If Robespierre thinks that I am capable of sacrificing liberty to an individual," he declared, "he mistook my intention. Those who have the proof in their hand realize better than we do the guilt of the men who have been arrested. . . ." Legendre died before the year was out. The newspapers attributed his premature demise to the heart-stopping fear inspired in him by Robespierre's terrible look. From that moment on no one in the Convention rose to Danton's defense.

St. Just assumed the rostrum after Robespierre and read out his report. Witnesses to this scene have recalled the monotonous drone of his voice and the sinister way in which he punctuated his accusations by a chopping gesture of his left hand, which, rising and falling suggested the blade of the guillotine. He announced the discovery of a great plot in Paris "by aristocrats more adroit and cunning than those of Coblenz." He pronounced Danton, "that servant of tyranny," to be the chief of this horde. But with the arrest of Danton and of the conspirators who surrounded him, "intrigue will never again touch this holy spot. You can then give yourselves up to legislation and government." Time and again Robespierre and St. Just promised the Convention an end of the "purges" if only the Convention would hand them one last faction. With Robespierre's threats and St. Just's promises they extorted Danton's head from his fellow deputies. "And then," St. Just concluded his speech, "there will remain nothing but patriots among us. . . ."

At the prison of the Luxembourg Danton's arrival caused a great sensation. "Gentlemen," he said to his fellow prisoners, "I had hoped to get you all out of this place. Unfortunately I'm now shut up in it with you." Thomas Paine, that ill-advised enthusiast, happened to be among the prisoners at the Luxembourg at the time of Danton's brief appearance there. To him Danton said in English, "I tried in vain to do for my country that which you did for yours. They are sending me to the scaffold. I shall go gaily." To another group of prisoners Danton spoke prophetic words, "If reason doesn't soon return to this poor country, what you have seen so far will be a bed of roses compared to what will follow."

Danton and his associates (Camille, Fabre d'Églantine, Philippeaux, Lacroix and a general named Westermann) remained in the Luxembourg only two days. On April 2 they received their formal act of accusation and were immediately transferred to the Conciergerie, that "antechamber of Death" where men and women who were on trial were lodged for the day or two that preceded their execution. A man named Riouffe, one of the few who survived to tell his tale, was imprisoned at the Conciergerie at the time of Danton's short stay there. He was not sympathetic to Danton or to any of his group, since he believed them to be responsible for his own plight and that of the other doomed occupants of the Conciergerie. He has left his impressions.

"Lacroix," relates Riouffe, "seemed more embarrassed than the others by the misery he saw about him. He affected astonishment at what he saw, which filled the witnesses to his emotions with indignation. He tried to make out that he was surprised by the filth of his surroundings and by the great number of prisoners there. One of these said to him, 'Do you mean to tell me that you've never seen the tumbrels filled with victims that leave this place every day? Do you mean to tell us that you didn't know that Paris has become a slaughterhouse?' Lacroix, who had been one of the most enthusiastic supporters of Revolutionary institutions, replied that he didn't. Even if his ignorance was not feigned, it was no less revolting. What is one to think of these destroyers who unleash their scourge over mankind and then don't deign to follow the progress of their destruction?"

With Danton's arrival at the Conciergerie, his vitality seems to have returned. Riouffe and others leave us with the impression of a man in the grip of primitive emotions. He flailed at his enemies with one hand and with the other he tore at his bonds. Certain of his words that have come down to us recall the volcanic utterances of the hero of August 10, the famous Tribune of the days when France had been menaced by invasion. "I am leaving a terrible mess behind me," he declared. "It is a pity I can't leave my legs to that cripple Couthon and my ——— to that eunuch Robespierre." Danton here used a vigorous French word to describe his masculinity.

"In times of Revolution power will always go to the worst scoundrel."

"The bloody beasts will cry *'Vive le Républïque!'* when they see me go by."

Amid these angry phrases another note can be detected. "A year ago I established the Revolutionary Tribunal. I ask pardon of God and men. I did it to prevent a renewal of the September Massacres, not to be the scourge of humanity."

"It is better to be a poor fisherman than a ruler of men," he cried out. And Riouffe assures us that "he spoke incessantly of trees, of the country, and of nature."

The Committee of Public Safety was well aware of the struggle that Danton was preparing to make. They had no intention of letting their prey escape. All possible loopholes were hurriedly closed. Fouquier-Tinville, the Public Prosecutor, and Herman, President of the Court, were warned that their own lives might be forfeit if they did not secure a condemnation. The jury was limited to seven men, all of them carefully chosen enemies of Danton. Robespierre once more demonstrated the devilish degree to which he had developed the technique of slander by implication. He saw to it that Danton and his followers, political prisoners, were put in the same dock as Chabot, the Frei brothers and several other men of shady reputation who were accused of the East India Company theft. The two cases had nothing in common, but by throwing them together in the same trial Robespierre knew that the public mind, always susceptible to vague or general impressions, would associate one with the other. The President and the Prosecutor were given orders that they were always to keep the East India Company group to the fore and the Dantonists in the shadows. Chabot and his colleagues therefore occupied the front benches when this shameful trial began on April 2. The fact that Danton was the real target of the proceedings would not have been apparent to an uninformed visitor to the courtroom.

Despite the court's precautions, Danton was determined to fight. He stated his intention to Camille shortly before the trial began. "We must try to reach the People," he declared. "We shall see what those —— look like when I'm through with them." He is said to have entered the courtroom "like an enraged bull" with his head lowered in a charging position. His eyes blazed with anger; his mouth was twisted with scorn. When Herman called out the prisoners' names and asked for their place of residence, Danton replied, "My residence will soon be in the Great Beyond. But you will find my name in the Pantheon of History." Camille Desmoulins, when asked his age, replied insolently, "Thirty-three, the same age as the sans-culotte Jesus Christ when they crucified him." (Camille was, in fact, thirty-four).

As soon as these formalities were finished, Herman and Fouquier turned their backs on Danton and his codefendants and addressed themselves to the matter of the East India Company. A long report was read off and this occupied most of the first day of the trial. Danton was given no opportunity to raise his voice as he had planned. The second day's session opened on the same theme as that on which the first had closed—the East India Company. Danton managed to interrupt the proceedings with a demand to be heard. Herman tried to drown his voice with the bell.

"Don't you hear my bell?" he rebuked.

"A man who is fighting for his life laughs at bells," Danton replied. "He bellows."

But the President (and behind him the two committees) finally had to face the dreaded moment when Danton was to be publicly accused.

"Danton," declared the President, "the Convention charges you with having favored Dumouriez, with not having informed it of that man's true character, and with having shared his schemes to murder Liberty such as that of marching on Paris with an armed force in order to destroy the Republican government and to re-establish royalty."

Danton's moment had come and his response was in the heroic manner of which he was the master. "My voice," he declared, "which has been so often heard speaking in the People's cause, will have no difficulty in thrusting this calumny aside. Will the cowards who have slandered my name dare meet me face to face? Let them show themselves and I will cover them with their own ignominy. . . . I demand that the Convention form a commission to hear my denunciation of this dictatorship. Yes! I, Danton, will unmask the dictatorship that is now openly revealing its existence."

The unexpected thrust behind these words caused the President to take alarm. "Danton," he declared, "boldness such as yours is characteristic of crime; calm is the proper attitude of innocence. . . ."

But the dam was broken and the water now flowed in torrents over it. Danton's voice drowned everything that stood in its path. A great crowd had gathered outside the Palais de Justice. It is related that Danton's defense could be heard in the Place Dauphine and even across the river as that stentorian voice rose and fell in rage and disdain. "When I see myself so grievously, so unjustly accused how can you expect me to restrain my indignation? Can you expect coolness from revolutionaries such as myself . . . ? You say I have sold myself. A man such as I am has no price! . . . Danton sold himself to Mirabeau and to Orléans? Let the men who have proof of that bargain step forward. . . ."

There is something magnificent about these unpolished chunks of rhetoric. They are somewhat disconnected because no official record of his defense was taken. A juryman, Topino-Lebrun, copied down Danton's words as quickly as he was able, but the flow was too fast for his hand. We thus have a sketch, similar to the one David did of Danton on his way to the guillotine, which, in a succession of swift, jagged lines, aptly suggests the tone of the whole.

Herman, Fouquier and the jury were appalled as the words boiled forth. More than once Danton approached dangerously near the sanctified precincts of the Committee of Public Safety. "I am in full possession of all my faculties when I summon my accusers to come forth. I demand the right to pit my strength against theirs. Let them show themselves, the vile impostors, and I'll tear away the mask that protects them from public chastisement!"

It is said that the audience burst into applause at these bold words. The President rang his bell to quiet the room, then attempting to calm Danton, he spoke words that only succeeded in enraging him further. "Danton, it is not by indecent outbreaks against your accusers that you will succeed in convincing the jury of your innocence. Address it in a language that it understands [*Parle-lui une langage qu'il puisse entendre*] and do not forget that the men who accuse you enjoy the public esteem. . . ."

This reference to the jury, a carefully selected group of prejudiced and perjured men, caused Danton to throw back his head. "A man accused as I am does not address himself to a jury, he answers before it. I defend myself and I slander no one. Neither ambition nor greed has ever had a hold on me. I have devoted my life to my country and I made that sacrifice gladly. It is necessary now, that I speak to you about three low cowards who have been the ruin of Robespierre. I have some very important information which I am now going to reveal to you. . . ."

Herman interrupted with alarm, ordering Danton to stick to his own defense and not to defame others. One wonders what information Danton might have revealed. The three "low cowards" were probably those bloodthirsty committee members Billaud-Varennes, Collot d'Herbois and St. Just. Up to this point in his trial Danton does not seem to have realized or in any case to have admitted that Robespierre was the real author of his ruin. He blamed St. Just and not Robespierre for the charges that were brought against him. "You, St. Just, you will answer to posterity for the slanders which you have cast upon me! When I hear that list of horrors my blood curdles. . . ." But one by one Danton began to answer these accusations, reducing them to the concoction of lies and malicious gossip that they were. He spoke for over an hour and before he was through it became apparent to the whole court, audience and participants alike, that the charges could not possibly be sustained.

The room burst into applause as, in a succession of bold and dazzling phrases, he routed his opponents: jury, judges, President and Prosecutor alike. A report was already spreading through Paris that Danton was to be acquitted. Herman and Fouquier-Tinville exchanged anguished, significant glances. They knew well their own fate should Danton be allowed to escape. And the Committee of Public Safety knew well that if he escaped they would probably be the next to be put on trial.

The General Security Committee, in defiance of all legal procedure, had sent three representatives to the Tribunal to observe the proceedings. These men, Amar, Vadier and David, openly mingled with the judges and jury, and in the opening days of the trial had looked at Danton with "leering, satisfied expressions." Only a few months earlier the wretched David had been one of Danton's close friends. He was an opportunist and would abandon anyone when association with him became dangerous to himself. But Nature endowed the hand of this despicable creature with genius. David may have been contemptible but he was a great artist.

When the three representatives of the government saw the way things were going, the "satisfied" expression on their faces turned to one of alarm. They were seen "rushing around the courtroom telling the judges, jury and witnesses that the accused, and particularly Danton, were all guilty wretches." They dispatched a message to the Committee about the unforeseen turn the trial was taking. Danton had grown so bold that he now seemed to shake a threatening fist in the direction of the Committee. "You will judge me, People, when I have told you everything, and my voice will reach not only you but the whole of France. . . ." A wave of applause greeted this assertion. He flung back his great head with a snort of disdain. "Danton an aristocrat! France will not believe that for very long!"

Beside himself with anxiety, Herman now scribbled a note to Fouquier-Tinville. "I am going to suspend Danton's defense in half an hour," he declared. That note alone (it still survives) is enough to strip away the few tattered shreds of legality that cling about that travesty of justice which was Danton's trial. In two months' time Robespierre's Committee was to eliminate entirely the time-consuming hypocrisy that characterized the pretense of legality at these trials before the Tribunal. With the Law of 22 Prairial (June 10, 1794) the "government" outlawed all defense. Accusation then became enough to secure condemnation. The example of Danton's trial frightened the Committee into legislating this terrible law which has few parallels in the voluminous history of tyranny.

Danton uttered a cry of despair when he found that the court was about to gag him by suspending his defense. "I am not allowed to call witnesses then?" he bellowed. "I might as well resign my defense!" And taking notice of the public response to his voice, he added the prophetic words, "The People will tear my enemies to pieces before three months are out!" Herman reluctantly promised him a further hearing on the following day, after the other prisoners had been cross-examined. The session closed in an atmosphere that was most favorable to Danton.

On April 4 Danton's codefendants rushed into the breach. The charges against them were so vague and so ill formed (Philippeaux was accused of "having criticized the government in his writings and of having calumniated Marat") that, encouraged by Danton's spirited defense, they were able to rout Fouquier with energetic defense tactics of their own. Like Danton they demanded that their witnesses be summoned. Danton again spoke up to support them, and in the ensuing commotion Fouquier and Herman realized that the case had gone out of their control. In Fouquier's words, "It was about to blow up in their hands." The clerk of court later recalled the "rage and terror" that were depicted on their "pallid countenances."

"It's time to put an end to this struggle, which is a scandal to the Tribunal and to those who hear you speak," declared Fouquier to the prisoners. "I am going to write the Convention to know what its wishes are. Those wishes will be carried out to the letter."

The Convention, or rather the Committee of Public Safety, to whom the Convention had handed over most of its prerogatives, was indeed the only agency that might now prevent the case from being dismissed from court. And Fouquier admitted so in the final sentence of the letter he now hurriedly wrote the Convention. "A terrible storm has been raging since the beginning of this trial," he declared. "The accused are behaving like madmen and demand the summoning of their witnesses. They are appealing to the People over the refusal which they pretend to have received. Despite the firmness of the President and the whole Tribunal, their repeated demands disturb the sitting and they declare that they will not be quiet until their witnesses are heard. We ask you what to do in regard to this demand. Our judicial powers do not furnish us with any means of refusing it." Fouquier, in other words, implored the Convention to tailor a new law to suit the case. The letter (which was to cost Fouquier his own head in the day of retribution that followed the Terror) provides all comment that need ever be made about "justice" as it was administered by the Revolutionary court of law.

In its chambers at the Tuileries, the Committee of Public Safety, to whom Fouquier's letter was delivered, had been in a state of consternation since the beginning of Danton's defense. Fouquier's appeal now drove them to quick and desperate action. St. Just, guided by Robespierre, managed the matter. It was decided that Danton's violent struggles suggested rebellion, and rebellion, to men of such paranoid inclination as Robespierre, suggested a hidden plot.

Lucile Desmoulins, in despair at Camille's arrest, was known to have rushed about Paris seeking the help of men who might save him. The poor woman had been seen several times wandering outside the prison of the Luxembourg when Camille had been imprisoned there. Such facts as these were enough to inspire St. Just with a Machiavellian plan.

A letter from a prisoner in the Luxembourg named Laflotte was suddenly produced. The letter dramatically unveiled a plot among the prisoners in that institution that had been concocted by the Danton-Desmoulins group to overthrow the Revolutionary Tribunal. Clutching this letter and waving a sheaf of important-looking papers in the air, St. Just hurried to the Convention and went to the rostrum. He did not read Fouquier's letter. Its naïve admission of the total illegality of the whole business would have embarrassed even the Convention. He read out instead a bold and falsified résumé of it. "The Public Prosecutor," he declared, "has just informed us that the *revolt* of the guilty men has forced him to suspend their trial until the Convention shall have taken measures. Citizens! You have just escaped the gravest danger that has ever threatened Liberty. All accomplices have now been discovered. . . .

No further proofs are needed. The very resistance of these wretches is an acknowledgment of their guilt!" After making a reference to "Desmoulins's wife, who has stirred up a movement for the assassination of patriots and of the Tribunal," and reading out Laflotte's letter, St. Just demanded the immediate passage by the Convention of a law decreeing that "every accused person who resisted or insulted the National Justice should be forbidden to plead."

The decree was duly voted and within minutes hurried from the Tuileries over to the Palais de Justice. Amar of the General Security Committee had Fouquier called from the courtroom and handed it to him.

"This," he said, "should make the job easier for you."

"Indeed we needed it," replied Fouquier with a smile. He hurried back to court, brandishing the decree and Laflotte's letter, which he read aloud. In the stupefied silence that followed, "judges, jurymen, spectators and the accused appeared dumfounded; they looked at one another in astonishment"; so declares an eyewitness.

Danton rose, a terrifying figure. "You are murderers!" he cried. He fixed his gaze on the three representatives of the General Security Committee, who looked back at him gloatingly. "Murderers! Look at them! They have hounded us to our deaths!" From this moment he had no doubt of the identity of the figure, still prudently hidden in the shadows, who had designed his ruin. "Vile Robespierre!" he cried. "You too will go to the scaffold. You will follow me, Robespierre!"

Poor Camille was in a far worse condition than Danton. In Laflotte's letter, which Fouquier had read aloud to the court, he heard Lucile denounced as "the leader of the conspiracy" that planned to secure his release. He was to go to his own death in the heart-wringing certainty of his wife's approaching anguish. "They are going to murder my wife!" he cried in horror.

Herman angrily rang his bell to put an end to the bedlam that had broken out. He ordered the session closed and the prisoners taken back to the Conciergerie. But Danton managed to release a parting shot. "I shall be Danton up to my last hour," he declared. "Tomorrow I shall fall asleep in glory."

Fouquier and Herman were determined that sentence should be imposed as soon as possible on the following day. And armed with their deadly decree, they were able to see that it was. "The debate will now end," pronounced the President after Fouquier had finished the remaining business of Chabot and the Frei brothers.

"End!" bellowed Danton. "End? How can it end? It hasn't even begun. You have not read a single document! You have not called a single witness!" A great cry went up from all the accused men. "We are to be sentenced without a hearing!" The uproar coud be heard on the streets.

Herman rang his bell, and Fouquier, pointing to the decree, demanded that the accused be removed from the room during the jury's absence. They were not even permitted to be present when sentence was imposed upon them. Desmoulins began to scream. He clung to his chair with such tenacity that it took three guards to carry him out of the courtroom. Danton departed, hurling fire at the Tribunal. They were taken back to prison, where Samson's tumbrels were already waiting to take them to the place of execution immediately after sentence had been pronounced.

Even at this juncture, however, and even among jurors as prejudiced as those who had been picked for Danton's trial, some restraining scruple seems to have manifested itself in the jury room. A rumor went about the court that the jury was not agreed and that a majority, indeed, was in favor of an acquittal. Fouquier and Herman now made their clumsy travesty of legal procedure complete by entering the jury room. They not only brought with them dire threats from the Committee of Public Safety, but also a mysterious letter that has never been explained and about which history knows nothing except that it extorted from the jury the decision that the Committee was determined to have. Some people believe that the letter may have had some reference to Marie Antoinette.

The jury returned to the courtroom with the faces "of madmen." "The wretches are going to die!" declared the foreman to the Clerk of Court. David, with an air of fierce joy, called out to everyone, "We've got them at last!"

The prisoners' benches were empty when Herman pronounced the sentence of death upon them. He ordered that the sentence be read to the condemned men "between the two turnstiles of the prison." It was imperative that the condemned be executed as quickly as possible.

36

"BIG GAME TODAY!" a guard called out when Samson entered the Conciergerie a few moments after sentence had been read to the doomed men.

Danton and his colleagues had already been shepherded to that grim room, still to be seen at the Conciergerie, where the executioner and his assistants prepared their "clients" for execution. Here, on a wooden bench the shirt collar of the victim was cut open, the hair at the back of the neck clipped and the hands of the victim bound behind his back. This preparation was archly referred to as "la toilette."

Samson found Danton in a mood of defiant cheerfulness, determined to play the rôle of "Danton" to the end. As he left prison, just before stepping into the tumbrel he is said to have declared, "What does it matter if I die? I've caroused, spent lots of money and loved women. Now it's time to sleep." Others claim to have heard him say, "I have the consolation of believing that the man who died as leader of the Indulgents will be treated mercifully by posterity." Dissimilar in spirit though the two remarks might superficially appear, they express perfectly the total character of this strange and passionate man. The difference between those two statements, like the difference between the prints in stereoscopic photography, projects Danton with an unexpected depth.

Poor Camille was less sanguine in his final hours. He resisted the scissors of Samson, cold foreshadow of the fatal blade, and raved incoherently about his wife and son. It became necessary to tie him to the bench. After they had bound his hands, he asked Danton, whose hands were not yet bound, to take from his neck a locket that contained the hair of Lucile and to put it into his hands. Camille

clutched this relic to the end and requested Samson (if we are to believe the memoirs of that cryptic personage) to remove it from his
body after he had been decapitated and to convey it to Lucile's
mother. Danton, who was the father of two sons himself and who
was leaving behind him a wife whom he loved dearly, uttered no
words about his own loss but applied himself to comforting the
distraught Camille with a tenderness and an understanding that
does him great credit. With Fabre d'Églantine, who was on the
other side of him in the tumbrel and who was nearly as distraught
as Camille, Danton was less tactful.

Fabre, vain littérateur to the end, was obsessed with the suspicion
that his literary rival, Billaud-Varennes, another playwright *manqué*,
might appropriate the manuscript of an unpublished play, *L'Orange
de Malte,* and pass it off as a work of his own. "There are such beautiful verses in it!" he lamented. "Such beautiful verses! [*de si beau
vers*]." Danton turned to him and with a Rabelaisian chortle made
a blood-chilling pun. In French the word *vers* means "worms" as
well as "verses." "Beautiful *vers*, indeed!" he laughed. "Before the
week is out you'll be making some beautiful *vers!*" Fabre's reply to
this ghastly play on words is not recorded.

Hérault de Séchelles, who was related to the Polignacs, observed
the affair with the wan irony appropriate to an aristocrat and a
philosopher. He scarcely uttered a word during the whole trip from
the Conciergerie to the Place de la Révolution. Here and there along
the way he nodded to friends. Despite his attitude of indifference, it
was noted by those who saw him that he was very pale.

The scenes that Danton glimpsed in his final trip across Paris
must have flashed upon his sight like some panorama of his past,
broken into fragments as though by a kaleidoscope. Surrounded by
a heavily armed *gendarmerie,* the tumbrels—there were three in this
procession, carrying eighteen victims to the slaughter—lurched out
of the Cour du Mai of the Palais de Justice over the Pont Neuf,
across the Quai du Louvre and into the rue St. Honoré, where they
turned leftwards, heading towards the rue Royale and the Place de
la Révolution. Danton thus passed near the site of his first lodgings
in Paris; passed within sight of the Café de Montparnasse, where
he had courted Gabrielle; passed not far from the Manège and the
Tuileries, where his voice had risen in patriotic exhortation. On the
rue St. Honoré he passed that place of evil omen, the Jacobin Club,

and a few doors down from it the house of Duplay the carpenter, where Robespierre lived in austere solitude. The shutters of Duplay's house were closed this day; like its shadowy tenant it had wrapped itself in noncommittal silence.

"Vile Robespierre!" cried Danton prophetically in a voice so loud it could have been heard within. "You will follow me. Your house will be leveled and the ground where it stood will be sowed with salt!"

Danton had always viewed the mob with a realist's eyes, and on his way to the scaffold he expressed his views. Camille, in a condition approaching frenzy, suddenly turned to the mob and shrieked out at it, "People! They have lied to you. They are sacrificing your servants! My only crime is to have shed tears." Danton turned to him and said, "Be quiet. Leave that vile rabble alone."

It was well after four o'clock by the time the procession finally reached the place of execution. The great square was filled as it was only on such momentous occasions as the execution of Louis XVI or of Marie Antoinette. A deep hush fell over the crowd as Samson helped his victims out of the carts and lined them up at the foot of the scaffold. Hérault de Séchelles was called first. He turned to embrace Danton and to say a few words of farewell to him. But time was pressing and Samson had eighteen heads to take off before nightfall. He separated them and hurried Hérault up the steps of the scaffold.

"Wretch!" exclaimed Danton. "You will not be able to prevent our heads from meeting in the basket."

Camille Desmoulins was the third to go. As his end approached he grew calm. He died clutching the locket of Lucile's hair, with Lucile's name reverently on his lips. Such he had promised in his last letter to her. "With bound hands I shall hold your hair. . . ."

The poet Arnault was among the crowd that filled the Place de la Révolution that mild spring evening. He watched the butchery until the end. Danton was the last. Daylight had already begun to fade when he stepped onto the scaffold. Beside the guillotine there stood an enormous statue of Liberty, done in plaster. Mme. Roland in her last minutes is said to have addressed it with the words, "Oh, Liberty! How they've duped you." The light of the sinking sun now caused it to "stand out in massive outline," as Arnault saw "something rise up that was like the shadow of Danton. In the dying light of day the great leader seemed to be rising out of his tomb as much as preparing to descend into it. Never was anything more bold than that athlete's countenance, never anything more formidable than the look of that profile which seemed to defy the knife. That great head, even as it was about to fall, appeared to be in the act of dictating laws. . . ."

At the last moment, the thought of his wife became unbearable, and he faltered. "Oh, my beloved," he murmured. "Shall I never see you again?" Then he took hold of himself and said, "Come, come, Danton. There must be no weakness." He turned to the executioner and said, "You must show my head to the People. It is worth it." A moment later he too was gone and his body thrown on top of the seventeen others that lay in a cart on the other side of the scaffold. He was only thirty-four years old, but he had warmed both hands well before the fire of life.

Danton, above all else, was a man of flesh and blood. Those historians who concern themselves with the events of history to the exclusion of the inner lives of the men who make the events, or those political theorists who are unable to see beyond the rigid categories that are fixed within the vocabulary of their personal convictions, will usually find Danton an awkward figure in the Revolutionary scene. He cut across parties and transcended the small consistencies of men less farsighted and less able than himself. In so doing he aroused the resentment of such bureaucrats as Roland and the rancor of such doctrinaire zealots as Robespierre. A certain school of historians can view him with no more charity than he was accorded by Robespierre. By these he has been contemptuously dismissed from the scene as "an opportunist." And that undoubtedly he was, but in so open, so bluffly cynical, so Gallic a manner as to suggest the presence in him of a deeper strain of altruism and honor. Society expects its opportunists to have the decency to wear the mask of hypocrisy. Had Danton done so, his counsels might have prevailed over those of Robespierre and France might have been spared the final and most terrible spasm of the Terror.

It is as a man that Danton ought finally to be judged. It is perhaps fitting that it should be an Englishman who pronounced the best and final sentence on him, since Danton spoke English with some fluency and had always been an admirer of the English people and of their laws and literature.

"He was brave and resolute," writes Macaulay, "fond of pleasures, of power and of distinction, with vehement passions, with lax principles, but with many kind and manly feelings. He was capable of great crimes, but capable too of friendship and compassion."

III. THE END OF ROBESPIERRE

JULY 1794

37

WITH THE DEATH of Danton France entered into that dark, brief period of its history that is called the Great Terror, a time that, in the words of Belloc, "leaves gaps which many men dare not bridge by reading." The Great Terror was to last for sixteen weeks, until the day known in the Revolutionary calendar as 9 Thermidor (July 27), when, with a desperate convulsion, the Convention finally overthrew Robespierre and his cohorts.

It is appropriate to the unreal atmosphere that surrounds this time that the familiar divisions of the year should have been altered and the months be made to begin on the twenty-first of the old calendar. These new months were given such fanciful names as Ventôse, Prairial, Messidor and Thermidor. In dating events that occurred during this period most historians make use of the Revolutionary calendar. Thus Danton was guillotined on 16 Germinal (April 5) and the terrible law that eliminated all defense before the Revolutionary Tribunal is known as the Law of 22 Prairial, June 10. Such terminology is confusing, but it captures a flavor suggestive of the period and of France's temporary alienation from the flow of history.

One immediate result of Danton's death was a firm tightening of the net held by the Revolutionary Tribunal. Herman, the "judge" who had presided over the trial of the Dantonists was rewarded with the portfolio of the Minister of the Interior a few days after the conclusion of the trial. His place on the Tribunal was taken by a man named Dumas, whom even Fouquier-Tinville spoke of as a "strangler," a brutal hatchetman totally submissive to the wishes of the Committee of Public Safety. From behind the screen of that all-powerful institution Robespierre let his will be known. "The

Tribunal," he pronounced, "must be as active as crime itself and conclude every case within twenty-four hours."

Henceforth most cases were concluded in less time, indeed, than twenty-four hours. The victims were shepherded to the courtroom in the morning and, no matter how many of them there might be, their fate was settled by no later than two in the afternoon of that same day. By three o'clock their hair had been cut, their hands bound and they were in the death carts on their way to the scaffold. Execution was almost always effected on the same day the sentence was imposed.

As Camille Desmoulins had foreseen, his wife soon followed his footsteps to the guillotine. Although her story is of no historical importance it nonetheless illuminates history with one of those flashes of human warmth and light that are always more significant than cold dates, statistics or political analysis. Lucile was arrested immediately after Camille's execution. It suited the Committee to support St. Just's story of a "dangerous conspiracy in the prisons." Along with having been seen in the vicinity of the Luxembourg (carrying the baby Horace in her arms in the hope that Camille might catch a glimpse of him), Lucile had gone to Robespierre's house and tried to gain admittance in order to plead with the Incorruptible on her husband's behalf. No man was less accessible to the pleas of wailing women than Robespierre, and his door remained adamantly closed. Such manifestations of despair conveniently lent themselves to St. Just's contention that revolt was afoot, and Lucile was accordingly arrested.

It is probable that the real villain in this sorry little tale was St. Just rather than Robespierre. St. Just had many reasons to hate Desmoulins, who had preceded him in Robespierre's unstable confidence. (Robespierre, in fact, had been chief witness at Camille's wedding and was actually godfather of little Horace.) Not least of these reasons was the fact that Camille, the too successful author, had once made a sarcastic reference to St. Just's epic poem *Organt,* and in so doing had compounded the insult by maliciously misspelling its portentous title. The fate of Lucile Desmoulins and of the orphaned Horace would have meant little to this cold theoretician who wanted all children removed from their parents' care soon after birth. St. Just looked on Camille's contented household with contempt.

Lucile was condemned to death on April 13, along with eighteen other victims. She accepted her sentence with serenity. "In a few hours I shall see my Camille again," she declared to her judges. "I am therefore less to be pitied than you, for at your death, which will be infamous, you will be haunted by remorse for what you have done." At the same trial the widow of Hébert was also condemned. The two women whose husbands had so bitterly hated each other struck up a friendship in the last few days of their life. "You are lucky," Mme. Hébert said to Lucile as they departed for the scaffold. "Nobody speaks ill of you. There is no shadow upon your character. You are leaving life by the grand staircase."

Lucile's mother was less philosophical about her daughter's fate. In less than a week's time this unfortunate woman had seen a son-in-law whom she loved dearly and a daughter who was the mother of her only grandchild put to death under the same axe. Upon hearing the news of her daughter's sentence she sent a frantic letter to Robespierre. "It is not enough for you to have murdered your best friend," she cried. "You must have his wife's blood as well. Your monster Fouquier-Tinville has just ordered Lucile to be taken to the scaffold. In less than two hours' time she will be dead. If you aren't a human tiger, if Camille's blood hasn't driven you mad, if you are still able to remember the happy evenings you once spent before our fire fondling our Horace, spare an innocent victim. If not—then hurry and take us all, Horace, myself and my other daughter Adèle. Hurry and tear us apart with your claws that still drip with Camille's blood . . . hurry, hurry so that we can all sleep in the same grave!"

No answer was vouchsafed this indiscreet cry of rage and grief. Lucile went quietly to her death. In the short time between her condemnation and her departure for the guillotine, she wrote a hurried note of farewell to her mother. It is one of the briefest, but surely one of the most poignant, of all the letters of the condemned written during the Terror.

Good night, dearest Maman. A tear falls from my eyes; it is for you. I shall fall asleep in the calm of innocence.

LUCILE

Mme. Duplessis never received this little cry from the edge of the grave. All such letters from the condemned were seized by Fouquier's clerks and thrown into the files of the Tribunal, an act not so much of deliberate cruelty as of bureaucratic indifference to human suffering. The heyday had now come of the *petit commissaire*, the traditionally rude and disaffected men who make life miserable for those who solicit consideration from the offices of government. But instead of handling visas, tax difficulties or postage stamps, the clerks of the Revolutionary Tribunal dispatched human life. In the welter of red tape and paper work with which they surrounded themselves, they were as insensitive to the grief of the bereaved as they were to the anguish of the dying. Lucile's last letter and many hundreds like it may be read today in the French National Archives, mute and terrible testimonies to the human suffering that was the price of the lifeless theories of such men as Robespierre and St. Just. Many of them are still stained with tears and in many others an unsteady hand betrays all too graphically the fear and despair of their doomed author.

During the months that preceded Danton's death the Tribunal had claimed 116 victims. In the following two months more than 500 were sent to their deaths. After the Law of 22 Prairial (June 10) was passed, the carnage began in earnest. Between June 10 and July 27, the day of Robespierre's downfall, 1,366 victims perished. There can be no doubt that if Robespierre had not been overthrown, these numbers would have greatly increased in the months after Thermidor.

This is the period of the Revolution that captured the attention of the Victorian novelist and gave birth to many anecdotes of a sensational sort. What makes such stories extraordinary is the fact that many of them are verifiably true. A spell of horror seems temporarily to have fallen over the city of Paris, a nightmare in which all communication with reality was suspended. It is impossible to read of this period without the impression that one is here confronted with forces more powerful than those controlled by men. "The Great Terror," declared one witness, "was a whirlwind that swept aside like a straw all human power that attempted to oppose it." Robespierre himself and even Fouquier-Tinville appear to have been shocked by the ocean of blood through which they now waded. The Public Prosecutor was crossing the Pont Neuf one evening when he was seen to stagger. "I am not well," he said to his companion.

"Sometimes I imagine that I see the shadows of the dead following me."

The politicians guillotined one another in order to escape the guillotine themselves, but what of the anonymous hundreds who were sent to their deaths for no better reason than that they were "under suspicion" and consequently under arrest, and because Fouquier had orders, as he phrased it, to "get heads"? Of what possible crime against the state can the seventeen-year-old hairdresser's apprentice Martin Alleaume have been guilty? Or the eighty-five-year-old Jacques Bardy? Or Marie Bouchard, an eighteen-year-old "domestic servant"? Thanks to Fouquier's meticulous clerks, the names and condition of nearly all the victims who died after Danton's execution are filed at the Archives. And one can only stand perplexed and appalled before the record of these indiscriminate butcheries that tossed together nuns, soldiers, ex-nobles, workmen, servant girls and prostitutes, not to mention the victims without number who belonged to no particular class or category, but who seem to have been caught like sardines in the meshes of an invisible net.

"I saw twenty peasant girls from Poitou," relates an eyewitness to a typical scene in the Conciergerie, "all of whom were to be executed together. Overcome by the fatigue of their long journey, they lay in the courtyard of the Conciergerie, sleeping on the paving stones. Their glances betrayed no understanding of the fate that awaited them, resembling those of oxen herded together in the market place. They stared fixedly about them without comprehension. They were all guillotined a few days after their arrival. At the moment these unhappy women were going to their deaths, a guard took from the breast of one of them the baby that she was nursing. . . ."

It is perhaps of parenthetic interest that someone named Helen Maria Williams confirms the story about the twenty peasant women from Poitou. Miss Williams was one of several English Liberals who, thrilled by the Revolution, hastened to Paris to be on the scene of great events. She applauded Danton's *coup d'état* of August 10 with a snowstorm of enthusiastic letters home to England. After the September Massacres, however, her enthusiasm began to wane. With Robespierre's ascendancy in the Committee, she was thrown into prison (all persons of English or foreign origin being declared "suspect"), where she began to experience herself some of the anguish that, in her transports of sentimental altruism, she had so callously overlooked in the fate of others. From that moment Miss Williams's revolutionary ardor is said to have "considerably cooled."

During the May that followed Danton's death the ardor of many another hothead appears to have cooled. Silence fell over the once animated rue St. Honoré, through which the death carts rumbled with their daily cargo of human cattle. A few months earlier this interesting procession had consisted of one or, on exceptional occasions, two tumbrels. Now it was not unusual to see three, four or five carts escorted by a shuffling, lackadaisical *gendarmerie*. The doomed went to their fate in stunned and submissive silence; the onlookers no longer gathered in quite so festive a mood. The execution of the Hébertists had put a damper on the enthusiasm of the vociferous canaille, while that of Danton had silenced the Old Guard of the Revolution, the Vieux Cordeliers. By June 1794 no walk of life had not been struck by that great blade that every afternoon rose and fell forty, fifty or sixty times on the Place de la Révolution. No one in the city of Paris could count himself safe, least of all the administrators of this indiscriminate and desperate slaughter. These knew full well that should the day of retribution ever arrive they would be made to walk that same path down which they had sent so many others.

So, in the heat of that terrible summer—hotter, it was said, than any in living memory—the people of Paris waited for deliverance.

38

"I saw paris in those days of crime and mourning," writes Joseph Broz, a future Academician who was then nineteen years of age. "From the stupefied expression on people's faces you would have said that it was a city desolated by a plague. The laughter of a few cannibals alone interrupted the deadly silence which surrounded you."

The history of a city in many ways resembles the life of an individual. Just as there are certain periods of crisis in the human life which alter what has gone before and determine, psychologically, what is to come after, so in the history of cities there is often a period in their evolution which is so violent or fascinating as to fix permanently a character that is compounded of atmosphere and association. The Terror was one of those periods in Paris. Today's visitor to the Conciergerie does not return from that relic of medieval construction thinking about its Gothic dining hall, one of the most perfect examples of medieval architecture to be found in Paris, but rather about the building when it was a prison during the time of the Terror. The anguish of its doomed occupants seems to have impregnated the walls of the place. It is not possible to see the Cour des Femmes, the Women's Courtyard, a part of the building that has been virtually unchanged since the Revolution, without receiving from it some sense of the scenes to which these grey walls have been witness. The fountain where the women washed their clothes and the stone bench on which they sat remain untouched. The bell rung by the jailers to announce the arrival of the tumbrels is still to be seen a few feet from the fountain and the grille through which the victims passed to their execution is the same grille to which Mme. du Barry clung in despair and which was touched by Lucile Desmoulins's dress as she too passed on her way out of life.

Such vestiges of the Terror as the Conciergerie abound in Paris, and to those familiar with the period they seem to exhale an almost palpable influence upon the imagination. So powerful indeed is the fascination of the period that it has given birth to a whole school of French historians. Led by the admirable Messrs. Cain and Lenôtre these historians have specialized in the geography of Paris as it was at the time of the Terror, and have devoted their life's work to searching for some forgotten house, some room or some fragment of wall which has an association with the human drama of the Revolution. Where, for instance, was the Hôtel Brittanique, where Roland and his wife "put up" when they came up to Paris from Lyons? It was on the rue Guénégaud, that is known, but which of the buildings was it on that short street, which has been relatively untouched by time? M. Lenôtre, at least, never found a satisfactory answer. But the fifth-floor room where Brissot and his friends often came to call, and where Robespierre chewed his nails over Mme. Roland's sugar-water tisane, may well still stand in Paris to day—a curious relic, if it does, whose walls would tell us more about the time than many an earnest tome devoted to the study of political effects at the expense of human causes.

This fascination, so singular a characteristic of the Terror, owes itself undoubtedly to the fact that the individuality of human flesh and blood was never overwhelmed by events. The appalling hecatombs of our own time resemble the numberless holocausts of ancient history, just as the dictators of our age resemble the cold and faceless tyrants of Asia Minor. Such men and such happenings are beyond the grasp of human comprehension. Individual anguish is engulfed by numbers that are inconceivable. Such, however, was not the case during the Terror. The methodical clerks of Fouquier-Tinville kept cold and careful record of the human cattle they had dispatched to the slaughterhouse. And thanks to those assiduous writers of memoirs, always at hand during critical periods of French history to record in detail the occurrences of their time, many of the condemned can be recalled in their flesh-and-blood appearance. The events of the Reign of Terror therefore in many ways seem closer to us than do the vast, inhuman cataclysms of our own era. Kaleidoscopic and disconnected in character, the anecdotes that may be culled from memoirs and the Paris archives throw a vivid light on life as it was lived within the prisons of Paris.

The closing years of the century of Voltaire saw pregnant women anticipating the moment of their delivery with horror. The pregnancy of a condemned woman secured her a temporary reprieve, but upon the birth of her baby she was dragged weak and tottering to the scaffold; the baby was sent to a state orphanage. Many women therefore declared themselves pregnant and managed, while waiting for an examination by the prison doctors, to grasp at another day or two of life. Such a case was that of the Princesse de Monaco, who had been born a Frenchwoman of the noble house of Choiseul-Stainville. Having secured a day's reprieve, she cut her hair with her own hands and was able to have it smuggled out of the prison and delivered to her children. "I inform you, Citizen, that I am not pregnant," she then wrote Fouquier-Tinville. "I did not soil my mouth with this lie from fear of death or because I wish to avoid it, but to secure a day's grace so that my hair would not have been cut by the executioner. It is the only legacy I am able to leave my children; it should at least be pure."

The Princesse was executed the next day. It is said that she rouged her cheeks so that she would not look pale should weakness overcome her at the last moment. Her maid died with her and she was heard to say to that unfortunate woman as she ascended the steps of the scaffold, "Have courage, my friend. Crime alone should show fear." She died along with forty-six others on 9 Thermidor, the day of Robespierre's overthrow, and she was therefore in the last "batch" (*journée*) to go to the guillotine.

The Maréchal de Mouchy was a man of eighty. He and his wife were in the prison of the Luxembourg when it was decided to empty such houses of detention by systematically transferring all occupants to the Conciergerie and dispatching them on the scaffold. Mme. de Mouchy was too old and too ill to comprehend what was happening. When the guard came to summon them for trial, her husband said to her in a gentle voice, "Madame, we must go now. God wishes it, let us therefore honor His will. I shall not leave your side. We shall depart together." The Maréchal de Mouchy and his wife had made themselves very much liked among their fellow prisoners at the Luxembourg. When they departed, their friends lined up before the gate to bid them adieu. "Courage, Monsieur le Maréchal!" cried one of these.

The Maréchal answered in a phrase that has the knightly ring of another day and age. "My friend," he declared, "when I was fifteen I went into the breach for my King. At eighty I go to the scaffold for my God. I am not unfortunate."

During the trial of this decrepit couple it was discovered that Fouquier's clerks had made a mistake and Mme. de Mouchy had never been legally arrested. There was, therefore, no formal accusation against her; she was on trial in flagrant defiance of all legal procedure. Such small details never troubled Fouquier-Tinville, however, and he ordered the trial to proceed. "It will all come to the same anyhow," he remarked to the court with a chuckle.

So nonchalant a dismissal of people's lives was commonplace before the Revolutionary Tribunal. Another instance of it took place at the same trial in which the Mouchy couple was condemned. There happened to be two women of the name Biron incarcerated in the Conciergerie. When Fouquier's clerks received orders to bring "the Biron woman" to trial they did not know which one he meant. An usher informed him that there were two women of this name in prison. "Take both of them, then," he replied. The two women were executed that very afternoon along with the Maréchal and Maréchale de Mouchy.

A certain woman named Mayet found herself condemned in a characteristic "batch" of fifty others. The fact that in calling her to her trial the illiterate guards had confused her with a Mme. de Maillé caused no consternation at all to Fouquier-Tinville. "Since she's here we might as well take her," was the answer to her protest. Mme. de Maillé survived the Reign of Terror and lived to recount her story only because when she herself was brought to trial she lost consciousness when she saw her sixteen-year-old son standing among the accused. She had to be removed from court. Her case was deferred for a day or two and during that time Robespierre was overthrown. The boy died bravely. It is said that when he heard his sentence he turned to a guard and, offering his hand, declared, "Do you think that I am nervous? See, my hand does not tremble."

Such great names as Monaco-Choiseul, Mouchy and Maillé give the false impression that the victims of the Great Terror were largely representative of the former nobility. That was far from the truth.

All walks of life were to be found in those great "batches" of forty and fifty souls. Science was represented by the chemist Lavoisier, who is said to have requested a short reprieve of his sentence in order to complete an experiment on which he was working. "The Republic has no need of scientists," came the brusque reply, and Lavoisier was forthwith guillotined, his experiment uncompleted.

Poetry's most famous victim was André Chenier, who died under a mistaken accusation (the authorities confused him with his brother Sauveur). Chenier's father had tried to secure André's release from the prison of St. Lazare, but in writing the authorities had only succeeded in reminding them of the existence of André, who through some clerical error had been overlooked. He was guillotined on 7 Thermidor (July 25) two days before Robespierre's downfall. Chenier was a revolutionist of the school of Charlotte Corday and had never quite recovered from the mystical exaltation that he had experienced on the day of her death a year earlier. He was an outspoken opponent of the Terror. He might, therefore, have been condemned on more accurate charges than he was, had Fouquier-Tinville troubled himself to uncover them.

Journalists and all snoopy or opinionated folk were anathema to Robespierre. "Repress the journalist impostors," he wrote succinctly in his private notebook. In consequence a great many men of the press were hailed before Fouquier-Tinville and condemned—most of them for opinions that they had expressed many months earlier, since all newspapers but the official *Moniteur* had been banned by the time of the Great Terror. Robespierre's naïve egotism is perfectly revealed in the sentence that immediately follows his note about "journalistic impostors." "Diffuse good writings," he declares, with hardly a pause. In his eyes journalistic impostors" were those who might criticize him, while "good writings" were those that were disseminated from the office of *l'esprit publique,* which was under his thumb. The fate of one journalist, a man named Paisan who had once been editor of a forgotten publication called *La Feuille du Jour,* is characteristic. The accused was asked if he hadn't once written in his paper that "in France they plant Liberty trees, but they don't pay much attention to the roots of the tree."

"I don't remember if I did," stammered the bewildered man. "But I don't think that I did."

"That's enough from you," snapped the President of the court.

"You have no right to speak [*tu n'as pas la parole*]." Paisan was condemned with no further hearing.

When we read the record of these "trials," the fate of the so-called lower classes somehow seems worst of all. These unfortunate creatures, many of them hardly aware of what was happening to them, were often arrested and brought to trial on the whim of their neighborhood Section leaders. Denunciations inspired by a neighbor's jealousy or some personal quarrel were generally at the root of their ruin. A man named Marc Bardier, tailor, was tried and guillotined because a neighbor claimed to have heard him say that "the men who work in government offices are all wretches." A seventy-two-year-old widow, Françoise Bridier, a domestic servant, was condemned to death when, because of a neighbor's denunciation, it was discovered that she had concealed ten ells of linen in her room. An ignorant creature named Germaine Quetier made the mistake of saying in front of malicious witnesses that she needed a spinning wheel. The word for spinning wheel (*rouet*) sounded on her lips like the word for king (*roi*) and accordingly she was guillotined. A young carpenter's apprentice lost his temper while playing cards in a café. His opponent unctuously rebuked him, saying that "good patriots don't talk like that." Understandably angered, Jabin yelled out "F—— good patriots [*je me f—— des patriotes*]." He was immediately arrested, brought to trial and guillotined.

The Abbé de Salamon relates a story in his memoirs of a devoted old servant named Blanchet who had been in his employ for many years. During the Terror she found herself in the Prison des Anglais with several once fashionable *ci-devants* of the *ancien régime*. These women, who in more tolerant times had frivolously (and ineptly) played with the fire of Rousseau and political theory, were now, under the shadow of the guillotine, able to appreciate the outcome of their misbegotten enthusiasms. Despite their shallow "liberalism" (an up-to-date expression of *noblesse oblige* was all that this usually was) and despite their condition in prison they remained fully aware of the difference between themselves and working women such as Blanchet. One of them, the Duchesse de la Rochefoucauld, turned to old Blanchet and said, "Citizeness Blanchet, it seems you are going to be guillotined just like one of us. . . ."

"I am quite aware of that," snapped Blanchet; "but there is a difference between you and me. I shall die for your cause, which you have abandoned, and you will die for having embraced the cause of these so-called 'patriots' . . . it will be more degrading for you to die thus. No one will be sorry for you, but honorable people who hear of my fate will pray for me. I have always been an aristocrat myself, and you, you were the friend of that despicable Condorcet, about whom I could tell you a thing or two."

Blanchet, in fact, survived the Terror and died eleven years later in the arms of her master.

Public drunkenness, in ordinary circumstances a rather rare sight in France, increased greatly during the culminating throes of the Terror. "Drunkenness has fearfully multiplied," reported one of the Committee's spies. "You can't walk five steps down the street without meeting a drunk." Inflamed by spirits and urged on by some obscure but exciting sense of danger, many men and women courted death by incautious oaths spoken on the street. More than one instance is recorded of people raising their voices in the cry *Vive le roi!* An atmosphere of madness induced by the reek of blood and a sense of horror hung over Paris like a blanket in the stifling summer nights that preceded 9 Thermidor. Brandy, therefore, was not the only stimulant that prompted men to self-destruction. Those who most fear heights will often leap from them. So many a deranged soul, fascinated by the ghastly scenes that were daily enacted about him, would plunge to his death in the very courtroom of the Tribunal by rising from his seat among the spectators and crying out *Vive le roi!*

In many ways it was better to be in prison than "free" in a city paralyzed by terror and suspicion. In prison, at least, the worst was over. One could fairly well count on death. "Out of prison you could not venture to meet, speak to or scarcely look at your friends, so terrified were you of compromising one another." So writes Pasquier, Napoleon's future Chancellor. "If you heard a knock on the door you immediately imagined that Revolutionary *commissaires* had come to take you away. But behind bars you re-entered society, as it were. You were surrounded by your relatives and friends and could converse freely with them."

The beautiful city of Paris, only a few years earlier the beacon light to Europe of all that was free in spirit, elegant in manner and tasteful in form, lay gutted and dead. "Tant de plaisir, tant de grâce, tant d'étouderie!" sighed those who had once loved it. "All this

337

handed over to inquisition, fanaticism and stupidity." The famous tree-lined boulevards that encircled the city were now empty of all traffic. The theatre, once the most animated expression of the perceptive and paradoxical French spirit, was now at the mercy of the heavy-handed and vulgar censorship of the Commune far stricter than anything ever seen under the monarchy. All of Molière was banned and most of Voltaire was "altered." At the Comédie Française a play was given in which the line *"et les plus tolérants sont les plus pardonnables"* was spoken. A Jacobin who happened to be in the audience rose from his seat red-faced with anger and yelled at the players, "No tolerance in politics! Tolerance is a crime!" The audience indignantly silenced him, but he hurried away and denounced the performance to the Jacobin Club. All the actors and the author were immediately placed under arrest and no doubt would have been guillotined had not the Terror ended before their trial.

Understandably the theatre, like every other expression of the free human spirit, withered away and died in this unpropitious climate. Someone suggested to the dramatist Ducis that he write a tragedy. "Why talk to me of writing tragedies?" he replied. "If I stir out of my house I'm up to my ankles in blood. . . . Farewell to tragedy, then. It is a rude drama when the People become the tyrant and it can only end in Hell." Jacobin tirades and vulgar burlesques of religion entered the vacuum left by such men as Ducis. By all accounts these productions must have been asphyxiating. Even the *Moniteur,* the government's official publication, protested the low state into which the theatre had fallen and in all seriousness suggested that the decline could probably be traced to the machinations of the agents of Pitt, who were employed to demoralize the public spirit with boring plays.

The Opéra limped along, but in no better shape. The music played there was usually revolutionary in spirit and of the patriotic kind to which the audience would be expected to respond by enthusiastically joining the chorus. "Group activities," always the sign of a dying or dead culture, enjoyed a brief vogue they have never known before or since in France. A horrible community function known as the Fraternal Supper was instituted during the Great Terror. Everyone in a neighborhood was expected to show up at these weekly gatherings, each bringing a contribution of food. Neighbor would sit beside neighbor at a communal board, and all were expected to join in the merriment, flinging arms about one another's shoulders and singing lustily. Timid or self-conscious spirits were at a serious disadvantage during these *agapes*, for too aloof an attitude hinted at snobbishness or at aristocratic propensities, while an overly eager appearance suggested insincerity or hypocrisy to the watchful eyes of the local Sectional leaders.

Some small compensation for the humiliation and fear the *convives* at these ghastly affairs must have endured was the food. Despite famine and an unpropitious setting, it appears to have been excellent. We have the account of a Mme. Rataud to testify to this fact. She relates that she did not know what to bring to her neighborhood Fraternal Supper. She was afraid that a simple dish like braised beans and leeks would offend the Jacobins present while more elaborate fare such as a roasted partridge with *choucroute garnie* might provoke an inspection of her too ample larder. She resolved the dilemma by bringing both dishes, and both were eaten with gusto and without incident.

It may thus be seen that the French did not totally lose possession of their senses during this unnatural time. Along with this example of their instinctive respect for the pleasures of the table it is to be noticed that they never went in for mass calisthenics or for folk dancing, those stern recreations which are the familiar expression of dictatorship in the Saxon or Slavic community.

The reports of the ubiquitous spies of the Committee of Public Safety filed in the Archives give us a partial picture of life in Paris during those days. "Children under five or six years of age should not be allowed to enter the courtroom of the Revolutionary Tribunal," complains one such report, "for they make a great deal of noise by crying during the trials. Vendors of apples, *petits pains* and brandy should also be banished, for they make so much noise calling out their wares that you can't hear what is being said." Having seen the trials, these infants of five or six were usually taken to the scaffold to witness the denouement.

Spies were everywhere. Not only the Committee's spies, but Robespierre's private agents, who were employed to spy on the official spies. They would join the conversation of men and women in public places like street corners or cafés and attempt, in this way, to net a potential victim for the Tribunal. A facial expression could be enough to arouse suspicion. A depressed or unhappy look would attract attention and often prompt an inquiry into the identity and circumstances of anyone who had such a dissatisfied air. "Taciturn faces, obviously those of men who are tired of life, are sometimes to be seen in promenades or groups," declares a spy in one report.

There were times, however, when a too contented look would awaken their suspicion. Such a time was the period just before the arrest and trial of Hébert and Danton, when Robespierre fell ill. Whether feigned in order to remove himself from the scene of open combat or whether genuine (and considering Robespierre's character, these seizures could well have been psychosomatic in origin), Robespierre usually took to his bed before a major crisis such as Danton's arrest. Paris always knew when he was ill. "Near the Jardin des Plantes," reports a spy at the end of February, "a sizable group was discussing Robespierre's illness. Most of them seemed concerned, but I noticed that while these sans-culottes discussed Robespierre's illness, certain well-dressed men who were listening wore a look of satisfaction on their countenances and didn't join in the conversation of the patriots."

A peculiar manifestation of the Terror were the *tricoteuses,* women who were supposed to have knitted at the foot of the guillotine. Dickens made them famous in *A Tale of Two Cities.* These women, clad in rags and half demented, came to the attention of the police spies. "People notice that certain women have become bloodthirsty," they report. "These creatures preach nothing but blood. There are more and more of them who are constantly around the guillotine or at the Tribunal. . . ." Racing about with denunciations on their lips and demanding constant attention, these drunken, crazy old harridans (the ancestresses, no doubt, of many of today's concierges) were a source of irritation even to Robespierre. One of them rose in the gallery of the Jacobin Club one day and complained that her repeated denunciations of a certain "aristocrat" had not been listened to. She was silenced, one reads with pleasure, "with a rebuke." Those of them who were vendors of violets or brandy at street corners were a singular nuisance to passing strollers. One declined to buy their wares at the risk of being publicly called an "aristocrat." They roamed the streets in small, vociferous packs, and anyone who happened to catch their attention would be obliged to sing a patriotic song or do a dance to the accompaniment of their ribald laughter. They seem to have enjoyed themselves immensely throughout the Terror, probably the only class of people who did.

The population of Paris during the Terror was about 650,000. Of this number at least 125,000 were National Guard. The greater portion of the city's citizenry was "well-to-do" (it is believed that 100,000 or more could even be called rich). A group of about 30,000, however, were "without means," and 9,000 of these were men. This latter segment was made up of unemployed domestics, dissatisfied workers and beggars and idlers of various kinds who left their families at home to starve while they attended Section meetings, for which they were paid a few sous out of the coffers of the Commune. There were 6,000 members of the Jacobin Club in Paris, most of whom were drawn from this group of 9,000 men.

Though these figures can only be general, there is no doubt that the majority of the heterogeneous population of Paris was moderate and law-abiding, and deplored the turn of events which had put the city at the mercy of a few politicians and agitators. The weight of numbers was in the favor of those who secretly opposed Robespierre and the system of the Terror, but until those numbers had been brought together in common cause the will of the united minority would prevail. Although Might, as the events of 9 Thermidor were shortly to demonstrate, makes Right, Might is rarely composed of the efforts of a prudent, frightened majority. Only when the battle's lost or won does Mr. Everyman of history's revolutions open the cellar door and come upstairs to join his equally prudent neighbors in the flag-waving and the cheering. Revolutions are made by politicians, visionaries and audacious opportunists, not by the majority of a city's populace.

And so too, as Robespierre was shortly to learn, are counterrevolutions. After the Law of 22 Prairial, swift and skillful hands began to weave the web of his ruin.

39

Although there exist many eyewitness accounts of life as it was lived in the prisons or on the streets of Paris during the Terror, we have only one description of an actual execution. The kind of person who wrote memoirs or kept a diary may well have found this gory spectacle too much to stomach. Many of these scribblers were all too close to the fatal axe themselves to view so gruesome a spectacle with equanimity or curiosity.

The one narrative which remains to us was written by an abbé, a certain Père Carrichon, who was attached to the family of Noailles, one of the great noble houses of France. At the time of the Terror three Noailles women inhabited the Hôtel de Noailles in the rue de l'Université (another *hôtel particulier* belonging to the cadet branch of their family was in the rue St. Honoré and is today the Hôtel St. James et d'Albany). These women were the elderly Maréchale de Noailles; the Duchesse d'Ayen, a pious and gentle soul of fifty-five who was the Maréchale's daughter-in-law; and the Vicomtesse Louise de Noailles, Mme. D'Ayen's daughter, who was thirty-six years old and the mother of three young children.

The old Maréchale had once played a prominent role at Louis XV's court, where she had been mentor on matters of etiquette to the Dauphine Marie Antoinette. The giddy young Dauphine had disparagingly dubbed her "Mme. l'Étiquette" and made her the butt of droll stories with which she indiscreetly amused her intimates behind the Maréchale's back. The family of Noailles had all been hostile to the Queen. Those matters of genealogy and etiquette with which she had bored the Dauphine became a mania to the Maréchale in the days just before the Revolution. In her dotage she seems to have gone harmlessly mad. She entered into a correspondence with the Virgin Mary in which she questioned the Queen of Heaven on the minutiae of precedence in the Kingdom of God. The Maréchale was looked upon leniently by a society only too familiar with the various manifestations of eccentricity, and her confessor would humor her by answering these letters, which he always signed "Mary," as though the Virgin were of royal or ducal rank. In one of them he made a small error of form, which the Maréchale's alert eye quickly detected. "One cannot expect too much of her," commented the old lady. "After all she was only a bourgeoise from Nazareth. It was through marriage that she became attached to the House of David. Her husband, Joseph, would have known better."

To the old Maréchale de Noailles the events following the execution of Louis XVI can only have seemed to be part of some bizarre nightmare out of which she soon would awaken. The Maréchale's daughter-in-law and her granddaughter saw matters with clearer eyes, and one day during the months of house arrest that preceded their incarceration in the Prison of the Luxembourg, they turned to their friend the Abbé Carrichon and made him promise that he would follow them to the guillotine and somehow give them absolution should they be condemned to death.

"If God gives me the strength to do so," he replied, "I shall accompany you to the scaffold. That you may be certain to recognize me I shall wear a dark-blue coat and a red waistcoat."

On April 6, 1794, the day following Danton's execution, many men and women who had been under house arrest in various parts of Paris were rounded up and taken to prison. Among these were the three Noailles women. It is said that when the old Maréchal de Mouchy heard that his sister-in-law the Maréchale de Noailles had arrived at the Luxembourg, he blanched.

"That crazy old woman doesn't talk with discretion," he declared. "She'll get us all beheaded."

His presentiment may have been correct. We catch fleeting glimpses of Mme. de Noailles hurrying to pay deference to the Duchesse d'Orléans, who was then at the Luxembourg, snubbing other noble prisoners who took liberties of address with her that their rank would not have permitted in another day, and babbling incoherently to the turnkeys and guards about genealogical subtleties.

The Maréchal de Mouchy and his wife were removed to the Conciergerie and sentenced to death on June 27. The Noailles women (*les femmes Noailles,* as they are collectively called on the prison records) followed them three weeks later. The Abbé Carrichon was at home when the tutor of Louise de Noailles's children burst into the room to inform him of the fact that they had been called up for trial.

On the twenty-second of July, which was a Tuesday, I was at my house between eight and ten o'clock in the morning. I was just on the point of going out when I heard a knock on my door. I opened it and saw the children of the Vicomtesse de Noailles with their tutor.

The tutor was pale and very agitated. "Let us go into your bedroom," he said, "and leave the children in your study for a moment." We went into my bedroom and he flung himself into a chair. "It's all over, my friend!" he declared. "The ladies are before the Revolutionary Tribunal at this very moment. I have come to summon you to keep your word to them. I will take the poor children out to the Park of Vincennes, where I will prepare them for their terrible loss."

For a moment I was overwhelmed. . . . I recovered myself and after some inquiries I said, "I must change my clothes, then, and prepare for this. What a mission! I pray to God that he may give me the strength to execute it."

When the tutor and his charges had departed I was nearly overcome. "God have pity on them!" I cried. "And upon me, too!" I changed my clothes and went out, my heart heavy with a sickening weight. I reached the Palais de Justice between one o'clock and two and tried to enter. It was impossible. But I got news [of the outcome of the trial] from someone leaving the court. I tried not to believe what I was told, but all hope was finally destroyed. I could no longer have any doubts. . . .

Anyone familiar with Paris need have no difficulty picturing the general scene that met the Abbé's eye at the Palais de Justice. Standing on the Boulevard du Palais in front of the iron gate that separates the spacious cobbled courtyard of the Palais de Justice from the street, one looks today on a sight that has been almost unaltered since the time of the Terror. Samson's waiting tumbrels were always

344

drawn up near the small entrance, which is to the right of the main staircase leading up to the central entrance. The victims left the Conciergerie by this door. In those days the courtyard was generally filled with various officials attached to the Tribunal, clerks rushing about on their business, lawyers hurrying to and fro, the *gendarmerie* on permanent assignments to the Conciergerie, ushers, bailiffs and guards. The trial and execution of fifty people a day involved considerable bureaucratic bustle.

Before the Law of 22 Prairial the People were permitted to enter the courtyard, where they would lean over the balustrade of the main stairway and hurl imprecations down on the condemned as they left the Conciergerie and mounted Samson's death carts. At the time of the execution of the Noailles women, however, no one without a pass was permitted inside the Cour du Mai. The mob watched from the street on the other side of the wrought-iron grille.

Because of the great increase in the number of victims that was its result, the Law of 22 Prairial necessitated other changes in procedure. The place of execution, formerly on the Place de la Révolution, was moved. The proximity of the Place de la Révolution to the rue St. Honoré filled the respectable citizenry of that quarter with horror. The spring of 1794 was unusually humid and from the blood-soaked stones of the square (it is said that cattle refused to cross it) rose a terrible vapor, menacing the health as well as destroying the peace of mind of those who lived near it. The value of real estate in that once desirable district began to depreciate. Its denizens finally summoned up the courage to complain. Their complaints were no doubt fortified by the fact that certain important officials of the Committee of Public Safety, including Robespierre, resided in the same area. The guillotine was first moved to the poor quarter of the Place de la Bastille, where it was indignantly rejected by the residents of that vociferous neighborhood. It was finally moved to the Place du Trône, now known as the Place de la Nation, a vast unvisited public square that is far beyond the Place de la Bastille at the remotest end of the rue du Faubourg St. Antoine. Far from the sight of respectable property owners, yet publicly displayed for the benefit of those who enjoyed watching the executions, the guillotine could here unapologetically go about its business. And go about its business it did. In the six weeks of its installation at the

Place du Trône, more than thirteen hundred people were executed. It was here, not on the Place de la Révolution, that Abbé Carrichon was to witness the death of the Noailles women.

The executions of July 22 appear to have been delayed. Customarily the procession was on its way to the scaffold by four o'clock in the afternoon. Carrichon had to wait until nearly six. Lenôtre, ever assiduous in his pursuit of such details, believes that Samson may have had to requisition an extra tumbrel or two. It may have been that the systematic pillaging of the personal effects of the condemned took more time than usual. Samson's victims went to their deaths stripped of everything but their shoes and clothing (these too were removed at the time of burial and divided among the grave-diggers). An inventory of the objects removed from the forty-four condemned of 4 Thermidor (July 22) may be seen at the Archives. It lists such articles as "four wedding rings, a tortoise-shell snuffbox, a pair of gold buttons, a brooch, five or six watches. . . ." Under the heading *Femmes Noailles,* we read that "a gold snuffbox" was taken, "twenty livres of money, a pin of silver and gold and a gold repeater watch."

Outside the Palais de Justice the Abbé waited.

My continual thought was, "In an hour or two these women will be no more." I cannot describe how this thought oppressed me. With so dreadful a cause for waiting never did an hour seem to me to be so long or so short as that which I passed between five and six o'clock of that day. . . . Finally by the noise which came to my ears I judged that the prison doors were about to be opened. I took a position near the gate, since for a fortnight it had been no longer possible to gain entrance into the courtyard. The first cart was filled and moved near to where I stood. It contained eight women who were unknown to me. The ninth in the cart was the Maréchale de Noailles. The absence of her daughter-in-law and granddaughter gave me a faint ray of hope. But, alas! They immediately entered the second cart. The Vicomtesse de Noailles was dressed in white, which she had not ceased to wear since the death of her relatives the Maréchal de Mouchy and his wife. She appeared to be only twenty-four years old at the most. Her mother, Mme. d'Ayen was in a striped deshabille of blue and white. Six men joined them in the fatal car and took their places near them. Scarcely had the two women entered the cart when the Vicomtesse de Noailles began to exhibit the most tender and eager interest in her mother. This was noticed by the bystanders. I heard people near me saying, "Look at that young lady. Do you see how agitated she is and how she talks to the other one?"

I knew that the women were looking for me. I even seemed to hear what they said. "Mama, he is not here!"

"Look again."

"He is not here, Mama, I assure you."

The carts finally started off. The women did not notice the Abbé in the crowd that surrounded them as they turned into the street and crossed the nearby Pont au Change. Carrichon, who was running a great risk, did not dare make a sign or motion that might attract public attention to himself. He decided to run ahead of the carts and meet them in the area near the Place de la Bastille.

I arrived before the carts did in the rue St. Antoine. Thunder was heard in the distance and a violent wind suddenly arose. The storm burst with flashes of lightning and the rain then began to fall, in torrents. I sought shelter in the doorway of a shop, which I still vividly remember and which I have not seen since without the most painful emotions. In an instant the street was cleared. There were no more people . . . the horsemen and the musketeers began to advance more quickly and the tumbrels too. When the second cart passed by the shop door I suddenly stepped forward and found myself alone and quite near the ladies who recognized me with many smiles. All my irresolution ceased. Though drenched with perspiration and rain, I had no thought for anything but the ladies and continued to walk near the carts.

Near the Collège de Saint-Louis there is an open space and several streets enter into it. The storm was now at its height and the wind had grown more violent. The women in the first wagon were much disturbed by it, especially the Maréchale de Noailles. Her large cap was thrown back and showed her grey hair. Their hands were tied behind their backs so that they lurched on their rough plank seats. At this spot a crowd of men recognized the Maréchale de Noailles and began to insult her with cries: "There she goes, that fine-feathered Maréchale who used to prance around in her big carriage—look at her now! She's in the cart just like all the others!"

We reached the street crossing just in front of the Faubourg St. Antoine. I went forward, looked around and said to myself, "This is the spot to afford them what they desire." I stopped and turned toward them. I made a sign to the Vicomtesse de Noailles, which she understood perfectly. Immediately they bent their heads with an air of contrition, tenderness and piety.

The Abbé then pronounced the words of absolution "in a low voice but very distinctly." The storm subsided a moment later. The carts moved implacably on towards their destination. His obligation fulfilled, Abbé Carrichon might well have returned home at this point. But he remembered that he had promised the women he would stay near them until the last moment. In a daze he followed the carts up the rue du Faubourg St. Antoine and into the Place du Trône, where, at a point farthest from human habitation, he saw the scaffold. A crowd of curiosity-seekers stood in a circle about it, impatiently awaiting the day's "batch." The tumbrels rolled up almost to the foot of it. On the platform stood three executioners, "the master and his two valets," putting a few final touches to their machine. The Abbé noticed that the chief executioner was young and short in stature with the dandyish air of a *petit maître manqué*. One of his valets was "fat, coarse and dark-complexioned," his sleeves were rolled up to his shoulders and his hair was pulled in a pigtail behind his neck. This individual fussed over the machine with a professional hand, all the while chewing on the stem of a red rose that he held between his teeth. Behind the scaffold stood an enormous low-slung cart painted red.

The executioner's two assistants now stepped down from the platform and began to empty the tumbrels. They went about this work with "swift gravity," lining up their victims in double file in front of the steps leading up to the scaffold. The order of execution was probably decided by the two black-robed and black-hatted *huissiers* who represented the Tribunal at every execution. These bailiffs, who, like wine waiters, wore a silver chain about their necks, always stood at the foot of the scaffold throughout a mass execution, holding a sheaf of papers in their hands. It was their signature at the back of

348

an order for execution that transformed each death warrant into a death certificate. After the execution these vouchers were handed back to the Tribunal, where they were filed.

Considerately, the victims, who had been exchanging farewells, were lined up with their backs facing the guillotine so that they would not have to see "what it was like." When all forty-five had been put in line, the executioner drew a blood-stained smock over his clothes and gave a signal to his two assistants, who seized the first victim, "a tall, rather fat old man with a kindly face," and half lifted him up the steps to the scaffold. The executioner held him by the right arm, the assistant held him by the left arm and the third assistant took him by the feet. "In an instant the man was thrown against the plank onto his stomach. There were three dull thuds, that of the plank going forward, that of the neck clamp falling into place and that of the axe falling. . . ." The man's body and head were tossed into the great straw-lined tumbrel. The whole business took less than two minutes. The valets seized the second victim and dispatched him with the same proficiency. "The Maréchale de Noailles was the third to mount this altar. It was necessary to cut the upper part of the neck of her dress so as to expose her throat. I felt as though I could stand there no longer, yet I had to keep my word. I implored God to give me the strength to keep my senses in the face of this ghastly sight. . . . Mme. d'Ayen was tenth in line. She seemed to look pleased that she was to die before her daughter. When she mounted the scaffold, the chief executioner pulled off her bonnet. As it was fastened on by a pin which he did not trouble to take out, the pain of having her hair pulled was evident in her expression. Then she too died. . . . How I grieved to see her daughter, dressed all in white and looking far younger than her years, follow. The same thing happened in her case as in her mother's. The same oversight as to the pin, the same pain, the same calm, the same death! 'Now she is happy!' I cried to myself when I saw her body thrown into the horrible straw-lined tumbrel."

When at last, with Louise de Noailles's death, Abbé Carrichon was free to leave, he found that his limbs were half paralyzed with horror. He left the place of butchery as quickly as he was able. Night was already beginning to fall, but the executions would continue for at least another hour. On the following day, fifty-eight more people were to die in the same manner, and on the day after that there were to be fifty-two. . . . It is no wonder that plans were afoot for a great *sangueduct,* or gutter, to carry away the rivers of blood that were daily shed on the Place du Trône.

40

MANY REASONS may be found for the drama of 9 Thermidor and for the downfall of Robespierre, which was to be its outcome. Danton, when he warned Robespierre that the system of the Terror could not last "because it was repugnant to the French temperament," probably put his finger on the most conspicuous and important reason. Sooner or later, however it may have come, the end was inevitable.

Another reason is the deterioration of Robespierre's character. In the hundred days of his dictatorship, we are witness to an almost perfect illustration of Lord Acton's famous maxim. Power corrupted him in a degree that seems to have been almost exactly proportionate to the extent of his power. For men like Robespierre who are abnormally disposed towards jealousy, there can never be an end to the people who arouse that passion. In each successive battle with some rival—Brissot and the Girondins first, Danton and his followers next—Robespierre consoled himself with the reflection that "this will be the last." But no sooner was one enemy dead than another rose to take his place. Jealousy is an appetite that in persons of a cold sexual disposition often replaces desires that are popularly believed to be "normal"; moreover like lust it is an appetite that grows by what it feeds on. Like many other pathologically jealous people, Robespierre was a man of very mediocre parts, totally lacking in any insight into his own real motives—and consequently into the motives of others. That combination of faults is a dangerous one for men who have achieved a position of power that can only be maintained by a cold and realistic awareness of the conditions on which their supremacy rests.

Scarcely was Danton dead when the Committee of Public Safety became rent with quarrels of the most personal and bitter sort. Since Robespierre's entrance into the Committee in July of the previous year, its energies had been devoted to acquiring more and more power for itself. In November, at a moment when it was close to achieving total supremacy, the Dantonists and the Hébertists had risen to defy its authority. In the face of common danger the members of the Committee laid aside their many private differences and temporarily joined hands. With Danton's death they again turned on one another. For reasons of public interest (and their own safety) these quarrels were at first kept "within the family" and took place behind the locked doors of the room at the Tuileries where the Committee sat. But no amount of discretion could conceal them from public notice. They reach our own ears muffled and confused, but according to the few accounts we have of them, they must have been violent in the extreme. When Carnot and St. Just were not screaming at each other in open rage, a far more explosive atmosphere prevailed in which the members of the Committee glared at one another with suspicion and hatred.

It cannot have been easy for a man of Robespierre's temperament to share with others the fruits of his political acumen. He considered himself—and with reason—to be the "head" of the Committee of Public Safety, although that position was nowhere officially admitted or acknowledged. To sit in proximity to such a man as Collot d'Herbois, a gross and bloodthirsty "Hébertist," was more than his hypersensitive temperament could support. In the friendship of Collot d'Herbois and Billaud-Varennes, he saw the beginnings of a new faction and of another conspiracy to undermine him.

Robespierre, who always conquered by division, had an instinctive dread of collusion between those whom he considered his enemies or, indeed, even between his friends. The mere sight of two associates of his talking together or walking arm in arm was enough to awaken fears of conspiracy. Once when he came into the offices of the Committee he found Collot d'Herbois and Billaud-Varennes deep in conversation. The expression on their faces seemed to him to be "guilty." Robespierre's antipathy to Collot was known to the public. "Robespierre detests Collot," wrote a citizen of Lyons, who knew people close to the Committee. "He can hardly bring himself to look at him in the Committee and only tolerates him there out of consideration for the powerful party [the Hébertists] that Collot has managed to gather about himself in Paris."

Carnot, a very different personality from Collot d'Herbois, had also aroused Robespierre's rancor. Carnot was a capable man, concerned with military affairs and indifferent to the petty factional disputes that occupied Robespierre's shallow mind. Almost from the moment of Robespierre's appointment to the Committee he had hated Carnot. An ill-concealed jealousy of Carnot's military capacities was probably at the root of the animosity. Carnot, in any case, was one of those exasperating men who concentrate on their work and appear to be oblivious of the ill will of those who are jealous of them. Only St. Just's hysterical accusations could arouse his temper. His calm only fanned the coals of Robespierre's resentment. Carnot usually stayed in the Committee's offices later at night than anyone else. Robespierre was certain that he did so in order to read any dispatches that might arrive before the other members of the Committee got to them. This suspicion is reflected in a report of one of Robespierre's agents, a man named Deschamps, who wrote to a friend: "Carnot is a wretched scoundrel who remains purposely all night at the Committee in order to open all missives that arrive. . . ."

No member of the Committee dared leave the office for fear that a rival would gain an advantage in his absence. The "triumvirate" of Robespierre and his two loyal satellites, St. Just and Couthon, began to make preparations for the next of those battles that concluded on the public scaffold.

Robespierre's nerves appear to have given way in the weeks preceding this final duel. We read of sudden fits of weeping, of a variety of strange worries and irrational terrors. He refused to ride horseback because of an excessive fear of falling. He began to take long walks in order to steady his unstable nerves, but a deep dread of assassination diminished any refreshment or benefit he might have received. An informal sketch taken of him on 9 Thermidor, while he was addressing the Convention, clearly indicates the toll that ambition and apprehension had exacted from him. It is the picture of a prematurely old man whose face has been pinched and withered by sleepless nights and fear-ridden days. Robespierre himself began to make frequent reference to his inner tribulations. "How could I have borne my struggles," he once cried out at the Jacobins, "that would have been beyond endurance, had I not raised my spirit to God?"

Consciously, at least, he nowhere appears to have been bothered by any thought of the fifty or sixty men and women who perished every day on the Place du Trône. That terrible mechanism, his conscience, handled any remorse he may have felt about those ghastly scenes—which, incidentally, he probably never saw. But somewhere, unseen by himself or by those historians who have tried to look for it, there may have been a horror too deep for him to recognize at the blood-drenched conclusion of Rousseau's pure dream. Nature had not made Robespierre a monster. Circumstances, many of which were of his own making, had done that. It is a pity that he did not share Danton's love of Shakespeare. He might have discovered in Macbeth's tragedy much that was pertinent to his own. He had waded too far through blood and could not go back; after Danton's death he could only press blindly on towards the other shore.

The nature of his political position after Danton's execution encouraged him, at the same time, to indulge himself in vanity and delusions, appetites of the spirit that are far more dangerous than the more commonplace indulgences of the flesh. Self-delusion is the most ruinous of all such temptations and it is often the ultimate indulgence of dictators. It is the one they can least afford.

Viewed in the light of the man's character, the real measure of the weakness or strength of his situation, Robespierre's house after April 1794 stood on a very flimsy foundation. All that was needed was a man of courage and sagacity to push it over. And such a man had, in fact, arrived in Paris on April 6, the day after Danton's death.

His name was Joseph Fouché.

41

Joseph Fouché, whose name is little known outside a relatively small circle of historians, amateurs of French history and specialists in the period that the universities too comprehensively label "the French Revolution and Napoleon," is one of the most curious men of his age. In that long and disturbed period of French history in which he was to play so significant and so varied a role he is undoubtedly one of the most fascinating figures. "A somber, profound and extraordinary man whom few people have ever really understood," pronounced Balzac. Balzac viewed the characters of history with the penetrating eye of a great novelist. It gave him an advantage that historians have not always enjoyed. "Fouché," Balzac declares again, "was one of those persons who have so many aspects and so much depth beneath each aspect that they are inscrutable in the moment of action and only become comprehensible long after the event."

It is indeed long after 9 Thermidor that we are best able to see how deadly an adversary this master of intrigue and consummate politician must have been. One cannot appreciate the Joseph Fouché of 1794 without some glimpse of the Duc d'Otrante of 1815, who juggled with dazzling dexterity his two former masters: Louis XVIII, for whose brother's death he had been in part responsible, and the Emperor Napoleon, for whose downfall he was in even greater part responsible.

It is sometimes difficult to believe that this Duc d'Otrante, whose inscrutable glance caused the Emperor himself to tremble and blanch, whose fortune was reckoned in the millions and who moved like a shadow across the marble vestibules first of the Empire and then of the restored Bourbons, was none other than Joseph Fouché, the man who once butchered "aristocrats" at Lyons and who over-threw Robespierre on 9 Thermidor. Between the conspirator of Thermidor and the minister of Louis XVIII lay the wreckage of six different governments, each of which Fouché had not only helped destroy but from out of the ruins of which he generally emerged more powerful than before. "He would work hard for a government so long as it was to his advantage to work for it rather than to betray it." M. Madelin expresses the matter succinctly. Fouché betrayed the Directory to the Consulate, the Consulate to the Empire, the Empire to Louis XVIII and Louis XVIII back to the Empire, all in so smooth and adroit a manner that only long after the event did his dupes become aware of the mind that had mastered them.

The Duc d'Otrante, who once tipped his hand to the extent of re-marking, "I know men well and I am quite familiar with the base passions that motivate them," never professed, like Robespierre, any great respect for human nature. He looked on human virtue as an old wives' tale. "He could not but conclude that with very few ex-ceptions the world is made up of scoundrels who are more or less hypocrites and of imbeciles who are more or less happy." So skepti-cal an attitude about his fellow kind did not endear him to his contemporaries and has brought the contempt of an idealistic pos-terity down on his head. Those who like their heroes to be white and their villains to be black will always find Fouché either incom-prehensible or abhorrent, for the elements "good" and "bad" were of equally small weight to him in the measurement of political force. He was that *rara avis,* the totally amoral man.

Those, on the other hand, who are able to view history and life with Fouché's dispassionate eye may find it difficult to resist the con-clusion that this cynical, unscrupulous, but intelligent man did less harm to humanity than the well-intentioned but bigoted, ignorant, and self-deluded Robespierre. Fouché regarded the vicious and the virtuous alike with the calm tolerance of total indifference. Unlike Robespierre his response to people was never personal. "Like" or "dislike" were considerations that never entered his estimate of men. He took their measurement with insight and accuracy, and when it was necessary he used what he saw for his own ends. Jealousy or rancor never obscured his calculations, though he was perfectly aware of the rôle that these emotions often play in the lives of other men—and profited from that knowledge accordingly.

356

It is well to remember the significant fact that the duel between Fouché and Robespierre was but one episode, the initial one, in the highly eventful life of the future Duc d'Otrante. Fouché was to survive all the men of the Revolution, as he survived most of those of the Directory and of the Consulate. One did not cross swords lightly with Joseph Fouché. Robespierre did not live to profit from this lesson, which others who followed him were to learn at their cost.

In the management of the innumerable intrigues that are the story of his life, it was always Fouché's instinct to hug the shadows. Darkness was the element in which he worked best. Like the spider he wove his web at night and out of sight of his prey. The exact extent, consequently, of his part in the events of 9 Thermidor still remains unclear. Indeed, many a respectable account of that dramatic day has been written without so much as a mention of his name. Nonetheless it is in relationship to this shadowy personage that the story of 9 Thermidor acquires its fullest dimension of interest. One might compare his role in it to that of the director of a play, a figure who is indispensable to the presentation of the show, but who is not seen by the audience, who hovers in the wings of the theatre, discreetly superintending the movements of his cast, controlling the inner rhythm of the drama. The satisfactions of the director belong to that subtle order which is related to authority and power; the actors, on the other hand, are usually satisfied by a burst or two of applause and that superficial appearance of importance which the publicity of their situation momentarily gives them. Fouché was a director *par excellence*. The pleasures of celebrity or exhibitionism did not interest him in the slightest. He was attracted by the actuality of power, never by its appearance.

Curiously enough his path had crossed Robespierre's in the years just preceding the Revolution. They had both been members of the Society of the Rosati, that club by the river's bank dedicated to wine and the rose. Fouché was then a professor of physics attached to the Oratorian priesthood and had been sent to Arras to administer the Oratorian seminary there. Through the Rosati he met Robespierre. It had been said that he courted Robespierre's sister Charlotte and aroused her fading hopes by a proposal of marriage. He is reported to have broken the engagement soon after. If the story is true, then Charlotte Robespierre probably has the distinction of being first in the long line of the duped and the betrayed that Fouché was everywhere to leave behind him. Some men have tried to find the source of the fierce enmity which raged between Fouché and Robespierre in this episode. It seems unlikely. Their differences were tempermental and these quickly became apparent in the arena of politics.

Fouché was at Arras when the Revolution began. In his memoirs he claims to have lent money to Robespierre to defray the threadbare deputy's traveling expenses to the States-General. Soon after Robespierre's departure for Versailles, Joseph Fouché returned to his native town of Nantes in Brittany, where he threw off his clerical garb and prepared to set sail on those stormy seas through which in the course of the next twenty-five years he was to navigate his frail vessel with such skill and sagacity. It is probably no accident that this consummate politician should have been the descendant of a long line of Breton mariners. The courage that informs so much of his political life is akin to that of the sailor. His senses were always sharpened by challenge; danger made him bold and decisive. Under stress he became a brave man. Robespierre was always a coward.

In September 1792 Fouché was elected to represent Nantes at the Convention in Paris. He arrived in the capital to find it in the grip of unsettled political weather. Paris was still burying the bodies of those slain in the September Massacres. Marat had crept out of his burrow, and Robespierre, pitting rival against rival, had begun his laborious ascent towards power. The ferocious partisan battles that were to discredit and finally to destroy the Revolution were about to be fought in the Convention. In the opening sessions the Girondins appeared to be dominant. Prudently seating himself nearer the Girondins than the men of the Mountain, Fouché examined the trend of things at his leisure and calculated the direction in which he ought to move.

It did not take him long to see that the Girondins, divided by conflicting ideologies and weakened by frivolous personal animosities, were doomed. One can be certain that he observed Danton's overtures to them with particular attention, for he of all men would have realized that an alliance with that powerful and disaffected arm of the Left was all that might have saved them. Watching the Girondins flounder in an ocean of words and confused intentions, the former professor of physics (who profitably applied the laws of force and resistance to the affairs of men) saw that the pendulum had not yet completed its leftward swing. "In times of revolution," Danton once declared, "power will always go to the biggest scoundrel." There are other ways of phrasing it. Fouché would have had reference to the formulae of mathematics or of the exact sciences. But however the matter may have been expressed, the deputy from Nantes realized that the time had come for him to shift his position on the benches of the Convention.

He broke with the Girondins at the trial of Louis XVI. On the insistence of Robespierre and Marat the votes of the deputies on the King's sentence had to be publicly uttered. The purpose behind this maneuver was to separate the sheep of the Convention from the goats. It was an awkward moment for many of France's senators. In case of a restoration of the monarchy (which many a blatant Republican secretly believed possible), a deputy's future would be irrevocably compromised by a vote for death; a vote for mercy, on the other hand, would put his immediate present in danger. Fouché, as was his habit in all situations admitting of no compromise, took a firm stand. His vote was for death. The moment marked a turning point in his life. Under the Empire and under the restored monarchy it forced on him a political orientation from which he could never escape. Many years later the Emperor once tried to humiliate him by referring to his vote.

"You voted for the death of Louis XVI, didn't you, Duc d'Otrante?"

"That is true, Sire," came the disconcerting retort. "It was the first service I was able to render your Majesty."

Future consequences apart, Fouché's vote had an immediate effect during the Revolution. Overnight the prudent moderate became an advanced radical. Having calculated his course, Fouché now took his position—to the left of Robespierre. And what, one wonders, did Robespierre think of this sudden swerve? One can only suppose that he observed it with contempt and suspicion. Like all fanatics he abhorred turncoats and opportunists. His animosity towards Fouché, which was to erupt in the spring of the following year, probably began to smoulder at the time of the King's trial. He took note of the man and remarked what he no doubt knew before: Fouché was not to be trusted.

With the downfall of the Girondins and Marat's assassination by Charlotte Corday, the dam which had heretofore contained the violence of the Extremist party was broken. Fouché foresaw with accuracy the cataclysm which was about to strike France and his alliance with the radical Left grew more pronounced. What he did not foresee was Robespierre's ultimate ascendancy in the Committee of Public Safety and his approaching control of the Convention through legalized terror. Many issues were still unsettled, many battles were still to be fought. The climate of Paris was not suitable for a man of Fouché's calculating temperament. He decided therefore to quit the theatre of political combat for a spell and to solicit an appointment as representative of the Convention in the provinces. Civil war had broken out over half of France, and the Convention was sending many of its deputies into the countryside to work with the army in quelling the rebellions. By absenting himself from the scene of the partisan quarrels that raged in Paris, Fouché could wait to return to the capital until just before the conclusion of the struggle and ally himself with the party that promised to be victorious. To reap the full harvest of benefit from these disputes, an experienced opportunist will always appear on the scene of combat just before the battle has come to its end—soon enough to give those on the winning side the impression that he has fought with them, late enough so that there will be no danger of finding himself trapped among the losers. Timing is all, and timing was the deepest instinct of Fouché's genius.

The summer of 1793 found him traveling from one provincial capital to another. As the Extremist party waxed strong in Paris, just so did Fouché's administration in the provinces grow severe. By October, at the time of the anti-Christian outbreaks, we find him looting churches and desecrating sacristies. The hour of the Hébertists, just as he had foreseen, had come round. Manifestos of a violent and communistic complexion now spilled from the pen of the future duke, who was destined to become one of the richest men in Europe. "Every man who is animated by cold self-interest," he pronounced, "every man who considers what profit he may derive from a piece of land, a political post or a talent, every man whose blood fails to boil at the mere mention of tyranny or wealth . . . must flee the soil of liberty, for he will be unmasked and will water it with his impure blood." Stern words that very soon, and at Fouché's hand, were to have a stern application.

In October 1793 the city of Lyons, which had been in active revolt against the Jacobins of Paris, finally capitulated to the army of the Convention. The vengeance that the Convention, the self-appointed advocate of humanity, now exacted from a helpless and defeated city can only be compared with the atrocities of antiquity. "An example must be given to show that the French Republic punishes most severely those who have revolted against the tricolor," pronounced the Convention. It was forthwith decided that "the city of Lyons shall be destroyed. All the dwellings of the rich shall be razed to the ground . . . and the name of Lyons shall be erased from the list of the towns of the French Republic. Henceforth such houses as remain standing there shall be known as Ville-Affranchie. Above the ruins of the city there shall be raised a pillar that will announce to posterity the crime and the punishment of the culprits who once lived there. It shall bear the inscription: 'Lyons made war against Liberty. Lyons is no more.'"

In a book called *Lyon n'est Plus,* the late Édouard Herriot, that distinguished *Lyonnais* of our own time, has described in detail the terrible fate that befell his native city during the winter of 1793-94. Lyons, the second largest city in France, was put to the sword. In "batches" numbering in the hundreds, citizens were dragged to the plain of Brotteaux outside the gates of the city, where they were put to death by cannon fire, by bayonets and by clubs. Hecatomb followed hecatomb. The bodies of the dead were tossed into the Rhone. "Let their bleeding corpses strike terror on both banks of the river as they drift toward the cowardly city of Toulon." The moans of human anguish that arose from the stricken city were drowned by the detonation of explosives as the "dwellings of the rich" were systematically blown up. The beautiful Place Bellecourt, designed by Mansart and admired throughout Europe as one of the most perfect expressions of eighteenth-century public design, fell first before this savage outburst of vandalism. "The demolitions in this abominable city are going too slowly," it was reported to Paris. "Republican impatience demands more rapid methods. Nothing but the explosion of mines and the use of fire can give full expression to the omnipotence of the People. . . ."

The Committee of Public Safety appointed two men to administer its "expression of the omnipotence of the People." One was the sanguinary Collot d'Herbois, who was the representative of the Hébertist party on the Committee. The other was Joseph Fouché.

Not far beneath the surface of most of the violent scenes of the Revolution there may be found an underlying web of political cause, whose strands are woven into future political effect. Lyons is no exception to this pattern. The tragedy there did not occur in a vacuum. Both its cause and effect were closely related to the political battles that were being fought in Paris. Lyons capitulated to the Convention at that moment when Robespierre's Committee of Public Safety found itself caught between the opposing demands of the Hébertists and the Dantonists. Danton was just then preparing to return to Paris from Arcis to become the champion of clemency. Hébert's excesses had begun to manifest themselves in atheistic revels before the high altar of Notre Dame. Robespierre faced a crisis, and no one, not even so astute an observer as Joseph Fouché, could tell what the outcome might be. Acting on the principle that in times of Revolution the middle party is the one that is crushed, Fouché continued to place his bets with the Hébertists, who were then clearly in the ascendant. In so doing he underestimated Robespierre, as events in Paris were shortly to demonstrate. But here is to be found an explanation of Fouché's savagery at Lyons. He was not bloodthirsty by nature, but he was a man who when obliged to take a position took it firmly without qualm or tremor. "Compromise," he once declared, "is always best. But there are times when extreme measures become necessary." This in his eyes was one of those times. He became a man without compassion or remorse.

In December, when the butcheries in Lyons were at their height, Fouché's associate in crime, Collot d'Herbois, returned to Paris. Reports had reached Paris of the horrors that were being perpetrated at Lyons, and Collot, learning of the ticklish political situation in the capital, thought it wise to give an explanation. "We shot down two hundred criminals at a time," he declared, "and now we are told that this was a crime! How can anyone not see that it was an act of mercy? When twenty culprits are guillotined, the last of the executed dies twenty deaths, but the two hundred we shot down all died together!"

The Convention appears to have been impressed by this interesting manifestation of humanitarianism and ordered the executions at Lyons to continue. Collot d'Herbois, however, did not return to Lyons. He stayed on in Paris, where political developments of a critical kind were taking place. At Lyons, Fouché, who heretofore had hidden behind Collot's back, had to go about the bloody business alone. When the day of retribution finally dawned, Fouché was to put the blame for the massacres of Lyons on Collot's shoulders. During the time that Collot had been at Lyons, Fouché had encouraged his loud-mouthed, imprudent and vulgar associate to sign his name to most of the death sentences and extremist decrees. After the middle of December, however, Fouché had to bear sole responsibility. No words, and Fouché was a master *par excellence* of words, ever succeeded in washing the bloodstains from his hands. "His behavior," writes M. Herriot bluntly, "was revolting."

For Fouché, who kept a careful eye on the scene in Paris, the situation was delicate indeed. On the one hand, should the Dantonists succeed in their campaign, he would be open to the charge of extremism; on the other if he abated the flow of blood he would be accused of moderatism by the Hébertists. Robespierre observed with contempt the veerings of the brazen opportunist between these two courses. Towards the end of January, Fouché realized that the party of Hébert was lost. The executions at Lyons began immediately to diminish. On February 9, Fouché ordered that the firing squad be discontinued. Pronouncements of a mild and moderate tone, tailored to the mood of Danton's so-called Tribunal of Mercy, now began to issue from the offices of the *gauleiter* of Lyons. He dissolved most of the radical clubs in the city, including the local branch of the Jacobin Club, whose members he denounced as "anarchists and rioters."

The Jacobin Club was a society which one offended at the risk of one's life during the Reign of Terror. The officious self-appointed guardians of patriotism who comprised its membership behaved like petty tyrants, knights who were bound in fealty only to the parent club in Paris and to its sovereign, Robespierre. Fouché's high-handed dismissal of the local "patriots" of Lyons (who must have been a continual irritant to him during his stay there) aroused the greatest indignation. The Jacobins instantly dispatched several representatives to Paris, where they reported their grievances to headquarters and to the Master himself, Robespierre. Robespierre heard their story with astonishment and expressions of outrage. M. Herriot is doubtless correct in pointing to this incident as the formal opening of battle between Fouché and Robespierre. Heretofore Robespierre had observed Fouché's shifty behavior with scorn as he watched him ally himself first with the Girondins, next with the Hébertists and then with the Dantonists (all of them parties hostile to Robespierre). He was well aware of the annoying gnat that buzzed about his head, but during the critical months of December and January larger insects had distracted his attention. Now, without warning and in the midst of a crisis, the gnat had settled on him—and had stung. He grew alert. Next time he was prepared to swat.

On March 15 Robespierre finally struck at the Hébertists. The arrest of Danton followed fifteen days later. The Incorruptible had navigated his ship with skill and success through those narrow shoals that separated the Scylla of moderatism from the Charybdis of extremism. With Danton's arrest he must have breathed a deep sigh of relief as he found himself safe again in the open sea. Now he could put his attention on those lesser threats to his peace of mind— Collot d'Herbois, Billaud-Varennes and Joseph Fouché. A host of other names was inscribed on this private death list: Tallien, the representative of the Convention at Toulouse who was misbehaving there with his beautiful mistress Therezia Cabarrus; Barras, another philanderer who walked around with a cynical sneering expression on his face; Bourdon de l'Oise, who back in November had dared suggest that the Committee of Public Safety should be renewed. A motley crew of turncoats, opportunists and men without Virtue. In Robespierre's eyes Fouché was neither the most prominent nor the most offensive of them. Collot d'Herbois probably enjoyed that distinction. Collot had been useful to him in trapping Danton. Collot was an Extremist and had had a certain influence over the noisy gutter element of the city. Without loyalty or prudence he had shortsightedly sacrificed Hébert and many of his former allies in order to get Danton's head. With Danton gone and the back of the Hébertist party broken, Collot was no longer useful and could no longer be considered dangerous. His presence on the Committee now became an insufferable affront to Robespierre's sensibilities.

On 12 Germinal (April 1), thirty-six hours after Danton's arrest, an order from the Committee of Public Safety was delivered to Fouché at Lyons. It commanded him to restore all authority to the local Jacobin Club and immediately to resign his commission at Lyons. He was ordered to return to Paris at once to "explain certain matters respecting the administration of the affairs at Ville Affranchie." This ominous missive was signed by Robespierre.

The French Revolution, which is not deficient in irony, offers no irony more startling than the fact that Joseph Fouché, the infamous *mitrailleur* of Lyons, was about to be charged with the "crime" of moderation. There were more than two thousand citizens of Lyons who might have vehemently testified to the contrary, but these witnesses were all dead and their broken corpses rotting along the banks of the Rhone.

Fouché arrived in Paris on April 6. It was probably in Paris, therefore, that he learned that Danton, the man whose principles he was accused of sharing, had been guillotined the day before.

42

Joseph fouché cannot have slept well on the first night after his return to Paris. One can only imagine the appraisals, the calculations, the possibilities of action and their alternatives that must have occupied his active mind. On the following morning he made his first move.

Instead of justifying himself before Robespierre and the Committee of Public Safety, who were his real accusers, he boldly took himself to the Convention. The meaning of that gesture was lost on neither body. Constitutionally the Convention was still the governing body of the Republic. By ignoring the Committee of Public Safety and laying his case directly before the Convention, Fouché publicly, and not very subtly, depreciated the authority of Robespierre and his upstart Committee. The move was analogous to that of a lesser employee in some office who dares appeal to the president of the company over the head of a too authoritarian vice-president. It was an audacious and resourceful step, but in politics as on the field of battle the shrewdest strategy will misfire when it has been executed on the basis of insufficient or inaccurate intelligence. Fouché's information respecting the true state of affairs in the Convention was, in this case, at fault—as a glance at the empty benches of so many vanished deputies, men of both the Right and the Left who had been mowed down, might have informed him. A grey pall of fear had settled over the eviscerated body of the Convention. The halls that only a year before had too lustily rung with the jeers and cheers of discord and dissension were now silent. Only the pronouncements of Robespierre or his mouthpiece, St. Just, were greeted with animation, and these invariably brought the house down with wild applause. Like a school of frightened fish, deputy cowered behind deputy, trusting to the obscurity of a mass identity for their individual safety.

Fouché had been absent from Paris for over ten months. He did not realize how powerful the Committee had become nor how debased the Convention. The deputies, appalled, listened to his justificatory speech. A deathly silence followed. No one knew what to say. One deputy, more courageous than his fellows, finally proposed that Fouché's report be passed on to the Committee of Public Safety without comment by the Convention. The alacrity with which this suggestion was accepted can have left Fouché in no doubt about the debilitated status of the Convention. The sea had cast him back upon the shore from which he had striven to escape. He lost the opening round.

It was one of Fouché's strong points that in addition to being fearless, he was also without self-respect or pride. He was a man who could eat humble pie with equanimity and grovelingly implore the mercy of those whom he had injured or whom he planned to injure. In the evening of the very day on which he had received the ominous check from the Convention, he made his way to the residence of the carpenter Duplay on the rue St. Honoré, where Robespierre lodged. An afternoon of agitated reflection had determined him to sue for Robespierre's pardon, to make terms with the dictator of the Committee of Public Safety, whose power he had so woefully underestimated. Fouché never left an account of this interesting interview, but it probably differed in few details from a blood-chilling *mauvais quart d'heure* which the man Barras (Fouché's associate on the "death list") had undergone a few days earlier. Barras, like Fouché, had just been recalled from the provinces. In the company of another potential victim, Fréron, he had hurried to pay court to the offended dictator. His vivid and vitriolic description of the event gives a swift but unforgettable glimpse of Robespierre at home.

"Robespierre," he writes, "lived in a little house, in the rue St. Honoré almost opposite the rue St. Florentin, that was owned and occupied by a carpenter of the name Duplay. . . . In order to reach the eminent guest who deigned to inhabit this miserable hole it was necessary to pass through a long alley which led to an inner yard full of planks, the owner's stock in trade. On this day we perceived the daughter of the owner Duplay in the yard, spreading out laundry to dry. Opposite her sat Mother Duplay between a pail and a salad basket, busily engaged in plucking salad herbs. Two soldiers standing close to her in a respectful attitude seemed to be taking part in the duties of the household and obligingly picked herbs in order to be free to chat more unrestrainedly under the shadow of this homely occupation. . . ."

Duplay's daughter, with some reluctance, finally ushered the two petitioners into Robespierre's presence. "We found Robespierre standing, wrapped in a kind of chemise peignoir: he had just left the hands of his hairdresser who had combed and powdered his hair. He was without the spectacles he usually wore in public. Piercing through the powder that covered his face, already so white with a natural pallor, we could see a pair of eyes whose dimness the glasses had until then concealed from us. Those eyes fixed themselves on us with a glaucous stare that was expressive of utter astonishment at our presence. We saluted him, but he showed no recognition of this courtesy. He took a small knife and began scraping off the powder. Then, doffing his peignoir, he flung it on a chair close to us in such a way as to soil our clothes without apologizing to us for this action and without even appearing to notice our presence in the room. He washed himself in a basin which he held with one hand, cleaning his teeth and spitting repeatedly on the ground right at our feet. . . ."

Fréron finally summoned up enough courage to speak to him, using the Republican *tu* form, which "by an almost imperceptible shadow of pain on his countenance" Robespierre indicated he found an impertinence. Fréron hurriedly substituted *vous,* but "this did nothing to warm the chill of our interview. Robespierre did not deign to reply by a single word, nor did his face reveal any trace of emotion. I have never seen anything so impassive as his expression, neither in the frigid marble of statuary nor in the faces of the dead already laid to rest . . . such was our interview with Robespierre. I can hardly call it a conversation, for his lips never parted. Tightly pressed though they naturally were, he pursed them even tighter. From them I noticed that there oozed a bilious froth that boded no good for Fréron or myself. I had seen all I wanted of this person. I had had a view of the man who has been so accurately described as the *chat-tigre."*

Like Barras, even the steel-nerved Fouché must have emerged from his interview reaching for his salts. After the manner of so many cowards, Robespierre was pitiless towards those whom he had at his mercy. Fouché's ill-timed interview seemed to Robespierre to be a groveling admission of the sneaky turncoat's helplessness. Accordingly he kicked his petitioner with contempt. Why should the victor make terms with the vanquished? In Robespierre's eyes the battle was already won. The Torquemada of Rousseau's mystic creed was no longer called upon to make compromises with such despicable creatures as Fouché or Barras. With Danton's death he had been carried above the squalid machinations of men without religious faith or elevating ideals. The hour had come when the God of Virtue, with Robespierre as His high priest, was about to reveal Himself to the Republic of France.

The hour had come when Robespierre seems to have gone mad.

Religious mania must almost necessarily be the outcome of a devouring vanity, the illusion of power without limit, and a natural disposition towards paranoia. God the Omnipotent has always exercised a peculiar fascination over those who have an insatiable appetite for power over men. When their will had been fully done among mortals, the Roman emperors usually declared themselves to be God. It was the inevitable conclusion to an uncontrollable hunger for power and an excessive indulgence in those concomitant passions of the soul: hatred and jealousy. To the insane (as, indeed, to the sane) God manifests Himself in many ways. The provincial, lower-middle-class French lawyer did not picture Him in quite the same way as did the Emperor Caligula. But the source of their hallucination was probably the same: madness.

Robespierre's deity was called the Supreme Being. Although Robespierre on occasion still referred to Him as God, his preference, as a prophet of Rousseau, was for the title Supreme Being. Under that name there was no danger of the Divinity being confused with the discarded idol that had been superstitiously worshiped by the rest of Christendom for the past seventeen centuries.

No one knows at precisely what date Robespierre decided to legislate the Supreme Being into existence. It was undoubtedly a dream that he had cherished for some time. The death of Hébert and Danton removed the restraints that had obliged him to keep his plans to himself. It is possible that his interview with Fouché prompted him to a final decision about the matter. For not least among the many things about Fouché that aroused Robespierre's hatred was that the man was a militant atheist. Fouché, the former Oratorian, had been an associate of the contemptible Chaumette, the man who had organized the Festival of Reason and had led the atheistic revels that Robespierre and Danton had so severely denounced back in November. In the provinces Fouché had caused a notice to be inscribed over the portal of a cemetery, "Death is an eternal sleep." Such a sentiment caused Robespierre (who, unlike many dictators, seems to have realized that he himself might die one day) to quiver with indignation. Worse than this, without authority from the Committee of Public Safety to do so, Fouché had spoken disparagingly about God in certain of his official manifestos at Lyons. Any slight against God was taken by Robespierre as a slight against himself! To have such blasphemies uttered in the name of the Convention was more than he could bear.

By restoring God to France and by enacting legislation making atheism a civil offense and in consequence a crime liable to the death penalty, Fouché and his kind could be netted with ease. At the same time as it advanced the Supreme Being's interests on earth, such a law would be serviceable in striking down a few of Robespierre's political enemies. Killing two birds with one stone had always been a specialty of this resourceful idealist.

Dogmatic and literal, Robespierre had always been suspicious of men who fancied themselves to be *bels esprits* or philosophers. Their glib tongues and their irreverent attitude towards the serious things of life aroused his ire. A number of these flippant atheists seemed to wear a cynical or mocking expression. At a deeper level Robespierre's hatred of atheism and of the so-called *philosophes* may perhaps be traceable to Voltaire's sarcastic treatment of Rousseau. M. Herriot, indeed, has seen in the conflict between Fouché and Robespierre a perfect example of that profound split between the Classical and the Romantic attitudes which divided France in the latter half of the eighteenth century: on the one hand, Robespierre, intuitive and moved by the promptings of an inner voice; on the other, Fouché, skeptical, self-controlled and moved only by the considerations of cold logic. Whatever the case, the atheists, Fouché most prominent among them, were in for a sharp shock on May 6, 1794. On that day Robespierre announced to the Convention that in the name of the French people the Committee of Public Safety had decided to recognize the existence of God.

The Revolutionary Tribunal had already sent Chaumette to the guillotine under the charge that he had "tried to establish the French government on the principles of atheism." Danton's friend Hérault-Séchelles had gone to his death escorted by an accusation of St. Just that he "did not believe in the immortality of the soul, which had been the consolation of the dying Socrates." Now it was openly to become grounds for a death sentence not to believe in God! The cowardly Convention, which had veered this way or that as the winds blew from the Committee of Public Safety, was now suddenly obliged to make another right-angle turn. Five months earlier the Convention had been vociferous in its denunciation of religion. Now it was asked to be equally vociferous in its denunciation of those who had disparaged religion. The terrified deputies once again hurriedly scrambled for shelter. A wild burst of applause greeted Robespierre's speech. Hats were flung in the air and feet were stamped in a mood of unrestrained enthusiasm suitable to the announcement of the millennium. There were no doubt many ashen faces among those who so enthusiastically clapped, but of all deputies Joseph Fouché had most reason to blanch. In the middle of his speech Robespierre had publicly castigated him.

"Tell us then," the Incorruptible had suddenly declared, lifting his spectacles and fixing his blood-freezing gaze on Fouché, "you tell us, then, who ever commissioned you to announce to the People that God doesn't exist? . . . What right have you to snatch from innocent people the scepter of Reason and give it to the hands of Crime? Only a villain who is contemptible in his own eyes and horrible in the eyes of others feels that nature cannot make him a better gift than annihilation."

The terrible words would have reduced a lesser man to water. It was a public declaration of hostility. Filing out of the hall, Fouché's fellow deputies must have shunned him as they would carrion. In the eyes of most of them he must have appeared as a man already dead.

In the weeks that followed Robespierre's announcement of God's imminent return to France, Fouché vanished from sight. No doubt Robespierre supposed that, like so many other of his victims who had been marked for death, Fouché trembled immobilized, like a bird before a snake. Robespierre was not familiar with his adversary's technique. Fouché had the agile feet of a mongoose; he would let the cobra strike in one spot, then dart nimbly out of its range, only to appear unexpectedly in another spot. The snake thus grew gradually exhausted while the mongoose waited for the propitious moment when its enemy lost its balance and, by a quick blow from behind, could be killed. Strategically speaking, the unexpected was Fouché's specialty. He was always most dangerous when he was not seen. Behind Robespierre's back, out of sight, he began to work furiously. Whispering, negotiating, seeing his colleague in crime, Collot d'Herbois, at one moment and certain important Jacobins who were disaffected by Robespierre's religious presumptions at the next, he went about his furtive business. On June 6 he was ready to give Robespierre an answer to the accusations of May 6. On that day Fouché was elected president of the Jacobin Club!

Robespierre recoiled at this news as though struck. He could scarcely credit his senses. For Fouché to have sought refuge in the very sanctuary of the Revolution, the holy of holies over whose altars he himself presided, was a piece of audacity that was as unexpected as it was alarming. The move was worse than defiant. It was a threat. From this moment Robespierre realized that he had underestimated the resources of his enemy. Fouché was as bold as he was crafty. But before taking steps to have him deposed from the presidency of the Jacobins, Robespierre had two audacious moves of his own to make. The first of these was the so-called Fête de l'Être Suprême, or Festival of the Supreme Being, which was held on June 8. The second was the death-dealing Law of 22 Prairial, submitted to the Convention on June 10.

The Festival of the Supreme Being has often been described. It is one of the most eye-catching vignettes of the Revolution and one of the most curious. Embellished by a convulsion of pasteboard devices and symbolic effigies done in papier-mâché, attended by flourishes, processions and hymns to Nature, this huge celebration was held in honor of God's return to France—and of Robespierre's appointment as His high priest there. It marks the zenith of Robespierre's power. Since he could not preside over the festivities as leader of the Committee of Public Safety, an admission of fact that it was not yet propitious to make, he appeared there as President of the Convention. When the deputies filed out of the Tuileries into the gardens, Robespierre, conspicuous in a pair of jonquil-colored knee breeches and a silk coat of robin's-egg blue, led the procession. He is said to have given the impression of a man totally absorbed in some blissful inner thought. After an interminable sermon, replete with the usual expressions of aspiration and menace, he seized a torch and set fire to an effigy representing Atheism. Egotism and Insincerity were incinerated with it. Out of the ashes the figure of Wisdom, slightly scorched, teeteringly arose.

The scenery and automata of the festival were designed by David. From the Tuileries the procession moved on to the Champs de Mars, where an enormous cardboard mountain, embellished with rocks and trees, had been erected. Girls bearing flowers, and boys bearing wands of oak escorted the parade. The deputies carried sheaves of corn and other agricultural produce. As they approached the mountain, Robespierre, impatient for the climactic moment, is said to have indiscreetly hastened ahead of his fellow deputies. In any case he was first to ascend the mountain. It was not by accident that his was the place closest to the summit. His fellow deputies willingly accorded him first place and encouraged him to stand alone and conspicuous. He suspected their motives, but vanity overcame prudence. From the height upon which he stood he could look down on more than 300,000 people. Their cries of "Vive la République!" and "Vive Robespierre!" wreathed the mountaintop like clouds of incense and obliterated the rankling recollection of the unpleasant murmurs he had heard before he began to scale the mountain. The grumbling of certain jealous deputies had been quite audible. Such words as "Brutus" and "dictator" had even reached his ear. Glimpsed in the crowd, Fouché's impassive face was a disagreeable reminder of the business he would have to deal with as soon as the festivities were over. But, on the summit of the cardboard mountain, the voice of the People, the faceless masses whom he loved as he could love no individual human, assuaged his doubts. The adulation of so vast a multitude gave him courage to face the approaching battle. It would be the last. After that the Republic would be cleansed of her impurities and the Reign of Virtue could finally begin.

Draped in hangings of rich velvet, the guillotine too took a holiday during the Festival of the Supreme Being. On the next day, however, it was back at work. And on the day after that, Robespierre detonated a bomb beneath the feet of the unwary Convention with the Law of 22 Prairial. "The Law," declared Article 16 of this fearsome legislation, "accords no defense whatsoever to conspirators. Patriots who have been calumniated can rest assured that they will be defended by a patriotic jury." Not only were all witnesses and all defense eliminated, but (in Article 18), "no accused shall have his case set aside until the Committee of Public Safety and the General Security Committee have examined that case." With this appalling law the Committee saw to it that there would never again be a recurrence of the awkward moments that had characterized Danton's trial. The Law of 22 Prairial brought every head in France under the sword. Arrest was now tantamount to death. Every loophole was closed in the snare that was to be used to catch the next batch of political heretics. The Law of 22 Prairial was Robespierre's answer to the intriguing Fouché. It remained now only to have him expelled from the Jacobins and then, when the moment was suitable, to destroy him.

Backed by the testimony of the Lyons Jacobins who hated Fouché, Robespierre appeared on the following day at the Jacobin Club with a scathing denunciation of his enemy. His attack was so violent that he nearly succeeded in toppling his adversary that very evening. Fouché, however, presided over the meeting as president. It was his prerogative to close a debate. He declared the hour to be late and hurriedly retired from the scene. He did not appear there again. The cobra raised its head to strike on the following evening, but the mongoose once again had vanished. Infuriated, Robespierre demanded that Fouché be summoned to the next meeting of the Jacobins. Fouché, who was no public speaker, was familiar with Robespierre's ability to mesmerize his audience. He had no intention of meeting his enemy face to face. He therefore dispatched a letter to the Jacobin Club requesting that it withhold judgment until he had written another justificatory report, which he would submit to the two Committees. Clutching Fouché's letter, Robespierre rose in the Jacobin Club and delivered himself of an outburst of rage and hatred.

"Fouché the individual does not interest me in the slightest," he began in an affectedly calm tone of voice. "If I denounced him here, it was not so much on account of his past crimes, but because of those that he is about to commit. I believe him to be the ringleader of a conspiracy which we must thwart. I have carefully studied this letter which has just been read and I perceive that it was written by a man who refuses to justify himself before his fellow citizens. That is how systems of tyranny get their start. A man who refuses to answer to a popular society is a man who attacks the institution of popular societies." Then, with characteristically personal rancor, Robespierre declared, "Is this man afraid that his terrible face will reveal his crimes? That, fixed on him, our eyes will read his soul and will uncover the thoughts which it is in his nature to conceal? Is this man afraid that hesitations and contradictions in his speech will unmask his guilt? A man who cannot look his fellow citizen in the eye is guilty! I demand that Fouché be called to judgment here!"

In an outpouring of invective the serpent reared back and began to spit venom: "Vile impostor! Despicable intriguer! A man whose hands are stained with loot and dripping with blood and crime!" When the diatribe finally ended, it was greeted with applause. By unanimous vote Joseph Fouché was ignominiously expelled from membership in the Jacobin Club. From that moment he was marked for the guillotine as a tree is marked for the axe.

43

ROBESPIERRE'S TRIUMPH at the Jacobin Club cannot have come as a surprise to Fouché. From the moment of his first public collision with Robespierre in the precincts of the Club Fouché knew that he would lose any further dispute there. He was in hiding therefore when Robespierre toppled him from his post. In the obscurity in which he worked best he had begun to prepare his final desperate move. In constant fear of arrest, he never slept in the same place for two consecutive nights. He worked through most of each night. When dusk had fallen over the fear-gripped city he would cautiously make his way from the residence of one deputy to that of another, from one furtive meeting place to another. And in every ear he dropped the terrible words, "Robespierre is preparing another proscription. You are on the list." Tunneling the ground beneath Robespierre's feet, he worked with the courage of a man who knows himself to be doomed and with the cunning and caution of an intriguer who had no peer.

In the month that preceded 9 Thermidor, the Convention is said to have been in an indescribable state of panic. More than fifty deputies, men like Fouché, dared not return to their homes at night. Such men as still appeared in the Convention sat mute and ashen-faced, their wills paralyzed by fear. During the months of May and June it was no secret that new proscriptions were being planned. The terrible Law of 22 Prairial, which abrogated the few remaining legal shelters accorded France's deputies, hung like the sword of Damocles over them all. No man was safe. In menacing tones Robespierre himself hinted at an approaching "purge." "The Convention *in general* is pure," he pronounced one night at the Jacobin Club. "The Convention can therefore be above fear as it is above crime. It has nothing in common with the conspirators it presently shelters in its midst. . . ." It was hardly a statement to allay fear. Who, exactly, were those conspirators? Menace and uncertainty crept through the city like a thickening fog. No doubt that was as Robespierre intended it should be. Vague terror of this sort was a weapon he had heretofore used with effective skill. But in this instance it was a serious tactical blunder. He had not reckoned on Joseph Fouché.

It is one of the virtues of poison that, artfully distilled, it can often be used to heal. Toxin, in the proper dosage, becomes antitoxin. By using the Terror Robespierre had isolated men one from the other. Each deputy trembled in his private hell of fear and foreboding and hurriedly dissociated himself from his doomed neighbor. Everywhere in the Convention there were men who hated or feared Robespierre. There were violent men like Danton's friend Legendre; gentle men like the government's financial advisor, Cambon. There were supple intriguers like Barras. There were stalwart Republicans like Carnot, and men of power like Collot d'Herbois and Billaud-Varennes, who sat in the council chambers of the Committee of Public Safety. But who, after all, had been more violent than Hébert, more gentle than Vergniaud, more stalwart than Brissot, more powerful than Danton? Robespierre had mowed them all down. They had hated one another more than they had feared him. Factional differences continually divided his enemies. The system of the Terror, the outcome of these differences, now isolated them even further from the possibility of any understanding.

It was Fouché's great feat that by using Robespierre's own weapon, the Terror, he was able to unite men who had heretofore been bitterly hostile to one another. An acute fear for their own lives now brought together such enemies as the Hébertist Collot d'Herbois and the Dantonist Legendre. When the cards are on the table most men are more interested in saving their skins than they are in the "isms" or the "ists" of political ideology. Though they may not hesitate to sacrifice other men in the name of their beliefs, their enthusiasm does not often extend to a sacrifice of their own lives. It was on this truism that Fouché now acted.

Fanning the panic that smouldered in the Convention, he began to move to and fro, spreading his snare. He fixed one end of his web on the remnants of the men of the Extreme Left. The other he attached to what remained of Danton's party. Between them he tied

377

together such loose ends as men like Barras and Tallien, who, like himself, were loyal to no man or no party. He went to other men such as those on the General Security Committee who hated Robespierre for having abrogated their prerogatives and who feared him because he was planning a reorganization of their committee. He went to the Plain, the mass of nonentities who sat in the center of the Convention and who committed themselves to nothing. We do not know and we will never know the secret bargains that were made or the threats and the promises that were proffered in these desperate negotiations that set the stage for 9 Thermidor. As usual Fouché's web was woven in the dark. Danger of the most deadly kind at all times threatened its delicate strands. The slightest false move and the whole conspiracy would have been torn to shreds. Though he was invisible in the moment of action and though his tracks have long since been covered by time, there can be no doubt that Fouché's capable hand designed and directed the plot. Robespierre himself recognized this when at the Jacobin Club he announced, "Fouché is the leader behind this conspiracy." One day Robespierre's ubiquitous spies glimpsed Fouché at work in the very corridors of the Convention (he had long since ceased to attend sessions there) in a furtive huddle with four other suspect deputies. Robespierre read the report with a grimace and hurried to complete his own plans. Fouché slipped back into the shadows.

An important filament of the conspiracy hung on Collot d'Herbois and Billaud-Varennes, who were members of the Committee of Public Safety. Shortly before 9 Thermidor, Fouché heard that these two cowards were considering a last-minute reconciliation within the Committee. He hurried to them with a bit of reasoning that the fate of Hébert and Danton all too vividly illustrated.

"And when you have let Robespierre have our heads," he demanded, "who will remain to protect yours? Our corpses will only nourish Robespierre's arrogance and ambition, and when we are gone he will strike you down with the weapon that you have lent him."

And that was the argument that over and again he used with each wavering deputy. And each, remembering the fate of Danton and what had followed, succumbed to his reasoning. In a true sense of the expression, Danton's ghost now rose from his grave. His bloody specter was a reminder to all those quavering politicians of the fate that sooner or later might befall them.

Cold courage was the quality most needed in the weaving of Fouché's conspiracy. And Fouché was a brave man, though his courage more resembled that of the rat or the weasel than of the lion. He dodged danger whenever possible. But when he was cornered he fought without fear. A few days before the denouement an event occurred that strung his unyielding nerves even more tightly. His firstborn child, a little girl hardly a year old, died of fever. It is not least among the unexpected elements at work within this complex man that he was a devoted husband and father. During his days of glory under Napoleon his hearthside resembled that of some Victorian paterfamilias. The sight of the terrifying Duc d'Otrante dandling his children on his knee never failed to astonish the few people who chanced to witness it. He loved his ugly wife and his ugly children ("wolf whelps," Barras sarcastically called them) with a tenderness that he never expressed to anyone in the world outside the limits of his foyer. The death of his little daughter was a blow that under the same circumstances might have caused a lesser man to falter. It only steeled Fouché to face his possible forfeit of the game with indifference. Hunted by Robespierre, he had not dared visit his dying child's bedside. But on 6 Thermidor he accompanied the little coffin to the cemetery. The sight filled him with the courage of despair.

On the following day he was back at work, moving from deputy to deputy, tightening the strands of his web, communicating his implacable intention to those who might weaken at the last moment. "Tomorrow we must strike," he whispered. "Tomorrow must be the day." He knew well that on the morrow, which was 8 Thermidor, Robespierre was planning to spring his own trap.

The end had come at last.

Since mid-June the animosities within the Committee of Public Safety had grown more bitter by the hour. A terrible scene took place there immediately after the passage of the Law of 22 Prairial. We do not know what precipitated the quarrel. Some historians believe that Robespierre had asked for the heads of Tallien, Barras and Fouché and had met with unexpected resistance. His colleagues on the Committee would have been understandably reluctant to hand him the rope with which he planned to hang them. In his move to strike down Fouché and company they may have glimpsed the opening move of Robespierre's attack on themselves. In any case Robespierre, after a fit of wild weeping, left the room in a rage. He did not return to the Committee for over a month—a fact that has been used by his latter-day advocates to show that he had little to do with the hecatombs of June and July. Their evidence is not persuasive, for during the period of his absence from the Committee he kept in very close touch with the sinister Police Bureau, a new office that was instituted soon after Danton's death and that, though nominally under the authority of the whole Committee of Public Safety, was, in fact, under Robespierre's thumb.

The Police Bureau had been set up over the head of the General Security Committee, another group that was a thorn in Robespierre's side. The General Security Committee had heretofore been in technical control of such matters as surveillance, arrest and the administration of justice. In the atmosphere of impending crisis Robespierre had no intention of letting so important a weapon remain in the hands of his enemies. Hence the institution of the Police Bureau, which was in direct communication with the Revolutionary Tribunal and Fouquier-Tinville. Throughout his absence from the meetings of the Committee of Public Safety, Robespierre continued to closet himself for long hours with the mysterious affairs of the Police Bureau. The door was perpetually guarded by a gendarme who had orders signed by Robespierre to admit no one but himself or his agents. St. Just was off on mission during part of June, but when he was in Paris he would take Robespierre's place in the offices of the Police Bureau (which are believed to have been located in an attic room in the Pavillon de Flore). On such days the velvety-eyed young man would usually be seen hurrying towards the Incorruptible's residence on the rue St. Honoré. The two men would retire for hours behind locked doors. It was hardly a sight to alleviate the apprehensions of their fellow committee members.

Robespierre's angry departure from the sittings of the Committee of Public Safety finally brought into the open the bitter quarrels which had heretofore been confined within the walls of the Committee's offices. Robespierre turned to his faithful followers in the Jacobin Club for support. Collot d'Herbois and his colleagues turned to the disaffected members of the General Security Committee and to the remnants of the Mountain in the Convention.

By the first week of July the tensions which gripped the Committee of Public Safety had communicated themselves to all of Paris. Everyone knew that a crisis was imminent. In the two weeks preceding 9 Thermidor (July 27) the sense of suspense in the city, blanketed that summer by one of the worst heat waves in its history, became almost unendurable. At the Jacobin Club Robespierre or his satellites, St. Just and Couthon, uttered warnings dark with menace.

"I am going to speak to you now of certain cabals that are secretly conspiring against the Revolutionary government," Robespierre declared one evening at the Jacobins. "My purpose is to warn all good citizens about certain snares that are being laid for them. There are men at work who are trying to persuade the members of the Convention that the Committee of Public Safety has proscribed them. Good citizens must be on their guard against these intriguers." Robespierre was clearly aware of Fouché's clandestine activities.

Couthon, through whose mouth Robespierre often spoke, made a characteristic pronouncement of his own at the Jacobin Club a few days before the storm broke at last. "Within the Convention," he declared, "there are certain impure men who are trying to corrupt the political morals of the deputies and to raise the throne of Crime over the tomb of Virtue . . . all good citizens must rally together. Pure deputies must detach themselves from these impure intriguers."

Agitated by these sinister insinuations, the Jacobin hive was soon humming angrily. The Jacobins owed their power to Robespierre. Without Robespierre most of those "gross and vulgar men" would have been nothing. Robespierre, in his turn, owed his power to the Jacobins. And this he tacitly admitted as the crisis approached. He turned to them for support against his "impure" colleagues on the Committee of Public Safety. The inner circle of the Jacobins, who knew well that their own ruin would be included in Robespierre's, gave him their support without reservation.

The Commune, once the fearsome instrument of Marat and Hébert, was another piece of artillery that Robespierre wheeled towards the field of battle. The Commune was now Robespierre's. After Hébert's death he had carefully filled the Hôtel de Ville with his own men: Hanriot, head of the Paris militia, and Fleuriot, the mayor.

381

Robespierre could count on the Commune to be loyal in the approaching struggle. Unfortunately for Robespierre, however, the Commune was no longer the savage beast it had been in the days of Marat and Hébert. Robespierre himself had pulled its fangs after Hébert's death. Its wild-eyed leaders, the anarchists of the Extreme Left, were many of them now dead. The Paris mob was no longer what it used to be. Certain of the Section leaders may have been loyal Jacobins, but the men beneath them were either apathetic or sullenly resentful of Robespierre's appropriation of their sovereignty. But on the surface, at least, the Commune still presented a formidable threat to Robespierre's opponents. It could be assumed that the quaking deputies of the Plain would abandon all resistance should it become apparent to them that they might be treated as the Girondins had been treated in June of the preceding year.

In the offices of the Committee of Public Safety, Carnot countered Robespierre's threat of the Commune with a hurried move of his own. He ordered a sizable troop of men out of Paris and put men whom he knew to be loyal to himself in charge of ammunition stores.

But what makes the events of 9 Thermidor so singular is that this bitter battle for power, as critical as any in the history of France, was not fought with guns or ammunition, but with words. The field of battle was the Convention. Intrigue, moral courage and mastery of the emotions won the day. Cowardice, opportunism, treachery and fear were the weapons. The precept that Might makes Right, basic to every *coup d'état* that had occurred during the Revolution, is at no time more undisguisedly apparent than during 9 Thermidor. In the events of 8-9 Thermidor, one is witness to a battle for power reduced to its barest fundamentals. Had the struggle concluded in a fist fight, its *reductio ad absurdum* might have been more obvious. But as it was the *reductio* could not have been more complete. Might, in this instance, remained almost entirely within the realm of the psychological.

Knowing well that the battlefield would have to be the Convention, Robespierre, before firing his opening shot, took last-minute steps to see that the men of the Plain, the majority in the Convention, would come to his support when the cards were on the table. Until this moment he had never much troubled himself with that faceless

mass. The great struggles in the Convention had always been between the Left and the Right. The Center had heretofore been of
little interest to him. He had silenced them with terror and then
dismissed them with contempt; they had never dared resist his
wishes. Now, thanks to Fouché's underground activities, the Terror had become a weapon that might backfire in his hands. For the
first time he had to go to representatives of the Plain with promises
rather than threats. Well did he know, however, that terror still remained the most important weapon in his arsenal. Behind those
promises the fangs were still visible. And in this estimate of the
cowardly Center, Robespierre was undoubtedly accurate. They could
be counted upon to side with whichever faction won the battle.

On 8 Thermidor Robespierre opened fire. Within the Committee
of Public Safety and the General Security Committee a desperate
attempt at reconciliation had taken place on 6 Thermidor (July 24).
St. Just is believed to have been behind this maneuver. But matters
had now gone far beyond any hope of repair. Robespierre was convinced that Collot d'Herbois's protestations of loyalty to him and
his pleas for understanding were a confession of weakness and a
stalling for time. He decided, therefore, to appear before the Convention and demand the arrest of the "conspirators" who were threatening the government. We will never know exactly whose arrest he
was determined to have. Those names were to have been revealed
on 9 Thermidor and on that day Robespierre was silenced. One can
make a shrewd guess, however. Robespierre's pattern of attack never
varied. He always isolated his enemies and then attacked them separately. At so critical a juncture in his political life as this he would
not have dared ask for any great hecatomb. He would have struck
at those men who at a future date might come to the defense of his
hated rivals. Fouché was certainly on the list; Tallien and Barras
were on it too. Collot d'Herbois, Billaud-Varennes in the Committee
of Public Safety and four or five of the Hébertists on the General
Security Committee would have probably completed that particular
batch. With those men gone, he could at his leisure strike down Carnot and others who dared oppose him. In the end St. Just and
Couthon would probably have gone down the path where they had
sent so many others. We will never know. The pattern of individual
human behavior repeats itself with variations like the themes of a

symphony. It was not in Robespierre's nature to share. The presence even of such devoted followers as St. Just and Couthon would eventually have precipitated another quarrel.

St. Just is said to have read Robespierre's speech of 8 Thermidor before Robespierre delivered it to the Convention, and there is reason to believe that St. Just may have considered it impolitic. Though he wholeheartedly approved of Robespierre's plan to rid the Convention and the Committee of Public Safety of the rebellious personalities that had risen to resist the Incorruptible's wishes, he may not have approved of Robespierre's method of achieving that goal. "The Angel of Death" was more down to earth than his doctrinaire master and had less confidence in the efficacy of moral exhortations and threats.

Everyone in the Convention knew that 8 Thermidor was to be an important day, that Robespierre was going to speak. Since dawn, clusters of apprehensive deputies had been gathering in the corridors of the building. Many of them were silent; others whispered together in low, tense voices. Here and there among the crowd moved the "conspirators," hurrying from one group to another, instilling their frightened colleagues with courage. Tallien was conspicuous among them. It is said that his mistress, the famous and beautiful Therezia Cabarrus, who now languished with her friend Josephine de Beauharnais in the prison of the Carmes, had sent him a dagger the night before, exhorting him to use it.

Fouché was nowhere in sight. The stage was now set and the curtain was about to rise. The stage manager had therefore retired to the wings.

The sitting opened at eleven o'clock. A few moments afterwards Robespierre entered. He was dressed in the same attire he had worn on the day of the Festival of the Supreme Being, a coat of sky-blue silk and jonquil-colored knee breeches. His hair was carefully powdered and dressed, but his face was deathly white and drawn. He had been up all night preparing his speech. Indeed it had been many nights since any of the deputies, Robespierre included, had enjoyed a refreshing sleep. The faces of most men in that assembly of 8 Thermidor were almost as haggard as Robespierre's. Soon after his entry into the hall, Robespierre announced that he wished to speak. The silence which this announcement induced was palpable. A faint sigh like that of expiring life rippled through the room as Robespierre, with slow, solemn steps ascended the rostrum.

In his hand he held the manuscript of his speech. Silence deepened as with studied care he spread the sheets out before him. Those in the hall whose names were somewhere written in those papers knew that they could count themselves dead. Like a cat toying with a mouse, Robespierre let that awareness sink in. He searched for his spectacles, fitted them on his nose and then raised them to his forehead. He scanned the room with his myopic eyes, encompassing the Right, the Center and the Left with that terrible menacing stare. No one stirred. His audience sat as though hypnotized, mute and immobile. Then at last he lowered his spectacles and began to speak.

The speech lasted for over two hours. Every phrase was characteristic of its author. It began on a note of self-praise and self-pity. "They say that I am a tyrant. Rather I am a slave. I am a slave of Liberty, a living martyr to the Republic. I am the victim as well as the enemy of crime. I confess to you that I am sometimes afraid that my name will be blackened in the eyes of posterity by the impure tongues of perverted men. . . . I have promised to leave a redoubtable testimony to the oppressors of the People. I shall leave them the terrible truth—and Death!"

Preparatory to revealing the "terrible truth," Robespierre paused a moment to ingratiate himself with the Plain and an uncertain group whom he called the *hommes probes,* or "honest men" of the Convention. No matter where such men might sit, he declared in a humble tone of voice, he stretched out his hand to them in respect and friendship. His eye rested on the Center. "Virtuous men," he said, "need have nothing to fear." It must have astonished the men of the Plain, whom he had once contemptuously dismissed as "cowardly moderates" and "money-minded bourgeois," to hear themselves courted in these obsequious terms.

Then he let the axe swing. Mentioning no names, but dropping hints of a most sinister kind, he unveiled the existence of a vast plot against "public Liberty." "The intrigues of this criminal coalition extend into the very bosom of the Convention," he declared. "The conspirators have accomplices in the General Security Committee . . . certain members of the Committee of Public Safety are also guilty. . . . These traitors must be punished, the General Security

Committee must be reorganized, the Committee of Public Safety must be cleansed!"

Alternately breathing flame and spreading unction, Robespierre's speech is expressive of the dilemma in which he found himself. It concluded, two hours after it had begun, with an exhortation to the People. "People! You should be informed that there exists within your bosom a league of scoundrels who are at war with public Virtue!" To the end Robespierre indulged himself in the illusion that the People was a virtuous and well-intentioned entity separate from the human beings who comprised it. In addressing himself thus to this idealized abstraction he no doubt recalled the great faceless throng that had saluted him on the day of the Festival of the Supreme Being. He supposed that at his command this mass of humanity would hurry to his support.

The Convention, which had listened to his words in dead silence, upon the conclusion of his speech sat as though stupefied. Instead of relieving tension, Robespierre, by not mentioning any names, had heightened it. He had virtually pointed the finger at certain men such as Cambon, head of the Financial Committee. To ingratiate himself with the Plain, the "money-minded bourgeoisie," he had denounced Cambon's financial administration as "corrupt and incompetent." Other men, such as Carnot, he had denounced in somewhat vaguer terms by criticizing the management of the war. Most of the Committee of Public Safety had fallen under the shadow of the axe; so had the General Security Committee. A great many deputies could thus imagine themselves inscribed on that fatal, but as yet unseen, "list." Robespierre's speech brought to white heat the atmosphere of panic that Fouché had been assiduously fanning for some weeks.

In the critical moment of silence that followed the delivery of the speech, the hearts of Barras, Tallien and other "conspirators" present in the Convention must have stopped beating. Now was the time for someone to rise and protest. But no one rose. All at once, there was an outbreak of applause, led probably by the Jacobins in the gallery. Like a wave it gathered volume and swept towards the front of the hall. Robespierre had once more won the day. Everyone present knew that on the morrow St. Just would appear at the rostrum and demand the heads that Robespierre wanted. When the applause died away, one of Robespierre's Jacobin satellites rose to propose that his speech be printed. The servile majority, those men of the Center on whom Fouché had counted, voted in favor of this proposal without a murmur. But just before the vote was recorded, one of the conspirators, Bourdon de l'Oise, who had been informed by Fouché that his name was on the list, suddenly rose from his seat on the Mountain.

"I am opposed to the printing of this speech!" he declared. "There are many grave accusations in it that ought to be clarified."

Stunned by these bold words, Robespierre momentarily lost his power of speech. He stood in the rostrum "as though petrified." The moment gave Cambon of the Finance Committee, the only man whom Robespierre had actually named in his diatribe, the opportunity he needed to seize the rostrum. He flew forward in a frenzy.

"Before I am dishonored," he cried, "I will speak to France . . . ! It is time that everyone here should know the truth. One man paralyzes the will of the National Convention. *That man is Robespierre!*"

The words struck the room like a thunderbolt. They rent to shreds the spell of silence and fear that Robespierre had so skillfully woven. Billaud-Varennes next went to the rostrum.

"The mask must be torn away!" he declared. "I would rather my corpse should serve as the throne of an ambitious man than that by my silence I should become the accomplice of his crimes!"

Another deputy, Panis, took Billaud-Varennes's place. He dared mention the mysterious list. "Robespierre has drawn up a list and my name is said to be on it. . . ."

"The list! The list!" went up the cry.

"Name those whom you have accused!" demanded a deputy.

"Name them! Name them!" echoed the Convention.

Recovering his voice, Robespierre declared that he did not wish to reveal any names at that moment. In so saying he made a serious blunder. He did not realize that by mentioning ten men he might have reassured three hundred. From the back of the room somebody called out, "And Fouché? What about Fouché?"

Instead of admitting that Fouché's name was indeed on the list and thereby relieving the apprehensions of those whose names were not on it, Robespierre replied vaguely that he was too busy to discuss the matter. "I listen only to the call of duty," he stated sanctimoniously.

The session of 8 Thermidor closed at five o'clock in the afternoon. Robespierre had lost the first round. But he had by no means lost the game. That evening, after a short stroll in the Champs-Élysées during which he calmed his nerves ("Fine weather for tomorrow!" he remarked to his companion, Éléonore Duplay), Robespierre repaired to the Jacobin Club. The events of the day at the Convention were well known to the Jacobins. The hive was humming angrily when Robespierre at last made his appearance. Rebuffed by the Convention, Robespierre now planned to incite his fellow Jacobins into terrorizing the Convention on the morrow. He was greeted by loud cheers and carried on a wave of triumph to the rostrum of the Jacobin Club, where he read again the speech he had delivered that morning before the Convention.

Collot d'Herbois and Billaud-Varennes, interested to know the mood of the Jacobin Club and hopeful of winning some members of it to their side, were present while Robespierre read his interminable speech. Dumas, Robespierre's "strangler" on the Revolutionary Tribunal, saw them and saluted them with a gloating leer, "I look forward to seeing you two in the Tribunal tomorrow," he said. The Jacobins who were loyal to Robespierre suddenly turned on them and with loud cries of "To the guillotine!" fell on them. Billaud managed to escape before he was assaulted, but Collot d'Herbois was knocked down and his clothes torn to shreds. The enthusiasm with which the Jacobins had rushed to Robespierre's support can have done little to assuage the apprehensions these two men must have felt about the outcome of events on the morrow.

"We must deliver the Convention from these scoundrels!" Robespierre declared. "If we fail, you will see me drink the hemlock with calm."

Hanriot, the drunken ex-valet who had led the mob on June 2, 1793, when Marat had driven the Girondins from the Convention, now promised Robespierre that he would have his cannon in readiness.

David rushed forward and embraced Robespierre. "If you drink the hemlock I shall quaff it with you!"

"We all will! We all will!" echoed the Jacobins.

Robespierre left the Club in high spirits. He was home before midnight in a mood that Duplay later described as "optimistic." Since the important speech on the morrow was to be delivered by St. Just, he retired to bed soon after his return.

While Robespierre slept his associates and enemies were in the midst of frenzied preparations for the *crise* that was to take place in the morning. In a room adjoining the offices of the Committee of Public Safety, St. Just brazenly penned the accusations he planned to deliver before the Convention in a few hours' time. The scratch of his implacable pen was audible to Carnot and to several other members of the Committee. Shortly after eleven the door of the Committee's room burst open and the disheveled Collot d'Herbois and Billaud-Varennes, who had just escaped from the upheaval at the Jacobin Club, staggered in.

St. Just looked up from his work. "What's new at the Jacobin Club?" he asked in a teasing tone, implying that he was well aware of the answer.

"You dare ask us what's new!" cried Collot. "You! You're the one who would know that. You, who with Robespierre and Couthon, are planning to kill us! You are here to spy on us and to denounce us to your colleagues. You have been drawing up an accusation against us!"

St. Just answered boldly. "You are not entirely wrong," he replied. With a cold malicious smile he turned to Carnot. "I shan't forget you, either. You'll find that I've dealt with you in a masterful way."

Beside himself, Collot seized St. Just by the throat and began to shake him. "Show us the report!" he cried. "You are not going to leave here until you've shown us your report!"

Carnot separated the two men. St. Just, taking alarm, promised his fellow committee members that he would show them his report before he read it to the Convention. He returned to his work. Dawn was breaking when at five o'clock he finally rose from his desk and took his departure. He left assuring the Committee that he would return before noon and read his report before giving it to the Convention. With his departure, Collot d'Herbois, Billaud-Varennes, Carnot and Barère put their heads together and began to make their own plans.

All through that hot summer night Fouché had been tirelessly at work, fusing the remnants of the Dantonists with the Hébertists, weaving the Mountain and the Plain into common cause, assuaging animosities, negotiating alliances and preparing the ground for tomorrow's battle. By dawn his task was done. With daybreak he retreated back to the shadows.

44

THE CONVENTION was scheduled to open its session at the usual hour of eleven o'clock. Since seven in the morning its galleries had been filled to overflowing. The corridors seethed with *tricoteuses* and with men armed with pikes or pistols. These ragged spectators were by no means united in purpose. Many in the crowd were Jacobins who had come to lend Robespierre their support. Others were remnants of Hébert's Commune who had come to support Collot d'Herbois and Billaud-Varennes. Led by Danton's loyal follower Legendre, many of the old Cordeliers moved among the surging mob in the galleries, uneasily aligning themselves with their enemies the Hébertists. At its periphery, too, Fouché had mined the battlefield well.

Nature that day reflected the anxious condition of men. After two weeks in which the thermometer had risen steadily, 9 Thermidor dawned in a sky that was the color of molten lead. The air was heavy with impending storm. As the day advanced, thunder could be heard in the distance. The storm, when it finally came, was destined to play a small rôle in the events of that famous day.

In the offices of the Committee of Public Safety, Robespierre's enemies, haggard from their night's vigil, feverishly awaited St. Just's return. Shortly after eleven a note from him was delivered. "You have blighted my heart," he declared. "I have decided therefore to trample my cowardly promises under foot and open my heart directly to the Convention." With cries of "Traitor!" and "We've been duped!" the committee members hurried to the hall of the Convention, where they found the corridors crackling with excitement. They were able to thrust their way through the crowd only with difficulty. Before entering the assembly room, Tallien hurried up to them and exhorted them to maintain their courage and resolution. Collot d'Herbois was already in the Convention. Whether by accident or design, he presided over that day's meeting in the capacity of President. It was a very high card in the hands of the conspirators.

Robespierre, Couthon and St. Just had arrived at the Convention a few moments before the Committee. From the galleries, "a volcano with a boiling crater," an outburst of wild applause from Robespierre's Jacobin followers greeted their arrival. Robespierre answered these plaudits with the satisfied expression of one who is certain of victory. He was dressed in his jonquil-colored breeches and his coat of robin's-egg blue. St. Just wore a pair of dove-grey breeches and a white waistcoat. In one report he is described as wearing a pair of gold earrings. Robespierre seated himself in the front of the room with the Center. He did so in order to see the rostrum more clearly, but his presence there was undoubtedly intended, too, as a compliment to the Plain. St. Just went immediately to the rostrum. His face was cold and impersonal.

"The course of events," he began, "has indicated that this rostrum may be the Tarpeian Rock for the man who . . ."

Tallien, hurrying towards the rostrum, suddenly interrupted him. "I demand to be heard!" he cried out. St. Just stared in astonishment at this interruption. When he opened his mouth to protest, Collot drowned out his voice with the President's bell. Tallien then stepped up to the rostrum and pushed St. Just aside. "I demand that the curtain be torn away!" he declared. It was the signal for attack. In the hall other conspirators arose. "It must be!" they echoed.

Billaud-Varennes ran forward to take Tallien's place in the rostrum. He denounced the scene that had occurrred at the Jacobin Club on the preceding night. "These people are planning to murder the Convention!" he declared. A gasp of horror filled the room at this announcement. He looked up at the galleries. "I see one of those men who dared menace the Convention sitting among us now."

"Arrest him! Arrest him!" came the cry. In a flash the police seized the man and bore him off. The dispatch with which this operation was effected filled the Jacobins in the gallery with consternation. And after each such successful assault on the Robespierrist citadel the conspirators were joined by more and more of the opportunists. *"Vive la Convention!"* rose the cry. One of Robespierre's followers, Lebas, then tried to approach the rostrum, but he too was boldly shoved aside. Tallien took his place. "I asked a moment ago that the veil be torn aside," he said. "It is now ripped asunder! The conspirators are soon to be unmasked and annihilated. Liberty will triumph!"

The words threw Robespierre's wavering partisans into further consternation and uncertainty.

"I too was at last night's meeting at the Jacobin Club," continued Tallien. "As I watched I shuddered for my country. I saw the army of a new Cromwell being formed! I have armed myself with a dagger which shall pierce this man's breast if the Convention does not have the courage to decree his arrest." And with these words Tallien suddenly pulled forth a dagger, presumably the one sent to him by Therezia, and waved it wildly in the air. The Convention gasped at this melodramatic sight. "Down with the tyrant!" someone cried. The cry was sporadically echoed through the hall. No one had yet dared mention "the tyrant's" name.

At these words Robespierre, "his face congested," sprang to his feet and made a dash for the rostrum. But a well-designed plan, carefully followed by the conspirators, lay behind much that seems chaotic on 9 Thermidor. All of these men knew that it was of vital importance that Robespierre be kept from the rostrum. Under no circumstances should he be given an opportunity to speak. He was speaking as he tried to step up to the rostrum. Collot drowned his words by a furious ringing of his bell. Barère took Tallien's place in the rostrum. And Barère was succeeded by another conspirator. Collot stepped down from the presidency for a moment and handed over his chair to Thuriot, one of Danton's friends and followers, who with inexorable gestures also refused to let Robespierre speak. Tallien appeared in the rostrum again. He suddenly demanded the arrest of Hanriot, Robespierre's "general" at the Commune, and of Dumas, the President of the Revolutionary Tribunal. With continual cries of "À bas le tyran!" the Convention quickly decreed their arrest. No one had yet struck directly at Robespierre, but, divested in one stroke of his army and his court, he was now vulnerable. Once again he rushed towards the rostrum. His color was ashen and great beads of sweat poured down his face. Once again his voice was drowned by implacable ringing of the bell.

An obscure deputy named Louchet suddenly rose and uttered the historic words, "I demand the arrest of Robespierre!" The word was finally spoken! The Mountain answered it with cries of "Down with the tyrant!" The President's bell clanged without cease above the pandemonium. Robespierre, with a desperate effort, finally made himself heard.

"For the last time," he cried at Thuriot, "will you let me be heard, President of Assassins!"

Like most famous phrases this one was reported in several forms. Others present thought that they heard Robespierre say, "By what right have you made yourself the president of these assassins?" Whatever his words may have been, they gave the President a pretext to put his arrest to the vote. "The monster has insulted the Convention!" declared Tallien indignantly.

With a beseeching gesture of his hands, Robespierre now rushed from the rostrum towards the benches on the Left, towards the Mountain, where he had always sat. "Get away from here!" someone cried. "The ghosts of Danton and Camille Desmoulins reject you!"

He tried again to speak, but his voice was drowned in the pandemonium. "The blood of Danton is choking you!" cried another deputy.

Rebuffed by the Mountain, he turned in dismay to the Center. "Men of purity," he implored. "Men of Virtue! I appeal to you. Give me the leave to speak which these assassins have refused me!" But the Plain, which had heretofore sat "on the watch," by now had had a chance to count the hands on the Left and on the Right and saw that Robespierre's fate was already decided. They, too, indignantly repulsed him. Like a trapped animal he scrambled up the empty seats on the Right and fell panting onto a bench. The remnants of this party who had escaped the guillotine withdrew from him in horror.

"Monster!" one of them screamed. "You are sitting where Condorcet and Vergniaud once sat!"

Driven from one end of the room to the other, repudiated by all, the frantic creature rose to his feet for the last time and turned with a despairing glance towards the galleries, where he supposed that the People, the idealized mob of his vain fantasy, sat. But the People, heedless of what Robespierre may have imagined them to be, had now disintegrated into their contemptible human components. The Dantonists and the Hébertists who were among them screamed down imprecations from the galleries. Those of them who might have been loyal to Robespierre had the winds blown in his favor, no doubt the greater portion, now hurriedly abandoned the doomed leader.

"Arrest him!" they cried. The loyal Jacobins among them—those, in other words, who were too deeply implicated to extricate themselves from their association with Robespierre—hurriedly left the room. They went to the Hôtel de Ville, headquarters of the Commune, which had now become the last bastion of Robespierre's hopes.

"Brigands! Hypocrites! Scoundrels!" screamed Robespierre at the Mountain.

"Arrest him!" came the pitiless answer.

Robespierre's arrest, along with that of St. Just, Couthon and several others, had by now been decreed. An usher went up to the bench where he had sought refuge and handed him the order. Robespierre, overwhelmed by the tumult, did not seem to notice it. "He refuses to obey the Convention's decree of arrest!" announced the President indignantly.

"Then carry him down to the bar!" cried the Convention and the galleries. Robespierre, St. Just and Couthon were accordingly brought down to the bar in front of the President's chair, where the decree was read to them. A few minutes later, escorted by a cordon of guards, the men were led away.

"The brigands have triumphed!" Robespierre declared just before he departed. Those were the last words he ever spoke in the Convention. In every sense they were among the truest.

Overwhelmed by relief and an intoxicating sense of liberation the Convention stamped its feet and cheered without restraint. Robespierre had entered the Committee of Public Safety on July 26, 1793. His rule had lasted one year to the day. No wonder that the deputies, suddenly relieved of the fear that had gripped them for so many long months, should have abandoned themselves to an outburst of emotion. What they did next, however, defies all rational explanation. In the midst of one of the most significant *coup d'états* in history, the French National Convention declared a two-hour recess for dinner. It was five thirty in the afternoon. The dinner hour in those days was at five.

Most deputies must have realized that although they had won a major battle, the war was not yet over. In the eastern sector of Paris, the Commune, led by desperate men who knew that their own ruin would be comprehended by Robespierre's, had already declared itself to be a provisional government and had begun to assemble a mob army whose purpose was to "liberate" the Convention from the conspirators and to restore Robespierre and his Jacobin cohorts to power.

The Commune learned of Robespierre's arrest at about the time that the overly confident deputies had begun to address themselves to their leisurely two-hour dinner. The mayor, Fleuriot, instantly dispatched an order to all the prisons in Paris forbidding them to receive any prisoners. At the same time he sent an urgent message to the Jacobin Club requesting that a posse of brawny arms, "including women," be sent to the Hôtel de Ville. Then he ordered the ringing of the tocsin. By six o'clock in the evening a formidable mob had gathered in front of the Hôtel de Ville. It waited impatiently for the appearance of Hanriot, on whom the last hopes of the Commune now depended.

Unfortunately for the Commune Hanriot had been drunk since early morning. By three in the afternoon he seems to have taken total leave of their senses. When he learned that his arrest had been decreed by the Convention he leaped onto a horse and, wildly flailing his sabre in the air, screamed: "Kill all policemen! Kill! Kill!" He then vanished in the direction of the Revolutionary Tribunal, whose president, Dumas, had just been apprehended in the courtroom over which he presided. Indifferent to the storms that were raging in the Convention, the Revolutionary Tribunal continued to go about its implacable business with cold efficiency. The arrest of its President startled no one. Since its inception that court had been witness to too many dramas to be astonished any further. Dumas quietly departed; the trials continued. Forty-two prisoners were sentenced to death. By four o'clock their hair had been cut and they were ready to be sent on their way. But Samson, aware of disturbances in the St. Antoine quarter of the city, suggested to Fouquier that the executions be deferred until the morrow.

"Justice must take its course," snapped the Public Prosecutor. "Do your work."

And so the last "batch" lumbered off in the direction of the Faubourg St. Antoine and the Place de la Nation. With the exception of the Princesse de Monaco, they were nearly all obscure and humble members of the *petite bourgeoisie*. Hanriot, waving his sabre, conducted the procession to the place of execution. By seven o'clock that evening, as the minutes of the military escort poignantly show, the unfortunate victims, who had been so close to deliverance, had all been executed.

Hanriot galloped back towards the Tuileries to deliver Robespierre. "Today must be another June 2!" he cried. "Three hundred of those criminals sitting in the Convention must have their throats cut!" In front of the Palais Royal, where he had assembled a crowd, he was pulled from his horse by gendarmes sent by the Convention, trussed up with cords and carried to the Tuileries, to be shut up in the offices of the Committee of Public Safety. The Commune, learning of this mishap, dispatched a party of two hundred gunners to rescue him. The deputies had just returned from dinner when that alarming battalion burst into the Tuileries and released Hanriot. Most of the senators, as they acknowledged later, were terrified. They all believed themselves lost. Collot d'Herbois still presided. "The moment to die has come," he announced.

But instead of marching the two hundred gunners directly into the hall of the unarmed Convention, as a cooler leader might have done, Hanriot made the inexplicable mistake of returning to the Hôtel de Ville. That decision gave the Convention the short reprieve it needed to assemble a small army of its own from the nearby Sections. Barras was appointed leader of this force. The Convention then declared the Commune to be in a state of rebellion and outlawed it and all its supporters. A copy of this decree, along with an order for Fleuriot and his adherents to appear at the bar of the Convention, was dispatched to the Hôtel de Ville.

Fleuriot read both the decree and the summons with scorn and tore them up. "Tell the Convention," he said to the usher who had delivered them, "that we shall soon come, but that we shall bring the people with us." The Commune, in its turn, then pronounced the leading members of the Convention to be outlaws.

Everything now depended on the armed force that each disputant might be able to raise from the Sections. The Convention hurriedly dispatched emissaries to the Sections that it knew to be wavering and tried to rally them to its side. Towards eleven o'clock it sent twelve of its members, attired in the uniform of their office, out into the streets, where, accompanied by gendarmes bearing torches, they read

396

out the decree of outlawry. The Sections were as ambiguous in their loyalty as the mob had been that afternoon in the galleries. Some, too deeply committed to do otherwise, hurried to the Commune and put themselves at the disposal of the Hôtel de Ville. Others, sensing the direction in which the winds had begun to blow, went over to the Convention. Many, such as the so-called Section of the Roi de Sicile, were divided among themselves. The leaders went to the Convention, the gunners went to the Commune. A fear of being on the losing side prompted most of these men to their decision. And by eleven o'clock the Convention was in the ascendant. The leader of the Hôtel de Ville's forces, Hanriot, was still in an apparently demented condition. The mob that had responded to the mayor's summons shuffled about aimlessly, waiting for some order or direction from their leader.

Robespierre, the man in whose name the Hôtel de Ville was preparing its insurrection, seems to have been in a worse state of mind even than Hanriot. When he and his colleagues had been ignominiously led from the Convention they were taken to the nearby offices of the General Security Committee, where they were given dinner. It was then decided that they should be separated and sent to different prisons. Robespierre was taken to the Luxembourg, where the authorities—obeying Fleuriot's order that no prisoners be received—refused to accept him. Robespierre's escort, at the request of Robespierre, himself, then took him to the *mairie*, the mayor's residence behind the Palais de Justice, a point midway between the Hôtel de Ville and the Tuileries. Here he knew he would be among friends, but would not have to become involved in the approaching struggle. His decision was characteristic of that too prudent man. Now that the moment for action had come, Robespierre fell victim to the same fatal lassitude that had overcome the leaders of each preceding party at the moment of crisis. Like Louis XVI, like the Girondins and like Danton, Robespierre found himself unable to make a decision. He had never been a man of action. He had always profited passively from the successes or failures of those who moved in the world of action. By temperament he was a combination of visionary and lawyer, a specialist in the minutiae of doctrine, and an intriguer. At the *mairie*, the latent weaknesses of Robespierre, now stripped of his power to terrify those about him, became all too apparent. The idealistic abstractions that were so large a portion of his thinking—Virtue, the People, Public Liberty—suddenly collapsed in a heap like deflated gasbags.

When Fleuriot and the Commune learned that Robespierre had sought refuge at the *mairie,* they dispatched an urgent appeal to him to come to the Hôtel de Ville and put himself at the head of his party. Robespierre clung stubbornly to the temporary safety of his asylum. With Hanriot demented and Robespierre trembling in his burrow at the *mairie,* the Commune lacked even the appearance of leadership.

An hour later Fleuriot sent Robespierre a second message. "You no longer belong to yourself," he said. "You belong now to your country." Robespierre still refused to budge. As the hours passed the mob waiting in front of the Hôtel de Ville began to grow impatient. In despair, Fleuriot sent an armed force with his next message. "We need your advice," he declared. "You must come here at once." Backed by the bayonets of the Commune, the note had more the tone of an order than an appeal. Robespierre, under guard, reluctantly set out for the Hôtel de Ville. He arrived there around eleven o'clock.

During the three hours that had been wasted on these negotiations between the Commune and Robespierre, the Convention had managed to raise a respectable little army. Barras divided this force into two columns and it was already preparing to march on the Hôtel de Ville when Robespierre finally arrived there. More and more Sections had by now begun to declare for the Convention and to join its ranks. The Convention's decree, outlawing all who had aligned themselves with the Commune, frightened many waverers into joining the Convention's army.

Towards midnight the news that the Sections were going over to the Convention reached the mob in front of the Hôtel de Ville. These "patriots" had waited too long for some decision from those whom they had volunteered to serve. Furtively, one by one at first and then in groups, they began to slink away. The thunderstorm that had been threatening all day suddenly broke. The rain was brief but it fell in torrents. It gave the remainder of the crowd an excuse to abandon the sinking ship. By one o'clock the square was deserted. Even Hanriot's gunners had departed.

Inside the defenseless Hôtel de Ville chaos had broken loose. Robespierre and his advisors huddled in one room. A delegation from the Jacobin Club agitatedly conferred with the officials of the Commune in another. Ushers, messengers and guards rushed from room to room. For over an hour Fleuriot had been urging Robespierre to sign an appeal to the army and the Sections to come to the help of the Commune. But the cautious legalist—who of all men should have been the first to realize how little the law matters when things have reached this state—hesitated to sign the paper. "In whose name am I to sign it?" he protested.

Barras's army entered the Hôtel de Ville at the very moment he finally decided to sign the paper. He had written the first two letters of his name when the door burst open. The bloodstains that are still to be seen on this extraordinary document (it hangs today in the Musée Carnavalet) evoke the moment with dramatic immediacy. They do not, however, propose an answer to the mystery that still obscures it.

Did Robespierre shoot himself? Or was he shot by one of Barras's *gendarmerie* (a man named Merda, who claimed to have done the deed)? Historians who have examined the matter are not agreed, though most of them believe that, temperamentally, Robespierre was not the kind of man to attempt suicide. The bullet struck Robespierre's jaw and shattered it. The bloodstains indicate that his head dropped onto the table towards the paper which he was signing. The wound was not fatal.

Pandemonium followed Barras's victorious army as it swarmed into the Hôtel de Ville. Robespierre's brother Augustin, who was present, flung himself from a third-story window into a courtyard below. The fall crippled but did not kill him. Philippe Lebas, the carpenter Duplay's son-in-law, shot himself. According to some accounts, St. Just turned to him a moment before and implored Lebas to kill him first, whereupon Lebas blew out his own brains with the words "Fool! I have more important things to do." The crippled Couthon left his wheelchair and crawled under a table. The Convention's army discovered him there and flung him down a staircase, where he lay hurt and senseless. Hanriot hurled himself from a window. His fall was broken by a manure pile, and he lay there drunk for several hours before being discovered.

By five o'clock in the morning the broken bones and mangled flesh of the men who only twenty-four hours earlier had caused all France to tremble had been removed from the Hôtel de Ville and brought back to the Tuileries. Only St. Just, his hands bound but his head held high, was able to walk. The Convention was still in session when Barras made the dramatic announcement: "The coward Robespierre is outside. Do you wish him to enter?"

The Convention, safe now from the possibility of any reprisals, indulged itself in one of those pompous retorts that were so much to its taste. "To bring a man covered with crime into our hall would be to diminish the glory of this great day. The body of a tyrant can only bring contagion with it. The proper place for Robespierre and his accomplices is the Place de la Révolution!"

He was therefore carried to the offices of the Committee of Public Safety and laid upon a table. That table, another memento of those turbulent hours, may also be seen today at the Musée Carnavalet. So, on the very spot where he had ordained the slaughter of so many of his fellow men, Robespierre now lay himself, a piteous object whose shattered head was supported by a wooden box filled with samples of army rations. The sky-blue coat and the jonquil-colored breeches, symbolic of his pristine aspirations on the day of the Festival of the Supreme Being, were torn and stained with blood and dirt. His shirt was open and his stockings had fallen to his ankles. His hair was clotted and in disarray.

"This man," recalled a deputy who saw him lying there, "who had occasioned so much anguish to others, suffered in the long hours that preceded his execution all that a mortal can suffer of what is painful and poignant."

The pain that his body suffered may well have been surpassed by that which his spirit was obliged to endure. During the six hours that he lay in the offices at the Committee of Public Safety, a crowd of curiosity-seekers shuffled by, jeering at him and insulting him. Many of these ignoble wretches were of the very class he always believed most devoted to his cause: working men, soldiers and the poor.

"Your Majesty appears to be suffering," laughed one of them with an ironic wink in the direction of his fellow sightseers. Another approached and gazed for a long time at his broken jaw. "Yes, Robespierre," he declared in an awe-struck tone, "there is a God."

Robespierre listened impassively to these cruel taunts, but it is related that when someone of a more charitable disposition brought him water with which to bathe his wound he lapsed into a pre-

Republican form of courtesy. "Thank you, monsieur," he whispered, forgetting that all Frenchmen were now Citizens.

Towards noon Robespierre and his "accomplices," twenty-two men in all, were rounded up and taken to the Conciergerie and the Tribunal. Because they had been declared outlaws (*hors la loi*), identification was all that was needed to secure their condemnation. Robespierre and St. Just had themselves to thank for the speed with which they were sentenced to death. They had devised the legislation that condemned outlaws to death without trial. Fouquier-Tinville, who well knew that his own approaching doom was written in the orders for execution that he was obliged to sign that day, was present in the court during the identification of the victims. His features are described as having been "convulsed" and his complexion "livid." The prisoners were sentenced at two in the afternoon; they were not guillotined until seven in the evening. The delay in their execution was probably due to a decision of the Convention that on such a momentous occasion when all Paris rejoiced in its deliverance, the guillotine should be restored to its former site on the Place de la Révolution. The mechanics of transporting that cumbersome machine across Paris and reassembling it took more time than the legal formalities before the Tribunal.

The gates of the Conciergerie swung open towards six o'clock. Samson had three tumbrels waiting. Robespierre was carried to the second. His fractured jaw was supported by a bandage that went under his chin and was tied at the top of his head. He sat on a plank at the side of the cart. Couthon lay on the floor of the third cart, where he was trampled by his fellow victims. Augustin Robespierre, half dead, sprawled on the floor of the first. Hanriot, caked with manure and with one eye falling from its socket, lay beside him. "Never have I seen such a disgusting sight," wrote one witness of this scene. "A vast mob screaming curses followed them right up to the scaffold."

Only St. Just retained command of his dignity. His fawn-colored breeches were unspotted, his white waistcoat was unwrinkled. He faced death, as he had life, with the cold impassivity of a being wrought in marble. He was twenty-seven years old and of all the personalities of the Revolution the most enigmatic.

The mob was thickest along the *via dolorosa* of the rue St. Honoré. Here a holiday atmosphere prevailed: hats were flung in the air, men and women joined hands and sang. Clusters of laughing people leaned from every window. The procession halted for a moment in front of Duplay's shuttered house. A group of women danced a *ronde* about the carts while one of the crowd spattered Duplay's door with blood that had been fetched in a bucket from a neighboring butcher's shop.

But there were many in that crowd who had no room in their hearts for holiday-making. The men and women who had been bereft of those whom they loved (one wonders where Lucile Desmoulins's mother might have been that day) could only curse and revile. At one spot along the way a grief-crazed woman broke through the cordon of *gendarmerie* surrounding the carts and tried to assault Robespierre.

"Monster!" she shrieked. "I am drunk with joy to see you suffer. You are going to Hell with the curses of all wives and mothers following you!"

So, escorted by the cruel laughter and bitter maledictions of the People, to whom he had so ignorantly and so selfishly pandered, Robespierre went to his death. We are distant from the violent passions that informed that ignoble spectacle. For us therefore it is difficult not to tender some expression of pity to that suffering soul and broken body. But in doing so we must remember that on the day that Robespierre was executed nearly eight thousand people filled the prisons of Paris. Had he not died, it is probable that most of them would have been guillotined in his stead. He was a man to whom the suffering of others seems to have meant little. Mankind was everything to him; men were nothing.

Of the twenty-two prisoners executed that evening Robespierre died twenty-first. He was thus given ample opportunity to appreciate the much-vaunted "humane" death that was dealt by the guillotine. It took nearly ten minutes to dispatch the crippled Couthon; he had to be guillotined lying on his side. When Robespierre's turn finally came he was obliged to mount a scaffold covered with the blood of those who had preceded him. A deathly hush fell over the mob as, assisted by Samson's men, he stepped towards the plank. Just before throwing him under the knife, Samson reached out and ripped away the bandage that supported his broken jaw. Robespierre's scream of pain, "like that of a slaughtered animal," was heard from one end of the great square to the other. An instant later, mercifully, he was dead.

The Reign of Terror died with him. Certain historians have been tempted to use this fact to support their contention that Robespierre alone was responsible for the Terror. Such was not the case. He was a willing accessory to the audacious or bloodthirsty schemes of others, and without conscience or remorse he incited bolder men than himself to acts of violence or illegality of which he was not capable. But the political conditions on which the Reign of Terror was built were established by stronger hands than his.

History is made by men. So by studying the Terror on its human rather than its economic, political or military level one is able to discern certain causes of that upheaval which are often overlooked. The insanity of Marat, the ignorance of Charlotte Corday, the spite of Mme. Roland, the self-indulgence of Danton, the vanity of Camille Desmoulins contributed as much to the tragedy as the malice, and jealousy and the ambition of Robespierre.

Yet all who played a rôle in the drama, even Marat, believed themselves motivated by patriotic or altruistic impulses. All in consequence were able to value their good intentions more highly than human life, for there is no crime, no murder, no massacre that cannot be justified, provided it be committed in the name of an Ideal.

BIBLIOGRAPHY

The National Archives in Paris is the principal repository of unpublished primary sources of information about the French Revolution. In France these are known as *documents inédits* and are held in high esteem by French historians. The announcement *"avec des documents inédits"* is almost mandatory on the cover of books of history or biography that are published in France. In consequence little that is of interest or importance now remains *inédit*.

For the author of so general a study as *Paris in the Terror*, in which human motives have been more closely examined than political causes, the chief value of the papers in the Archives lies in the powerful sense of immediacy that they impart to far-off events. The mysterious difference between the written and the published word becomes dramatically apparent when one compares the dossier of Charlotte Corday that is in the Archives with an excellent work of Vatel, published in 1861, called *Dossiers du Procès de Charlotte Corday*. Vatel's work contains, word for word and line for line (with orthographic errors respected), all the material in the Archives. It is a superior piece of editing. It is deficient nonetheless in that curious quality of actuality that often distinguishes original documents. A small instance makes this apparent. When she left the Hôtel de la Providence to kill Marat, Charlotte discovered that she did not know her victim's address. The driver of the hack that she had hailed on the Place des Victoires made enquiry among his fellow cabbies. When he returned with this information he gave it to Charlotte and set out for Marat's residence. Charlotte, always methodical, made a hurried notation of the fact on the back of a scrap of paper. That paper is still in the Archives (Vatel has made note of it in his work). There is something about Charlotte's penciled scrawl, in which one seems to detect the jogging motion of the carriage, that suddenly brings the events of that hot summer's evening of July 13, 1793, very close to the present.

Series W, or the *Section Judiciaire,* in which Charlotte Corday's dossier is only one of many, is particularly fascinating. Within this series is contained the file of nearly every case tried before the Revolutionary Tribunal. Among other cartons the author has had reference to Series F ^{7} 1069, 4660, 4443-6, 4687-92. These papers largely pertain to the trials of Danton and the Hébertists.

The following are among the more interesting, helpful or important secondary sources that were consulted:

Acton, Lord: *Lectures on the French Revolution*
Alger, John G.: *Paris in 1789-94*
Aulard, A.: *The French Revolution*
          La Société des Jacobins
Barthou, Louis: "Danton et les Massacres de Septembre" (*Revue de Paris,* 1932)
Belloc, Hilaire: *Danton, A Study.*
Bessand-Massenet, P.: *Robespierre, l'Homme et l'Idée*
          La France après la Terreur
Beugnot, Comte: *Mémoires*
Bowers, Claude: *Pierre Vergniaud, Voice of the Revolution*
Brink, Jan ten: *Robespierre and the Red Terror*
Cain, Georges: *Coins de Paris*
          À travers Paris
Calvet and Mathiez, editors: *Vieux Cordelier*
Campardon, Emile: *Histoire du Tribunal Révolutionnaire*
Caron, Pierre: *Paris pendant la Terreur*
Cassagnac, Granier de: *Histoire des Girondins et des Massacres de Septembre*
Castelnau, Jacques: *Le Tribunal Révolutionnaire*
Chuquet, Arthur: "L'Assassinat de Marat" (*Revue Hebdomadaire,* 1916)
Claretie, Jules: *Camille et Lucile Desmoulins*
Clemenceau-Jacquemaire, Madeleine: *The Life of Madame Roland*
Corday, Michel: *Charlotte Corday*
Dauban, Charles: La Démagogie en 1783 à Paris
          Les Prisons de Paris sous la Revolution
          Étude sur Madame Roland et Son Temps
Duras, Duchesse de: *Prison Journals during the French Revolution*
Fleischmann, Hector: *Behind the Scenes in the Terror*
          Charlotte Robespierre et Ses Mémoires

Garat, D. J.: *Mémoire sur la Revolution*

Gaudel, Louis: "Le procès de Danton" (*Révolution Française,* 1937)

Gaxotte, Pierre: *The French Revolution*

Gershoy, Leo: *Bertrand Barère, A Reluctant Terrorist*

Gooch, G. P.: *History and Historians of the Nineteenth Century*

Gottschalk, Louis: *Jean-Paul Marat, A Study in Revolution*

Green, F. C.: *Jean-Jacques Rousseau*

Greer, Donald: *The Incidence of the Terror during the Revolution*

Hamel, L.: *Histoire de Robespierre*

Harmand de la Meuse: *Anecdotes*

Herlaut, General: *Deux Témoins de la Terreur* (Clavreuil, 1958)

Herriot, Édouard: *Lyons n'est Plus*
           "Fouché et Robespierre" (*Révolution Française,* 1936)

Lamartine, Alphonse de: *Histoire des Girondins*

Lenôtre, G.: (ed. Perrin) *Le Jardin de Picpus*
           La Maison des Carmes
           Robespierre et la Mère de Dieu
           Vieilles Maisons, Vieux Papiers
           Paris Révolutionnaire
           Le Tribunal Révolutionnaire

Madelin, Louis: "La Dernière Année de Danton" (*Revue des deux mondes,* 1914)
           Danton
           The French Revolution
           Fouché
           Mémoires de Fouché (ed.)

Maromme, Loyer de: "Mémoire de Charlotte Corday" (*Revue Hebdomadaire,* 1898)

Mathiez, Albert: *Girondins et Montagnards*
           La Révolution Française
           Autour de Danton

Mercier, Sébastien: *Nouveau Tableau de Paris*

Moore, John: *A Journal during a Residence in France*

Morand, Pierre: *L'Énigme Robespierre*

Morton, J. B.: *Camille Desmoulins*

Palmer, R. R.: *Twelve Who Ruled: The Year of the Terror in the French Revolution*

Peltier, J.: *The Late Picture of Paris*

Pol, Stéphane: *Autour de Robespierre*
Pope-Hennessy, Una: *Madame Roland, A Study in Revolution*
The Reign of Terror, A Collection of Authentic Anecdotes
Robinet, Dr.: *Danton, Mémoire de sa Vie*
Robiquet, Jean: *La Vie Quotidienne au Temps de la Révolution*
Roland, Madame: *Mémoires* (ed. Perroud)
              Lettres (ed. Perroud)
Rudé, George: *The Crowd in the French Revolution*
Russell, John: *Paris*
Scherr, Marie: *Charlotte Corday and Certain Men of the Revolutionary Torment*
Shearing, Joseph: *The Angel of the Assassination*
Sorel, Albert: *L'Europe et la Révolution Française*
Taine, Hippolyte: *The French Revolution*
Ternaux, Mortimer: *Histoire de la Terreur*
Thompson, J. M.: *Robespierre*
              The French Revolution
Tourneux, Jean M.: *Bibliographie de l'Histoire de Paris pendant la Révolution*
Vatel, C.: *Dossiers du Procès de Charlotte Corday*
Villiers, Chéron de: *Charlotte de Corday*
Wallon, Henri: *Histoire du Tribunal Révolutionnaire*
Walter, Gérard: *Marat*
              Robespierre, La Vie et l'Oeuvre
Warwick, Charles: *Danton and the French Revolution*
Webster, Nesta: *The French Revolution, A Study in Democracy*
Wendel, Hermann: *Danton*
Williams, Helen Maria: *Letters*
Zweig, Stefan: *Joseph Fouché, Portrait of a Politician*

INDEX

Buzot, François, 206, 213, 217, 218, 236, 256

Cabanès, Dr., 92
Caen, 13, 21, 23–24, 25, 27, 36, 43–45, 55, 57–58, 68–72, 98, 107–9, 115, 117, 118, 120, 124, 127, 129, 130, 218, 245
Cain, M., 332
Calvados, 14, 15
Cambon, 386, 387
Carlyle, Thomas, 87
Carmes prison, Paris, 79–80, 226
Carnot, Lazare, 352, 353, 377, 382, 383, 386, 389
Carrichon, Abbé, 342–44, 346–49
Carrier, Jean-Baptiste, 213, 288–89
Chabot, François, 132–35, 246, 286–287, 309, 316
Chains of Slavery, The (Marat), 87, 88
Champagne, 154
Charpentier, Gabrielle, 161–63, 168, 223–26, 231–34, 247–49, 252–53
Charpentier, M., 161–63
Châtelet, The, Paris, 81
Chaumette, Pierre-Gaspard, 226, 370, 371
Chauveau-Lagarde, Claude-François, 144–45
Chenier, André, 146, 335
Civil war, 245
Collot d'Herbois, Jean-Marie, 76, 165, 226, 232, 288, 289, 297, 298, 352–53, 361–64, 372, 377, 378, 380, 383, 388–92, 396
Comédie Française, 338
Committee of Public Safety, 42, 77, 131–32, 137, 155, 183, 236–38, 240–43, 251, 254, 255, 257–59, 263, 278, 279, 281, 283–85, 288, 290–91, 293, 295, 297, 301, 305, 308, 311–14, 316, 325, 339, 351–353, 361, 362, 364, 366–67, 370–371, 374, 378–83, 385–86, 389, 390, 395, 400

Committee of Surveillance of the Commune, 76, 77, 207–8
Conciergerie, Paris, 81, 139, 256, 258, 307–8, 315, 317, 318, 329, 331, 333, 343, 345, 401
Condorcet, Antoine-Nicolas, 173, 214
Confessions (Rousseau), 27, 29–30, 177
Constituent Assembly, 11, 42, 49
Constitution (1791), 48
Constitutionalists, 49–50
Contrat Social (Rousseau), 31, 37, 47, 267, 274
Corday, Abbé de, 18
Corday, Charlotte, 13, 23, 218, 403
  at Abbaye-aux-Dames, 35–38, 41–43, 45, 47
  appearance, 39, 40
  arrest, 131–39
  birth, 15, 17
  at Caen, 57–60, 65–69, 99, 103–4, 108–14
  execution, 145–47
  Marat, 121–27, 128–30
  murder of Marat, 241, 245
  in Paris, 115–18, 119–27, 128–36
  return to Mesnil-Imbert, 54
  trial, 115, 121, 137, 140–45, 245
  youth, 17–20, 21–22, 25–27, 34
Corday, Éléonore de, 17, 26, 55–56
Corday family, 15–20, 21, 24–26, 35, 55, 68, 156
Corday, Marie-Charlotte de; *see* Corday, Charlotte
Corday, M. de (Charlotte's father), 15–18, 21, 24, 25, 35, 54–55, 68, 113, 137, 148
Cordeliers, 42, 84, 165–66, 246, 390
Cordeliers' Club, 61, 142, 170, 171, 193, 246, 250, 258, 278
Cordeliers' District, Paris, 91, 163, 165–67, 170, 200, 213
Corneille, Pierre, 18–19, 20, 21, 27, 34, 37, 72, 120, 137, 159, 181
Couthon, Georges, 254, 308, 353, 381, 383–84, 389, 391, 394, 399, 402

415